How to get the Most Out of Your Divorce Financially

HOW TO GET THE MOST OUT OF YOUR DIVORCE FINANCIALLY

G. Edmond Burrows, FCA

THE DUNDURN GROUP
TORONTO · OXFORD

Publisher: Anthony Hawke
Copy-editor: Edna Barker
Designer: Jennifer Scott
Printer: Transcontinental

National Library of Canada Cataloguing in Publication Data

Burrows, G. Edmond (George Edmond), 1934—
       How to get the most out of your divorce, financially

Rev. ed.
Previous ed. published under title: Getting the most out of your divorce, financially.
Includes bibliographical references and index.
ISBN 1-55002-386-1

1. Equitable distribution of marital property — Canada. 2. Pensions — Law and legislation — Canada. 3. Divorce settlements — Canada. I. Title. II. Title: Getting the most out of your divorce, financially.

KE574.B87 2002   346.7101'66   C2002-901074-8

1   2   3   4   5   06   05   04   03   02

 Canada

THE CANADA COUNCIL | LE CONSEIL DES ARTS
FOR THE ARTS | DU CANADA
SINCE 1957 | DEPUIS 1957

ONTARIO ARTS COUNCIL
CONSEIL DES ARTS DE L'ONTARIO

We acknowledge the support of the **Canada Council for the Arts** and the **Ontario Arts Council** for our publishing program. We also acknowledge the financial support of the **Government of Canada** through the **Book Publishing Industry Development Program** and **The Association for the Export of Canadian Books**, and the **Government of Ontario** through the **Ontario Book Publishers Tax Credit** program.

Care has been taken to trace the ownership of copyright material used in this book. The author and the publisher welcome any information enabling them to rectify any references or credit in subsequent editions.

J. Kirk Howard, President

Printed and bound in Canada.✿
Printed on recycled paper.
www.dundurn.com

Dundurn Press
8 Market Street
Suite 200
Toronto, Ontario, Canada
M5E 1M6

Dundurn Press
73 Lime Walk
Headington, Oxford,
England
OX3 7AD

Dundurn Press
2250 Military Road
Tonawanda NY
U.S.A. 14150

Acknowledgements

This book could not have been completed without the kind assistance of many people, including:

Celia Pearce, my eighty-nine-year-old mother-in-law, who read the whole book and corrected my grammar just two months before she died.

Janine Ernst for the endless typing and re-typing of the manuscript along with her many other duties in the office.

Penny Hebert and Kim Maika for checking technical content.

My wife, Claire, for her encouragement and assistance.

Brian Randle, C.A., C.B.V., for editing the chapter on business valuations and the glossary for same.

Stephen Grant of McCarthy Tétrault for reviewing the Chapter on Disability Benefits.

Bernice Lever for introducing me to her publisher and recommending that they publish this edition.

It's really wonderful that all of these people found time in their busy day to help make this book as error free and readable as possible. Any remaining errors are the fault of the author only.

Table of Contents

Introduction

There are, on average, 80,000 divorces per year in Canada and about twenty times that number in the United States. (About 36 percent of marriages end in divorce in Canada and close to 45 percent in the United States.) So if you are going through a separation or divorce, you have lots of company.

Most provinces, and states, now have laws in place to ensure that property acquired during the marriage is shared equally when the marriage breaks down. This may seem like a simple and straightforward process. However, in many cases, it is complicated and difficult and causes great problems, holding up the divorce for years.

For about 45 percent of the working population, one of the most valuable assets acquired during the marriage is the pension, which will be received after retirement. The working population in Canada (with only a few exceptions) will also receive a pension from Canada Pension Plan. The value of a pension acquired during the marriage may be very high or very low depending on a number of factors. Experience indicates that pensions, and their valuation for marriage breakdown purposes, are not understood by very many people. Even lawyers and judges are having tremendous problems trying to establish what is the proper value for a particular person's pension on marriage breakdown. Experience also shows that many divorces are settled using wrong values for one or both partner's pensions. In some cases this costs one of the parties many thousands of dollars.

You may be trying to avoid the costs of a lawyer or valuator in dealing with the value of your pension or your spouse's pension. If so, you are probably being penny wise and pound foolish. At the same time you should not just dump everything on your lawyer's desk expecting him to do his best job for you if you have not investigated your pension fully. If you are to be treated fairly, you must understand something about pensions and their valuation. Many factors affect the value of a person's pension on marriage breakdown, and I will attempt to explain these in this book. It will be necessary for me to use technical terms in some cases. Please do not allow this to confuse you.

A glossary of the most common terms is provided at the back of the book. Or check the meanings of terms or phrases in a good legal dictionary. These can be found in most libraries.

The goal of this book is to ensure you are treated fairly in the equalization of assets on marriage breakdown, particularly with respect to pensions, but also with respect to some other employment-related assets, and to real estate and businesses. The book will also help you with the necessary arguments for a higher or lower value for every pension. And I hope the book will help you obtain your divorce sooner and at less cost.

There have been many cases where the divorcing couple thought they would save legal fees and valuation costs by keeping it simple. They agreed to not spend money on valuations. Invariably, total costs of the divorce are higher, and the process is slower. Usually one of the spouses does not get his fair share of the assets. Some people end up with less than 10 percent of what they were entitled to because they did not have their spouse's pension valued properly.

In this second edition, I have expanded the information about pensions and added information about other financial concerns, for example, support, disability benefits, common law spouses, and death.

Some factual situations and actual cases have been used to illustrate problems people may encounter. While all the circumstances described are real, the names, places, and some facts have been changed to protect clients' privacy and the confidentiality clients expect from professionals. While this book deals mainly with the laws in force in Ontario, many parts of it will be appropriate in other provinces and many states.

This book is not intended to teach you how to prepare a proper pension valuation or to look after all of the financial aspects of your divorce or separation yourself. This requires specialized knowledge and years of experience. However, it does point out contentious issues that must be checked to ensure that a person's pension is valued properly.

Throughout the book, reference to the masculine gender should be taken to include the feminine gender where applicable.

Chapter 1

Thousands of People are not Getting their Fair Share of the Assets on Marriage Breakdown

This is especially true when one of the parties has a pension to be valued. This chapter will discuss:

- attempts made to ensure that pension valuation becomes standardized
- reasons there is considerable confusion about pension valuations
- how a pension should be valued
- some horror stories I have seen where values have been grossly overstated or understated
- other possible employment related assets to watch for
- how numerous people lose their right to a CPP pension
- some valuation questions that are still unanswered, and
- how to ensure that you are not one of the thousands of people who do not get a fair share of the assets on marriage breakdown.

When the current Ontario Family Law Act became law on January 1, 1987, it clarified the fact that pensions are subject to equalization when a marriage breaks down. Since then, pension valuators, lawyers, and judges have been struggling to understand how pensions should be valued for this purpose. Pension valuators have been disagreeing with each other and in many cases producing widely divergent values for the same pension asset. Often the pension valuator acting for the member has produced a very low value, while the pension valuator acting for the non-member spouse has produced a very high value, even though both valuators are working from the same basic facts. Lawyers will either argue the extreme or try to negotiate a value somewhere in the middle, often resorting to the courts to settle the matter. The courts, in their attempt to consider all of the facts presented to them, have often arrived at a value that is not fair to either party and their decisions have been inconsistent. If each party is to receive their fair share of the assets, the pension value must be determined properly, as it is often one of the largest assets involved in the equalization of property on marriage breakdown.

ATTEMPTS AT STANDARDIZATION

There are many reasons why different values are presented for the same pension, and some attempts have been made to standardize the valuation process.

In 1993, after five years of extensive study and debate and after discovering that different actuaries were producing widely divergent values for the same pension, the Canadian Institute of Actuaries issued standards for their members to follow in valuing pensions. Unfortunately these standards are ambiguous and poorly written and do not cover all facets of the valuation. They are also out of date.

These standards also allow the valuator to vary from them, as long as he discloses that he has done so. Although there is a general requirement that the values produced be fair to both parties, I have seen many cases where the requirement has been ignored.

In 1995, the Ontario Law Reform Commission studied this area of pension valuation intensely and identified many problem areas in the valuation process. They did produce some excellent recommendations. However, Mr. Harris has been too busy with health, education, and other matters to deal with these recommendations.

The recommendations are clear and should help, if they are ever introduced into law.

There have been many short articles published dealing with the valuation of pensions for equalization on marriage breakdown. There have been only three books written. One is *Pension Division and Valuation, a Family Lawyers' Guide*, by Jack Patterson of Actuarial Consultants of Canada Limited. Another is *Division of Pension* by Pask and Hass, and the third is this book. The first two books are out of date.

The Law Society of Upper Canada has presented several seminars dealing with the legal aspects of pension valuations. I have given several seminars to lawyers explaining the mathematical methods and how to ensure that their clients are treated fairly.

REASONS FOR CONFUSION

One reason pension valuations have been misunderstood is that the process is complicated and difficult to understand. It involves determining how much pension benefit has been earned during the marriage, projecting that benefit to payments in the future, after retirement, and predicting the future without taking into account post-separation events.

Unfortunately short phrases have been penned to describe some pension valuation methods. In the process these descriptive phrases have been used to mean different things. This has led to considerable confusion, and I refer you to Justice Kurisco's 104-page decision in the case of *Bascello v. Bascello*[1] for a lengthy discussion of this matter and some excellent clarification of terminology and valuation methods.

Another source of confusion as to the proper value of a pension for marriage breakdown purposes is that a pension, like other assets, has a different value for different purposes. A pension may have three or four possible values for equalization on marriage breakdown; these are difficult enough to calculate and explain. It has another and often much different value for literal termination of employment, for division of the pension, or on death.

Many employers issue a letter stating the "commuted value" or "termination value" of the employee's (or member's) pension earned during the marriage. The member's lawyer, suggesting that this is the value for equalization, presents this letter. This would very rarely be true. Normally this commuted value on termination of employment is much less than the proper value for equalization on marriage breakdown. This is because the two values are calculated quite differently. When the employer is calculating the commuted value, he uses every legal means to keep the value to the lowest amount possible in order to reduce the amount that will be transferred out of the employer's pension fund when the employee terminates.

Another source of confusion is the fact that many valuation reports are based on estimates or are prepared on a biased basis. Even though these facts are disclosed in the report, the values produced are often used in the equalization process.

There are simple computer programs available for calculating the value of a pension for equalization. There may not be anything wrong with these programs; however some people are feeding in different information until they get the answer they want for their client. I have reviewed many of these computer-generated reports, but I am yet to find one that was prepared properly and produced the right values.

CONSIDERATIONS IN VALUING A PENSION

Besides knowing all of the methods used to value a pension, being familiar with all the appropriate legislation and being aware of all court decisions, before proceeding to do a particular pension valuation, it is necessary to gather all the details of the particular pension plan and the appropriate details of the particular individual.

DETAILS OF PENSION PLAN

There are thousands of pension plans in Ontario, many of which have their own nuances, which can affect the value. Before preparing a valuation report, the valuator must review the particular pension plan carefully to determine at least the following:

- how the pension benefit is calculated
- how years of service are defined
- what amount of indexing is provided
- any history of ad hoc indexing
- the normal retirement age
- any and all other ages at which a person may start receiving an unreduced pension
- if any bridging benefits are available to eligible members.

All this information may be needed as it was for the particular pension plan at the date of valuation, since these details can change from time to time and the pension must be valued at a specific point in time.

DETAILS OF INDIVIDUAL

Of course each individual has his own particular details to be considered in a valuation. This would include at least the following:

- date of birth
- date of hire
- date of joining the pension plan
- date of marriage
- date of valuation
- contributions and interest to the date of valuation, if applicable

- state of health
- sex
- amount of accrued service to date of marriage and to date of valuation
- earned pension benefit to date of cohabitation and to date of valuation
- other income to be considered in the tax allowance.

HORROR STORIES

I won't delve into the long, complicated valuation process, which is explained later in this book. In fact, due to the proliferation of pension plans, and the different details of different individuals, I could not possibly cover all possibilities.

Here are a few short examples of some cases I have seen in practice:

One case involved a member of the INCO Hourly Paid Employees' Pension Plan. We were acting for the non-member and wanted to be sure that the values had not been understated. The valuation report presented by the member's lawyer showed four possible values ranging from $15,800 to $95,000. Unfortunately, the pension valuator ignored a provision of INCO's pension that guarantees a minimum pension benefit. We were able to issue a proper report showing that the value could be as high as $142,500. This made our client, the spouse, very happy.

In another case, someone used a simple computer program to prepare a two-page valuation report and arrived at the conclusion that the value of the pension was $29,500. The person used the wrong benefit rate, the wrong income tax rate, the wrong contributions and interest, and ignored the early retirement provisions of the pension plan. Again we were acting for the non-member, and were able to show that the proper value ranged from $44,000 to $47,000.

In another case, again involving the simple computer program, the member's lawyer claimed that the value was $35,000. We were able to show that it could be as high as $60,000.

In a case involving the president of a large company, the report prepared by an actuary suggested that the value could be as low as $49,500. We were able to show that the value could be as high as $382,000.

In another case, the actuary used the projected amount of benefit that the member could expect to receive after retirement rather than the actual benefit earned. He showed that the value could be as high as $89,000. By using the proper amount of benefit and preparing a proper report, we showed that the value could not be higher than $10,000.

We recently had a case where the pension administrator said, "[Y]ou are correct in assuming that our pension plan is strictly employer contributions; the amount on the statement is in fact, the value of the pension." The value shown on the statement provided by the pension administrator was $53,700. Acting for the spouse, we were able to prove that the proper value was more than $96,000.

There was one court case in Sudbury where a letter from INCO stated that the value of the member's pension was $6,600. The judge recognized that this could not possibly be the proper value, and he valued the pension at $63,000.

These are just a few examples of the many cases I have seen where people would have lost thousands of dollars if they had not insisted that the pension be valued properly.

DEATH BENEFITS

As required by law, all pensions make provisions for payment to be made if the member dies before retiring. Most plans provide that this benefit must be paid to the spouse first, if there is one. If there is no spouse, the payment goes next to the dependants, and if there are none, the payment is made to the member's estate.

The courts have tended to recognize that the payment of this benefit is of no value to the member if he cannot designate the beneficiary. When a plan does stipulate that the payment goes first to the spouse, second to the dependants, and third to the estate, it can be argued that the member cannot designate the beneficiary. Therefore, you should ensure that the value of this benefit is not included in the value of your pension. This benefit is usually referred to as the *non-spousal death benefit*. Since many pension valuators are including this in the value, you should watch for it in the report.

Pensions also provide that when the member dies a percentage of the pension payments will continue to the spouse, unless the spouse has waived this right in writing. Therefore, if you retired before the date of separation, you should insist that your spouse's survivor benefit also be valued and included in your spouse's assets.

ESTIMATES

Many pension valuation reports are prepared based on estimates that may be arrived at from a recent annual pension statement. Of course, the end values shown in the report can be only as accurate as the estimates used. Using estimates rather than accurate information can affect the value of the pension substantially. I have seen many cases where the value of the pension was overstated or understated because the basic information was not confirmed and improper estimates were used in the valuation. It is important to confirm the information with the pension administrator to ensure that the right information is being used in the calculations.

INCOME TAX ALLOWANCE

When a person retires and pension payments are received, they must be included in income for income tax purposes. Therefore, it has been generally recognized that the value of a pension should be reduced by a reasonable income tax allowance. The amount of this allowance can affect the value substantially. There is considerable disagreement among pension valuators, lawyers, and judges as to what constitutes a reasonable allowance.

Sometimes an arbitrary flat rate of 20 percent or 25 percent is used for the income tax allowance, with little justification for the rate other than that this rate was used in some reported cases and considered reasonable by a presiding judge.

There have been many other approaches to estimating a reasonable allowance. Some valuators attempt to allow for proposed income tax changes that are being considered by the federal government but may never become law.

In my opinion, the tax allowance should be based on known facts and on the Income Tax Act as it existed at the date of valuation. It should take into account the person's expected pension payments, CPP, Old Age Security, and other income they can expect to have after retirement, for example from RRSPs owned at the date of separation.

RRSPs

These days a large percentage of the population has an RRSP. This can sometimes be a substantial asset. Cases have been fought over whether the value of the RRSP should be reduced by an income tax allowance.

There is no doubt that when money is taken out of the RRSP it will be taxable income to someone.

Some people argue that the Ontario Court of Appeal case of *Sengmueller v. Sengmueller*[2] established that no such reduction in value should be allowed. I believe that this case established just the opposite and that a reduction can be justified with the proper arguments.

OTHER EMPLOYMENT-RELATED ASSETS

Besides pension a person may earn several other employment-related assets, which must be valued and included in the equalization calculation. This assets could include:

- accrued sick leave gratuity for a teacher or a municipal employee
- retiring allowance for an Ontario or a federal government employee or an employee of a quasi-government organization
- lieu time for a police officer
- accrued paid vacation for any employee
- paid absence prior to pension for a Bell Canada employee or a member of the armed services
- Security Reserve Fund for an INCO salaried employee
- Stock Purchase Plan for salaried employees of General Motors
- Deferred Profit Sharing Plan for employees of Canadian Tire or numerous other companies
- new plan for sharing profits for employees of Sears
- stock options, both exercisable and non-exercisable, of A & P, Apple Computer, INCO, Joseph Seagrams, Northern Telecom, and Canadian Pacific
- group RRSPs
- some disability benefits
- executive pension plans or top-up pension plans for employees of Air Canada (and some other companies)

whose pension would otherwise exceed the maximum allowed by Revenue Canada

- Senior Executive Incentive Plan for employees of Canadian Pacific
- Income Program for Older Workers for laid off employees of Algoma Steel
- Supplementary Retirement Benefit Plan and Voluntary Defined Contribution Plan for employees of CAMINCO and other companies.

There is a case where severance pay received three years after the date of separation was subject to equalization, and a case where winnings from a lottery ticket purchased after the date of separation were subject to equalization.

This list of possible employment-related assets goes on and on, and even a lawyer must be extremely careful and knowledgeable to ferret out all the assets and have them included in the member's Net Family Property Statement. More about this in another chapter.

CANADA PENSION PLAN

The Federal Government has made it easy for couples to share Canada Pension Plan credits when a marriage breaks down.

A person need only inform the Canada Pension Plan administration of the divorce, and the matter will automatically be taken care of. This is accomplished by transferring Canada Pension Plan credits from one of the parties to the other, so they both have the same amount of credits accumulated during the marriage.

Canada Pension Plan records indicate that very few people avail themselves of this equalization of credits. This may be because people are not aware of this possibility. In fact, in a divorce there is often no discussion of Canada Pension Plan credits accumulated during the marriage, and the credits are not considered in the equalization of assets. The credits are considered property but are not included in the accounting of marriage period assets.

Many people lose thousands of dollars because they do not have Canada Pension Plan credits equalized.

OTHER BENEFITS LOST BY THE NON-MEMBER SPOUSE

Many attempts are made to settle the equalization debt by dividing the pension at source or dividing the pension payments when they are received. This is generally very attractive to the person with the pension but is often disastrous for the non-member spouse.

The Pension Benefits Division Act (PBDA) became law a few years ago. This Act provides for the division of certain federal government pensions into two pensions so that each party has a pension. This may be an appropriate way to satisfy the equalization payment in some cases. However, as Justice Catherine Aitken pointed out in a talk she gave to judges in Ottawa in 1998, there are many reasons the value calculated by the government for this purpose is probably not the proper value for equalization on marriage breakdown. I had one case where the value of the pension accrued during marriage according to the PBDA was $80,880. On acting for the spouse of the member, I was able to prove that the true value earned during the marriage period, as determined for marriage breakdown purposes, was $150,000.

Many pensions are not eligible for the splitting of the pension under the PBDA. In Ontario, at least, most private pensions cannot be accessed in this way.

This leads to the drafting of agreements or orders to divide the pension payments if and when they are received. This topic is discussed more fully in Chapter Seventeen.

Even the most diligent lawyer can do nothing about the fact that the non-member spouse loses many things in the equalization process because of the operation of the law. For example:

1. The equalization value of the pension is often based on a pension being paid in the future in deflated dollars. While the value is settled on this basis, the member normally receives a pension in dollars that keep pace with inflation to at least the date of retirement. The non-member spouse has to settle for a value in deflated dollars.

2. These days many employers provide dental and other health benefits. The value of these is not included in the equalization of assets. Even though the member continues to benefit from these plans, the non-member spouse is cut off from them.

3. Many pensions provide for a substantial payment to be made to the spouse if the employee dies before retirement or shortly thereafter. The divorced non-member spouse gives up the right to these possible benefits.

4. All pensions in Ontario must include a provision that, on the death of the member *after* retirement, at least 60 percent of the pension payments must continue to the person who was the spouse when the member retired. The non-member spouse gives up this very valuable asset on the breakdown of the marriage *before* retirement of the member. The loss of this asset for the non-member spouse is not considered in the equalization process.

The whole process of valuing a pension for equalization on marriage breakdown is considered mainly from the viewpoint of the member. There is little consideration for the non-member's viewpoint.

QUESTIONS STILL UNANSWERED

Even though several years have gone by since the current Ontario Family Law Act came into effect, there are still several matters that must be resolved to ensure that each party receives a fair share of the assets on marriage breakdown. Here are some of these unanswered questions.

Vesting

Until such time as a pension vests, the member has no right to receive a pension. Is it possible that a pension can have no value the day before it vests, and a large value the day after? Some valuators say yes. Others say that the value accrues gradually.

Retirement Age

At what age do you assume that the member will retire and start to receive his pension? This is an important consideration. The earlier he starts to receive his pension, the more money he will receive, and the higher the value is for equalization.

Indexing

When valuing someone's pension, how do you provide for inflation and the indexing provisions of the particular pension plan, including both plan-provided indexing and ad-hoc indexing? In final average plans and flat rate plans do you consider the fact that salaries and flat rates tend to keep pace with inflation over the long term?

Contingency Discount

Should provision be made for the possibility that for many reasons the member may not be able to retire early? If no such discount is provided in the valuation, the pension may be overvalued.

SUMMARY

I sympathize with lawyers who must deal with the equalization of assets on marriage breakdown when a pension is involved. I recommend that they keep the following points in mind:

1. Some pension valuation reports are issued on a biased basis and must be read carefully. Even careful reading may not make it clear that the correct value could be higher or lower.
2. Many valuation reports are based on estimates, and details have not been confirmed. If the estimates are wrong, the final values may be wrong.
3. Most valuation reports show more than one possible value. Negotiating a value somewhere between the highest possible value and the lowest possible value may not be fair.
4. There are valid ways to justify a higher value or a lower value for most pensions. These valuation methods can be supported by reference to court decisions and can be argued on a logical basis. To provide the best possible service to a client, a lawyer must be familiar with these methods.
5. There are many problems associated with dividing the pension or sharing the pension payments if and when they are received.
6. Even if the pension is being divided or shared on an if and when basis, it still must be valued to ensure that both parties receive what they should.
7. The cost of a proper pension valuation is very small compared to the possibility that without one you may lose many thousands of dollars and look to your lawyer for restitution.
8. When your lawyer is presented with a pension valuation report, you should always insist that another pension valuator review it. We have often been able to help lawyers argue a higher or lower value by doing this.

9. The valuation of a pension for equalization on marriage breakdown requires that the valuator be a specialist who spends all his time, or close to it, in this complicated area.

Some day we will have a profession of certified pension valuators who will clear up all the problem areas and help ensure that every person receives a fair share of the assets on marriage breakdown.

Notes

1. *Bascello v. Bascello* (1995) CarswellOnt 1282, 18 R.F.L. (4th) 362.
2. *Sengmueller v. Sengmueller* (1994) 111 D.L.R. (4th) 19.

Chapter 2

Resolving Your Differences

INTRODUCTION

When you and your spouse reach an impasse and are unable to resolve your differences without professional assistance, there are three possible approaches you might use: the conventional adversarial process, a mediated settlement, or a collaborative approach.

TRADITIONAL OR ADVERSARIAL METHOD

The adversarial approach is the one best known to everyone. With this approach each party retains a lawyer and other experts. The two lawyers negotiate, each fighting for the best interests of his client. If the lawyers are not able to negotiate a settlement both clients agree with, the case goes to court and a judge makes the decisions. In this approach, divorce is perceived as a fight and emphasizes competition, winners and losers while suppressing any co-operative impulses.

The adversarial method is generally most costly and generally requires the greatest length of time to complete. It may create animosity and unpleasantness between the parties, who may end up being enemies. This makes it very difficult to share in such matters as the raising of the children.

However, this does not have to be the case. A good lawyer may be able to negotiate an excellent settlement for you provided you and your spouse are reasonable. To accomplish this, you and your spouse need to know the rights of both parties. Your lawyer will advise you in this regard. He will also help you make your decisions. If you and your spouse are not able to negotiate with each other successfully, an adversarial approach may be your only choice.

MEDIATION

You may find some people, including your lawyer, suggesting that you and your spouse try mediation as a means of resolving your differences without having your day in court. This section explains the process of mediation and sets out some of the advantages that may be expected.

Some findings about mediation could be of concern.[1]

1. Spouses with more tangible resources (more income, more education or vocational skills) experience advantages in mediation. They are better able to purchase expert legal advice prior to or during mediation, or to threaten to terminate or extend the process. They also demonstrate a far greater expertise at negotiations, as well as a greater knowledge of tax and financial matters.

2. The power a spouse may have in an intact marriage (a person's emotional or psychological dependence upon a spouse) evaporates after separation, making an imbalance in tangible resources even more important.

3. Intangible factors, such as status, are extremely important. Status disparity between husband and wife becomes important to divorce mediation because high-status people have authority, command automatic deference, and exert subtle and covert control over lower-status people.[2]

4. Depression renders an individual almost incapable of representing his own interests in negotiation or mediation. The

skills that enhance effective negotiation (healthy self esteem, problem-solving ability, willingness to take risks, strong inter-personal skills, and strategic thinking) are lacking in depressed people. More women than men suffer from depression, and the process of divorce enhances the likelihood for women to become depressed. Women experience role overload and financial vulnerability, for example.[3]

5. Women's low perception of their entitlement to a share of assets or to reasonable spousal support payments influences their ability to negotiate for a good result.

6. Individuals who are unfamiliar with competitive bargaining strategies tend to do more poorly in mediation.

7. The goal of a result, any result, is highly valued in the medi-ation process. Whether the result is fair and just is some-times secondary. The results of mediation are private, and this privacy has an impact on developing jurisprudence and principles of law.

8. The blending of issues (custody of children, division of assets, child support, spousal support) leads to the potential for women to trade away economic entitlements for custody of children, regardless of the likely court outcome. Men have historically experienced fantastic negotiating success as a result of threatening a custody application.

9. Probably one of the most important and fully discussed barriers to fair mediation is the presence of violence within the marital relationship and the devastating impact of the dynamics of abuse.[4]

10. Women are seldom advised that agreeing to one compo-nent of mediation will have an impact on other compo-nents. For example, a mother agreeing to shared custody (custody discussions will always precede support discus-sions) is not necessarily going to be aware of the operation of section 9 of the Child Support Guidelines, and the

financial impact of her decision. Her spouse, on the other hand, may have been motivated by his knowledge of how the guidelines work.

THE PROCESS

Generally there will be one mediator who meets with both you and your spouse at the same time. This mediator does not represent either of you and must maintain impartiality. The mediator's goal is to reach an agreement that is acceptable to both of you, while at the same time ensuring that you are well informed throughout the negotiation process.

The mediator will make every effort to help you and your spouse communicate more clearly with each other. You may still want to retain a lawyer who will advise you as to your rights and duties and review your final agreement with you before it is signed in order to ensure that you understand the agreement.

Mediation has been used for some time in labour disputes and is becoming more widely used in family law and commercial disputes. The process is becoming more popular as more people understand the process and as mediators become more knowledgeable and experienced.

MEDIATION SERVICES AT FAMILY COURT LOCATIONS[5]

Mediation for family law matters is provided at all Family Court locations. These services include mediation of all legal issues arising upon family breakdown: custody, access, support, and equalization of net family properties. Services are delivered in accordance with the Ministry of the Attorney General's Policies for Government Funded Mediation Services.

External service providers who have been awarded a contract by the Ministry provide the services. Mediators who provide services in connection with the Family Court are required to have qualifications at least comparable to those of a "practicing mediator" as set out by the Ontario Association for Family Mediation (OAFM) as follows:

- Professional degree or equivalent
- Minimum of 60 hours of family mediation training (basic and advanced skill course)
- Minimum of 100 hours of supervision and/or
- Minimum of 5 cases mediated to the point of agreement where a practicing OAFM mediator has provided supervision and/or consultation.

Mediation is available on-site in the court facility, and off-site in the mediators' offices. User fees are charged to clients on a sliding scale.

Mediation is voluntary. In order to ensure that cases are appropriate for mediation, mediators are required to screen their clients to ensure that:

- abuse has not occurred that has rendered either party incapable of mediating
- no harm will come to either party or the children as a result of mediation
- the parties' desire to mediate is voluntary
- any inequality in bargaining power can be managed so as to ensure that negotiations are balanced and procedurally fair
- parties are psychologically ready to mediate and have the capacity to do so
- the complexity of the case does not exceed the mediator's education, training and competence.

ISSUES FOR MEDIATION[6]

The adversarial process is designed to resolve legal issues, not reconcile people or help them change the attitudes and habits that led to the dissolution of the relationship or marriage. A wide variety of issues can be resolved through the mediation process.

- ongoing arrangements for the care, control, and parenting of the children
- responsibility for the financial support of the children
- obligation to support each other
- possession of the matrimonial home
- equalization and division of property

LAWYERS

Lawyers play an important role in the mediation process. Lawyers may advise their clients concerning the suitability of the dispute for mediation, make the mediation referral, and be available to the parties throughout the process. Most important, both parties need legal advice concerning the rights and entitlements and the implications of the contemplated agreement.

It is preferable for each party to be represented throughout the mediation process. At a minimum, both parties are encouraged to seek independent legal advice so they can make informed choices during mediation.

Mediation does not replace or supplant the protection the legal system can provide. In fact, it works within the legal system.

CONFIDENTIALITY

In mediation, the parties seek to reach a settlement based on full and frank disclosure of all relevant information between them. Therefore, it is important that all discussions take place off the record or without prejudice.

The mediator, unless otherwise agreed to by the parties, will not voluntarily disclose the substance of any of the discussions that take place in mediation or the content of any document prepared or exchanged during the mediation process.

In rare circumstances, the parties may jointly choose to proceed with open mediation. The process remains confidential, but if there are issues unresolved, the mediator will present both opinions and positions in a written report, which may be used in any subsequent legal proceedings.

Steps of Mediation

There are five steps to a successful mediation.

1. The mediator will help you identify the issues on which you and your spouse agree so these can be set aside. The mediator will then help you identify the issues on which you disagree. This may include who will remain in the family home, how the furniture and property will be divided, where the children will live, and what arrangements need to be made so the children can spend time with each parent.

2. As the issues you do not agree on are defined, the mediator will help you look at different ways of solving each problem. You and your spouse can then negotiate on the different issues and make joint decisions as to how you will settle them.

3. You and your spouse, it is hoped, will work together to make decisions that will allow the issues to be settled. The success of mediation will depend on your willingness, and your spouse's willingness, to give and take a little to find solutions.

4. Once you and your spouse have reached your decisions the mediator will put them down on paper. This draft agreement will contain specific detailed information on how you have agreed to resolve each problem.

5. You and your spouse will review the draft agreement carefully. Perhaps each of you will have the agreement reviewed by a lawyer of your own choosing. If the agreement is satisfactory, it can then be finalized and signed by both parties.

WHEN MEDIATION MAY NOT WORK

Successful mediation requires two individuals who are able to put their emotions aside and find solutions that allow each of them to achieve an acceptable result. In some situations, mediation may be difficult or even impossible. For example:

1. if there has been child abuse by one of the parties.
2. if there has been family violence and one spouse has reason to fear the other.
3. if there is a significant financial imbalance in the marriage or if one spouse is substantially more powerful than the other.
4. if one spouse won't co-operate and act fairly in the negotiations.

BENEFITS[7]

People who consider using mediation as a way to resolve their differences often want to know what the process offers. While mediation cannot guarantee specific results, there are trends that are characteristic of mediation. Some benefits of mediation, broadly considered:

- Mediation is generally less expensive when contrasted to the expense of litigation or other forms of fighting.
- In an era when it may take as long as a year to get a court date, and multiple years if a case is appealed, the mediation alternative often provides a more timely way of resolving disputes. When parties want to get on with business or their lives, mediation may be desirable as a means of producing rapid results.
- Parties are generally more satisfied with solutions that have been mutually agreed upon, as opposed to solutions that are imposed by a third party decision-maker.
- Parties who have reached their own agreement in mediation are also generally more likely to follow through and comply with its terms than those whose resolution has been imposed by a third party decision-maker.
- Mediated settlements are able to address both legal and extralegal issues. Mediated agreements often cover procedural and psychological issues that are not necessarily susceptible to legal determination. The parties can tailor their settlement to their particular situation.
- Parties who negotiate their own settlements have more control over the outcome of their dispute. Gains and losses are more predictable in a mediated settlement than they would be if a case is arbitrated or adjudicated.
- People who negotiate their own settlements often feel more powerful than those who use surrogate advocates, such as

lawyers, to represent them. Mediation negotiations can provide a forum for learning about and exercising personal power
or influence.

- Many disputes occur in the context of relationships that will
  continue over future years. A mediated settlement that
  addresses all parties' interests can often preserve a working
  relationship in ways that would not be possible in a win-lose
  decision-making procedure. Mediation can also make the
  termination of a relationship more amicable.

- Parties who mediate their differences are able to attend to
  the fine details of implementation. Negotiated or mediated
  agreements can include specially tailored procedures for
  how the decisions will be carried out. This often enhances
  the likelihood that parties will comply with the terms of the
  settlement.

- Interest-based mediated negotiations can result in settlements that are more satisfactory to all parties than simple
  compromise decisions.

- Mediated settlements tend to hold up over time, and if a
  later dispute results, the parties are more likely to utilize a
  co-operative forum of problem solving to resolve their differences than to pursue an adversarial approach.

Mediation is impartial and confidential, whereas court proceedings can be attended by any member of the public, and your court
file can be reviewed by anyone. If the mediation process is successful, you and your spouse create your own agreement rather than
being told by a judge what to do. The mediation process is apt to
leave less animosity between the two of you than if you went
through adversarial proceedings such as a court case.

With mediation you are not bound to settle based on someone
else's decision. In fact, you can walk away from mediation at any
time if you don't like the way it is proceeding.

THE ROLE OF THE MEDIATOR[8]

The mediator's role is to do anything and everything necessary to assist parties to reach agreement. In serving this end, the mediator may take on any or all of the following roles:

Convener

The mediator may assist in contacting the other party or parties to arrange for an introductory meeting.

Educator

The mediator educates the parties about the mediation process, other conflict resolution alternatives, issues that are typically addressed, options and principles that may be considered, research, court standards, and so on.

Communication Facilitator

The mediator seeks to ensure that each party is fully heard in the mediation process.

Translator

When necessary, the mediator can help by rephrasing or reframing communications so that they are better understood and received.

Questioner and Clarifier

The mediator probes issues and confirms understandings to ensure that the participants and the mediator have a full understanding.

Process Advisor

The mediator may suggest procedures for making progress in mediation discussions. These may include caucus meetings, consultation with outside legal counsel, and consultation with substantive experts.

Angel of Realities

The mediator may exercise his or her discretion to play devil's advocate with one or both parties, to assess the practicality of solutions they are considering or the extent to which certain options are consistent with participants' stated goals, interests, and positive intentions.

Catalyst

By offering options for considerations, stimulating new perspectives and offering reference points for consideration, a mediator serves as a stimulant for the parties reaching agreement.

Responsible Detail Person

The mediator manages and keeps track of all necessary information, writes up the parties' agreement, and may assist the parties to implement their agreement.

INTERESTING WEB SITES

- The Network: Interaction for Conflict Resolution www.nicr.ca
- Academy of Family Mediators www.mediators.org
- Society of Professional in Dispute Resolution www.spidr.org
- Association of Family and Conciliatory Courts (AFCC) www.afccnet.org
- Arbitration and Mediation Institute of Canada (AMIC) www.amic.org
- Canadian Bar Association (CBA) www.cba.org
- Canadian Department of Justice – Dispute Resolution Services www.canada2.justice.gc.ca

- Access to Justice Network www.acjnet.org
- Canadian Centre for Mediation www.ccmediation.com
- Ontario Mandatory Mediation Programme www.attorney-general.jus.gov.on.ca
- Mediation Training Institute Canada www.mediation works.com

ORGANIZATIONS

There are at least three well-known professional mediation organizations. You can contact them for more information or for brochures about mediation and also to obtain referrals to mediators in your area. These organizations are:

Family Mediation Canada
123 Wallwich Street,
2nd Floor,
Guelph, Ontario
N1H 3B1
Telephone: (519) 836-7750
Facsimile: (519) 836-7204

Association of Family and Conciliation Courts
329 West Wilson Street
Madison, Wisconsin
53703, U.S.A.
Telephone: (608) 251-4001

The Academy of Family Mediators
4 Malicha Drive
Luxenton, Mass.
02173, U.S.A.,

Telephone: (617) 674-2663
Facsimile: (617) 674-2690
or visit their web site: http://www.igc.apc.org/afm

(For a list of mediators interested in mediating family law, please refer to the Appendix.)

AGREEMENT TO MEDIATE[9]

This bulletin provides general information concerning mediation of civil (non-family) disputes. It is not intended to suggest that all disputes are suitable for mediation.

Once the parties to a dispute have selected a mediator, the mediator and all the parties will sign a written agreement outlining the terms on which the mediation will proceed. A draft copy is usually given to the parties by the mediator before the first mediation session. It is often signed after the parties have agreed to mediate but before the first meeting. Alternatively, it might be signed at the beginning of the first mediation session.

Each mediator is likely to have his or her preferred form of agreement, but all agreements should contain some common provisions. Typically, an agreement will include a brief description of the process, the neutral and impartial role of the mediator, the subject matter of the dispute, and the objective of reaching a collaborative resolution.

The agreement should be reviewed before it is signed to ensure that certain matters have been adequately dealt with.

- **Confidentiality**: The agreement should provide that information acquired and admissions made during the mediation process cannot be used in court, and that the mediator cannot be required to testify. Confidentiality in mediation means that you can speak freely; it will not prejudice your case if it goes to court.

Sometimes during mediation, the mediator will meet with the parties separately. Therefore, the agreement should also clarify whether or not the mediator is free to share information disclosed by one party with the other party.

- **Full disclosure**: A clause requiring full and frank disclosure of all relevant information and all relevant documents is central to the agreement. Depending on the nature of the case, it might be desirable to have a specific term agreeing to the exchange of summary reports and all relevant documents seven or ten days before mediation is scheduled to begin.

- **Fees and costs**: The agreement will retain and instruct the mediator, specify the mediator's fee, identify other possible charges, and clarify who pays. Experienced, legally trained mediators usually charge hourly rates running from $150 to $200 per hour, although a few are outside this range. You may also find that rates are negotiable, and that daily rates are available.

- **Role of legal counsel**:Most agreements suggest that parties either have legal counsel involved in the mediation, or recognize that they have the option of obtaining independent legal advice before committing to an agreement. The opportunity to obtain independent legal advice is very important if parties attend mediation without legal counsel.

- **Ending mediation**: A clause stating that the mediation may be ended at any time by any party, or by the mediator, is common. This confirms the voluntary nature of the process.

Sample Agreement to Mediate

BETWEEN:

_____

(name of party involved in dispute)

AND:

_____

(name of party involved in dispute)

AND:

_____

(the "Mediator")

Because:

The parties wish to settle matters in dispute between them without resorting to the adversarial process.

The parties, their lawyers, and the Mediator will make a serious attempt to resolve all issues fairly in mediation.

The Parties Agree:
1. Process

Mr./Ms._____
will be the Mediator.
The Mediator will act as an impartial facilitator to assist the parties in a negotiation aimed at the resolution of issues between them. All parties will work with the Mediator to isolate points of agreement and disagreement, to identify their interests, to explore alternative solutions, and to consider compromises or accommodations.

2. Disclosure
There will be full and timely disclosure by each of the parties to the other, and to the Mediator, of all information and documents relevant to the matters under discussion.

3. Exchange of Documents
At least seven days before the mediation conference, the parties will exchange all relevant information and documents.

4. Summary Reports
Each party (or their counsel) will prepare a brief summary of the issues in dispute and their views on them. The parties will deliver the summaries to the Mediator at least seven days before the mediation begins.

5. Without Prejudice Communications and Inadmissibility
All communications between the parties, either with one another or with the Mediator privately, are settlement negotiations conducted on a without prejudice basis. All communications occurring in the context of the media-

tion are confidential, and are inadmissible in any legal proceeding. No party will subpoena the Mediator to testify or to produce records or notes. No party will disclose or attempt to compel disclosure of:

a) any views expressed or suggestions made by another party in respect of the possible settlement of the dispute;

b) any admissions made by a party in the course of the mediation;

c) the fact that another party had indicated a willingness to accept a proposal made by any party to the mediation.

6. Confidentiality of Information Disclosed to the Mediator

Parties will discuss with the Mediator the matter of confidentiality of information disclosed to the Mediator.

7. Authority to Settle

To have an effective mediation it is important that a representative of each party with authority to settle a dispute be present at the mediation conference.

8. Effecting a Settlement

Where a settlement is reached in the dispute, the parties and their counsel will formalize the terms of the settlement agreement as soon as possible, either in a written agreement or in a court order.

9. Independent Legal Advice

The mediator does not act as legal counsel for any party during the mediation. Each party is encouraged to secure independent legal advice to ensure that legal rights and obligations, and the consequences of any potential settlement, are fully understood.

10. Ending the Mediation

Participation in mediation is voluntary. A party or the mediator may end the mediation at any time.

11. Mediation Fees

Mediation costs will include the mediator's fees and any out-of-pocket expenses incurred by the mediator for telephone calls, correspondence, and so on. The Mediator's fees will be calculated as follows:

The parties will share the fees and expenses as follows:

(Signed by all parties, counsel, and the mediators)

COLLABORATION

Many family law lawyers have found that the bitterness and acrimony engendered by the process of divorce has long-term harmful consequences on those who participate in it. They have found that participating in this process was having a deleterious impact not only on their client's emotional health and psychological lives, but also on their own lives, as well. As a result, lawyers began to explore alternative avenues for resolving disputes. One of these processes is now known as Collaborative Divorce and Separation.

In 1990 Stewart Webb and a group of lawyers decided they were sick of practicing family law in the traditional way. They were convinced that they were not really helping their clients. Litigation forced both parties to take extreme positions and to dig in their heels. Months or years later and after a fortune in legal fees, the wife and husband hated each other as never before, and the kids were caught in the middle. The adversarial process was tearing families apart, and these lawyers hated being a part of the process. There had to be a better way. This was the birth of collaborative law, and it is revolutionizing family practice. It is also being considered for other practice areas. It is sometimes referred to as "divorce without bloodshed."

The idea of collaborative law spread quickly from Minneapolis to California, Minnesota, Texas, Ohio, and many other states. It also spread to British Columbia and Ontario. There are now Collaborative Family Law Groups in Vancouver, Toronto, and Ottawa.

Collaborative family law is the latest development since mediation. Mediation is helpful but is often not sought until communication breaks down and conflict is adversarial. In mediation, the "do it my way or else" threat is ever present and undermining. But what if the context for negotiation itself could be changed? What if there was a way to approach a person with whom one had a perceived conflict with request for an honest and detailed examination of the problem, in a way that also offered an absolute and irrevocable commitment to do so, in a non-adversarial manner? That is collaborate.

HOW IT WORKS

There are many ways a collaborative divorce process can work. The first phase starts with each spouse visiting a collaborative lawyer. The creation of a working team is the next step. Once all relative professionals are on board, an agreement is then reached between the professionals and the couple that allows the team to work together collaboratively. The degree to which each type of professional is involved will depend on the unique needs and circumstances of the family.

As in any interdisciplinary team, spouses waive confidentiality so that team members can communicate with each other. However, all professionals involved are still held to the standards of confidentiality of their respective professions. The rules of all parties are clearly laid out and discussed until both spouses fully understand the process. The signing of an agreement means that the professionals can communicate with each other; if the collaborative process is not successful, the spouses have agreed that all records are protected from future use in court proceedings. The team then meets as necessary, either in person or by teleconference.

In the second phase, information is gathered at meetings, with professionals who help family members address pertinent issues and help all professionals in making recommendations. Four-way meetings are held as necessary. These meetings can include both spouses and collaborative lawyers or spouses and divorce counselors. A financial specialist or child specialist can also be included if necessary. Since they are neutral, these specialists are valuable in dealing with difficult areas. These meetings offer brainstorming and problem solving in difficult situations.

The third phase involves negotiating and settling issues. Collaborative family law is a process where both spouses are represented by lawyers whose express goal is to settle the divorce out of court in a way that is fair to you both. Spouses and lawyers commit themselves to settle the case without court or the threat of going to court. The well-being of your family is the number-one goal. The lawyers must settle your case or withdraw from your case. Custody issues will be negotiated in a way that protects the children from the dispute. Both parties have skilled lawyers committed to collaborative family law.

In practicing collaborative family law, the lawyers for both parties in a family dispute agree to assist in resolving conflict using co-operative strategies rather than adversarial techniques and litigation. The process involves analysis and reasoning to solve problems, to generate choices and to create a positive context for settlement.

While no two cases or collaborative lawyers are alike, the emphasis in the approach is to find a way in which the lawyers can work with the parties to achieve a satisfactory settlement in an efficient, co-operative manner. The philosophy is that as much effort should be exerted towards settlement as is traditionally spent in preparation for and conducting a trial.

The role of the lawyers is to facilitate the development of a voluntary settlement without the threat or use of power. This is in contrast to the traditional approach of lawyers in prosecuting and defending legal causes of action. The single most important characteristic of this system is the commitment to achieve settlement without the use of any form of litigation. The most challenging and controversial aspect of this approach is the contractual obligation of the collaborative lawyers to withdraw from the case if any party chooses to abandon the collaborative law approach. This is a disincentive to a party who enters the process without good faith. The commitment of the lawyers to withdraw if litigation breaks out is a check against the lawyers' tendency to resort to well-developed adversarial skills when the going gets tough.

Another major and distinguishing characteristic of this system is its focus on educating and empowering the client to become proactive in all phases of the dispute resolution process, especially the settlement. This contrasts starkly with the traditional approach, where the legal process plays such a dominant role in the path to trial or separation that the client is frequently seen as getting in the way of the strategies of the lawyer who is charged with the responsibility for aggressively pursuing the interests of that client.

In the collaborative process the lawyers should:

- advise their clients of the law that applies to their circumstances
- model honesty, mutual respect, and dignified behaviour
- guide their clients through a process of co-operative conflict by using disagreement as a way to find creative solutions to problems
- model listening skills for each party so the interests of both parties are promoted; lawyers represent their client's interest while mediating the other party's interest, as well
- bring stability and reason to emotionally charged situations; serve as agents of reality for unreasonable clients; use clear, neutral language in speaking and in writing
- co-operate fully with each other to provide all necessary disclosure and discovery
- understand that court involvement is not an option, and refrain from using adversarial techniques or tactics
- show they are committed to finding effective ways to reach agreement and overcome impasses, using mediation or neutral experts to provide a third opinion when necessary.

The collaborative method has an immediate appeal to lawyers. Instead of using confrontation tactics and intimidating demands, collaboration reaches for the basic goodness in individuals and looks for win-win solutions. Collaboration aims to create a renewed respect for and a better understanding of the other party, and a general feeling that the agreement is a job well done.

Not all negotiations will end in agreement, of course, but in the collaborative process most will because of the determination of all participants, the collaborative lawyers especially, to reach the goal through fair and open dealing. It is also being said that the risk of having to start all over with new lawyers usually convinces about 95 percent of all couples to settle. If settlement still eludes them, the parties will have the satisfaction of knowing that every reasonable effort was made and that the lack of success was not for want of trying. They will also have a clearer understanding of the issues involved; if the matter is to be litigated, they will be in a better position to instruct their trial counsel on the crux of the case so time and money are not wasted.

Collaborative law provides clients and their lawyers with a new formal and strictly non-adversarial approach to resolving legal disputes. It encourages mature, co-operative, and non-combative behaviour as the parties contract to eliminate litigation as an option.

In collaborative law, your lawyer's continued employment depends on the ability to design acceptable settlement options. If the collaborative law process proves unsuccessful or either party wants litigation, both lawyers must withdraw from the case.

THE BENEFITS

In the 1700s, the average length of a marriage was only seven years; then one of the spouses died. Today, we have the opportunity to be married to the same person longer than ever before in history. During the 1940s and 1950s divorce overtook death as the leading cause of the termination of a marriage. Continued co-operative relationships between former spouses have become important particularly when there are children involved.

It is not the divorce itself that is the most destructive element for the family, but rather the level of distress, conflict and loss that can occur as a function of the divorce process. Next to death or disability, divorce results in the most radical and permanent reorganization a family is likely to face. If divorce is necessary you owe it to your children and yourself to do it as sensitively and as sanely as you can.

Beneficial aspects of collaboration include:

1. a more affordable and less emotionally draining process for clients
2. less stress for lawyers practicing family law
3. settlements that last longer
4. less stress on family relationships
5. strong incentives to reach a settlement
6. a blend of mediation and negotiation
7. rules of conduct that discourage hostile, intimidating, or power-based tactics.

As well. there are other advantages.

1. The process is generally costs less and takes less time than litigation.
2. You are a vital part of the settlement team.
3. Your lawyer supports you both, and you work co-operatively with your spouse and his lawyer to resolve your issues.
4. The process is much less frightening than court proceedings or the threat of such proceedings.
5. Everyone can focus on settlement without the imminent threat of going to court.
6. There is no lengthy wait for a court date.
7. You control the proceedings; your destiny is in your hands rather than in the hands of the courts.

Collaborative family law creates a co-operative environment where communication remains open. In this setting, you can work with your spouse to meet your children's needs regardless of their ages. There is a tone of open communication and a hope of reduced conflict in the future. There is a team instead of adversaries. Your lawyer supports you and your spouse's lawyer supports him, but all of you work together, and, in doing so, you each retain control of the process. In matters requiring expert opinions, both parties jointly hire one independent consultant. This helps shorten the duration of the case and also reduces the overall expense. You and your spouse shape the agreement together, which means you are both more likely to keep the agreement. This diminishes the parental conflict the adversarial system generates and helps protect children from the anguish and divided loyalties that result. You avoid the fear and anxiety associated with going to court. You also avoid having confidential matters become public through the court proceedings.

WHO SHOULD ATTEMPT COLLABORATION?

Collaborative family law works best when both spouses are:

- interested in reaching a fair settlement that considers the rights and needs of everyone
- committed to devoting the time and effort to participate actively in a co-operative negotiation process
- able to respect and treat the other fairly and honestly throughout the process
- able to believe that a settlement negotiated by the parties themselves is inevitably better than one imposed by the courts
- able to believe that a dispute is a problem to be solved together, not a battle to be won
- able to agree to scrap the idea of the adversarial system of law and work at every phase of the dispute resolution process in a collaborative, co-operative way
- convinced that problem solving is more important than fighting.

WHAT CAN BE RESOLVED?

Collaborative family law should be able to resolve:

- separation and divorce
- child custody and visitation
- spousal and child support
- division of property
- non-marital relationship break-up
- guardianships
- adoption.

HOW TO GET STARTED

1. Talk with your spouse about collaborative family law and share information about the benefits.
2. Choose a lawyer who is committed to the collaborative family law process.
3. Meet with your lawyer to discuss how collaborative law will work in your situation.
4. Sign a participation agreement with your lawyer, your spouse, and your spouse's lawyer.
5. Attend the first collaborative meeting.

PARTICIPATION AGREEMENT

Once you and your spouse have agreed to use collaboration, the two of you and your lawyers should sign a participation agreement. This agreement will set out the process for the parties involved in the dispute, for their collaborative lawyers and any experts or consultants they may retain to assist them. The agreement should create for the parties and their lawyers the best possible conditions for fully and fairly appraising and resolving the dispute without adversarial threats or actions. The agreement should contain provisions that explicitly commit the parties and their lawyers to resolve their dispute in an atmosphere of honesty, co-operation, integrity, and professionalism without court intervention. The most important part of the agreement is the formal agreement not to litigate. Under the agreement, if any party or collaborative lawyer takes a formal legal adversarial action, all collaborative lawyers and their firms are automatically disqualified from further representation of the parties. (The automatic disqualification is enforceable by the courts.) The agreement should spell out the parties' obligations to disclose crucial information to one another and to maintain the confidentiality of such disclosures. The agreement should obligate each to provide good faith responses to any good faith questions and requests for information from the other party or parties. A good faith question or request for information is one that is reasonably calculated to assist in accessing the merits or value of a party's claim or to otherwise further the process of reaching a settlement of all issues.

The agreement to confidentiality is an important complement to the participation agreement. It enables candor by strictly forbidding the disclosure of any statement, comment, or admission made by any party or lawyer during the collaborative law process to any court for any purpose. Only in the event of an impasse in the collaborative law process and subsequent litigation, and then only through completely independent formal discovery, can information revealed in the collaborative negotiations be used against a party.

The agreement should include provisions:

- prohibiting a party from unilaterally initiating litigation
- governing the use of experts independently or jointly during the collaborative law process and disqualifying the same experts from taking part in any subsequent litigation

- permitting the parties to enter temporary agreements and making such agreement enforceable in court
- allowing any participant to call for the assistance of another collaborative lawyer or a mediator before an impasse is declared.

If either party is unwilling to commit to the provisions of the participation agreement, chances might be high that the collaborative law process would not be successful. The willingness of both parties and counsel to agree to adhere to the participation agreement provisions bodes well for successful collaboration.

SAMPLE PARTICIPATION AGREEMENT[10]

This is not to be construed as being legal advice or a form to use in any particular case. It is merely a sample. A lawyer should draft any agreement.

I. Introduction

1.01 The essence of collaborative law is the shared belief of the participants that it is in the best interests of the parties and their families in typical family law matters to commit themselves to avoiding litigation. We seek to adopt a conflict resolution process that does not rely on a court-imposed solution. The process does rely, however, on an atmosphere of honesty, co-operation, integrity, and professionalism geared towards the future well being of the parties and their children.

1.02 One of our major goals in adopting the collaborative law process is to minimize, if not eliminate, the negative economic, social, and emotional consequences of protracted litigation to the participants and their families. We commit ourselves to the collaborative law process and agree to seek a better way to resolve our differences justly and equitably.

II. No Court or Other Intervention

2.01 By electing to treat their family law matter as a collaborative law case, the parties and their attorneys are committing themselves to settling the case without court intervention. The parties agree to give complete, full, honest, and open disclosure of all information, whether requested or not, and to engage in informal discussions and conferences for the purpose of reaching a settlement of all issues. All lawyers, accountants, therapists, appraisers, and other consultants retained by the parties will likewise be directed to work in a co-operative effort to resolve issues without resort to litigation or any other external decision-making process.

III. Limitations of Collaborative Law Process

3.01 In electing the collaborative law process, we understand there is no guarantee of success. We further understand we cannot eliminate concerns about the disharmony, distrust, and irreconcilable differences that have led to the current conflict. While we all are intent on striving to reach a co-operative and open solution, actual performance may fall short.

3.02 Even though they have adopted the collaborative law process, the parties are still expected to protect their respective interests and not to allow themselves to lapse into a false sense of security in the assumptions and expectations each hold about the other. The parties may continue to act in their own best interests and not in the other party's interests in areas outside the dispute, such as in changing estate plans and future financial and other activities.

IV. Participation with Integrity

4.01 As participants in the collaborative law process, we are concerned about protecting the privacy, respect, and dignity of all involved, including the parties, lawyers, and consultants. Each participant shall uphold a high standard of integrity, and specifically shall not take advantage of inconsistencies and others' miscalculations, but shall disclose them and seek to have them corrected.

V. Experts and Consultants

5.01 In selecting outside help, the parties are encouraged to retain joint experts and consultants. In the event each party retains a separate expert, each shall be directed to follow the spirit and direction of these principles and guidelines, and to collaborate with each other, meet and confer, and, if possible, render joint statements on the issues in dispute.

5.02 In resolving issues about sharing the enjoyment and responsibility of the parties' minor children, the parties, lawyers, and therapists shall make every reasonable effort to reach amicable solutions that promote the best interests of the children. The parties agree to act quickly to mediate and resolve all differences related to the children in a manner that will promote a caring, loving, and involved relationship between the children and both parents.

VI. Negotiation in Good Faith

6.01 The parties understand that the process, even with full and honest disclosure, will involve vigorous good faith negotiation. Each party will be expected to take reasoned positions in all disputes, and, where such positions differ, each party will be encouraged to compromise where necessary to reach a settlement of all issues. Although all parties should be informed by their lawyers and consultants about the litigation process and the result it may attain, no party or lawyer may use threats of going to court as a way of forcing settlement.

VII. Abuse of Collaborative Process

7.01 Collaborative counsel are encouraged to withdraw from a case as soon as possible if they learn that their client has withheld or misrepresented information or otherwise acted so as to undermine or take unfair advantage of the collaborative law process.

Such actions may include, but are not limited to, the secret disposition of community, quasi-community or separate property, failure
to disclose the existence or the true nature of assets and obligations, ongoing emotional or physical abuse of the minor children
of the parties, or withholding a secret plan or intention to flee the
jurisdiction of the court with their children contrary to an agreement or existing court order.

7.02 All understand that the ultimate sanction against lawyers
who abuse the collaborative law process, or condone or encourage
such abuse by their clients, is the diminution of that lawyer's reputation in the legal community.

VIII. Disqualification by Court Intervention

8.01 The parties and their lawyers have signed this document
and have agreed to be bound by its specific terms and provisions.
The parties understand that their lawyer's representation is limited
to the collaborative law process. Thus, while your lawyer is your
advisor, confidant, counselor, advocate, and negotiator, he cannot
represent you in court, go with you to court in person, or be named
as your lawyer on any document filed with the court other than a
mutual stipulation or agreement of the parties.

8.02 In the event a party or lawyer deems it necessary or
unavoidable that a filing with the court be done, the lawyers will be
disqualified from further representing their clients. Except upon
mutual written agreement of the parties to the contrary, in such event
all consultants will be disqualified as witnesses, and their work product will be inadmissible as evidence in the case after it ceases to be a
collaborative law case.

IX. Withdrawal of Lawyer

9.01 If a lawyer deems it appropriate to withdraw from the case
for any reason, he agrees to do so immediately by a written notice
of withdrawal to the court and all parties and their lawyers. This

may be done without terminating the status of the case as a collaborative law case.

9.02 The party losing his or her lawyer may continue in the collaborative law process without an attorney, or retain a new lawyer who will agree in writing to be bound by this agreement.

X. Election to Terminate Collaborative Process

10.01 If a party or lawyer decides that the collaborative law process is no longer appropriate and elects to terminate the status of the matter as a collaborative law case, he agrees to do so immediately by using written notice of the termination election to the court and all parties and their lawyers.

10.02 The termination of status may also occur automatically in the event a party deems it necessary to proceed to court in an emergency to protect his property, himself or his children.

XI. Selection of New Lawyer; Additional Fees

11.01 Once the status of the case as a collaborative law matter is terminated, the lawyers agree to aid their respective clients in the selection of a new lawyer.

11.02 The parties understand that in retaining new lawyers in the event of the termination of the status of the case as a collaborative law matter, each party will incur additional legal fees in an amount equal to or exceeding that paid to his or her current lawyer.

XII. Pledge

12.01 All parties and lawyers hereby pledge to comply with and to promote the spirit and written word of this document.

Dated:_____   Dated:_____

———————————————

———————————————

Petitioner   Respondent

———————————————

———————————————

Lawyer for Petitioner   Lawyer for Respondent

———————————————

Notes

1   P.E. Bryan, *Killing us Softly: Divorce Mediation and the Politics of Power* (1992) 40 Buffalo L. Rev. 441.
2   *Ibid.* At 458.
3   *Ibid.* At 468 – 469.
4   Dr. H. Astor, *Mediation and Violence Against Women* (Paper prepared for the National Committee on Violence Against Women, Australia, December 1991).
5   www.attorneygeneral.jus.gov.on.ca/html/family/family mediation.htm
6   Durham Family Court Clinic.
    http://www.dfcc.org/brochure2.html
7   http://mediate.com/help/mediation.efm
8   Family Mediation Canada
    http://www.mediation.com/help/mediation.cfm
9   www.ag.gov.bc.ca/dro/bulletins2000/agreement.htm
10 "Collaborative Law," www.nocourt.org/principles.htm

Chapter 3

What About Financial Support?

INTRODUCTION

Besides equalizing the assets that have been accumulated during the marriage, it is often necessary to determine whether one of the parties should pay support. This may take the form of child support or spousal support.

CHILD SUPPORT

After it has been determined who will have custody of each child, it is necessary to establish whether child support will be paid, and if so, how much, and for how long. For many years couples have resorted to the courts to make these decisions for them.[1] Judges consider:

1. both spouses' financial obligation to maintain the child or children
2, the need to apportion support between the spouses according to their abilities to pay
3. the parents' current assets and means.
4. the child's current assets, and any assets he is likely to have in the future
5. the child's capacity to contribute to his support
6. the child's age and physical and mental health

7. the child's aptitude for and reasonable prospects for an education
8. the child's need for a stable environment.

In 1997 the federal government introduced the Federal Child Support Guidelines, which have been adopted by all provinces, with slight variations. These guidelines tend to set minimum amounts of child support to be paid depending on:

- the province of residence of the payor
- the income of the payor
- the number of dependant children
- who has custody
- undue hardship, extraordinary expenses, and cases where the payor has income in excess of $150,000.

These guidelines apply to both married and unmarried couples. The following is a brief summary of the provisions.

THE FEDERAL CHILD SUPPORT GUIDELINES[2]

The Guidelines

The guidelines are a set of tables and rules that prescribe the amount of child support a non-custodial parent should pay to the custodial parent. Tables set a specific amount of support depending on the income of the non-custodial parent and the number of children. Rules set out when and how the amount in the table should be modified to address special situations. The guidelines also explain the determination of the payor's income, the variation of present support orders, and the requirements for the parties to provide information about their incomes and expenses.

The Purpose of Guidelines

The four objectives of the guidelines are (1) to establish a fair amount of support for the children of divorced parents; (2) to reduce conflict by having the amount of support more objective; (3) to improve the legal process by providing guidance in setting the amount of child support; (4) to ensure similar treatment for similar situations.

Basis of the Guideline Tables

The tables are based upon the average costs of raising children. As those costs vary with income, the amount of support varies with income of the non-custodial spouse. The income of the custodial parent is not considered in the table. The reasoning is that the custodial parent will spend a similar share of his income to meet the costs of raising the children. The tables are based upon a tax system where the support payments are not tax-deductible to the payor or tax-includable for the recipient.

The Exceptions in the Guidelines

Certain situations allow the court to deviate from the amount set out in the tables. Those situations are defined specifically in the guidelines or the Divorce Act. The guidelines set forth what should be considered in determining the new amount, though there is not always a specific arithmetic formula. Some brief explanations of the exceptions:

> *Previous order or agreement benefiting a child*
> The court may order an amount different from the table if it finds it would be fair to do so because in a previous order

or agreement there was a property transfer or a financial responsibility that directly benefited the child.

Incomes over $150,000

The court may extrapolate from the table or order an amount different from the table.

Children over the age of majority

The court may use the tables. If, however, it believes the table amount is inappropriate it may order an amount different from the table after considering the income and needs of the parents and the child over the age of majority (which in Ontario is eighteen).

Special or extraordinary expenses

The court may order a parent to pay for certain expenses beyond the amount set out in the table. Those expenses are (a) child-care; (b) extraordinary medical; (c) post-secondary education; (d) extraordinary extracurricular activities. These expenses are to be shared in proportion to the parties' respective means. These expenses are calculated after tax, and subsidies are applied.

Undue hardship

The court may deviate from the table amount of support if it finds there is undue hardship because of four defined circumstances: (1) one spouse has assumed a proportionally high amount of debt from the marriage; (2) access expenses are unusually high; (3) one spouse must support another person under a court order or separation agreement; (4) one spouse has a legal duty to support another child (as in a second marriage).

In determining the new amount of support, the court

must ensure that the household standard of living of the spouse pleading undue hardship is not greater than the household of the other spouse. There is a prescribed test in the guidelines to decide the standards of living. A court must give recorded reasons if it deviates from the table because of undue hardship.

Split Custody

The support will be the difference between the amount each spouse would pay based upon the table and the special or extraordinary expense determination.

Shared Custody

The court may deviate from the tables after considering the appropriate amounts set out in the tables, the extra expenses of a shared custody arrangement, and the means and expenses of all the parties.

Determination of Income

The guidelines set out specific rules to determine the income of the payor spouse. The rules start with income that would be reported on an income tax return. Income then may be adjusted under certain circumstances to reflect fairly what moneys are available for the payment of support. Those circumstances include the situation where the payor spouse is a shareholder, officer, or director of a company or where the payor's income is increasing or decreasing for three years. Courts may also impute income for many stated reasons. Some of those reasons include intentional unemployment or underemployment, where assets are not being properly utilized, where there has been a failure to reveal income, or where there is a different tax rate than normal.

Variation of Support Orders

These guidelines may apply to all agreements and orders retroactively to the date that the guidelines become law. Once the guidelines become law, an application to vary should be made if an outstanding agreement or court-ordered amount of child support is different from what the guidelines will state.

Obtaining Financial Information

The guidelines require the recipient spouse of an application to file specified financial documentation. Such documentation includes tax returns, notices of assessments and reassessments for a three-year period, a statement of earnings from an employer, financial statements where the spouse is a self-employed business or controls a corporation, and confirmation of income when a spouse is a partner of a partnership. An applicant spouse must file the same information if his income is an issue under the guidelines, for example in the issues of special expenses, undue hardship, and incomes over $150,000. Failure to comply with the disclosure requirements will result in an adverse inference against that party or an order to comply. Failure to comply with an order to produce documents may result in an order to strike that party's claim, a contempt order, an adverse inference at trial, or an order for costs.

EIGHT STEPS TO CALCULATING CHILD SUPPORT[3]

These eight steps can help you estimate how much child support is appropriate in most cases.

Step 1 Determine if federal guidelines apply to you.

Step 2 Determine the number of children.

Step 3 Determine the type of custody arrangement.

Step 4 Choose the appropriate federal table.

Step 5 Calculate annual income.

Step 6 Determine the table amount.

Step 7 List any special expenses.

Step 8 Explain any undue hardship.

CONCLUSION

The introduction of the Federal Child Support Guidelines is a major change to family law in Canada. The guidelines should result in fairer, more objective, and more consistent support agreements and orders. They will reduce the emotional and financial costs of spouses' separation.

SPOUSAL SUPPORT

This article appeared in *Reader's Digest* recently.

Till Death Do Us Part?[4]

A woman who shot her husband in the face at close range, leaving a bullet lodged near his spine, has filed a claim for spousal support over a year after her release from prison, where she served time for attempted murder. "As if the shooting wasn't enough, now she's after me for what I've got left," says victim David Alexander.

Alexander, 51, has difficulty controlling his facial muscles and cannot fully close his jaw. His former wife, Christine Ann Alexander, 52, shot him with a .22

caliber hunting rifle as she moved her belongings out of the couple's Bowmanville home in November 1995, shortly after they separated.

Christine was convicted of attempted murder, assault and firearm offences, and was sentenced to two years less a day in addition to the two years she spent in pretrial custody. She served 16 months, then was released in April 1999.

In court documents, Alexander says he is in fear of his former wife, and her support claim has "rekindled many of the anxieties and concerns that he strived to put behind him."

Alexander's lawyer has asked the court to dismiss the claim "as five years have passed since the date of separation" and "as a consequence of the unconscionable treatment he received throughout the course of their marriage, including numerous acts of violence and [Christine's] ultimate attempt to terminate [Alexander's] life." The attempt on Alexander's life constitutes an "obvious and gross repudiation" of the couple's marriage, and even if she is entitled to support, "it ought to be fixed at zero."

Court records show the couple separated after a "long period of physical violence and abuse perpetrated by [Christine]." Alexander won custody of the couple's two sons, and the Alexanders have since divorced.

The lawyer representing Alexander says the claim is going forward on a "peculiar wrinkle" between Ontario's Family Law Act, which allows the court to reconsider conduct of one spouse towards another, and the federal Divorce Act, which decrees conduct is not relevant and prohibits a judge from considering it.

"It's an unusual case, there's no doubt about that, " concludes Alexander's lawyer.

The parties are awaiting a judge's ruling.

There tend to be three types of spousal support to consider:

1. compensatory support
2. needs and means support
3. contractual support.

COMPENSATORY SUPPORT

Compensatory support may be claimed where a dependant can prove and quantify future or past economic loss that is due to the roles adopted in the marriage. The support would be awarded to compensate the dependant for the future economic loss. For example, a wife who has suspended her career to assume responsibility for a home and child care may be entitled to support to compensate her for the future economic loss she will suffer due to the role she adopted during the marriage. Compensatory support considers the economic advantages and disadvantages to the spouses flowing from the marriage. The underlying premise of matrimonial property legislation in Canada is that equalization of property will compensate each spouse for the role adopted in the marriage. If the equalization of the assets does not fairly redress economic disadvantage during the marriage, the court may award an unequal property distribution or compensatory support. Compensatory support tends to be difficult to prove and hard to quantify.

NEEDS AND MEANS SUPPORT

Needs and means support considers the disparity between the needs and means of the two parties upon marriage breakdown. If it can be shown that one party needs support and the other party has the ability to pay support, the courts will normally order that the support be paid.

Needs and means are based on a party's projected income and expenses as set out in the financial statement each must complete. The form of these statements differs for each province. In the appendix you will find the current financial statement format required in Ontario. This tends to be fairly representative of what is required by all provinces.

Where the parties have had a long-term traditional marriage with the result that the dependant spouse is without job skills or income, the rule is that the dependant spouse is entitled to a standard of living equal to what she or he could have expected had the marriage continued. Of course, this rule will only hold true to the extent that the other spouse has sufficient income to pay the support required.

Because your needs and ability to pay support will be determined based on the projections you show in your financial statement, you will want to devote considerable time to the preparation of that statement. You should also be prepared to prove each item of income and expense with documentation. Remember that your spouse's lawyer and possibly the courts will review your financial statement. Any overstatement of expenses or understatement of income could extend the time required to finalize your divorce and could increase your legal fees and other costs substantially. It is best to be as fair as possible in the preparation of your financial statement. At the same time you should be careful to ensure that you have not forgotten anything.

CONTRACTUAL SUPPORT

Contractual support may be payable due to an express or implied agreement between the parties concerning their financial obligations to each other. This agreement may be written or oral. For example, one spouse may have requested that the other spouse stay at home to care for the children and look after the household duties so the first spouse may work towards advancing his career. Any agreement to pay support must of course be adhered to. As always, oral agreements may be difficult to prove.

OBJECTIVES OF SUPPORT

The Divorce Act of Canada lists four objectives for spousal support. It provides that an order for support should:

1. recognize any economic advantages or disadvantages to the spouses arising from the marriage or its breakdown
2. apportion between the spouses the financial consequences arising from the care of any child of the marriage over and above the obligation between the spouses with respect to child support
3. relieve any economic hardship of the spouses arising from the breakdown of the marriage, and
4. in so far as practicable promote the economic self-sufficiency of each spouse within a reasonable period of time.

Four questions generally arise in connection with the consideration of spousal support.

1. Who can afford to pay support?
2. Who deserves support?

3. How much support should be paid?
4. How long should support payments continue?

The provisions of the Divorce Act of Canada apply only to legally married spouses. However, the principles described in this chapter apply to legally married spouses and common-law spouses.

The amount of support awarded by the courts is quite unpredictable. The best way to resolve this question is for the couple to come to some agreement themselves.

Support payments will generally continue until the recipient becomes self-sufficient, but may be varied at any time if the circumstances of either party change sufficiently.

- Over the years the courts have tended to develop important considerations in the area of supposal support, with respect to assessment of need and calculation of the amount:
- In determining a reasonable standard of living, the court must consider the spouse's ability to pay. In one case the court decided that it was unconscionable to reduce the husband's standard of living below the poverty level in order to provide the wife with a reasonable standard of living. This was so even though the parties were married for thirty years and the wife was unable to work full-time.
- A wife asking for support is not expected to take just any job in an effort to meet her own needs.
- The objective of a spousal support order is not to equalize the incomes of the two spouses.
- The need for spousal support should be assessed after the determination of the division of the family assets. If the division of assets leaves the spouse with sufficient means to meet reasonable needs, the court will not order support, or it will order a lower amount than it might otherwise have done.

- Will the prudent investment of the assets through property division at marriage breakdown and the spouse's qualifications for work reduce the need for support from the other spouse?
- Spousal support has been denied in cases where there was a lengthy marriage but both spouses were employed throughout and after the marriage breakdown, and the funds from the sale of the matrimonial home generated additional income.
- Each spouse should make every reasonable effort to become economically self-sufficient as soon as is reasonable.

SUMMARY

The awarding of support by the courts will almost always be based on the need of one party to receive additional income and the ability of the other party to pay support. That is why the careful and proper preparation of your financial statement is extremely important when it comes to consideration of spousal support.

With regards to income tax, spousal support is generally income of the recipient and deductible by the payor.

Notes

1 *Surviving Your Divorce*, Michael G. Cochrane, LL.B.
2 The Federal Child Support Guidelines, http://www.thepascoediffernce.com
3 http://canada.justice.gc.ca/en/ps/sup/steps/int8stps.html
4 Reader's Digest, August 9, 2001, Chris Eby in *National Post.*

Chapter 4

Equalization of Property: How it Works

INTRODUCTION

This chapter explains the system for equalizing assets on marriage breakdown. It explains what property is subject to equalization and what property is exempt. It also provides a sample completed Net Family Property Statement, similar to the one that must be completed by each party to a divorce or separation.

THE LAW

Every province and territory in Canada has enacted legislation to establish property-sharing rights between spouses on marriage breakdown or divorce and, in some provinces, on death. These sharing rights raise three questions:

1. What kind of property is shared?

2. How is the property to be valued?

3. How will the sharing of the property be achieved?

Provincial and territorial statutes differ considerably in content and approach. Therefore it is impossible to provide details of all provisions dealing with matrimonial property for all provinces in this book. This book will deal mainly with the laws in Ontario, which represent the most comprehensive legislation on matrimonial property rights in Canada.

In general terms the fundamental objective of the Family Law Act in Ontario is to ensure that, on marriage breakdown or death, each spouse will receive a fair share (usually an equal share) of the value of the assets accumulated during matrimonial cohabitation. About sharing or equalization of property, the Ontario Family Law Act says,

> The purpose of this section is to recognize that child care, household management and financial provisions are the joint responsibilities of the spouses and that inherent in the marital relationship, there is equal contribution whether financial or otherwise by the spouses to the assumption of these responsibilities entitling each spouse to the equalization of the net family properties subject only to the equitable considerations set out in sub-section 6.

The Ontario Family Law Act provides that, on marriage breakdown, the spouse whose net property is the lesser of the two net properties is entitled to one half the difference between them. Note that the Act does not say each partner to the marriage has a 50 percent claim on each. There is merely a right to equalization of total net value of all assets.

WHAT KIND OF PROPERTY IS SHARED?

When dealing with the equalization of property, it is important to know what constitutes property and to know what property, if any, is excluded from the equalization process.

The Ontario Family Law Act defines property as any interest, present or future, vested or contingent, in real or personal property. This includes, in the case of a spouse's rights under a pension that has vested, the spouse's interest in the plan including contributions made by other persons.

Some examples of property that may be included in the net family property calculation:

- accrued sick leave gratuity
- accrued retiring allowance
- accrued vacation pay
- automobiles
- bank accounts
- boats, snowmobiles, ATVs
- business interest
- cottage
- furniture
- investments
- jewelry
- matrimonial home
- pension
- RRSPs
- disability benefits

Some examples of property that is excluded from the equalization process:

- any asset, other than the matrimonial home, that was owned in advance of the marriage
- a gift or inheritance, other than the matrimonial home, that was received during the course of the marriage
- a court award or settlement for damages for personal injuries suffered (for example in a car accident)

- items of exclusively personal value (for example a professional degree)
- proceeds from a life insurance policy
- property the spouses have agreed by a domestic contract is not to be included in the spouse's net property
- assets that are acquired after the date of separation.

The process of equalization involves having each spouse complete a net family property statement. This entails assigning proper values to each of the assets. Examine your spouse's net family property statement to ensure that all assets have been included and properly valued. Pay particular attention to the value shown for any pension. (Pensions are discussed more fully later.)

In preparing your own net family property statement, make sure you describe each asset fully and value each asset properly. There is no point in trying to undervalue an asset, as your spouse, your spouse's advisors, and possibly the courts will closely scrutinize the content of your statement. Undervaluing or attempting to hide any assets will affect your credibility; as well, it may delay matters and increase your costs. Be reasonable in all your valuations and obtain assistance from professionals where necessary. This is particularly true when it comes to valuing your pension or your spouse's pension, since the pension is generally one of the most valuable assets, and valuing it is a complicated matter.

If you and your spouse are unable to agree on the value of a particular asset, for example the matrimonial home, the judge may order that it be sold and the proceeds be used in the equalization of property.

Make sure you identify all your assets that are exempt from equalization, and be prepared to prove it. Even assets that can be specifically identified as having been purchased with the proceeds from the sale of exempt assets may themselves be exempt.

You will also want to check carefully all assets for which your spouse is claiming an exemption.

Since you are allowed a deduction for liabilities you are responsible for, you should ensure that you disclose all your liabilities and their balance as at the valuation date. These may include:

- mortgage on matrimonial home
- mortgage on cottage
- debt owing on automobile, boats, snowmobile, ATV
- credit cards
- income taxes
- bank loans.

You will also be allowed a deduction for the value of any property you owned at the date of marriage other than a matrimonial home.

You should review your Net Family Property Statement and that of your spouse in detail with your lawyer, your accountant, and your other professionals.

The sample Net Family Property Statement sets out examples of various assets that may be included. It also shows debts, property owned on the date of marriage, and excluded or exempt property.

NET FAMILY PROPERTY STATEMENT

Court file no._____

ONTARIO COURT (GENERAL DIVISION)

BETWEEN:
      John Public   PETITIONER
                                     (Husband   )

(Court seal)
                       and
      Mary Public   RESPONDENT
                                       (Wife   )

___Husband's___ **NET FAMILY PROPERTY STATEMENT**
Wife's or Husbands

Valuation date   June 1, 200?   Statement date   August 1, 200?

(Complete columns for both husband and wife, showing your assets, debts, etc. and those of your spouse).

1. VALUE OF ASSETS OWNED ON VALUATION DATE
(a) Land

Nature and Type of ownership *State percentage interest where relevant*	Nature and Address of Property	Estimated Market Value on valuation date	
		Husband	Wife
Joint tenancy 50%	Matrimonial home, Peterborough, Ontario	$75,000.00	$75,000.00
	Total a)	$75,000.00	$75,000.00

(b) General Household Items and Vehicles

Item	Particulars	Estimated Market Value on Valuation Date	
		Husband	Wife
General household contents excluding special items			
(a) at matrimonial homes	Refrigerator, stove, washer, dryer, furniture, etc.	$ 4,000.00	$ 6,000.00
(b) elsewhere			
Jewelry	Diamond ring (gift)		1,200.00
Works of art			
Vehicles and boats	1994 Station wagon 1999 Ford	15,000.00	6,500.00
Other special items			
Total (b)		$19,000.00	$13,700.00

(c) Savings and Savings Plan, Pensions, RRSPs

Category	Institution	Account Number	Amount on Valuation Date	
			Husband	Wife
Bank Account	Royal Bank	123456	$ 1,000.00	$ 1,300.00
RRSP	Royal Bank	78910	5,000.00	2,000.00
Pension	Federal Government		150,000.00	85,000.00
Total (c)			$156,000.00	$88,300.00

(d) Securities, Bonds

Category	Number	Description	Estimated Market Value on Valuation Date	
			Husband	Wife
Stocks Bonds	350 Shares 3 x 5,000	Bell Canada CS45 - Mature Nov. 2002	$20,000.00 7,500.00	 $7,500.00
		Total (d)	$27,500.00	$7,500.00

(e) Life and Disability Insurance

Company and Policy No.	Kind of Policy	Owner	Beneficiary	Face Amount	Cash Surrender Value on Valuation Date	
					Husband	Wife
Sun Life Group	Life	Husband	Wife	$100,000	no cash surrender value	
				Total (e)		

(f) Accounts Receivable

Particulars	Amount on Valuation Date	
	Husband	Wife
None		
Total (f)		

(g) Business Interests

Name of Firm or Company	Interest	Estimated Market Value on Valuation Date	
		Husband	Wife
None			
	Total (g)		

(h) Other Property

Category	Particulars	Estimated Market Value on Valuation Date	
		Husband	Wife
Accrued Sick Leave	Federal Government	$12, 500	
Gratuity Accrued	Federal Government	10, 000	5, 000
Retiring Allowance Accrued	Federal Government	2, 000	1, 000
Vacation Pay			
Total (g)		$24, 500.00	6, 000

Total value of assets owned on valuation date	TOTAL 1. (Sum of a, b, c, d, e, f, g, h)	$302, 000.00	$190,

2. VALUE OF DEBTS AND OTHER LIABILITIES ON VALUATION DATE

Item	Value of debts and other liabilities on Valuation Date	
	Husband	Wife
Mortgage on Residence	$20,000.00	$20,000.00
Royal Bank Visa	1,000.00	
Total (f)	$21,000.00	$20,000.00

3. NET VALUE OF PROPERTY, OTHER THAN A MATRIMONIAL HOME, OWNED ON DATE OF MARRIAGE

Item	Husband	Wife
a) Land	$4,000.00	$2,000.00
c) Savings and savings plan, pensions	10,000.00	2,000.00
d) Securities		
e) Life and disability insurance		
f) Accounts receivable		
g) Business interests		
h) Other property		
TOTAL 3	$14,000.00	$4,000.00

4. VALUE OF PROPERTY EXCLUDED UNDER SUBS. 4(2) of the FAMILY LAW ACT

Item	Husband	Wife
1) Gift or inheritance from third person		$1,000.00
2 Income from property expressly excluded by donor or testator		
3) Damages and settlement for personal injuries, etc.		
4) Life insurance proceeds		
5) Traced property		
6) Excluded property by spousal agreement		
7) Other excluded property		
TOTAL 4		$1,000.00

5. NET FAMILY PROPERTY
(TOTAL I MINUS TOTALS 2, 3 AND 4)

	Husband	Wife
Total	$267, 000.00	$165, 500.00

Name, address and telephone number of solicitor or party
Joan Public
Peterborough, Ontario

SUMMARY

This Net Family Property Statement indicates that the value of the husband's net family property is $267,000 and the value of the wife's net family property is $165,500. The difference between the two is $101,500. Therefore the husband must transfer assets equal to half of this amount (that is, $50,750) to the wife in order to satisfy the required equalization of assets on marriage breakdown.

The sample statement gives an idea of what property is shared and what property is exempt from equalization. How property is to be valued and how the sharing of property will be achieved is covered later in this book.

In this example, Mr. and Mrs. Public could agree to equalize their Net Family Property by selling the house and splitting the net proceeds. Then Mr. Public would transfer shares and bonds worth $50,750 to Mrs. Public.

Chapter 5

Pensions:
A Brief Explanation

INTRODUCTION

Most people understand that a pension is something you accumulate and earn while you are working and from which you will start to collect monthly payments when you retire and no longer have income from employment. What they don't understand is that pensions are not all the same. There may be vast differences between two pensions. Some pensions are better than others, and therefore more valuable than others.

There are thousands of pension plans in Canada, and probably no two are word for word the same. Some provide generous pensions on retirement and some do not. The exact provisions of a particular pension plan can affect the values substantially. The provisions of each plan are generally explained in a booklet given to each member of the pension plan. A more accurate and complete description is available only by reading the pension document itself. Reading the booklet will help you understand your particular pension. However, for complete accuracy, reference must to be made to the pension documents. Both the booklet and the documents can be obtained from either the employer or, in Ontario, from the Financial Services Commission of Ontario. You will probably need signed authorization from the member to obtain a copy, and there may be costs involved. Read the booklet and documents carefully.

Not all pension plans make the same provisions for contributions by the member. Many plans require the member to contribute a percentage of his salary each year to the pension fund with the employer either matching the employee's contributions or providing whatever other funds are required so money will be available to pay pension payments as required. Some plans do not require any contributions from the member; the employer provides all funds. All contributions are invested in safe, restricted investments, in order to maximize income while minimizing risk of capital loss.

Normally it is true that the more contribution required from the member the higher the value of the pension. However, contributions do not determine the value of the pension. They just allow the pension plan to be more generous.

DEFINED CONTRIBUTION PLANS

Some pension plans state merely that the contributions of the worker or the employer will be invested and accumulated until the worker retires. These plans are known as defined contribution plans. In this type of plan a separate record is kept of the contributions made by, and for, each individual member. When the member retires, the accumulated amount in that member's account is used to buy whatever pension can be purchased with that amount of money at that particular time. This is a very simple type of pension, and very little consideration is needed to prepare a valuation. In many cases the value of a defined contribution pension will be the amount accumulated in the particular person's account less a reasonable allowance for income taxes at any time. However, in some cases it may be necessary to value the underlying investments to ascertain the value of the pension.

At the very least you must determine the account balance at the *exact* valuation date. Then you can determine the projected pension that can be purchased on retirement. Use this figure to calculate the income tax allowance.

DEFINED BENEFIT PLANS

A more complicated type of pension is known as a defined benefit pension plan. This type of plan sets out a formula for determining the actual amount of pension the member will receive each year after he has retired. This type of pension requires very careful consideration when being valued for marriage breakdown purposes. The value of this type of pension rarely has any direct relationship to the accumulated contributions and interest of the particular member.

One of the popular types of defined benefit pension plans is the average earnings plan. Pensions of teachers and municipal employees, for example, are of this type. In these plans the member's pension on retirement will be equal to a percentage of average earnings multiplied by years of service. The actual percentage and the definition of average earnings and years of service will be set out in the pension document and in the explanatory booklet.

Another popular type of defined benefit pension plan is known as a flat rate pension plan. This type of pension is provided by General Motors, Ford, INCO, Falconbridge and many other companies, mainly to union employees. In this plan, the pension the person receives on retirement is equal to a flat rate times years of service. The flat rate generally increases over time; years of service are defined in the pension document. In this type of pension, the member generally does not make any contributions. The proper value for marriage breakdown purposes still may be substantial.

Different pension plans make varying provisions for indexing pension payments after they have commenced, in order to keep pace with inflation. Some make no provision for indexing. Others, for example pensions for teachers and government employees, are indexed 100 percent. Most have indexing that is somewhere in between.

Generally speaking the greater the amount of indexing provided by the plan, the more valuable the pension.

Many pension plans provide for retirement on a full (or "unreduced") pension at a particular age, usually sixty-five. They provide that the person may retire at fifty-five with a reduced pension benefit – because the person will be receiving the benefit for a longer period. Some pensions provide that a person may retire with an unreduced pension at an earlier age, or perhaps when their age and years of service added together equal a certain number. Teachers' pensions are an example: when a teacher's age and years of qualifying service total eighty-five, the teacher may retire on an unreduced pension.

Generally speaking, the earlier a person can retire on an unreduced pension the higher the value of his pension will be. This is because he will be receiving the payments for a longer period of time.

Some pensions provide that members who retire before age sixty-five will receive a higher monthly pension from the age of retirement until age sixty-five; their pension ise reduced when they start receiving Old Age Security and Canada Pension Plan benefits. Generally speaking, the higher the amount of this bridging provided, the more valuable the pension will be.

Some people say that once a person retires and starts receiving his pension payments ("pension in pay"), the pension becomes an income stream and is no longer an asset for equalization on marriage breakdown. Nothing could be further from the truth. Pensions in pay are property. They must be valued and included in the recipient's assets for equalization purposes.

COMBINATION PLANS

Some pension plans combine defined contribution and defined benefit. Some defined contribution plans provide a guaranteed defined benefit.

SUMMARY

There can be many different provisions in any pension plan. All provisions must be considered carefully in preparing a valuation. Pension provisions are discussed more fully later, with explanations of how they can affect the value of a pension.

Chapter 6

How a Pension is not Valued: Beware

Introduction

You may think any valuation report is a valid report of the proper value of the pension. However, you should not automatically accept someone's valuation of your pension or your spouse's pension.

Pension Valuators of Canada offers to review any valuation reports that have been presented to support the value of someone's pension on marriage breakdown. If we cannot help the person who orders the review by justifying either a higher or lower value, depending on which is desired, there is no charge for the service; we inform you that the suggested values are appropriate. We review numerous valuation reports and prepare full calculations of the value of the particular pension for marriage breakdown purposes. In about 25 percent of cases, we find that we can justify a different value than the value shown in the report. This may be for several different reasons.

- Some pension valuators take whatever information is provided to them and use it to estimate the information they use in their calculations. Such a report is suspect.
- The value being suggested may be the commuted value, or transfer value, as reported by the person's employer. Transfer value is rarely appropriate for this purpose.
- The suggested value may be the value determined for purposes of the Pension Benefits Standards Act or the Pension

Benefits Division Act. This will almost never be the value for this purpose.

- The report may be biased basis in favour of the person it was prepared for.
- The report may have been prepared on a computer program that was not meant for this purpose.

ESTIMATES

Some pension valuators take a member's annual pension statement or other information and use it to estimate details, which are then used in their calculations. We are often asked to review such reports for accuracy. The following are examples we have had recently:

Values Based on Estimates	Values Based on Facts
$42, 598 to $72, 403	$106, 139
$84, 314	$93, 727
$30, 744 to $68, 293	$106, 139

In many cases, the valuator has incomplete information and uses estimates to do his calculations. If his estimates are wrong, the values he provides will be incorrect. If the valuator had taken the trouble to confirm the information with the pension administrator, he would have arrived at different values than those produced using estimates. I have seen many such cases.

If your pension valuation report or your spouse's pension valuation report uses the word "estimated," insist that the basic information be confirmed in writing.

COMMUTED VALUE OR TRANSFER VALUE

Many people suggest that there is no need to spend the money on a proper valuation report when the person's employer will value the pension at no cost. But an employer's valuation is not an appropriate valuation for marriage breakdown equalization of assets. The employer's valuation is for the purpose of termination of employment only.

When you terminate employment before reaching retirement age, the law requires the employer to give you three choices about your accrued pension.

1. You may accept what is called a deferred pension. This means that no more contributions will be made to your pension, and you will start to collect it at a later date, in most cases the normal retirement age for your particular plan.
2. You may transfer the value of your pension to a special RRSP that restricts you from withdrawing any funds until you reach a certain age, in most cases the normal retirement age for your particular plan.
3. You may transfer the value of your pension to a life insurance company, which will purchase an annuity with payments that start at a later date, in most cases the normal retirement age for your particular plan.

The value of the pension for these purposes is often referred to as the commuted value, the transfer value, or the termination value. This value is not calculated using the criteria used in valuing a pension in a marriage breakdown. The commuted value normally ignores the early retirement provisions of the plan, and often provides for no indexing of the pension. Thus the commuted value is rarely the best value to use in a marriage breakdown. We have had many cases where the letter from the employer gave a low commuted value; in working for the spouse of the member, we were able to justify much higher values.

If someone tells you the employer has valued the pension, be suspicious. It has probably been undervalued.

The following table gives some examples of the commuted value suggested by the employer and the value we were able to justify.

COMPARISON OF COMMUTED VALUES TO PROPER VALUES

Case No.	Years of Service	Commuted Value	Proper Value For Marriage Breakdown
1	5	$2, 250	$12, 810
2	20	64, 635	81, 025
3	20	48, 400	29, 050
4	25	10, 680	39, 710
5	18	1, 705	11, 550
6	24	6, 600	83, 235
7	18	7, 480	26, 485
8	20	13, 090	71, 665
9	27	10, 210	72, 670
10	22	15, 720	104, 370
11	23	13, 550	17, 460
12	24	14, 415	42, 450
13	20	54, 700	78, 165
14	25	128, 935	90, 025
15	15	4, 350	64, 015
16	14	6, 955	83, 235

In the unreported case of *Sauder v. Sauder*,[1] it was disclosed that a letter from INCO stated the commuted value of Mr. Sauder's pension was $6,653.77. Justice Meehan determined the proper value to be $62,974.

In each case in the table, the member worked for a reputable employer. The employer was asked for, and provided, a letter stating the value of the pension accrued during the marriage period. In some cases, the employer explained that the value was for termination of employment only.

In each case, the lawyer acting for the member presented the letter from the employer and said it gave the value of his client's pension for marriage breakdown equalization.

In each case, Pension Valuators of Canada prepared a proper pension valuation report proving the value was much higher than that shown in the employer's letter.

We have had several cases where the difference between the commuted value and the proper value for marriage breakdown purposes was $100,000 or more.

The commuted value or transfer value is usually considerably lower than the proper value for marriage breakdown. But this is not so in all cases. Here is an example of a commuted value that may be higher than the proper value for marriage breakdown purposes.

The pension administrator provided a letter saying that the present value of the pension was $68,000. Our calculations indicated that the value of the member's pension was $36,000. The remainder of the value was the survivor benefit, which had to be included in the spouse's assets, not the member's. Since the member retired before the date of separation, there were two separate assets, which needed to be accounted for separately.

BIASED OR QUESTIONABLE REPORTS

At Pension Valuators of Canada, we have reviewed many valuation reports. We often find that the proper value for marriage breakdown purposes is different from the value shown in the report. Some examples:

COMPARISON OF REPORTED VALUES TO PROPER VALUES

Case No.	Years of Service	Reported Value	Proper Value For Marriage Breakdown
1	19.5	$164, 745	$134, 115
2	23.5	124, 440	169, 375
3	23.5	61, 165	80, 600
4	20	56, 000	78, 165
5	29	10, 700	89, 770
6	?	91, 600	7, 060
7	25.1	70, 400	121, 885
8	26.1	81, 900	133, 120
9	23	75, 275	114, 025
10	10	41, 000	2, 200
11	20	24, 055 to 31, 345	13, 825
12	24	111, 300	32, 625

In Case Number 1, Mr. James was a member of the Public Service Plan. He had a pension valuation report prepared by an actuary and, since the values were high, he wanted a second opinion to see if anything could be done to justify a lower value. We reviewed the actuary's report and found that he had used the wrong discount rate. We also found that he had arbitrarily chosen a tax rate of 25 percent. He admitted that his choice of 25 percent was arbitrary but pointed out that the rate was often used in pension valuations under the Family Law Act. He made no effort to establish a proper rate of tax for Mr. James. We prepared a new valuation report and justified a much higher income tax rate.

In Case Number 2 we substantiated a much higher value; we also located an accrued vacation pay with a value in excess of $6,000.

In Case Number 3, the actuary who prepared the original report had not obtained an updated copy of the pension plan. The outdated copy he used contained wrong information.

Case Number 5 involved a report prepared on a computer program. The lawyer for the member suggested that the value of his client's pension was $10,700. We were able to justify a much higher value.

In Case Number 9, an actuary arrived at a value of $75,275. He misunderstood the indexing provisions of the pension plan and used the wrong discount rate. He also used the wrong income tax rate.

In Case Number 10, the actuary who prepared the report used the wrong mortality tables and the wrong discount rate.

In Case Number 11 a retired accountant prepared a report showing 26 different values ranging from $24,055 to $31,345. He used the wrong discount rate and mortality tables. He also used the wrong income tax rate.

Case Number 12 involved a four-page report prepared by a chartered accountant and business valuator who used the wrong discount rate and the wrong accrued benefit.

Then there is the interesting case of Mr. Thomas, who had been a firefighter for twenty-five years. He had been married for twenty-two of those years. Mr. Thomas had his pension valued by a chartered accountant, who reported that the value was $61,760. Mrs. Thomas had a valuation report prepared by an actuary, who said the value was between $199,855 and $327,050. Pension Valuators of Canada, asked for an independent valuation, proved that the proper value was $172,570.

When we review reports prepared by someone else, we can generally justify a different value in about 25 percent of the cases.

Some pension valuators think anything goes as long as they disclose in the report what they have done. Be sure to read the report carefully, and have it reviewed by a knowledgeable qualified pension valuator. (See Chapter Eleven.)

Many pension valuation reports are prepared to favour the person for whom the report is being prepared. Sometimes the valuator wants to favour his client. Sometimes the valuator has taken specific instructions from the client's lawyer. Sometimes the valuator has made mistakes in his calculations. Sometimes the valuator has estimated the figures used in his calculations and did not confirm his figures.

The time and cost involved in obtaining a second opinion may save you many thousands of dollars.

COURT CASES

Even judges who must decide the proper value of a pension for marriage breakdown purposeshave tremendous difficulty. In a recent case, a judge had this to say after reviewing the evidence presented to him:

> This case provides a classic example of the problems, which are inherent in the pension valuation process as related to matrimonial litigation. Both parties filed financial statements, which formed part of the trial record. One party's original sworn financial statement contained no valuation of her pension at all, not even an estimated one. The other party's sworn first financial statement was equally barren of information about pension values. The financial statements later filed at the opening of the trial, showed remarkable disparities. Each party filed several net family property statements. The hopelessly cluttered and conflicting evidence on pension values does not end here. Exhibit Two is a document brief containing, amongst other documents, no less than seven documents bearing on the value of the two pensions. This case is proof positive as to why the legislature must do something to quantify and simplify the pension valuation process in family law disputes. Existing legislation is forcing the courts to

guess and use palm tree justice in an area where
there is a dearth of clear-cut legislative guidelines
and an absence of agreement amongst pension valuators on some key issues.

In the now famous case of *Bascello v. Bascello*,[2] two well-qualified
pension valuators prepared reports of the value of the husband's pension. One of the experts arrived at a value of $24,231. The other
expert produced twelve figures for the value, ranging from $25,963 to
$146,580. Justice Kurisko, after reviewing cases and other sources of
information and after doing his own calculations, concluded that the
proper value was $59,500.

Taking your case to court will resolve the issue. However, there
is no guarantee that the courts will agree with your valuation.

YOU KEEP YOURS AND I'LL KEEP MINE

We had one case that involved two teachers who were getting a
divorce. It was explained to us that the male teacher was older and
had accumulated more service; the female teacher had a higher salary
and – because she was younger — a longer life expectancy. It was
suggested that the pensions were probably worth about the same.
We were able to show that the value of one pension was $25,000 and
the value of the other pension was $125,000. It would been unfair
not to consider the pensions in the equalization process.

If two pensions have about the same value, it is probably co-inci-
dence. There is no way to *estimate* the value of someone's pension. It
is probably never equitable for each party to keep his own pension.

In a recent case, the couple decided to have an amicable divorce.
They were intelligent people and were both satisfied that they could
divide their assets themselves and keep their legal costs to a minimum. Each took one car, and they split the furniture and other

assets more or less equally. They continued to live (separately) in the matrimonial home until it was sold. Then they divided the proceeds. The husband was a teacher; the wife had several years ago quit her job with the government. It was agreed that since the husband had stayed at a job that provided a pension and the wife had not, it was fair for him to keep his pension. Then the wife learned that, legally, the pension had to be included in the equalization process. We determined the value was $150,000. In their desire to save some legal fees, she lost almost $75,000.

A SPECIAL CASE

In another case, the husband had assets totalling about $300,000, plus he had a pension. The wife had assets totalling about $125,000. A report had been prepared suggesting that the husband transfer to the wife his equity in their house and $40,000 in RRSP funds. He also offered to pay the wife $7,000 annual support for his lifetime.

We found several errors in the report. We valued the husband's pension plan and revalued the assets. The total value of the husband's assets was $505,100. The total value of the wife's assets was $107,540. We agreed that the wife be given sole ownership of the home and $7,000 of annual support, as suggested. In addition, she should receive $175,000 of RRSP funds, instead of the $40,000 offered by her husband.

COMPUTER PROGRAMS

There are computer programs available for roughly calculating the value of a person's pension on marriage breakdown. They produce a two or three page report giving up to three possible values for the pension. These programs are not intended to be used to calculate the exact value of a person's pension on marriage breakdown. They are marketed as useful tools for calculating a rough estimate. In our opinion, the programs are not even useful for that purpose. To use the programs, you must be an expert in valuing pension plans on marriage breakdown. Anyone not familiar with the intricacies of pension valuations will probably never arrive at the proper value, because they will not input the correct information. And a small inputting error can cause a large error in the final value produced.

We have seen several reports prepared on computer programs and have yet to see one that used the proper information. In every case we have seen, the values produced by computer programs were incorrect because the person inputting the information did not have enough knowledge about pension valuations. In one case, Mr. Adams had a pension valued on a computer program. The person inputting the information put in the wrong benefit amount, the wrong indexing information, the wrong income tax rate, and the wrong retirement age. The program produced a value for the pension of $10,706. We produced our report using the right information and proved that the proper value was $89,770.

If you receive a pension valuation report that has been produced on a computer programs, we recommend that you obtain a second opinion.

CONCLUSIONS

Be cautious about accepting the figure that has been suggested as being the value of your pension or your spouse's pension. In every one of the cases we have cited, and in many other cases we have not mentioned, the cost of obtaining a second opinion was recouped many times. The cost of a proper valuation report is very small compared to the large loss you might suffer if you accept an incorrect valuation of a pension.

Notes

1 (1996) Court File No. A 4123/93 – in Sudbury.
2 (1995) 26 O.R. (3d) 342 (Gen. Div.), 18 R.F.L. (4th) 362 (Ont. Gen. Div.) (July 12, 1996) Doc. 09174-91 (Ont. Gen. Div.).

Chapter 7

How a Pension is Valued

INTRODUCTION

The Family Law Act of Ontario does not state how a pension is to be valued in the equalization of assets on marriage breakdown. A pension can be valued properly only by a qualified professional who uses accurate information and follows proper valuation procedures. This chapter will give a simple explanation of the process of pension valuations and discuss some contentious issues that create difficulties. The aim is to help you understand pension valuations a little better. Remember, the value of a person's pension entitlements will rarely have any relationship to the *contributions* the person has made to the pension plan. Many people think a pension's value depends on accumulated contributions and interest. This is rarely true.

TYPES OF PENSION PLANS

There are two basic types of pension plans, and all plans fall into one or the other of these two types or a combination of the two. Most pension plans are either defined *contribution* plans or defined *benefit* plans. The first defines the contributions made. The second defines the contributions and the pension benefits each member will earn.

DEFINED CONTRIBUTION PLANS

Defined contribution plans define clearly what contributions will be made, who will make them, and when they will be made. Some plans provide for contributions by the employee only; some provide for contributions by the employer only; some provide for contributions by both employee and employer.

In a defined contribution plan, each employee is given a separate account. The employee's contributions and the employer's contributions accumulate account and earn interest. In this way, the plan is similar to a bank account or an RRSP. A defined contribution plan does not establish the amount of pension benefit the member will collect. The benefit will depend on what can be purchased with the funds that have accumulated in the member's account.

For marriage breakdown purposes, the value of a defined contribution plan at any time will be the total of contributions and interest accumulated in the particular member's account less an allowance deducted for income taxes. There may also be an allowance for amounts not yet vested.

There are two major considerations in valuing this type of pension. First the actual amount accumulated in the particular person's account at the date of valuation should be confirmed with the employer or the pension administrator. This amount should never be estimated as it affects the value directly and substantially. It is important that the amount be determined at the exact date of separation, not some close date. It may also be necessary to value the underlying assets in the account (e.g., if the money is invested in Mutual Funds or Long Term Interest Bearing Securities).

The second major consideration is the income tax allowance. It is not proper to use an arbitrary rate of say 25 percent just because that rate was used in some reported court cases. The proper rate for the income tax allowance should be established by calculating the amount of annuity that can be purchased with the balance in the person's account and completing detailed future income tax calculations as described later in this book.

DEFINED BENEFIT PLANS

A Defined Benefit Plan sets out what contributions are to be made by the employee, if any. It states that the employer is to provide the balance of funds required to pay the benefits due to retired employees. Recent legislation ensures that a member's contributions do not finance more than half their particular pension, thereby ensuring that the employer pays at least half. (This is a simplification of the law; specific provisions are included in the Ontario Pension Benefits Act.)

In a defined benefit plan, the employer pays a lump sum to the fund; he does not put funds in separate accounts for each employee.

A defined benefit plan sets out a formula that makes it possible to calculate the amount of pension benefit a particular employee has earned at any particular time. (Remember that the amount may not be payable until the employee is of retirement age.) It is this earned benefit that must be valued for marriage breakdown purposes.

Example One shows a very simple way of looking at the valuation of a pension for marriage breakdown purposes. The value can be defined as being the net present value, after income tax allowance, of the projected accrued pension benefit the member can expect to receive—provided he is alive to receive each and every payment.

The value of a defined benefit pension could also be described as the estimated amount that must be set aside at the date of valuation so the amount, plus interest earned, will be just sufficient to make each and every pension payment when it comes due, taking into consideration that the person may die at any time, thus causing the payments to stop.

In the example we assume the member was born in 1935, became a member of the pension plan in 1960, was married in 1965, separated in 1995, and retired in 2000. We also assume that, to the date of valuation, the member has earned a pension of $1,000 per year, payable at age sixty-five. The pension payments commence in the year 2000, assuming a retirement age of sixty-five.

The amount subject to equalization is the value of the annual payments from the year 2000 to the year 2010, but only to the extent that the value was earned during the marriage.

EXAMPLE ONE

YEAR

1935	born	
1960	joins pension plan	
1960 - 1965	continues working	
1965	marries — net present value?	
1965 - 1995	continues working	
1995	separates — net present value?	
1995 - 2000	continues working	
2000	accrued pension earned	$1,000
2001	accrued pension earned	$1,000
2002	accrued pension earned	$1,000
2003	accrued pension earned	$1,000
2004	accrued pension earned	$1,000
2005	accrued pension earned	$1,000
2006	accrued pension earned	$1,000
2007	accrued pension earned	$1,000
2008	accrued pension earned	$1,000
2009	accrued pension earned	$1,000
2010	accrued pension earned	$1,000

In this example, we have been asked to calculate the value in 1995 of the accrued pension of $1,000 per year.

It would seem to be a simple matter to find the value of the pension by calculating the net present value in 1995 of the payments of $1,000 per year from the year 2000, when the member turns sixty-five, to the year 2010, which is the approximate life expectancy of this person, then deducting the before-marriage portion, plus an income tax allowance. Unfortunately an accurate valuation is never that simple. What must be considered to prepare a proper valuation of a pension?

THE PARTICULAR PENSION PLAN

There are numerous differences in pension plans. Each difference may have an affect on the value of the pension. A valuator should be familiar with the particular plan, and must refer to the plan *as it was at the exact date of valuation*. This is extremely important in determining the value of the pension accrued during the marriage. Remember, the provisions of pension plans change from time to time.

DATE OF BIRTH

Only the date of birth of the member is needed, not the date of birth of the spouse. If the valuator is considering the age of the spouse, be suspicious. The value shown in the report may be higher than it should be.

It is important to use the correct date of birth. The older the person is, the closer he is to retirement — and the higher the value of the pension. But the older he is, the higher his mortality rate, which reduces the value of the pension.

DATE OF JOINING THE PLAN

Many plans require that the person be an employee for a certain period before joining the plan. The particular plan may count service from the date employment started or from the date of joining the plan. Since length of service enters into the calculation of the accrued benefit, it is important to know which applies for the pension being valued.

The more service included in the calculation, the higher the value will be.

DATE OF MARRIAGE

This is important. Any pension value accrued before the date of marriage is allowed as a deduction in the Net Family Property Statement.

Three basic methods have been developed for valuing the portion of the pension accrued during the marriage: value added, pro rata on service, and pro rata on benefit. For now we will use the value added method. This means that we do indeed value the accrued pension benefit earned as at the date of marriage and deduct it from the value of the accrued pension benefit as at the date of separation, and we use the same procedures for both valuations. The pro rata on service method often produces a much lower value.

CONTRIBUTIONS

You will note we have made no mention of having to know the amount of contributions to value this pension. There is only one reason to know the amount of contributions and the interest earned thereon to the date of valuation: to calculate any excess contributions the member may have made. Excess contributions are prescribed by law; they increase the value. Make sure excess contributions are included in the valuation of your spouse's pension.

Some people contend that total contributions to date, plus interest, before tax allowance, equal the minimum value of a pension. This may be true, but a minimum value is not the appropriate value for marriage breakdown equalization purposes.

DATE OF SEPARATION

It is important that the value of the pension be determined as of the proper date. In Ontario, this is the date that parties believe there is no chance of reconciliation. There may be special considerations for periods of cohabitation before the marriage or after the breakdown. If there is disagreement about the proper date of separation, and if the two dates are less than six months apart, it is probably not worth arguing about—the difference in the two pension values would probably not be significant.

RETIREMENT AGE

First we must decide if sixty-five is the correct age to assume for retirement. Not all plans require that you work to age sixty-five to retire on an unreduced pension. Many plans include special provisions for earlier retirement. This might be a simple provision that the member may retire at an earlier specific age. For police officers and firefighters, the retirement age is sixty. The plan may provide that when age and years of service equal a certain number, the member may retire on an unreduced pension. Teachers can retire when their age and years of service total eighty-five. (This is called "the rule of eighty-five" or "the eighty-five factor.") Some plans provide that a member may retire on an unreduced pension when he has completed thirty years of service regardless of age. Many plans provide that a member may retire at age fifty-five with a reduced pension.

Once you have determined the age at which a member may retire on an unreduced pension, you must decide which retirement age fits your particular case. Courts often use the earliest date at which the member may retire on a unreduced pension unless the member can prove that he will not be able to retire until a later date. Some judges use a probable date of retirement.

If the two spouses or their counsel can agree on an assumed retirement age, a lot of argument will be avoided, and costs of the divorce could be reduced substantially.

ACCRUED PENSION BENEFIT

The amount of basic pension benefit earned to the date of valuation—in our example $1,000 a year—is usually a straightforward calculation. First, establish the exact amount of benefit earned to the date of valuation, as this is the basis for all other calculations. Confirm this amount with the employer or the pension administrator. The formula and rates are set out in the employer's pension documents. Make sure you refer to the right documents for the particular date of valuation; check your calculations. In most plans, the benefit is either a percentage of salary times service to date or a flat rate times service to date.

If assumed retirement is before age sixty-five, most pensions provide a bridge benefit payable from the date of retirement to age sixty-five. This is an effort to provide the member with a higher pension until he qualifies for CPP and OAS. The projected bridge benefit payments must be included in the calculations. The bridge payments cause the value to be higher, as the person has earned a higher pension.

DISCOUNT RATE AND INDEXING

To complete the calculation of present value, you need to know what rate of discount—also called the rate of interest—to use in the calculations. Some guidance for this is given in the standards set by the Canadian Institute of Actuaries. Most valuators follow these standards. However, the standards allow a certain amount of leeway.

If a pension plan provides full indexing for all pensions (for example, the pensions of federal and provincial government employees), the rate is the rate of return on Real Return Government Of Canada Bonds plus a quarter of a percent for the first fifteen years. After fifteen years, the rate is the rate of return plus 3.25 percent.

If the pension plan does not provide indexing, the standards say to use a rate related to the recent return on long term Government of Canada Bonds for the first fifteen years, then adjust the rate to six percent.

The rate of discount will have a great effect on the value. The higher the rate used, the lower the value. The higher the indexing provided by the plan, either contractual or ad hoc, the lower the discount rate used and the higher the value of the pension. This makes sense, of course, because the higher the indexing provided, the more valuable the pension. The rate of discount used in the calculations is often the item with the greatest effect on the value. It is also one area that should be agreed on by both counsel if arguments are to be avoided.

ACTUARIAL CALCULATION

Proper actuarial calculations take into account the possibility that a person may die at any time. They do this by reducing the annual payments each year by a certain factor and continuing the string of payments until death is a reality (age 105 to 110). This is called the actuarial method of calculating the value. This is the only area of pension valuation that requires the knowledge of an actuary.

INCOME TAX ALLOWANCE

Many valuators use a flat rate of 25 percent to allow for income tax that must be paid on pension payments when they are received. Our experience is that the rate can range from 0 percent to 45 percent; often the rate is between 18 and 23 percent. At Pension Valuators of Canada, we calculate future pension payments, then make appropriate allowance for CPP, OAS, and any other income that will be earned after retirement. If you have other sources of income, such as from an RRSP, it is important to tell the valuator. The extra income justifies a higher tax rate, and will therefore result in a lower value for equalization.

THE CALCULATIONS

Actuarial calculations are used to determine the net present value of each year's pension payments. Then each year's values are added together to give the proper value of the pension benefit for equalization.

Example Two shows the actuarial calculations. We assume the person retired in 1996 and started receiving his basic pension of $1,000 per year. For the first five years he also received a bridging benefit of $200 per year. Each year's pension payment is multiplied by the person's chance of surviving for one more year, then is adjusted for the discount rate of 6 percent for the first fifteen years and 3 percent thereafter. All results for the years from 1996 to 2040 are added together to determine the value of the pension in 1995.

EXAMPLE TWO
PROPER VALUATION

	Life Expectancy	Discount Pension	Rate	NPV
1995				?
1996	93%	1,000 + 200	6%	1,049
1997	92%	1,000 + 200	6%	1,038
1998	91%	1,000 + 200	6%	1,026
1999	90%	1,000 + 200	6%	1,015
2000	89%	1,000	6%	837
2001	88%	1,000	6%	827
2002	87%	1,000	6%	818
2003				
2004				
2005				
2006				
2007				
2008				
2008				
2010	75%	1,000	3%	727
2011	74%	1,000	3%	718
2012				
2013				
2040	0%	1,000	3%	0
TOTAL				?

In our example, we have simplified the valuation process considerably. There are sundry matters, for example refunds and buybacks, death benefits, survivor benefits, and vesting, which must be considered carefully. These matters are discussed in chapters eight and nine.

If the member married before joining a pension plan that includes early retirement provisions, a proper valuation report will show four values for the pension.

1. the value of the pension accrued during the marriage as if the member had terminated employment on the date of valuation (rarely the proper value for marriage breakdown equalization)
2. the value of the pension accrued during the marriage assuming the member will retire at the normal retirement age for the particular pension
3. the value of the pension accrued during the marriage assuming the member will retire at the earliest date he can start collecting a full or unreduced pension
4. the value of the pension accrued during the marriage assuming the member will retire midway between normal retirement age and the earliest date of unreduced pension.

Although the calculations take into consideration time periods outside the marriage, they consider and report only the value of the pension benefit earned or accrued during the marriage.

Which of these values is the correct value for equalization will depend on the facts of the particular case. You might want to look at reported court cases.

Chapter 8

Special Considerations

INTRODUCTION

This chapter provides detailed information and describes important considerations about the valuation date, the pension benefit that has accrued, the retirement age to be assumed, the life expectancy tables used, the indexing assumed and discount rates used, the value added method and the pro rata method, the income tax allowance, some special discounts to consider, and refunds and buybacks. All must be considered carefully to ensure that a pension is valued properly.

VALUATION DATE

Property division, in a marriage breakdown situation, is governed entirely by provincial law, and therefore varies from province to province. In Ontario, on marriage breakdown, assets are valued when two parties to a marriage separate and there is no hope for reconciliation. This seems simple enough in a traditional marriage where two people get married, start living together and later separate once and for all. There are many situations that are not quite this clear cut.

What if the two people separate once, reconcile their differences and get back together, then later separate permanently? Do you include any increase in value that took place during the period the couple was separated? The law is not entirely clear on this matter, and the courts have been inconsistent in their decisions.

If you are in this situation, ask your lawyer to review applicable court cases carefully.

These days many couples live together and never do go through the formal marriage ceremony. The Ontario Family Law Act, which provides for property division on marriage breakdown, defines "spouses" as people who are legally married. Therefore, in Ontario, unmarried couples who cohabit have no property rights under the Family Law Act on marriage breakdown. Many lawyers have found a way to argue that ownership of an asset includes more than registered legal ownership. They have argued beneficial ownership of an asset for their client; they have argued the other person is holding property in trust for their client. They have argued unjust enrichment. If you are separating after unmarried cohabitation, have your lawyer investigate this matter carefully. (See Chapter Twenty-Six.)

It is not unusual for a couple to live together for a period of time before they get married. The question that arises in equalizing the assets is whether you should include any increase in value that occurred before the marriage, during the cohabitation. Again the courts have been somewhat inconsistent on this matter, and it will be necessary for your lawyer to review all reported cases carefully.

Sometimes the couple cannot agree on when their marriage finally broke down. In most cases, if the dates in dispute are less than six months apart, there will usually not be a large difference in the value of the pension from one date to the other, and it is not worth arguing.

The Ontario case of *Oswell v. Oswell*[1] sets out criteria for determining the actual date of separation.

> 13(1) There must be a physical separation. Often this is indicated by the spouses occupying separate bedrooms... Just because a spouse remains in

the same house for reasons of economic necessity does not mean that they are not living separate and apart.

14(2) There must also be a withdrawal by one or both spouses from the matrimonial obligation with the intent of destroying the matrimonial consortium...or of repudiating the marital relationship.

15(3) The absence of sexual relations is not conclusive but is a factor to be considered.

16(4) Other matters to be considered are the discussion of family problems and communication between the spouses; presence or absence of joint social activities; the meal pattern.

17(5) Although the performance of household tasks is also a factor, help may be hired for these tasks and greater weight should be given to those matters which are peculiar to the husband and wife relationship outlined above...

18 Under the Family Law Act, the court must have regard to the true intent of a spouse as opposed to a spouse's stated intent... An additional consideration to which the court may have regard in determining the true intent of a spouse as opposed to that spouse's stated intentions is the method in which the spouse has filed income tax returns... If a mediator is consulted, the purpose for which the mediator was consulted may also be of assistance.

19 When a spouse makes plans for his or her assets as a separated person the courts consider this to be indicative that there is no real prospect of resumption of cohabitation under the Family Law Act.

ACCRUED PENSION BENEFIT

Valuing a pension means determining the value on a certain date of the amount of monthly pension benefit earned during the marriage, which will be payable sometime in the future. In other words, it is valuing the amount of pension payable in the future in the form of a monthly lifetime annuity commencing at an assumed or actual retirement date. Since the accrued benefit is being valued, it is important to ensure the accrued benefit has been calculated properly. Accrued benefit does not recognize service beyond the date of valuation or salary increases or pension plan improvements after the date of valuation. In some cases it will include the amount of benefit payable at retirement age and any bridging benefits or special allowances provided by the pension plan.

By law, every member of a pension plan is provided with an annual pension statement. (There are a few exceptions, for example federal employees.) This statement will show how much pension benefit has been earned by the person to a certain date. Compare the amount of accrued pension benefit shown in a pension valuation report to the earned benefit disclosed in an annual pension statement close to the valuation date. This will tell you if the valuation has been based on the proper accrued pension benefit.

The proper accrued pension benefit should be confirmed with the pension administrator, and not estimated by a valuator. Remember that pension administrators often quote only the amount of benefit accrued that is payable at normal retirement age, or only the benefit reflective of vested pension accruals. They do not mention or show bridge benefits or special allowances if a member has not yet qualified for those. If future bridging benefits and special allowances are not considered, the values will be understated. Make sure all bridging benefits and special allowances are considered in the valuation even if the person has not yet qualified for them. Adjustment can be made if they are not yet fully earned.

In formula pension plans, such as plans for teachers, municipal employees, and government employees, the amount of pension benefit is calculated as the number of years of service to the date of valuation, times a certain percentage, times the average salary of the person. The average salary used in the calculation is often the average salary earned in recent years.

For example, Mr. A has been a police officer for exactly ten years. His average salary for the last five years has been $50,000. A police officer's pension is 2 percent of his average salary for each year of service. Mr. A's accrued pension benefit is

$$2\% \times \$50,000 \times 10 = \$10,000 \text{ per year.}$$

If Mr. A. was married during the entire ten years he was a police officer, then the pension benefit accrued during this marriage period is $10,000, and this figure will be used in the pension valuation calculations.

In flat rate pensions, for example General Motors, Ford, INCO, and Falconbridge, the amount of salary earned does not enter into the calculation of pension values. The amount of pension benefit accrued is calculated as years of service to date of valuation times an established flat rate. In union contracts this flat rate generally increases with every new contract. Therefore, it is important to ensure that the rate used in the calculations is taken from the contract in effect at the date of separation.

For example, if Mr. A had been an hourly rated employee of General Motors for ten years, the amount of his average salary would not enter into the calculations. A General Motors' pension is based on a flat rate rather than salary. Assuming that the flat rate is $55.85 at the time, Mr. A's basic General Motors Pension would be

$$\$55.85 \times 10 \times 12 = \$6,702.00 \text{ per year.}$$

The accrued basic pension benefit used in the calculations would be $6,702.

If a person can retire on an unreduced pension before the normal retirement date, there generally is provision for "bridging benefits." These bridging benefits may be added to or deducted from the normal pension benefit. The bridging benefit is an attempt to provide the early retiree with additional income until he starts to receive Canada Pension Plan and Old Age Security. It generally is earned by working for a long time. (For example, after thirty years of service a government employee may be allowed to retire on an unreduced pension as young as fifty-five instead of sixty or sixty-five; the amount of his pension will be reduced when he does reach sixty-five.) If you include the amount of bridging benefit or special allowance, the value of the pension can sometimes double or even triple.

For example, Mr. A the General Motors employee might qualify for an additional pension of $2,160 per year because the General Motors pension plan provides for a bridging benefit of $18 per month for each year of service, payable from age sixty to age sixty-five.

The valuation of a pension must be based on the correct amount of accrued pension benefit. If the wrong amount of benefit is used in the calculations, the value produced will be wrong. That is why the benefit should be confirmed—don't estimate.

If the employee has not yet completed the requirements to qualify for bridging benefits, the employer will normally state the basic pension benefit that has been earned to the date of valuation and not mention any accrued bridging benefit or special allowance. Here is an example of the difference this can make to the value of the pension.

Mr. Roberts is forty-three years old and is an hourly rated worker at General Motors. He has worked for twenty-three years and has just separated from his wife. At the date of separation he has earned an annual pension of $13,160, with payments starting when he reaches sixty-five. If he quits before then, he'll receive the same pension, but it won't be indexed, and he won't get the bridging benefit or the special allowance General Motors provides in their pension.

If Mr. Roberts continues to work for General Motors for seven more years he can retire at fifty and qualify for a bridging benefit of $18 per month for each year of service, or $6,480 additional pension per year. The extra will be added to his basic pension benefit and will be paid to him from age sixty to age sixty-five.

If Mr. Roberts works the seven years, he will also qualify for a special allowance: from retirement at age fifty until he is sixty, he will receive a total pension of $34,260 per year. This amount could be higher by the time he retires, since the special allowance increases with each new union contract.

The value of Mr. Roberts's pension is quite different depending on whether the bridging benefit and the special allowance are included:

Value of pension if termination assumed: $ 14,165
Value if only basic pension payable at sixty-five: $ 37,595
Value including bridging benefit and special
allowance to the extent earned: $135,285

This is an actual case of a pension that was valued recently.

FOR A HIGHER VALUE

If you want to make sure the value of the pension has not been understated, make sure the accrued benefit has been calculated properly, and confirm it with the pension administrator. You should also make sure that all possible bridging benefits and special allowances have been included in the valuation.

FOR A LOWER VALUE

If you are attempting to argue a lower value for your pension, make sure the bridging benefit or special allowance has been included in the calculations only to the extent it has been earned. For example, if it takes thirty years of service to earn the bridging benefit, and you have worked for fifteen years, then only half the bridging benefit or special allowance has been earned, and only half should be included in the calculations. You might even argue that if you had terminated employment on the date of separation, you would not have been eligible for bridging benefits or special allowances. A value earned after the date of valuation should not be included in the value earned during the marriage.

It may be possible to argue that unvested pension benefits—those to which you do not yet have a right—should be discounted or excluded from the calculations. This approach has been used successfully in many reported court cases.

RETIREMENT AGE

Most pensions provide that normal retirement age is sixty-five. If this is the only retirement age to consider in the pension valuation, the process is considerably simplified. However, many pension plans provide for early retirement on a full (unreduced) pension. For example, a teacher may retire on an unreduced pension when his age and qualifying years of service total eighty-five. A General Motors hourly employee may retire at any age provided he has accumulated thirty years of service.

It is important to know which age of retirement to assume when you do the pension valuation, because different retirement ages can produce significantly different values for the pension.

Generally speaking, the earlier the age of assumed retirement on an unreduced pension, the higher the value will be for marriage breakdown purposes. If the pension benefit is reduced for early retirement, the value probably will not be any different than it would be for retirement at the normal age.

The retirement age to use is often a contentious issue between the parties to a divorce. The person who has the pension generally will argue that he cannot retire until age sixty-five or later. The non-member often will argue that the spouse always planned to retire as early as possible.

In the recent case *Bascello v. Bascello*,[2] Justice Kurisko was not provided with any evidence about when Mr. Bascello could be expected to retire. With no evidence to guide him, he settled for an age midway between Mr. Bascello's normal retirement age and the earliest age at which Mr. Bascello could retire on an unreduced pension. The judge suggested that if parties cannot agree on a proper retirement age, they can save considerable costs by agreeing to use the mid-age value. Many equalization payments are determined using that value. It is important that the mid-age value be calculated properly and not just be taken as the average of two values.

Remember, the earlier the age of retirement with an unreduced pension, the higher the value of the pension. In the case of Mr. Roberts, if we assume he will continue to work for General Motors until retirement is mandatory at age sixty-five, the value of his pension for marriage breakdown purposes is $37,595. If we assume he hates his job and can hardly wait to retire at age fifty, the value becomes $135,285. The difference in these two values is due entirely to the age of retirement assumed in the valuation calculations. Both values are based on the pension benefit accrued during the marriage and do not include any increase after the date of separation. Mr. Roberts probably will argue vigorously that he won't retire until age sixty-five, while Mrs. Roberts will argue just as vigorously that he will retire at age fifty.

FOR A HIGHER VALUE

Some arguments that support early retirement may be appropriate-to your situation. For example:

1. A plan that provides for the opportunity to retire early on an unreduced pension is obviously worth more than one that does not, provided a person can take advantage of the provisions. Assume the value of the early retirement provisions accrue over time; it is not reasonable to assume they are worthless until the day early retirement takes place, when they suddenly become very valuable.

2. Some people have always said they want to retire early. But remember, people can change their minds about retirement right up until the time they submits their resignation.

3. The earlier a retirement on an unreduced pension starts, the more a person will collect. Some people might be inclined to retire early so they can collect the highest amount possible and get the most from the pension.

4. In many court cases, an assumption of the earliest date of unreduced pension was supported.

5. Early retirement provisions of a pension plan are available whether a person takes advantage of them or not. It would not be fair for a wife to lose out because her husband decides not to retire early.

6. If the pension payments are generous and fully indexed, the person will not suffer a drastic reduction in his income on retirement.

7. A high percentage of people retire early.

8. A person in poor health or with a short life expectancy would be more inclined to retire early.

9. A person who hates work would be more inclined to retire early.

10. A person who has a hobby to follow will be more inclined to retire early.

11. A person who can retire young enough to get another job would be more inclined to retire early.

12. The older a person is, and the closer to qualifying for early retirement, the more likely the chance he will take early retirement.

13. The only way to know if a person will take early retirement is to wait and see. This is not practical.

14. Assume early retirement for everyone; the onus of proof otherwise should be on anyone who alleges otherwise.

FOR A LOWER VALUE

Some arguments may be useful in arguing a lower value for a pension:

1. The court case of *Sanders v. Sanders*[3] supports the idea that it is not always right to assume early retirement.

2. Some people cannot afford to retire early because they must make support payments.

3. Some people have not accumulated enough assets to be able to retire early.

4. The pension payments may be too small to live on until CPP and OAS begin.

5. The person may love work, or be a workaholic, or be unable to accept retirement psychologically.

6. The early retirement provisions of the pension plan may be cancelled or changed before a person qualifies.

7. A person may die, or the company may cease business, before he qualifies for early retirement.

8. Someone in good health want to continue working until retirement is mandatory.

9. Someone with a much younger spouse—someone he married after the divorce—might want to work until his new wife is eligible for retirement.
10. A person with no hobbies may find retirement unattractive.
11. Many people who retire early die shortly afterwards.
12. At early retirement age, a person might be too old to get another job.

LIFE EXPECTANCY AND PENSION VALUATIONS

Once pension payments start, they continue for the remainder of your lifetime. The longer you live, the more pension payments you will collect, and the more valuable your pension will be to you. So your life expectancy must be considered in the calculation of the value of your pension for marriage breakdown purposes. Some people think that this entails projecting a person's pension payments until they think the payments will stop. Actually, the calculations are much more complicated than that. They are based on the individual's probability of living one more year depending on age and life expectancy, with the probability being considered for each year in the future until death is a certainty, at age 110. A person's life expectancy—age at death—increases, as he grows older. In this chapter we consider the normal way of looking at life expectancy, and not the complicated calculations that are employed in valuing a pension plan.

The life expectancy tables accepted in recent court cases in Canada are known as the 1983 GAMS. These are the tables recommended by the Canadian Institute of Actuaries.

1983 GAMS

GAMS stands for Group Annuity Mortality Statistics. These tables were developed from life insurance company data on group annuity life insurance policies that covered working individuals. The tables include statistics gathered in Canada and the United States. The basic data for the tables was gathered more than fifteen years ago. They don't take into consideration new diseases that have reduced life expectancies or new medical discoveries and drugs that have lengthened life expectancies. The Canadian Institute of Actuaries requires their members to use these tables in their valuations.

FOR A LOWER VALUE

Life expectancy tables are based on average health. If you have had serious health problems, or if your family has a history of health problems, you may be able to obtain a doctor's certificate predicting that your life expectancy is less than the average. Using your personal life expectancy in the calculations would reduce the value of your pension for equalization purposes.

The 1983 Group Annuity Mortality Table used by most pension valuators does not give different mortality rates for smokers and non-smokers. Consequently, nor do reports prepared for family law purposes. If you are a heavy smoker, request that this be taken into account. Since it has been proven that smoking reduces life expectancy, this should reduce the value of your pension for equalization purposes. It has also been proven that working different shifts reduces life expectancy.

INDEXING AND DISCOUNT RATES

We value a person's pension on marriage breakdown in an attempt to establish how much money would need to be set aside now so that, with interest earned, it will be just sufficient to make the pension payments when they come due. First we establish the pension payments that must be made in the future, then we reduce (discount) them to allow for the interest that will be earned. The higher the rate of discount used, the lower the value of the person's pension will be. (If we assume the money will earn a higher rate of interest, a lower starting fund would be required.)

INDEXING

The extent to which indexing is recognized in the pension valuation calculations will probably affect the final values more than any other factor. Indexing is usually considered for two different periods: from the date of separation to the assumed date of retirement, and from the assumed date of retirement until death is certain.

If there was no inflation—if one dollar in the future would buy as much as one dollar today—our calculations would be considerably simplified. However, inflation has been with us for a long time, and we have to assume it will always be with us. A pension of, say, $3,000 a month now may look very good, but $3,000 a month may not buy very much ten or twenty years from now. Some pensions are indexed—increased—regularly so they keep pace with inflation, and some are not.

Some pensions, for example those provided by the federal government and the government of Ontario, are indexed 100 percent, so the payments always keep up to inflation. Many private pension plans have no indexing at all. And many pension plans provide indexing somewhere between 0 and 100 percent; the indexing may be guaranteed or ad hoc.

The more indexing provided by a pension, the more valuable the pension. Any indexing provided by the pension must be recognized in the valuation. We use different discount rates for different degrees of indexing, so we set different values. For example:

Mr. Michael is forty-four years old and has worked for twenty-four years. Let's look at values for three different indexing scenarios.

70 percent indexing assumed $93,800
90 percent indexing assumed $111,130
100 percent indexing assumed $116,285.

There are two time periods to consider when you allow for indexing—separation to retirement, and retirement to death. The rate of indexing will affect the values substantially. This is one of the most difficult parts of the pension valuation to understand, and the area in which pension valuators disagree with each other the most.

Often no indexing is assumed for the period from the date of separation to the date of assumed retirement. In some pensions, if the person quit work on the date of separation, his pension would not be indexed. This approach, which provides a lower value for the pension, is unfair to the non-member spouse. If the member continues to work until retirement, the portion of the pension earned to the date of retirement will be 100 percent indexed, because salaries and flat rate benefits tend to keep pace with inflation. The final amount of pension benefit—even the portion earned during the marriage—will also also keep pace with inflation. Recognition of this in the value of the pension earned during the marriage is simply recognition of the facts of life and past history. Assuming full indexing from the date of separation to the date of retirement does not, as some people suggest, add to the value something that is earned after the date of separation. Instead it recognizes the full value of the pension earned during the marriage.

The indexing assumed in the calculations for the period from date of assumed retirement to date of death must also be considered carefully. Most pension plans either state clearly the amount of indexing guaranteed after retirement, or they do not mention indexing, in which case none is guaranteed. Many pension plans add ad hoc indexing to pensions in pay.

When you review a pension valuation report, check into the history of indexing for the particular pension. (It should be in the report.) Check to see that the history has been assumed to continue in the calculations unless there is a valid reason to assume some other indexing.

THE STANDARDS

In an attempt to establish some uniformity in the values produced by different actuaries, the Canadian Institute of Actuaries has set guidelines that explain how to determine what discount rates to use in a valuation for marriage breakdown purposes. These rates are related to the rate of inflation at the valuation date.

The standards say:

> The following sets forth applicable economic assumptions for valuation dates of marriage breakdown at or after September 1, 1993.
>
> For non-indexed pensions the interest rate, for the first 15 years from the valuation date should be the month end value of the nominal rate of interest on long-term government of Canada bonds (CANSIM Series B14013) in the second calendar month preceding the month in which the valuation date falls adjusted as follows:

1. Add .50 %
2. Translate the resulting nominal rate, which is based upon semi-annually compounding, into an effective annual rate and
3. Round to the nearest integral multiple of .25 %.

After the first 15 years the rate should be 6 %.

For pensions which are fully indexed (that is where the pension increases by the same percentage as the Consumer Price Index) in both the deferral period and in course of payment the net rate of interest for the first fifteen years from the valuation date should be the month-end value of the real rate of interest on long-term government of Canada Real Return Bonds, in the second calendar month preceding the month in which the valuation date falls adjusted as follows:

1. Add .25 %
2. Translate the resulting nominal rate, which is based upon semi-annual compounding, into an effective annual rate and
3. Round to the nearest integral multiple of .25 %.

   After the first 15 years the rate should be 3.25 %.

According to the standards, the discount rate will fluctuate in accordance with fluctuations in the inflation rate or the Consumer Price Index. For example: for a valuation date in September 1990, when inflation was high, the rates are:

Fully indexed pensions: 7 percent for the first five years, then 3 percent thereafter. Non-indexed pensions: 11 percent for the first fifteen years then 6 percent thereafter

For a valuation date in March 1994, when inflation was low, discount rates are:

Fully indexed pensions: 3.75 percent for the first fifteen years then 3.25 percent thereafter. Non-indexed pensions: 7.5 percent for the first fifteen years then 6 percent thereafter.

For a partially indexed pension, the standards say to use rates appropriately between the rates for fully indexed pensions and the rates for non-indexed pensions.

THE APPROPRIATE DISCOUNT RATE

When the pension plan sets out the amount of indexing to be provided, the process of selecting the appropriate discount rates is fairly straightforward. However when the pension plan does not state the amount of indexing, or if the indexing is ad hoc, the valuator must to determine the appropriate rate. In these cases two valuators can produce two different valuations, though both attempt to adhere to the standards. Ignoring the ad hoc indexing produces a lower value for the pension. The standards say that any history of ad hoc indexing should be recognized in setting the discount rate (unless there is evidence that the indexing will not continue in future). This does leave some room for discretion.

There is some latitude in determining the discount rate when the value for age sixty-five—normal retirement age—is being determined. In some pensions, if the member terminates employment before age sixty-five, he will receive a deferred pension—his payments won't start until he is sixty-five. In these cases, the indexing of the pension payments often is reduced (sometimes to no indexing at all) when the person terminates employment before normal retirement age. Courts have said that a pension should be valued using the "termination method." Many pension valuators take this to mean that termination of employment should be assumed, and that there should be no recognition of indexing. Often this will produce a much lower value for the pension. The assumption of termination is unreasonable when you know the member is still working and probably will work until he reaches retirement age. Watch for this if you are checking the value of your spouse's pension. If two pensions are exactly the same in every detail except that one provides indexing between termination of employment and retirement age but the other doesn't, and if both members intend to work until they reach retirement age, why should one be more valuable than the other at the time of separation? Surely the values are different only if one employee quits before retirement age. A member who wants to argue for the termination value and the higher discount rates in the calculations should prove he will not be working until he is sixty-five.

FOR A HIGHER VALUE

Any pension valuation report should indicate which discount rates have been used in the calculations. The report should also state what indexing is provided by the pension plan, with a clear history of ad hoc indexing if appropriate. Make sure the appropriate discount rates have been used. If you can show the discount rates should be lower, this will increase the value of the pension.

To argue for a higher value, argue that the discounting should provide for indexing from the date of valuation, not just from the date of retirement.

FOR A LOWER VALUE

Argue for higher discount rates to establish a lower value for your pension.

Argue that the pension should be valued as though you had terminated employment on the date of valuation. In some cases this will mean no indexing of the pension payments at all and the value will be considerably reduced. You can point out that this will ensure no future increases in the value of the pension are included.

PRE-MARRIAGE PORTION

If the marriage took place after the member joined the pension plan, as it does in many cases, remember that only the increase in value during the marriage must be considered in the equalization calculation. Determine the value of the pensionon the date of separation. Then establish what portion of that value accumulated during the marriage.

The Supreme Court of Canada says that, to determine the portion of the pension earned during the marriage, the pro rata method must be followed, unless there is good reason not to. This means that the total value of the pension to the date of valuation is pro rated between the pre-marriage period and the marriage period, based on the amount of service accrued in each. However, there are many cases where the pro rata method would not be appropriate.

TERMINATION VALUE

Remember, only the increase in value during the marriage must be included in net family property and be subject to equalization. Some people think the only way to ensure this is to assume the member terminated employment on the date of separation. While this does ensure that no future benefits or increases are included, it presents other problems; it undervalues the pension for marriage breakdown purposes, and it is unfair to the non-member.

Many pension plans have benefits that are earned over a period of time and are lost if employment is terminated before a time requirement has been fulfilled. Let's look at a few examples.

In some pension plans, if you put in thirty years of service, you can retire on a full pension with bridging benefits and generous special allowances. If you terminate employment one day before you complete your thirty years of service, you lose all the valuable benefits. If you assume the valuation date is one day before you complete the thirty years, the value of the pension is low. If the date of separation is one day after thirty years of service have been completed, the value of the pension will be much higher. It hardly seems reasonable that the value should be considerably different based on one or two days' difference in the separation date. Here is an example.

Mr. Johnston had worked for General Motors of Canada for twenty years when he and his wife decided to end their marriage. If we assume Mr. Johnston stopped working on the day they separated, the value of his pension for equalization purposes would be $9,525. He was two-thirds of the way to qualifying for the generous early retirement provisions of his pension. If he worked for ten years after he and his wife split up, he would qualify for retirement at age fifty, and his monthly pension would start at $2,500, or more than $100,000.

Another example shows the difference between the value assuming termination of employment and the value assuming continued employment. Both values include only the pension benefit earned during the marriage.

Mrs. Jones had been a teacher for twenty-eight years when her marriage ended in September 1996. Valuing her pension as though she had quit the day she separated from her husband produced a value of $200,800. Assuming she would continue to teach for three more months, which she had contracted to do, produced a value of $271,600.

Many pensions state that if you stop working before you reach retirement age or early retirement age, your pension will not be indexed. Whether a pension is indexed can make a substantial difference to its value. In one of these pensions, if you quit work and separate from your wife one day beforeyou reach retirement age instead of one day after, the pension values are substantially different.

One or two days' difference in the date of separation should not have a substantial effect on the value of the pension. A proper pension valuation for marriage breakdown purposes should not assume termination of employment on the date of separation. Such things as bridging benefits and special allowances should be assumed to accrue on a regular basis. The right to indexing of a pension is earned gradually over time. A proper valuation should never take the position that the right to indexing is earned all on the day the requirements are met.

Consider the following example:

Mr. Smith begins working as an hourly employee at General Motors in January 1966, when he is twenty years of age. He is married at the time. Mr. and Mrs. Smith stay married for about thirty years, and Mr. Smith continues to work for General Motors the entire time. Both spouses are familiar with the terms of Mr. Smith's pension and are looking forward to Mr. Smith retiring at the earliest date he can receive an unreduced pension.

One day before Mr. Smith completes his thirty years of service with General Motors, the marriage breaks down, and Mr. and Mrs. Smith separate. Mr. Smith is left with his pension, which he has worked for and looked forward to for thirty years. Mrs. Smith must provide her own retirement fund. To simplify the case, we will assume that Mr. Smith's pension is his only asset. It is important that it be valued properly and shared fairly. The couple will not consider an If and When agreement.

During the thirty years of their marriage, Mrs. Smith worked part-time in some years but spent most of the time raising their children. She was unable to establish a meaningful career outside the home and did not build up a pension for herself. She was an excellent mother and wife.

Two days after separating from Mrs. Smith, Mr. Smith decides to go through with his lifetime wish. He retires. He is fifty years old and wants to enjoy the years remaining to him. From age fifty to age sixty Mr. Smith will collect $30,000 per year from his General Motors pension. This amount will be indexed. Until he is sixty-five, Mr. Smith will collect an annual pension of $23,940, about three-quarters of which will be indexed at 90 percent. After age sixty-five, Mr. Smith will collect $17,460 per year, indexed at 90 percent.

If Mr. and Mrs. Smith had not separated, and if Mr. Smith died, Mrs. Smith would receive $10,476 per year from the General Motors pension for the remainder of her life with indexing at 90 percent. (Called a survivor benefit.)

If Mr. Smith had stopped working the day he and his wife separated—two days before he qualified for early retirement—his annual pension would be $17,460. It would begin when he turned sixty-five; there would be no indexing. The lump-sum value of this pension would be about $32,800. If the termination value is used in the equalization settlement, Mr. Smith pays Mrs. Smith $16,400 and keeps his pension.

Since Mr. Smith did not retire until two days after the separation, he will collect the pension as set out above. The after tax value is about $248,000.

The difference in value between $32,800 and $248,000 is due entirely to assuming "literal termination" on the date of separation instead of valuing the pension Mr. Smith would receive if he retired two days later.

It is obviously not fair that Mr. Smith should pay $16,400 and then enjoy the pension the couple had planned on for thirty years while Mrs. Smith is left with little to invest for her retirement.

While the example may seem rather extreme, it clearly shows why the termination value is not the proper value for equalization purposes. This holds true not only for a flat rate pension. We refer you to Jack Patterson's article(*Money and Family Law*, March 1996; *Canadian Family Law Quarterly*, December 1996). Patterson warns lawyers to be careful of the termination method for valuing private sector pension plan entitlements for family law equalization purposes and explains why the termination method does not produce a value that is fair to the non-member spouse.

We also refer you to a paper by Ms. E. Diane Pask entitled "Drafting Pension Division Legislation," presented at a joint meeting of the Federal/Provincial Family Law Committee and the Family Law Section Canadian Bar Association. Pask says, "[To] share only the termination value on marriage breakdown overlooks the underlying structure of the plan and results in an unrealistic determination of the pensions value to the owner."

CONCLUSION

The Ontario Family Law Act attempts to ensure that, on marriage breakdown, the value of the assets acquired during the marriage is shared equally between the two parties. Using the termination value of a person's pension is not fair for the non-member spouse, as it ignores some values built into the pension. Chapnik, J. in *Salib v. Cross*[4] and Kurisko, J. in *Bascello v. Bascello*[5] were right in saying that if continued employment is to be assumed—as it normally should be—any uncertainties in connection with this value such as the possibilities of illness, early death, or change of employment should be provided for with a contingency discount. However, the standards issued by the Canadian Institute of Actuaries do not allow such a discount. If a mathematical approach is adopted, the value added by assuming continued employment could be reduced by recognizing length of service to date and future service needed to qualify for early retirement on an unreduced pension.

Valuing a person's pension on the assumption that he has terminated employment is similar to valuing a business based solely on the liquidation value of the assets and ignoring the additional value that is normally attributed to a successful business.

TERMINATION METHOD

The termination method is defined in the standards established by the Canadian Institute of Actuaries. When we use this method, we assume termination of employment only to find out the amount of pension benefit earned to the date of separation. The valuator is required to value and take into account bridging benefits and special allowances earned only by fulfilling time requirements. With the termination method, benefits earned after thirty years of service and the right to an unreduced pension when the ninety factor has been met are included in the value of the pension for marriage breakdown purposes. These values are shown separately from the value based on retirement at age sixty-five.

The termination method is distinguished from the retirement method, which attempts to value the pension as of the date of retirement, then pro rate the value to three different time periods: before marriage, during marriage, and after separation. The retirement method projects salary increases and creates a much higher value for a pension.

FOR A HIGHER VALUE

If your spouse's pension is being considered, ensure that early retirement provisions have been added into the value. Also make sure the calculations have assumed full indexing from the date of separation to the date of retirement.

FOR A LOWER VALUE

If it your pension is being considered, point out that benefits earned after the date of separation should not be included for marriage breakdown purposes. You may not be successful with this argument, but it may help you in your negotiations.

MINIMUM VALUE

The Pension Benefits Act of Ontario provides that the value of any pension paid for services rendered before January 1, 1987, must not be less than the member's required contributions and interest thereon. The act also provides that the member's contributions and interest for service after December 31, 1986, cannot provide more than half the pension for that service. These provisions establish a minimum value for a pension. In some cases the minimum value will be more than the value arrived at by calculating the value of a pension for marriage breakdown purposes. Some people contend that, in such a case, the minimum value rather than the calculated value is the proper value to use. This is not necessarily true. The minimum value assumes literal termination of employment, which probably didn't happen. Giving up your job to access the pension value would constitute giving additional consideration for the value received.

For a Higher Value

If you want to ensure the value is as high as possible, make sure the valuation report shows the minimum value of the pension. If that minimum value is more than the calculated net present value, argue that the minimum value is the proper value for marriage breakdown purposes, even though it probably isn't.

For a Lower Value

If the minimum value for your pension is more than the calculated value, you should point out that the minimum value is based on termination of employment at the date of separation. Argue that your pension should be valued, as a business is valued, on an ongoing basis. Point out that normally, by the time you retire, the value of your pension will be more than the minimum value, and the minimum value will be of no consequence.

SPECIAL DISCOUNTS

In the valuation of your pension, you may be able to justify some special discounts, which will reduce the value. A few possibilities:

Pension valuation calculations are based on the assumption that the individual will live the normal average life expectancy. If you have some special health problems, such as high blood pressure, high cholesterol, or a serious level of sugar diabetes, or if there is a history of these health problems in your family, you should attempt to have your pension discounted for the possibility that you may not live the normal life expectancy.

Ensure that only vested benefits have been included in the value of your pension. If non-vested benefits have been included, insist on a discount for the possibility that these benefits may never vest. Sometimes a pension's bridging benefits and special allowances are earned only if you complete a certain number of years of service. If the value of these benefits has been included in valuing your pension, suggest a discount to allow for the possibility that you may never complete the necessary service requirements or take advantage of these special provisions.

If your work is dangerous, or if you work different shifts, request a discount in the value of your pension on the basis that your life expectancy is less than the normal average.

Anything you can do to argue for a discount in the value of your pension will reduce the value, and therefore save you money in the equalization process. In some court cases these discounts were not allowed; in other cases, they were allowed. Tell your lawyer about any special circumstances.

REFUNDS AND BUYBACKS

Sometimes a pension plan member receives a refund of contributions to the pension plan. Some members repay the amount. Sometimes a member is allowed to "buy back service," if he starts working before he joins the pension plan. The timing of any of these events may affect the value for marriage breakdown purposes substantially. Pension Valuators of Canada has had cases where a person received a refund of contributions before the marriage and repaid them during the marriage. We have seen cases where service was accumulated before the marriage but the applicable contributions were made during the marriage. All possibilities must be investigated in the valuation.

SUMMARY

Many things affect the value of a pension. Make sure that anything special has been taken into consideration in the valuation of your pension.

Notes

1   (19900 74 O.R. (2d) 15, 28 R.F.L. (3d) 10, (Ont. H.C.J.) affd 12 O.R. (3d) 95n, 43 R.F.L. (3d) 180 (Ont. C.A.).

2   18 R.F.L. (4th) 362, 26 O.R. (3d) 342.

3   (1992) 42 R.F.L. (3d) 198 (Ont. Gen. Div.).

4   (1993/1995) 15 O.R. (3d0 521 (Ont. Gen. Div.) 18 R.F.L. (4th) 218, (Ont. Ct. of Appeal).

5   (1995) 26 O.R. (3d) 342 (Gen. Div.) 18 R.F.L. (4th) 362 (Ont. Gen. Div.) (July 12, 1996) Doc. 09174-91 (Ont. Gen. Div.).

Chapter 9

Other Considerations

INTRODUCTION

A few special matters may apply to your marriage, for example pre-judgement interest (interest on the settlement you have been arguing over), double dipping (when the value of a pension is shared and support is also paid), costs of disposition (sometimes a major deduction from the value of an asset), and death benefits.

PREJUDGEMENT INTEREST

In a divorce settlement, the payment of the equalization amount is often made years after the date of separation. In the meantime the spouse with more assets may see those assets increase in value considerably. Should that increase be shared by allowing interest on the equalization amount from the date of separation to the date of payment. This is usually referred to as prejudgement interest or PJI. See Chapter Twenty-Seven.

DOUBLE DIPPING

Some people suggest that when a person's pension has been included in his calculation of Net Family Property for equalization purposes, the payments from that pension after retirement should not be considered in the calculation of income to determine ability to pay support payments. They say that to do so would be "double dipping."

Early court cases concluded that double dipping should not be allowed. In more recent cases, it has been decided that a pension may be accessed twice if it is in keeping with the goals on which family law is predicated. On a property application, each spouse must account for the property benefits that have been accumulated during the marriage. If a spouse can claim that his need continues or that economic disadvantage rooted in the marriage exists after the separation, then the pension benefits may be accessed to provide maintenance. In these cases, the pension was considered property for the purposes of equalization of assets, and it was considered a source of income in a support action at the same time. If the person with the pension has sufficient income after equalizing the assets, and if the spouse has a need for income, the court decided the support should be ordered.

In the recent case of *Schaeffer v. Schaeffer*,[1] Justice Metivier found that Mrs. Schaeffer had been economically disadvantaged by the marriage and its breakdown. He also found that Mr. Schaeffer had the capacity to pay support. He divided the pension and also ordered support payments. Without the payment of support, Mrs. Schaeffer's income would be $42,000 and Mr. Schaeffer's would be $113,000. The judge ordered payment of $1,500 per month so Mrs. Schaeffer's income would be $60,000 and the husband's would be $95,000.

In the case of *Pacheco v. Pacheco*,[2] Heeney, J. said:

> Much of my concern arises out of the "double dipping" issue. Major J. recognized in *Best* (at pg. 62) that "double dipping" is a "serious problem when spousal support orders are based in part on an equalized pension" but held that those concerns did not arise in *Best* because the trial Judge did not consider the pension as a source of income for support purposes.

The "double dipping" issue is, I am advised, currently before the Supreme Court of Canada in *Boston v. Boston* [(January 17, 2001), Doc. 27682(S.C.C.) (heard and reserved January 17, 2001)], and that decision, when it is released, will hopefully settle the issue once and for all. Because the law is about to be clarified by our highest court, I do not propose to engage in an analysis of the case law for and against the proposition. However, since the spousal support order that I intend to make in this case will be reviewable, it is important that I set out the complete basis upon which I make that order and call for it to be reviewed. My opinion cannot, of course, tie the hands of the reviewing Judge, but it may be of assistance to the reviewing Judge to understand the underlying assumptions and reasoning that resulted in the order I am about to make.

The argument against "double dipping" seems, in my view, to be self-evident. The laws that govern property division and support are two parts of the same whole, the objective of which is the equitable distribution of the economic resources of the marital partnership. L'Heureux-Dubé J. put it thus in *Moge v. Moge* [(1992), 43 R.FL.L. (3d) 345 (S.C.C.) at pg. 374]:

Equitable distribution can be achieved in many ways: by spousal and child support, by the division of property and assets, or by a combination of property and support entitlements. But in many, if not most, cases the absence of accumulated assets may require that one spouse pay support to the other in order to effect an equitable distribution of resources.

Where, as here, a pension has been equally divided between the parties by means of a lump sum payment, the equitable distribution of that resource has been accomplished. It is redundant and unfair to effect a further distribution by carving out a support order from the other half of the pension remaining to the pensioned spouse, once payments begin.

Accepting as we do the accuracy of the appraisal evidence, it follows that, once the value of the pension has been equalized, the share that each party receives is actuarially equivalent. The only difference is the form that each share takes. The Wife's share is in the form of a lump sum, payable immediately. The Husband's share is in the form of a stream of monthly payments commencing on the deemed retirement date that was accepted by the court for purposes of valuation. Just as the Wife is free to enjoy her lump sum without fear of having to share it with the Husband in the future, so too should the Husband be free to enjoy his stream of payments without fear of having to share them with the Wife by handing over part of those payments as spousal support.

Even if Heeney, J. is right, there are other ways to deal with the concern of double dipping. Usually only a portion of the pension will have been considered in the equalization calculation. The other part is available to be considered as income. If one person is taking all non-income earning assets and the other person keeps only a pension, perhaps for support consideration purposes, income should be attributed to the non-income earning assets. This argument has been used successfully in some cases.

The Supreme Court of Canada, in *Boston v. Boston*,[3] carefully considered the whole question of double dipping. Their decision was rendered in July 2001. See Chapter Fourteen.

COSTS OF DISPOSITION

When valuing an asset, one question often arises. Should you deduct the estimated cost of disposing of the asset and converting it into cash? In valuing a pension plan on marriage breakdown, you *do* deduct an allowance for the income taxes that must be paid when the pension payments are received in cash. Should you deduct an allowance for income taxes and other disposition costs in valuing an RRSP? The question has been argued many times. The Ontario Court of Appeal case of *Sengmueller v. Sengmueller*[4] is useful reading in this regard. In *Canadian Family Law Quarterly*, Professor MacLeod, one of the leading experts on property law in Canada, says,

> Sengmueller stands for the following propositions:
> 1. Notional costs of disposition are to be deducted from a spouse's net family property as long as it is clear that these costs will be incurred.
> 2. If the costs of disposition are so speculative that they can be ignored safely, based on the evidence presented, they should not be considered in calculating net family property.
> 3. It is inconsequential whether the costs are considered to be a component of the valuation of the asset or they are segregated as a liability existing at the valuation date. The impact on net family property is identical.
> 4. The underlying circumstances of each matter should dictate the basis of calculating

notional income tax and disposition costs. Specifically the determination of the deduction will depend largely on:

a. the nature of the asset
b. the probable timing of the asset disposition
c. the probable tax and other costs of disposition which will be incurred at that date, and,
d. the perception of risk and how it is incorporated in establishing the correct discount rate to be used in establishing the present value or discounted value of the notional income tax and disposition costs.

In essence, the decision stands for the overall principal that notional disposition costs and income taxes are to be shared by spouses just as assets and other benefits are shared equally under the equalization scheme set out in the act.

In the case of *MacDonald v. MacDonald*[5] the court said that, because RRSPs will be taxable in any event, the parties should be entitled to some reduction. The court permitted the deduction on the entire amount even though there was no evidence at the date of separation of any necessity or intention to cash in RRSPs at that time.

Once you have determined that income tax should be deducted from the value of an asset, you must make sure the tax allowance is set at a reasonable rate. One way to do this for an RRSP is to calculate the annuity payments that would be received assuming the RRSP will be annuitized at the retirement age, then include these annuity payments in projected income to establish an average income tax rate after retirement.

Another way to provide a reasonable deduction for costs of disposition is to estimate the likely holding time of the asset. Then calculate the applicable tax and other costs inherent in disposition, and apply a present value discount.

For a more detailed discussion of costs of disposition, see the article by Neil Mairel. in the October 1995 issue of *Money & Family Law*.

For Higher Value

If your spouse's assets are being valued, make sure the deduction for income tax is reasonable. It should be based on detailed calculations that establish his average tax rate at the time the asset will be liquidated.

For a Lower Value

If your assets are under consideration, make sure all your expected income has been included in the calculation so the deduction for income tax allowance is as high as you can justify.

DEATH BENEFITS

The amount payable from a pension plan on the death of the member may need to be considered in equalization.

Pension plans provide for payments to be made on the death of a member. The provisions depend on whether the member dies before or after retirement. The courts have had to decide whether these death benefits should be valued and added to the value of the member's pension on marriage breakdown. They also have considered whether the value of these death benefits should be added to the non-member's assets on marriage breakdown.

It seems fair to assume that one of the member's economic goals would be to provide for the security of surviving dependants. This can be accomplished by accumulating assets or by purchasing life insurance, or by having a pension that pays death benefits. If you have a pension that pays death benefits, you don't have to buy life insurance or other assets to provide security for surviving dependants. It is generally agreed that the death benefits, payable before or after retirement, are of no value to the member of the pension plan unless he can designate the beneficiary of those death benefits. If the member has the right to designate the beneficiary under all circumstances, then the extra value attributable to the death benefit should be included in the value of the pension. However, many pension plans specify that the death benefit is payable first to the spouse of the member (if there is one). The member cannot designate the beneficiary, and there should be no extra value added to the value of the member's pension.

There are three types of death benefits provided by pension plans. One is on payment when the member dies before retirement. Another is on payment when the member dies after retirement but before the end of a guarantee period. The third is survivor benefits due to the pension being established on a "joint and survivor" basis.

DEATH BEFORE RETIREMENT

Pensions are valued on marriage breakdown. The valuation acknowledges the possibility that the member may die at any time after the date of separation, so the pension is discounted each year for the possibility that the member may die. The calculations also take into account the possibility of the future pension payments being received after retirement. These calculations take into account only the possibility of death based on accumulated statistics. They do not consider the amount that will be paid from the pension plan if the member does indeed die before retiring, and therefore, does not receive his pension.

All pensions provide for the payment that will be made if a member dies before retirement. The Ontario Pension Benefits Act requires payment of a pre-retirement death benefit. If the member has a surviving spouse with whom he was living when he died, the value of the pension accrued after 1986 must be paid to the spouse. The spouse may elect to receive either a cash lump sum settlement or an immediate or deferred life annuity. If the member was not living with a spouse when he died, he could have named another beneficiary. If there is no designated beneficiary and no spouse, the death benefit will be paid to the estate of the member. However, if the pension plan provides for a payment to a dependent child or to dependent children, that payment will be deducted from the death benefit. In other words, depending on the particular plan, you may or may not have any control over who the beneficiary is.

The value of the death benefit on death before retirement is not generally very high and should be shown separately (if at all) in a pension valuation. The courts have generally said this value should not be included in assets on marriage breakdown.

DEATH AFTER RETIREMENT

Pensions are payable for the life of the member. Most plans provide that the member may elect to have the pension payments continue to a named beneficiary or to his estate if he dies before the end of a specified guarantee period. If you choose a guarantee period, your monthly pension payments will probably be reduced. The longer the guarantee period, the more the pension payments are reduced.

You don't have to decide about a guarantee period until shortly before you retire.

If you haven't retired before you separate, the valuation will be based on gross pension payments. It will ignore any reductions because of a guarantee period. But if you have retired, and you did choose a guarantee period, and if the actual pension payments are being used in the calculation, it could be argued that the value of the guarantee should be added to the value of the pension. If the spouse is the beneficiary of the guarantee, this could be an asset for her.

SURVIVOR BENEFITS

Under the Ontario Pension Benefits Act, any pension that commences after 1986 must include a survivor benefit payable to the spouse unless the spouse waives the right thereto in writing before retirement. Usually, if a person dies after he has retired, a percentage of his pension will continue to be paid to his spouse until the spouse dies. Under federal pension legislation (Pension Benefits Standards Act Section 22, Sub Section 2) and provincial pension legislation (Ontario Pension Benefits Act Section 44) the spouse at the time of retirement is entitled to the member's survivor benefit. In many cases, a person retires, starts to collect his pension, then separates or divorces, then dies. Even though the couple is separated or divorced, the ex-spouse often has a right to the survivor benefit. The courts have held that the survivor benefit must be included in the non-member spouse's assets for equalization purposes.

If you retired before separating, make sure your lawyer checks into the possibility that your spouse has a survivor benefit to be valued and included in her assets.

SUMMARY

A pension valuation report may or may not consider the value of death benefits in determining the value of the pension for marriage breakdown purposes. Find out how this matter has been handled in the valuation of your pension or your spouse's pension. You might be able to argue that the value has been overstated or understated.

FOR A HIGHER VALUE

Argue that the value of all death benefits should be included in the value of your spouse's pension, particularly if he can direct who the beneficiary will be.

FOR A LOWER VALUE

Argue that the death benefit provided by your pension could not possibly be of any value to you, as you will never receive the money and you can't direct who will receive it. You can also argue that you can not both live and get the pension and at the same time die and have your beneficiaries receive the death benefit, and therefore the two values should not be added together in valuing your pension.

SPECIAL PROVISIONS

Some pension plans, for example those of General Motors of Canada, make provision for special allowances to be paid to a member regardless of age at retirement as long as he has accumulated thirty years of service. There is generally a rider attached to this provision that reduces the amount of the special allowance in the event the member earns employment income after retirement in excess of a stated amount. Should this special allowance be considered an unreduced pension? After all, it may be reduced under certain circumstances. The special allowance adds a considerable value to the member's pension.

If your pension is being valued, you may want to argue that if you do retire after thirty years of service and receive the special allowance, you will be earning employment income, and therefore, the special allowance should not be included in calculating the value of your pension.

HIRING THE RIGHT PROFESSIONALS

The costs of a divorce are high. There are lawyer's fees, pension valuation fees, real estate appraisal fees, and court costs. You may think you can save money by shopping around for people who will work for less. Or you may think you don't need any help because you can do it all yourself. If you try to save a few hundred dollars this way, you could lose many thousands of dollars in the process.

A qualified pension valuator, real estate appraiser, or business valuator may arrive at values that are much different than you expect. I have seen cases where the pension was worth one hundred thousand dollars more than the two parties thought it was. I have also seen cases where the value of the pension was far less than expected. The proper value of a pension—or other asset—can be determined only by a qualified valuator or appraiser.

A mediator or a lawyer can help you settle the equalization of your assets and your spouse's assets without the costly process of having a judge decide for you in court.

If you do go to court, you could end up paying not only your own costs but also some of your spouse's costs, and you may not be happy with the judge's decisions. The process of dividing the assets and going through a divorce is stressful and unpleasant. Hiring the right professionals to assist you in settling matters with your spouse will save you money and time.

Professionals generally charge based on the amount of time they spend with you and on your behalf. Sometimes there is an adjustment for the complexity of your case and the results that they achieve for you. You should choose your professionals carefully, as they can have a substantial effect on the results.

Ask the professional what his hourly rate is and what other charges could be involved, but don't necessarily choose the professional whose rates are the lowest. A more efficient professional may cost less, even though his hourly rate is higher. A well-qualified professional will generally get the best result.

Don't waste the professional's time telling him how rotten your spouse is. He has probably heard it all before.

Ask him what you can do to help. Complete your financial statement and Net Family Property statement. Provide full documentation to support your figures. Your lawyer will need your last five years of income tax returns and a copy of your marriage certificate. Gather all the information you can about any pensions, RRSPs, or businesses that are involved.

Be prepared to accept less than you think you should receive and to pay more than you think you should pay. Don't haggle over inconsequentials.

If you and your spouse disagree about the date of your marriage breakdown, and if the difference you are arguing over is less than six months, it will probably to cost you more to argue than the amount you are arguing over.

Keep in mind that, if you and your spouse cannot agree on who should get an asset such as the matrimonial home, a judge may resolve the matter by ordering that the home be sold. If you are unreasonable in your demands, you will run up more legal fees and other costs and may be required to pay interest on the equalization amount you owe.

SUMMARY

There are many considerations to keep in mind to ensure that you are treated fairly in the equalization process and that unpleasantness and costs are kept to a minimum.

Notes

1   (1996) File # 47942/94.
2   (2001) Docket: Woodstock 255/00 (Ont. Sep. Ct. of Justice).
3   (2001) SCC 43, File No. 27682 (S.C.C.).
4   (1994) 2 R.F.L. (4th) 232, 111 D.L.R. (4th) 19 (Ont. Ct. of Appeal).
5   (1995) Doc. # 45183/92 (Ont. Gen. Div.).

Chapter 10

The Standards

Because of the introduction of the Ontario Family Law Act 1986, it became clear that the value of pensions had to be included in the equalization calculation on marriage breakdown. Pension valuators set out to prepare pension valuations using their own judgement and drawing on their own experiences. They used many different methods—the termination method, the retirement method, the real interest method. The courts had to decide which methods would be fair to both parties yet abide by the spirit of the Ontario Family Law Act.

In 1988 a survey of actuaries who produced pension valuation reports indicated a wide disparity in the valuation of similar pension entitlements. And a review of reported court cases made it clear that different pension valuators, valuing exactly the same pension entitlements, often produced widely different values. All were prepared to support their particular value in a court of law. The same year, the Canadian Institute of Actuaries issued guidelines for its members to consider. These guidelines were debated until 1993 when the institute issued its *Standard of Practice for the Computation of the Capitalized Value of Pension Entitlements on Marriage Breakdown for the Purposes of Lump-Sum Equalization Payments* (otherwise known as Standard of Practice for Marriage Breakdown Computation). In adopting the standard of practice, the institute had three main goals:

1. to give some uniformity to the valuation reports being pre-

pared by its members

2. to reduce the need for litigants to hire separate pension valuators

3. to ensure that pension valuation reports are prepared and values are determined in a manner equitable to both the plan member and the member's spouse.

Unfortunately the standards have not resolved all the differences that exist among pension valuators. At present it seems the institute is waiting for direction from the courts, and the courts are looking for direction from the institute. The standards have increased the likelihood that a pension valuation report will be prepared properly. But it is still possible to adhere to the standards and arrive at different values for the same pension. In my opinion, the standards are poorly written and sometimes ambiguous. Some pension valuators still issue biased reports; they justify their work by qualifying their report.

The preamble to the Standards says, in part:

> The council for the Canadian Institute of Actuaries has approved the following Standard of Practice for conduct of a member (hereinafter called the actuary) when engaged to compute or specify the basis to be used for the computation of the value of a pension entitlement on marriage breakdown for purposes of lump-sum equalization payments under provincial family law acts or similar statutes. This Standard of Practice defines the approved principles by which an actuary shall determine the value of the entitlement of a plan member or the plan member's beneficiary (hereinafter collectively called the plan member). This Standard of Practice represents a basis that is not

biased in respect to either the plan member or the spouse of the plan member.

The standards define terminology, establish general principles and set out assumptions to be used. They include:

1. how to determine the interest rate to use to discount the future pension payments
2. salary increase assumptions to use under the retirement method
3. mortality assumptions to follow
4. assumed retirement ages for which values are to be reported
5. compliance with prevailing local practice on legal issues
6. content of actuarial valuation reports, for example, disclosure of client relationships, disclosure of assumptions and methods, disclosure of plan information, statement of compliance.

As set out in the *Report on Pensions As Family Property Valuation and Division*, issued by the Ontario Law Reform Commission in 1995, legal issues left unresolved by the standards include:

1. whether to use the retirement method or the termination method for valuing entitlements
2. the retirement age (or the pension commencement age) to be assumed
3. extent of recognition of benefits that were not vested on the date of separation, primarily termination benefits and early retirement privileges
4. when to recognize death benefits
5. when to recognize non-contractual inflation protection practices and other plan improvements
6. what adjustment for value at date of marriage to use—pro

rata, value added, or value of increase in pension during the marriage

7. issues related to allowance for income tax, for example
   (a) whether to adjust for income tax
   (b) whether to use average rate or marginal tax rate
   (c) which year's tax regime to use, year of separation or current year
   (d) recognition of increase in tax arising from incomplete indexing of tax brackets and exemptions

8. recognition of post-separation events, for example, change of employment, retirement, failure to retire when eligible, and plan amendments.

All these matters have been considered in court cases but the decisions have not been consistent. Policies and procedures have varied from valuator to valuator. Some valuators, in an attempt to be fair, produce several values, which causes confusion. The lawyers involved often choose a value somewhere in the middle, which may not be fair to either spouse.

Meanwhile there are still disparities in the interpretation of the standards, and there are still issues not dealt with. While the number of court cases dealing with the value of pension plan entitlements has diminished substantially, there still is a need for more clarification and guidelines.

At Pension Valuators of Canada, we have met some pension valuators who say they are minions of their clients who do mathematical calculations as requested. These valuators ignore the basic principal of fairness to both parties. Don't assume the values shown in a report are proper because the author of the report says he has adhered to the standards of the Canadian Institute of Actuaries.

A complete copy of the Standard of Practice can be purchased by sending $15 to the Canadian Institute of Actuaries in Ottawa, 360 Albert, Suite 820, Ottawa, Ontario, K1R 7X7.

Chapter 11

Who is Qualified?

If you live in Saskatchewan, Manitoba, Quebec, or New Brunswick, valuation of your pension is done by the pension plan administrator. However in Ontario, Alberta, Nova Scotia, Prince Edward Island, and Newfoundland, you must find someone to value your pension. Make sure you find someone well qualified.

Where do you go to have a pension valued? How do you know whether someone is qualified? Accountants, business valuators, economists, mathematicians, university professors, actuaries, and laymen prepare pension valuation reports. Some lawyers prepare pension valuations. None of these people is specifically trained to value pensions on marriage breakdown. A professional degree is no guarantee a person knows how to value a pension. Some accountants are qualified to prepare valuations, and some are not. Some actuaries are qualified, and some are not. If you were faced with the need to find a doctor qualified to perfom heart surgery, you would go to a specialist. The same is true when you are looking for someone to value a pension on marriage breakdown. You will get a properly prepared and unbiased valuation report only if the person who prepared it has the necessary knowledge and experience and specializes in valuing pensions for marriage breakdown purposes.

KNOWLEDGE

Anyone who states he is qualified to value a pension on marriage breakdown should have studied these books:

Actuarial Involvement in Divorce Litigation, Murray Proctor
Bankruptcy and Family Law, Robert A. Klotz
Valuation of Divorce Assets, Barth H. Goldberg
Lindey On Separation Agreements & Anti-Nuptial Contracts, Alexander
    Lindey and Louis I. Parsley
Pension Plans in Canada, Statistics Canada
Mercer Handbook of Canadian Pension and Welfare Plans
Pension Division and Valuation, Jack Patterson
The Value of Pensions in Divorce, Marvin Synder
Your Canadian Pension Plan, C.C.H.
Canada Employment Benefits and Pension Guide, C.C.H.
Canadian Family Law Guide, C.C.H.
Division of Pensions, Pask and Haas
Understanding your Pension Plan, The Ontario Pension Board
Development of the 1983 Group Annuity Mortality Table, Society of
    Actuaries
The Ontario Family Law Reform Commission Report
Getting the Most Out of Your Divorce Financially, G. Edmond Burrows

They should have studied and be familiar with these acts:

The Pension Benefits Act of Ontario, and the Regulations
The Pension Benefits Standards Act of Canada, and the Regulations
The Income Tax Act
The Teachers' Superannuation Act and the Teachers' Pension Act
    of Ontario, with the Regulations
Ontario Municipal Employees' Retirement Act, with the Regulations
Ontario Family Law Act

The Public Service Superannuation Act (Federal), with the Regulations

Executive Employment Transition Policy (Federal)

Master Agreement between the Treasury Board and the Public Service Alliance of Canada

Pension Benefits Division Act

Ontario Public Service Pension Act and Ontario Public Service Act, with the Regulations

Canadian Forces Superannuation Act

They should be familiar with all reported court cases that dealt with pension valuations since 1987.

They should know the provisions in releases issued by the Canadian Institute of Actuaries, including the Standard of Practice for the Computation of the Capitalized Value of Pension Entitlements on Marriage Breakdown for Purposes of Lump-Sum Equalization Payments, as well as notes for study of pension valuations on marriage breakdown. They should know what economic assumptions are used to calculate transfer values and marriage breakdown values relating to pension benefits. They should have read all recommendations for the preparation of actuarial reports and presentation of evidence before the courts and other tribunals. Every pension plan is established by a legal document that must be registered with Revenue Canada and with the appropriate pension board. Each plan issues a booklet or other explanation of the details of the plan. The person preparing the valuation should understand all this information. He should know the provisions of the income tax act that can affect the value of a pension. He should read *Money and Family Law*, the *Report of the Ontario Pension Commission*, reports issued by the Ontario Teachers' Pension Plan Board, reports issued by the Ontario Municipal Employees' Retirement System, and newsletters issued by other pension valuators. He should attend seminars on pension valuations. He should subscribe to and read the *Monthly Bank of Canada Review*, *Law Times*, *Lawyer's Weekly*, *Canadian Family Law Quarterly*, and *Benefits and Pensions Monitor*.

After he acquired all this knowledge, the valuator must apply what he has learned. He needs to learn how to combine the information with meaningful calculations that take into consideration the theory of probabilities.

EXPERIENCE

Someone who has not prepared very many valuation reports and does not prepare them frequently may not be up to date on court decisions. Only through experience can a person learn to apply practically what he has studied. It is only through issuing reports and having them critiqued by other pension valuators and questioned by lawyers and the courts that he can gain experience. The valuator also should have appeared as an expert witness in court with regards to some of his pension valuation reports.

SPECIALIZATION

Unless a person specializes in valuing pensions on marriage breakdown, it is unlikely he will have the knowledge and experience to prepare a good report. Valuing pensions is an evolving field of expertise that has changed dramatically over the last several years. The courts are still making precedent-setting decisions in determining pension values. Only through specialization can a valuator hope to keep himself up to date. Valuing pensions on marriage breakdown should be the valuator's only business.

CHECKLIST FOR REVIEWING A PENSION VALUATION

Whether the pension valuation has been prepared for your pension or your spouse's pension, make sure it has been prepared properly. Otherwise you could face serious problems. The following questions should help in your review. If you answer no frequently, you should consider ordering a new valuation.

	YES	NO
1. Does the valuator state **clearly** the propervalues to consider for marriage breakdown purposes (including age sixty-five and other retirement ages)?	____	____
2. Does the report provide **more than one but less than ten** possible values?	____	____
3. Does the report **explain clearly the details** of the particular pension plan, including provisions for eligibility, employer contributions, employee contributions, vesting, normal retirement age, possible early retirement, integration with CPP, normal retirement annuity calculation, bridging, indexing, and leaving the company or organization before retirement?	____	____
4. Is the report **professional in appearance, clearly written, logical and easy to understand**? A report should contain no less than fifteen pages to	____	____

provide appropriate case law references and necessary details.

5. Is the long-term history of any ad hoc indexing disclosed in the report? _____ _____

6. Does the report explain clearly the latest recommendations of the Canadian Institute of Actuaries and state that the valuator has adhered to them? _____ _____

7. Does the valuator **explain** and **justify** retirement dates, the discount rates chosen, the mortality tables used, the calculations of the income tax allowances, and any other assumptions? _____ _____

8. Has the **possibility of excess contributions** been considered? _____ _____

9. Does the valuator tell you not to use one flat, rounded rate for income taxes in all calculations? _____ _____

10. Does the report contain references to court cases and legislation? _____ _____

11. Does the report show total accumulated contributions with interest? _____ _____

12. Have the valuator's qualifications been stated, and is he qualified based on the criteria set out in this book? _____ _____

13. Has he **explained clearly his method of valuation**?   _____   _____

14. Does he consider refunds and repayments of contributions?   _____   _____

15. Does the valuator tell you not to use averaging to arrive at a proper value for settlement?   _____   _____

16. Does the report show the value for the mid-way age?   _____   _____

17. Has the termination value been included, as well as all other values?   _____   _____

18. Was information obtained from the pension plan administrator?   _____   _____

A good report may show as many as six or eight possible values for marriage breakdown purposes and equalization. You might be tempted to settle for the average of all of these values. Rarely would that be fair to both parties.

In most cases the correct value will be the net present value after adding excess contributions, deducting appropriate discounts, deducting the appropriate income tax allowance, and deducting the value earned outside the marriage according to the pro rata method. There also may be some discount for contingencies. Often this will leave you with the highest value shown in the report. Any suggestion to use some other value would need to be justified with good arguments.

Chapter 12

The Valuation Report

When all information has been gathered and confirmed with the pension administrator, the complicated calculations can be completed, and a report can be issued. The report should be easy to read and understand. It should be professional in appearance. It should include all information necessary for someone to be able to review the valuations, and should look something like the following.

PENSION VALUATION

MR. JOHN DOE

SIN: 111-111-111

AS AT JANUARY 1, 2001

PREPARED FOR: *Laura Lawyer B.A. (Hon.). LL.B.*
(File Number: 01-293)

Table of Contents

Opinion of Value

Based on our specific research and our review and analysis of all pertinent information received by us (the details of which are set out in this report), in our opinion, the actuarial net present value of the pension entitlements of **JOHN DOE** in the **ONTARIO MUNIC-IPAL EMPLOYEES RETIREMENT SYSTEM - NRA 60** as at **JANUARY 1, 2001** (after allowing for income taxes) was as set out on the following page.

Issued at Peterborough, Ontario, this December 12, 2001.

PENSION VALUATORS OF CANADA
G. EDMOND BURROWS, F.C.A.
Specialist in Pension Valuations

SUMMARY OF VALUES - PRO RATA METHOD

	MINIMUM VALUE	NRA	MIDPOINT	AGE 50 + 30 YEARS
Age	59.42	60.00	55.00	50.00
Payments Start	May-15	Dec-15	Dec-10	Dec-05
Gross NPV	$227,653	$218,555	$315,044	$434,500
Excess Contributions	16,189	18,678	12,958	9,395
	243,842	237,233	328,002	443,895
Accrued Prior To Marriage	7,942	10,683	14,458	35,900
	235,900	229,506	317,319	429,437
Income Tax	57,770	56,204	77,709	105,166
NPV During Marriage	$178,130	$173,302	$239,610	$324,271*
Tax Rate	24.49%	24.49%	24.49%	24.49%

Gross NPV refers to the net present value of the stream of future pension payments before adjustments.

The Minimum Value is the date of separation value of the accrued pension based on no further service accruals beyond the valuation date. This value, which implies literal termination of employment at the valuation date, may be more or less than the other values, which assume the member will remain in the plan to various assumed retirement ages.

The NRA (Normal Retirement Age) value is the date of separation value of the accrued pension based on the assumption that the member will continue employment from the date of separation to normal retirement age.

The Mid Point value is the date of separation value of the accrued pension for the mid-age between the normal retirement age and the age for the earliest unreduced pension, assuming continued employment. The value in the right column is the date of separation value of the accrued pension for the earliest date for an unreduced pension, assuming continued employment. These values do not include the value of a service discount. Please refer to the section of the report entitled "Service Discount" for details. Should you wish to consider values inclusive of a service discount, the after tax midpoint marriage period value is $ 228,357, and the after tax Earliest Age of Unreduced Retirement marriage period value is $299,087, including the service discount.

IMPORTANT CRITERIA

Plan Member:	JOHN DOE
Date of Birth:	November 13, 1955
Date of Enrollment:	June 3, 1975
Date of Marriage:	April 2, 1976
Date of Valuation:	January 1, 2001
Age at Valuation:	45.14 Years
Annual Payments Pre 65:	$ 32,666.52
Annual Payments Post 65:	$ 26,955.76
Average Earnings:	$ 63,837.12
Average YMPE:	$ 37,200.00
Credited Service:	25.59 Years
Earliest Age of Unreduced Pension:	50.00 Years

Pension Plan:

ONTARIO MUNICIPAL EMPLOYEES
RETIREMENT SYSTEM, NRA - 60

	Accumulated Contributions With Interest:
To January 1, 2001	$141,750.11

Important Rates at Valuation Date:

Discount Rates	
Fully indexed first period	3.75 %
reducing to	3.25 %
Not indexed first period	6.25 %
thereafter	6.00 %

Purpose of Valuation: To include in list of assets on marriage breakdown.

DETAILS OF PLAN

The basic provisions of the Ontario Municipal Employees Retirement System are as follows:

Type of Plan

OMERS is a multi-employer pension plan for employees of local governments in Ontario. It is a contributory defined benefit pension plan based on the member's final average salary.

Eligibility

Continuous full-time employees must join when hired by a participating employer. Other-than-continuous full-time employees may be required by the employer to join, or may choose to join when eligible. Municipal councillors may also join under certain conditions.

Member Contributions

The member's contribution rate as at January 1, 1998 is 4 percent of their contributory earnings up to the Year's Maximum Pensionable Earnings **PLUS** 5.5 percent of employee contributory earnings, if any, above the Year's Maximum Pensionable Earnings for NRA - 65 members and 5 percent of their contributory earnings up to the Year's Maximum Pensionable Earnings **PLUS** 6.50 percent of employee contributory earnings, if any, above the Year's Maximum Pensionable Earnings for NRA - 60 members.

Contributory earnings are the earnings on which the employee pays pension contributions, and may not be the same as actual income for income tax purposes. Overtime pay, lump sum or other payments and most lump sum termination payments are excluded from contributory earnings.

Maximum Contribution Period

No contributions are required from the member once he/she has earned thirty-five years of credited service. Contributory earnings will still be reported to OMERS and will be used to calculate the benefit.

Employer Contributions

The member's employer contributes equally to the indexed pension, paying an equal share of the member's contributory earnings. Any balance of the cost of the member's indexed pension is paid by the investment earnings of the OMERS Fund.

Normal Retirement Age

The normal retirement age for most police officers, cadets and fire-fighters is age sixty.

The normal retirement age for all other members is age sixty-five.

Early Retirement

Unreduced early retirement options are available if the member is within ten years of normal retirement age <u>and</u> 1) the sum of age in years and months, plus credited service in years and months equals ninety or more for normal retirement age of sixty-five, or eighty-five or more for normal retirement age of sixty or; 2) when thirty years of service is attained.

From November 30, 1997, through December 31, 2002, if the member is within ten years of normal retirement age (at least age fifty-five for NRA - 65 and at least age fifty for NRA - 60) and retires early, the early retirement 90 Factor will be an 85 Factor for NRA - 65 and the 85 Factor will be an 80 Factor for NRA - 60. (From May 6, 1999, to December 31, 2002, the member may be within fifteen years of normal retirement age and qualify for the 85 Factor and the 80 Factor.)

From January 1, 1999, through December 31, 2001, if the member is within fifteen years of normal retirement age (at least age fifty for NRA - 65 and at least age forty-five for NRA - 60) and retires early, the early retirement 90 Factor will be an 80 Factor for NRA - 65, and the 85 Factor will be a 75 Factor for NRA - 60.

Reduced early retirement may be chosen between ages fifty and sixty-five even if the 85 Factor, the 90 Factor, or thirty years of qualifying service conditions have not been met. The early retirement pension will be reduced by 5 percent by the least of: Normal Retirement Age less current age, the 85 Factor, or the 90 Factor, less the sum of current age, plus qualifying service, or thirty less qualifying service, all pro rated for partial years.

From November 30, 1997, through December 31, 2002, the 5 percent penalty applied to reduced early retirement pensions has been reduced to 2.5 percent (within *Income Tax Act* Limits) per year of point you fall short of: 1) the 85 Factor (for NRA - 65) or the 80 Factor (for NRA - 60) or; 2) thirty years of service or; 3) your normal retirement age.

Mandatory Retirement

There are no mandatory retirement requirements.

As a result of the March 1996 federal budget, payments made after the end of the year in which the member reaches age sixty-nine cannot be tax sheltered. This means that by the end of the year the member reaches the age of sixty-nine, Revenue Canada requires that pension contributions must stop and pension payments must begin.

Pension Amount

The member's normal retirement pension will be calculated as follows:

2 percent X pensionable earnings X years of credited service (max. 35 years),

Less at age 65

0.7 percent X (the lesser of AYMPE or Pensionable Earnings) X years of credited service from January 1, 1966.

Effective January 1, 1999 the age sixty-five pension offset will be calculated as follows,

0.675 percent X (the lesser of AYMPE or Pensionable Earnings) X years of credited service from January 1, 1966.

If the government approves the OMERS Board's most recent package of surplus proposals, the offset (retroactive to January 1, 1999) will be:

0.6 percent X (the lesser of AYMPE or Pensionable Earnings) X years of credited service from January 1, 1966.

Bridging

The member's normal retirement annuity provided until commencement of their Canada Pension Plan entitlement is 2 percent of their pensionable earnings for each year of credited service (to a maximum of thirty-five years).

Integration with Canada Pension Plan

The member's pension benefits become reduced after entitlement to a pension under the Canada Pension Plan, by a percentage of the average year's maximum pensionable earnings of the year of retirement and the two preceding years, to a maximum of final average earnings.

Definition of Pensionable Earnings

The member's pensionable earnings are his average annual contributory earnings during his sixty consecutive months of highest contributory earnings. Contributory earnings are the earnings on which the member's plan contributions are calculated, excluding overtime pay and lump sum or other payments.

Credited Service

Credited service is accrued in full months and is used in the calculation of pension benefits. It includes:
- all periods of service, including purchased leave periods, for which the member has contributed to OMERS, and has not had a refund of contributions, plus
- any period of past service with an eligible employer purchased, or provided by the member's employer, or
- any period of prior public service purchased as a buyback, or
- any period of credited service established as a result of the

transfer of funds from another public service pension plan, and

- any period of credited service established under a disability waiver of premium benefit.

Maximum Credited Service

There is a maximum of 35 years of credited service.

Definition of AYMPE

AYMPE is the average of the Year's Maximum Pensionable Earnings for the year in which the member retired and the two preceding years. Starting January 1, 1999, the AYMPE is the average of the Year's Maximum Pensionable Earnings for the year in which the member retired and the four preceding years. The YMPE, which is the maximum amount of the member's earnings on which he contributes to the Canada Pension Plan, is set for the CPP effective January 1 of each year.

Post-Retirement Indexing

The Act does not provide for indexing; however, the regulations are amended frequently to provide for it. As of July 1992, the accumulated indexing was adjusted to 70 percent of the percentage increase in the Consumer Price Index measured over the twelve months ending in September of the year prior to the increase date. Each year the OMERS Board will examine the plan surplus and, if it is sufficient, the Board may recommend to the Ontario government an ad hoc increase to pensions over the formula increase. These ad hoc increases could top up the increase to 100 percent of the CPI increase.

Prior to this date, the plan had a history of ad hoc increases.

The OMERS' Annual Report of 1996 had this to say about pension increases:

"OMERS paid ad hoc pension increases from the surplus in 16 of the 20 years prior to the introduction of guaranteed indexing in 1992, and has topped up the increase to 100 percent of the change in the CPI in every year since then."

As of January 1, 1999, guaranteed indexing is 100 percent of the consumer price index.

Pre-Retirement Indexing of Deferred Vested Pensions

The deferred pensions of terminated employees are equally indexed for inflation in the pre-retirement deferral period.

History of Ad Hoc Pension Increases

Prior to the 70 percent guaranteed inflation protection effective in 1992, there were regular ad hoc pension increases beginning in 1971, detailed as follows:

1971	10%	1979	0%	1987	4.2%
1972	5%	1980	0%	1988	4.2%
1973	5%	1981	4%	198	94%
1974	5%	1982	4%	1990	0%
1975	0%	1983	4%		
1976	10%	1984	4%		
1977	0%	1985	4%		
1978	3%	1986	6.5%		

Since 1992 ad hoc increases have increased the indexing each year to 100 percent of the increase in CPI.

Other Benefits

Provision is made for pre-retirement and post-retirement death or survivors' benefits and also for disability benefits.

When a plan member dies, the plan will pay survivor benefits. The type and amount of benefits depend on who the survivor is and whether the plan member dies before or after going on pension.

Vesting

Vesting is the right of an employee to leave his or her contributions in the plan on termination of employment in order to receive part or all of the earned pension. Vesting is usually in the form of a deferred annuity commencing at retirement age.

Benefits on Termination of Employment

Terminating employees have several options with respect to their pension entitlements and contributions and interest. They may choose any of the following options: continued OMERS membership, transferring their credited service to their new employer if it is another Canadian public service employer, deferring their pension by leaving it with OMERS, undertaking a commuted value transfer if the employee is not within ten years of their normal retirement age, or electing a cash refund of that portion of the member's total contributions plus interest that is not locked in.

ASSUMPTIONS AND EXPLANATIONS

We have prepared this report based on the information provided to us and on our review of the plan (Ontario Municipal Employees Retirement System, NRA - 60) and appropriate court cases.

We have applied the latest criteria, techniques, and standards established by the Canadian Institute of Actuaries to determine the net present value of the pension benefits using the actuarial present value approach, except where the courts have decided to vary therefrom.

METHOD OF VALUATION

This valuation has been prepared in such a way as to provide an equitable value of the accrued pension benefits based on objective statistical and economic factors. The pension benefits used in the calculations are as set out in the plan (Ontario Municipal Employees Retirement System, NRA - 60) on the date of separation and according to the information we received.

Since this is a defined benefits plan, we have used the termination method of valuation, which assumes that MR. DOE terminated employment on the date of separation, for purposes of calculating the amount of the accrued pension but continued employment for purposes of calculating the entitlement to early retirement.

These values are calculated for marriage breakdown purposes and may be different from those values associated with literal termination such as transfer value or commuted value. We have also included a value that assumes literal termination of employment. Our procedures were as follows:

We studied and summarized the detailed data, dates, etc.

We reviewed the plan (Ontario Municipal Employees Retirement System, NRA - 60).

We selected appropriate mortality tables and discount rates.

We completed full detailed income tax calculations.

We reviewed appropriate legislation and court cases.

Based on all of the above we completed present value calculations.

RETIREMENT AGE

In recent court cases, there have been three types of decisions regarding choice of retirement date. Some cases ruled to choose the earliest date at which the individual can receive an unreduced pension. Some ruled that if there is a disagreement as to the retirement date, is the earliest date at which the individual can receive an unreduced pension appropriate. The majority ruled to take what is determined as the most probable date for retirement.

In the recent case of *Bascello v. Bascello* in Thunder Bay (*Bascello*), Justice S.R. Kurisko decided that the appropriate age of retirement to assume in some cases is the age that is midway between the earliest date of unreduced pension and the normal age of retirement. This coincides with the recommendation by the Ontario Law Reform Commission in their report on pension valuations. We have included the mid-age value as another possible value for this pension, if there is a mid-age value in this case.

SERVICE DISCOUNT

When a person has the right to retire on an unreduced pension before normal retirement age, that right has value. The right to the additional value of the early, unreduced pension is earned by completion of certain criteria, for example age and years of service. At the date of early retirement, the value of that right is the difference between the net present value for the early retirement date and the net present value for retirement at normal retirement age.

We have also considered a service discount in our calculations in those cases where there are provisions for unreduced retirement prior to normal retirement age. We have noted the NPV During Marriage value inclusive of such service discount below our Summary of Values shown above.

DISCOUNT RATE

In valuing pension plan entitlements, a discount (or interest) rate is applied to the string of projected pension payments expected to be received, in order to estimate the present value of those payments.

In a fully indexed plan, the rate should approximate the difference between market interest rates for similar investments and the rate of inflation. For valuation dates before September 1, 1993, the Canadian Institute of Actuaries recommends starting with a rate arrived at by a formula related to the rate of increase in the Consumer Price Index for the first five years from valuation date. They say that this rate should then be adjusted to 3.00 percent for the remainder of the term. For valuation dates after August 31, 1993, the Institute recommends a rate related to Government of Canada Real Return Bonds for the first fifteen years, adjusting to 3.25 percent for the remainder of the term.

For non-indexed pension plans, the Canadian Institute of Actuaries recommends starting with a rate related to the rate of return on long term Government of Canada Bonds for the first fifteen years from the valuation date. They say that this rate should then be adjusted to 6.00 percent for the remainder of the term.

For partially indexed pension plans, the Canadian Institute of Actuaries recommends using a complicated formula to establish the discount rate. The formula combines the rate for fully indexed pension plans and the rate for non-indexed plans and depends on the degree of indexing in the particular plan. They also say that any history of ad hoc indexing should ordinarily be recognized.

We have followed the recommendations of the institute.

MORTALITY TABLE

Since the payments being valued in this report are subject to the survival of the employee, statistical probabilities must be applied in our calculations. These probabilities are derived from a mortality table. The 1983 Group Annuity Mortality Tables were recommended by the Canadian Institute of Actuaries in the Standard of Practice for the Computation of the Capitalized Value of Pension Entitlements on Marriage Breakdown for Purposes of Lump Sum Equalization. We have followed their recommendations.

We have assumed that the member is in average health for his age and does not have an unusual health history in his background.

FIFTY PERCENT RULE

On January 1, 1988, new regulations were established under the Ontario Pension Benefits Act. These regulations affect the value of pensions in Ontario. Before that date, in contributory plans, a member was entitled to at least his accumulated contributions with interest credited to the date of valuation.

The new legislation provides as follows:

> A former member's contributions to a pension plan made on or after the 1st day of January, 1987 and the interest on contributions shall not be used to provide more than 50 percent of the commuted value of a pension or deferred pension in respect of contributory benefits accrued under the pension plan on termination of membership or employment.
>
> A former member who is entitled to a pension or deferred pension on termination of employ-

ment or membership is entitled to payment from the pension fund of a lump sum payment equal to the amount by which the former member's contributions under the pension plan, made on or after 1st day of January, 1987 and the interest on contributions, exceed one-half of the commuted value of the former member's pension or deferred pension in respect of the contributory benefit accrued after that date.

Pension plans falling under the jurisdiction of the Pension Benefits Standards Act have similar provisions.

This adjustment has been accounted for in our calculations.

INCOME TAX ALLOWANCE

The courts have generally established that there should be an allowance for the income taxes that must be paid on pension payments when they are received. However, the discounts have ranged from 0 percent to 36 percent, often with no explanation of how the rate was chosen.

Recent cases used the projected average tax rate of the employee after retirement. This method is gaining support among pension valuators and in the courts.

We have estimated the amount of tax Mr. Doe would pay at age sixty-five on his pension payments assuming that his income would be these pension payments, any other known income, his Old Age Security payments, and his Canada Pension Plan payments.

We used the tax brackets, tax rates, and tax credits in effect at the date of calculation.

PENSION EARNED OUTSIDE THE MARRIAGE

Two methods have generally been used to estimate the portion of the pension value that was earned outside the period of marriage.

One method, the pro rata method, is to calculate the total value of the pension at the valuation date and then deduct for the portion earned before the marriage by pro rating the value based on the number of years married over the number of years of participation in the plan.

The second method, the value added method, is to value the pension earned before marriage and then deduct that value from the total value of the pension at the valuation date.

The recent Supreme Court of Canada decision in *Best vs. Best* (February 17, 1999, July 9, 1999, File No.: 26345) decided in favour of the pro rata method; this indicates that the value added method is no longer appropriate when valuing defined benefit pension plans.

DEATH BENEFITS AND OTHER BENEFITS

The plan, Ontario Municipal Employees Retirement System, NRA - 60, provides certain death and disability benefits. An argument could be made for placing a value on these benefits. Recent judgements have consistently refused to recognize any value to the pensioner of death benefits on the basis that they are funds that benefit someone else. We have assumed that the member will not become disabled before retirement. Therefore, we have not assigned any value to these benefits.

OTHER ASSUMPTIONS

We have assumed that Mr. Doe has not made any prior allocations of a portion of the pension on an "if, as, and when" basis.

DEFINITION OF NET PRESENT VALUE (NPV)

The Net Present Value of a pension is the estimated amount, which, if invested on the valuation date and on which any interest earned is reinvested, would be sufficient to provide for the pension payments, taking into consideration the fact that the recipient of the payments must be alive to receive each payment.

REFERENCES

Abate v. Abate (1988) Can. Rep. Ont. 308, 17 R.F.L. (3d) 251 (Ont. H.C.J.) Affd 17 A.G.W.S. (3d) 790 (Ont. C.A.).
Alger v. Alger (1989) 21 R.F.L. (3d) 211 (Ont. H.C.J.).
Andrews v. Andrews (1995) Can. Rep. B.C. 82, 11 R.F.L. (4th) 117 (B.C.S.C.).
Artus v. Artus (1985) (W.D.F.L.) (B.C.S.C.).
Aubie v. Aubie (1988) 91 N.B.R. (3d) 5, 14 R.F.L. (3d) 418 (C.A.).
Audley v. Audley (1993) 58 W.A.C. 127, 84 B.C.L.R. (2d) 390, 50 R.F.L. (3d) 274 (C.A.).
Aylsworth v. Aylsworth (1987) 9 R.F.L. (3d) 105 (Ont. S.C.).
Balyk v. Balyk (1992) Can. Rep. Ont. 391, File No. 353509427/92 before Justice J. de P. Wright in Thunder Bay (1994) 3 R.F.L. (4th) 282 (Ont. Ct. Gen. Div.).
Bascello v. Bascello (1995) 26 O.R. (3d) 342 (Gen. Div.), 18 R.F.L. (4th) 362 (Ont. Gen. Div.), (July 12, 1996) Doc. 09174-91 (Ont. Gen. Div.).

Beaudoin v. Beaudoin [1997] O.J. No. 5504 (QL).

Becker v. Pettkus (1980) 19 R.F.L. (2d) 165, 117 D.L.R. (3d) 257.

Belyea v. Belyea (1990) 30 R.F.L. (3d) 407 (N.B.Q.B.).

Berdette v. Berdette (1991) 81 D.L.R. (4th) 194, 3 O.R. (3d) 513, 47 O.A.C. 345, 41, E.T.R. 126, 33 R.F.L. (3d) 113 (C.A. leave to appeal to S.C.C. refused 85 D.L.R. (4th) viii, 55 O.A.C. 397n, 137 N.R. 388n.

Best L. v. Best M. (1992) 41 R.F.L. (3d) 383.

Best T. v. Best M. (1999) S.C.J. No. 40, File No.: 26345, (1997) 31 R.F.L. (4th) 1 (Ont CA), (1993) I.C.C.P.B. 8, 50 R.F.L. (3d) 120 (Ont. Ct. Gen. Div.) Court File No.: 32962-D.

Bourdeau v. Bourdeau [1993] O.J. No. 1751 (QL).

Bourdeau v. Bourdeau (1996) 26 R.F.L. (4th) 117 (Ont. C.A.).

Bracewell v. Bracewell (1994) 4 R.F.L. (4th) 183, 152 A.R. 379 (Alta Q.B.).

Brinkos v. Brinkos (1989) 20 R.F.L. (3d) 445, 61 D.L.R. (4th) 766 (Ont. C.A.).

Burgess v. Burgess (1995) 24 O.R. (3d) 547, 82, O.A.C. 380 (C.A.).

Cattran v. Cattran 45 R.F.L. (3d) 213, 119 N.S.R. (2d) 409 (S.C.).

Clarke V. Clarke (1986) 29 D.L.R. (4th) 492, 72 N.S.R. (2d) 387, 1 R.F.L. (3d) 29, (S.C.A.D.), revd 73 D.L.R. (4th) 1 (1990) 2 S.C.R. 795, 101 N.S.R. (2d) 1, 28 R.F.L. (3d) 113, 113 N.R. 321.

Cliche v. Cliche (1991) 36 R.F.L. (3d) 297 (Ont. C.A.).

Deane v. Deane (1995) O.J. No. 1150 (Gen. Div.), (1995) 14 R.F.L. (4th) 55.

Deroo v. Deroo (1990) 28 R.F.L. (3d) 86 (Ont. Supreme Ct. H.C.J.).

Dick v. Dick (1993) 46 R.F.L. (3d) 219 (Ont. Gen. Div.).

Flett v. Flett (1992) 43 R.F.L. (3d) 24.

Forster v. Forster (1987) 11 R.F.L. (3d) 121 (Ont. H.C.J.).

Gasparetto v. Gasparetto (1988) 15 R.F.L. (3d) 401 (Ont. H.C.J.).

Gilmour v. Gilmour (1994) 9 R.F.L. (4th) 365 (Sask. C.A.).

Gregory v. Gregory (1994) 113 D.L.R. (4th) 255, (1994) 7 W.W.R. 394, 92 B.C.L.R. (2d) 133, 22 C.C.L.I. (2d) 39, 3 C.C.P.B. 269 (S.C.).

Halman v. Halman (1993) Court File No. 3768/92, O.J. No. 2932 (Ont. Gen. Div.).

Hilderley v. Hilderley (1989) 21 R.F.L. (3d) 383 (Ont. H.C.J.).

Huisman v. Huisman (1994, 1996) 8 R.F.L. (4ᵗʰ) 145 (Ont. U.F.C.), 21 R.F.L. (4ᵗʰ) 341 (Ont. C.A.).

Kennedy v. Kennedy - (1996) - Court File No. C12114 (Ont. C.A.), 19 F.L. (4ᵗʰ) 454 (Ont. C.A.).

Knippshild v. Knippshild (1995) 11 R.F.L. (4ᵗʰ) 36.

Leeson v. Leeson (1990) 26 R.F.L. (3d) 52.

Levac-Vicev v. Vicev (1994) O.J. No. 17 Action No. 43152/92, Doyle, J., W.D.F.L. 352 (Gen. Div.0 (Q.L.).

Linton v. Linton (1990) 30 R.F.L. (3d) 1, 75 D.L.R. (4ᵗʰ) 637, 1 O.R. (3d) 1, 42 O.A.C. 328, 41 E.T.R. 85 (Ont. C.A.).

Marsham v. Marsham (1987) 38 D.L.R. (4ᵗʰ) 481, 59 O.R. (2d) 609, 7 R.F.L. (3d) 1 (Ont. H.C.J.).

Miller v. Miller (1987) 8 R.F.L. (3d) 113.

Moge v. Moge 43, R.F.L. (3d) 345 (1992) 3 S.C.R. 813 (1994) W.W.R. 481, 145 N.R. 1, 81 Man. R. (2d) 161, 99 D.L.R. (45ᵗʰ) 456 (S.C.C.).

Monger V. Monger (1994) 8 R.F.L. (4ᵗʰ) 157, O.J. No. 1650 (Ont. Gen. Div.).

Munro v. Munro [1995] O.J. No. 1769 (QL).

Porter v. Porter (1986) 1 R.F.L. (3d) 12.

Radcliff v. Radcliff [1994] O.J. No. 2874 (QL).

Radcliffe v. Radcliffe (1995) W.D.F.L. 188 (Ont. Gen. Div.).

Ramsay v. Ramsay (1994) 111 D.L.R. (4ᵗʰ) 312, (1994) 3 W.W.R. 562, 119 Sask R. 81, 2 C.C.P.B. 120, 1 R.F.L. (4ᵗʰ) 447 (Sask. Ct. Q.B.).

Rauf v. Rauf (1992) 39 R.F.L. (3d) 63.

Rickett v. Rickett (1990) 67 D.L.R. (4ᵗʰ) 103, 72 O.R. (2d) 321, 25 R.F.L. (3d) 188 (Ont. H.C.J.) supp. reasons 71 D.L.R. (4ᵗʰ) 734.

Rusticus v. Rusticus (1995) Court File No. 15829, Killeen J. O.J. No. 516 (Ont. Gen. Div.) (Q.L.).

Rutherford v. Rutherford (1979) 14 R.F.L. (2d) 41.

Salib v. Cross (1993/1995), 15 O.R. (3d) 521 (Gen. Div.), 18 R.F.L. (4th) 218 (Ont. C.A.).

Sanders v. Sanders (1992) 42 R.F.L. (3d) 198 (Ont. Gen. Div.).

Sauder v. Sauder (1996) File No. A4123/93, Meehan J. (Ont. Ct. of Justice - Gen. Div.) 23 R.F.L. (4th) 228.

Sengmueller v. Sengmueller (1994) 2 R.F.L. (4th) 232, 111 D.L.R. (4th) 19, 17 O.R. (3d) 208, 69 O.A.C. 312, 25 C.P.C. (3d) 61, (Ont. C.A.).

Shafer v. Shafer (1996) 25 R.F.L. (4th) 410.

Smiley v. Ontario (Pension Board) (1994) 4 R.F.L. (4th) 275, 116 D.L.R. (4th) 337 (Ont. Gen. Div.).

Spinney v. Spinney [1996] O.J. No. 1869 (QL).

Stevens v. Stevens (1992) 41 R.F.L. (3d) 212.

Valenti v. Valenti (1996) 21 R.F.L. (4th) 246 O.J. No. 522 (Ont. Gen. Div.).

Weaver v. Weaver (1991) 32 R.F.L. (3d) 447 (Ont. Gen. Div.).

Wiebe v. Wiebe (1988) 72 Sask. R. 17,18, R.F.L. (3d) 408 (Q.B.).

Yaschuk v. Logan (1991) (C.A. 1992) 33 R.F.L. (3d) 316 (N.S.S.C.), 39 R.F.L. (3d) 417 (N.S.S.C. Appeal Div.).

Canadian Institute of Actuaries ' "Standard of Practice for the Computation of the Capitalized Value of Pension Entitlements on Marriage Breakdown for Purposes of Lump-Sum Equalization Payments," Effective September 1, 1993.

Division of Pensions by Pask and Haas (Carswell).

Family Law Act of Ontario (R.S.O. 1990).

Ontario Municipal Employees Retirement System, NRA – 60.

Lindey on Separation Agreements and Anti-Nuptial Contracts.

Ontario Law Reform Commission, Report on Pensions as Family Property: Valuation and Division (1994).

Pension Division and Valuation - Family Lawyers' Guide, Jack Patterson, 1991.

Valuation of Divorce Assets, Garth H. Goldberg.

Value of Pensions In Divorce, Marvin Snyder.

Getting the Most Out of Your Divorce Financially, G. Edmond Burrows.

CREDENTIALS OF VALUATOR
G. EDMOND BURROWS, F.C.A.

- Acquired Chartered Accountant's designation for the province of Ontario in 1960
- Awarded Fellowship (F.C.A.) of the Institute of Chartered Accountants of Ontario in 1976 for outstanding contribution to the profession
- Chairman of numerous committees of the Institute of Chartered Accountants of Ontario
- Past president of Central Ontario Chartered Accountants Association
- Tax specialist and senior partner in a national accounting firm.
- Member of various committees of national accounting firm.
- Author of numerous articles on tax, business development, estate planning, amalgamations, and pension valuations on marriage breakdown
- Guest speaker at numerous functions and conventions
- Authority and specialist in pension valuations; issued more than five thousand reports on valuation of pension plan entitlements on marriage breakdown
- Accepted as an expert witness in court in cases involving valuation of pension plans on marriage breakdown
- Assisted in settling pension valuation disputes without resorting to court
- Author of *Getting The Most Out Of Your Divorce – Financially*
- Gave numerous seminars on pension valuation to lawyers
- Provided services to more than 1,400 lawyers

PENSION VALUATORS OF CANADA

Pension Valuators of Canada is meant to be synonymous with Pension Valuators International Incorporated and is completely owned and operated by Pension Valuators International Incorporated.

This report values the pension of Mr. John Doe, who separated from his wife on January 1, 2001. The report shows a normal retirement age of sixty, meaning Mr. Doe is probably a police officer or a firefighter.

The report gives full details of the particular pension plan and sets out all assumptions and explanations. The important criteria used in the valuation of the pension are set out on page five for easy checking. If any of these criteria are wrong, the values shown for the pension could be wrong.

Page four of the report shows four possible values for Mr. Doe's pension, each of which assumes a different age at which Mr. Doe will retire. Mr. Doe was only about forty-fivewhen he separated from his wife, and it is impossible to predict exactly when he will retire. Each column shows when the pension payments will start based on the assumed retirement age. The table then shows the Net Present Value (NPV) of the future pension payments, to which is added excess contributions. From this total is deducted the portion of the pension earned before marriage and a reasonable allowance for income tax. The final figure in each column shows the value of the pension earned during the marriage for the particular age of retirement assumed.

The value of the pension accrued during the marriage ranges from $173,302 to $324,271, depending on which age of retirement is assumed. From this you can see that a pension has more than one possible value, and it becomes extremely important to determine which age of retirement is the proper age to assume in valuing Mr. Doe's pension.

Column 1, Minimum Value

This value assumes that Mr. Doe stopped working the day he and his wife separated. (We know this did not happen.) Mr. Doe was just over forty-five years of age when he and his wife separated. He had accumulated 25.59 years of service. If Mr. Doe had stopped working on the date of separation, he would qualify for a deferred pension, with the payments starting at age 59.42. The value of the portion of that pension earned during the marriage would be $178,130.

Column 2, NRA

This column shows the value of Mr. Doe's pension earned during the marriage and assumes he will continue to work until he reaches the normal retirement age of sixty in November, 2015, with his payments starting in December, 2015. Under this assumption, the value of Mr. Doe's pension for marriage breakdown purposes is $173,302.

Column 3, Midpoint

This column shows the value of Mr. Doe's pension accrued during his marriage assuming that he will retire midway between his normal retirement age of 60, and the age of his earliest unreduced pension, which assumes continuous service, age 50. This value is $239,610.

Column 4, Age 50 + 30 Years

This column shows the value of Mr. Doe's pension earned during the marriage and assuming that he will continue to work until he has both accumulated thirty years service and reached fifty years of age. The value of his pension based on these assumptions is $324,271.

If consideration is given to the possibility that Mr. Doe may for many reasons not retire at fifty or fifty-five, these values should be reduced by a service discount, and will give values of $228,357 and $299,087 respectively. It is useful to compare all four values to Mr. Doe's accumulated contributions with interest to January 1, 2001, which is $141,750 before adjusting for the pre-marriage period and income tax. Clearly, the value of the pension for marriage break-down purposes has little relationship to the accumulated contributions and interest.

Since the four possible values for Mr. Doe's pension vary widely, it becomes important to know which age of retirement should be assumed in order to determine which is the proper value to include in his Net Family Property statement (NFP).

Chapter 13

Service Discount

Many pension plans allow the member to retire before age sixty-five on a generous pension provided he meets certain criteria. These early retirement provisions must be recognized in valuing the pension for equalization on marriage breakdown. Literal termination of employment at the date of separation should never be assumed except to determine the earliest date of unreduced pension. Most recent court decisions have recognized the right to retire early. The Court of Appeal in *Salib v. Cross*[1] and the Supreme Court of Canada in *Best v. Best*[2] decided differently, but only over when the member would reach his 90 Factor. In *Best v. Best*, the Supreme Court of Canada also ruled that future service should not be counted. However, there is always the possibility that assuming retirement at the earliest age of unreduced pension may be unfair to the spouse who has the pension. At the same time, not recognizing the value of being able to retire early may be unfair to the non-pensioned spouse.

It is also important to recognize that the early retirement provisions of a pension are not even vested until all requirements have been met, and the Family Law Act says that only *vested* pensions are property.

Obviously the best solution to this conundrum is to include the value of the early retirement provisions and then provide a service discount to arrive at a value that is fair to both parties, particularly if future service is being considered in determining the assumed retirement age.

As Justice Catherine Aitken said in a paper she delivered to Ontario judges in April 1998,[33,34]

> The age at which a pension plan member will commence receiving a pension has become one of the most contentious issues in pension valuations. Earlier case law under the Family Law Act[3] allowed for the application of a presumption in situations where the evidence regarding retirement date was contradictory. More recent case law, and especially the Court of Appeal decision in Kennedy v. Kennedy[4] has put an end to the use of any presumption. Each case is to be decided on its facts. The resulting lack of certainty in individual cases has resulted in increased litigation and unwillingness on the part of litigants to settle.

Usually the possible values based on different retirement ages apart differ by $100,000 or more. The provision of a reasonable discount to the early retirement values would reduce the gap in the values and thereby reduce the amount of litigation.

There are several other reasons providing a service discount in a pension valuation may be appropriate. The service discount approach has been suggested by some judges at trial and has been recommended by the Ontario Law Reform Commission in their extensive study of pension valuations. The service discount becomes particularly appropriate when the valuation has been prepared by providing indexing in the deferral period (that is, the period from the date of separation or valuation to the assumed date of retirement).

The fact that the early retirement pension has not vested at the date of valuation is another good reason for providing a discount for the possibility that it may never vest. Justice Kurisko in the case of *Bascello v. Bascello*[5] suggested this.

MATHEMATICAL CALCULATION

The service discount is a means of reducing the additional value of an early retirement provision so it is recognized only to the extent that it has been earned. For example, if the particular pension requires thirty years of service to earn the right to retire early, and the person has only worked fifteen years to the date of valuation, we would discount the additional value that is due to early retirement by half. We are recognizing that the person is only halfway to earning the right to retire early.

The actual calculation for reducing the value of the early retirement pension (assuming the person has only completed half the required service) would be to apply the discount rate to the difference between the value of the early retirement pension and the value of the pension based on retirement at the normal retirement age. This calculated discount would then reduce the early retirement value. Calculating the discount mathematically provides consistency.

CONTINGENCY DISCOUNTS

There are many possible reasons a person may not retire early. These reasons could include premature death, illness, and loss of employment. There is the possibility that the person's salary may not keep pace with inflation. It is also possible that when the person reaches the early retirement age, he is not able to retire for financial or other reasons. The discount rate used in the calculation may not be an appropriate estimate of future inflation. The service discount allows for these contingencies.

COURT DECISIONS

Such a discount was suggested and allowed by the judges in the cases of *Bascello v. Bascello, Salib v. Cross, Knippschild v. Knippschild, Madden v. Madden, Erion v. Erion, Richter v. Richter, Sauder v. Sauder, Fernich v. Fernich, Hilderley v. Hilderley, Weise v. Weise, Biblow v. Biblow, Deroo v. Deroo, Dorriesfield v. Dorriesfield, Harrop v. Harrop, Kalytuk v. Kalytuk, McBurnie v. McBurnie, Tucker v. Baudais,* and others.

The Ontario Law Reform Commission also recommended using the discount. It was considered in *Sauder v. Sauder.*

Bascello v. Bascello[6]

Justice Kurisko carried out considerable research and was very thorough in his reasons, which were set out in a 104-page decision. He determined that pensions should be indexed in the deferral period, and then a 30 percent discount should be applied to allow for the possibility that Mr. Bascello might not, for various reasons, take advantage of the early retirement value of his pension.

The 30 percent discount was applied to the difference between the value of Mr. Bascello's pension assuming early retirement and the value assuming continued employment until normal retirement. The 30 percent discount was somewhat arbitrary, and Justice Kurisko explained that he had no basis on which to determine a more accurate discount.

Madden v. Madden[7]

Justice Pardu noted that the valuations presented to him made no deduction for the contingency that Mr. Madden's income may not keep pace with inflation between valuation day and retirement, nor for the risk that disability or some other reason other than death in that period could result in an earlier loss of employment. He applied a 15 percent discount to the *total* value of the pension as otherwise calculated.

Salib v. Cross[8]

In this case, Justice Chapnik said, "In my view it would be inappropriate to accept a method of calculation which utilizes maximum figures without regard to contingencies which might affect those figures such as ill health, early death or change of employment and without taking into account the length of the particular period of service involved."

This statement supports the provision of a service discount particularly when the deferral period has been indexed. The service discount recommended here acknowledges the length of the particular period of service involved, as it is based on the number of years the individual still has to work to qualify for early retirement. The Ontario Court of Appeal agreed.

Knippshild v. Knippshild[9]

Justice Klebuc said,

> Where the pension benefit is to be distributed by way of a lump-sum payment the value of the non-member share, arrived at using the retirement method, is to be discounted by the member's future income tax liability, loss of opportunity and borrowing costs (if any), premature death risk, loss of employment risk, the risk of an error in interest and

inflation rate assumptions, and by the benefit of a cash payment to the payee (if any).

Justice Klebuc is supporting the deduction of the service discount, at least when indexing is provided in the deferral period.

Sauder v. Sauder[10]

Justice Meehan said, "I am of course bound by the evidence led before me, even if it is by report and as a result, I am not willing to use the approach set out in *Bascello* because of the reluctance of Mr. Dibben to do so. If I had used that method, I would have allowed a 20 percent contingency for possible loss of indexing and other imponderables." Another statement of support for the service discount.

Ferniuk v. Ferniuk[11]

Justice Scollin said, "There must be some discount, necessarily arbitrary, for the various economic, social and personal changes which may occur between now and the year 2002."

Richter v. Richter[12]

Justice Lawton allowed a discount of 6 percent for contingencies.

Erion v. Erion[13]

Justice Gagne said, "These funds are not cash in the Petitioner's hands and cannot be cash in her hands at the present time, so to arrive at a present-day value, these must be adjusted for contingencies. To this end, these funds must be reduced by another 15 %."

Hilderley v. Hilderley[14]

Mr. Hilderley, a teacher, was forty-nine at the date of trial. If continued service was included in determining his 90 Factor, he could retire at age fifty-five. Justice Osborne decided to assume retirement at age fifty-five. He said,

> Mr. Rudel's approach is flawed because it does not take contingencies into account in any realistic way. There are a number of contingencies that were referred to in the evidence.
>
> One of them is the contingency of a change of employment [although Mr. Hilderely had, in fact, continued to teach and reach age 55 at the date of trial]. There are other contingencies, which are referred to in the evidence, which I have not reviewed. Having in mind those contingencies and attempting to discard from the calculation what we now know, it seems to me that even Mr. Aseltein's approach [actuary for Mr. Hilderley] was too generous.

He then deducted what he called a "reasonable contingency deduction" without specifically identifying the amount.

Weise v. Weise[15]

After reviewing *Best, Hilderley, Alger,* and *Rickett,*Justice Granger said,

Following the Hilderley approach, if the evidence on a balance of probabilities establishes that Mr. Weise would continue his employment with the Elgin County Board of Education and take early retirement at age 56, the present value of his pension at separation would be $230,479 subject to reduction by 25 % for contingencies.

Biblow v. Biblow[16]

Justice Schiebel said,

> There is ample authority to reduce the pension value for taxes and for contingencies. The respondent suggests a 30 % adjustment for taxes and 6 percent for contingencies. In my view, both figures give an advantage to the petitioner and I am prepared to accept this recommendation made by the respondent.

Deroo v. Deroo[17]

Justice Misener accepted the recommendation of Mr. Asselstine, an actuary, who suggested a discount of 11 percent in case employment was terminated before the earliest age of unreduced pension.

Dorriesfield v. Dorriesfield[18]

Justice Meehan referred to the fact that service discounts had been considered in other cases and allowed a 10 percent deduction.

Harrop v. Harrop[19]

Jusitce Osborne said,

> In this case the actuary, Louis R. Martel, using the discount rates based on the recommendations of the Canadian Institute of Actuaries for the computation of the capitalized value of pension entitlements on marriage breakdown, testified that the discount factor in this case should be 21.4 per cent for income tax, with a contingency factor of 5 per cent. As this was the uncontradicted evidence of the actuary Martel, who was qualified as an expert in this area, I intend to apply these percentages to the value of the pension based on the termination method.

Kalytuk v. Kalytuk[20]

Justice Dickson allowed a 6 percent reduction for prepayment advantage and future contingencies.

McBurnie v. McBurnie[21]

Justice McGarry said,

> A further reduction of 5 percent was allowed for the contingency that the husband would not reach the early retirement date. Having listened to the husband's evidence, noted his excellent health and the little likelihood of his changing jobs, it would seem

to be a fair deduction.... In this matter I am satisfied that a 5 percent contingency is appropriate and I note that it was not challenged at trial.

Tucker v. Baudais[22]

Justice Dixon said,

> Many contingencies may reduce the value of his share; premature death and inflation for example. A reasonable reduction of the petitioner's share should be made to offset the advantage she will enjoy from a cash payment and to allow for the contingencies faced by the respondent. In my opinion, a reduction of 6 % would be fair and reasonable.

ONTARIO LAW REFORM COMMISSION

The Ontario Law Reform Commission studied pension valuations in 1995 and issued a report. Their recommendations can be found on page 268 of their report. They said, "[The] calculation should include a discount to reflect the possibility of termination of plan membership prior to the member reaching retirement."

INDEXING IN THE DEFERRAL PERIOD

When a pension is valued and indexing is provided in the deferral period, future inflation is being estimated. Actual inflation could differ from the estimate. The provision of a contingency discount allows for any error in estimating. It also allows for the possibility that the salary or flat rate used in the pension benefit calculation may not keep pace with inflation.

OTHER OPINIONS

Many pension valuators suggest that if the early retirement values were being considered in a pension valuation, it probably would be appropriate to provide a discount for the possibility that the member may not retire early. However, they do not provide for the discount in the values they produce in their report. Here are some comments from valuators:

> If a mathematical approach is to be adopted because a most likely retirement age cannot be established, it seems to me that it should take into account the length of service to date and the additional future service required to qualify for an undiscounted pension. In this way very little recognition would be given to early retirement for a short service member who is likely not going to remain with the same employer until retirement; and almost full recognition would be given to early retirement for a long-service member who would actually be expected to remain; gradual partial recognition would be given to situations falling between those two extremes.[23]

This thinking coincides with our suggestion of a service discount.

> The selection of the most appropriate scenario among those discussed above would depend on, for example, relevant case law and such factors as [the client's] lifestyle and financial circumstances, as well

as any economic climate that might affect continued employment for any appreciable period after the date of separation.

I would point out that the figure based on age 56 is predicated on [the client] (a) continuing to teach until reaching that age (she was 48 at the valuation date); and (b) retiring at that age if she does so remain rather than, for example, continuing in employment until attaining a higher age.

If the figure for age 56 is to be taken into account, some discount should presumably be applied in order to reflect the possibility of either or both of the situations mentioned in (a) or (b) not materializing.[24]

This is a strong recommendation for a service discount.

Retirement Age Assumption

Court rulings have varied on the extent to which early retirement benefits should be recognized for purposes of the Ontario Family Law Act.

Some courts have applied a strict interpretation of the termination method under which non-vested early retirement rights are excluded from consideration. Other courts have ruled that the amount of pension should be determined using the termination method, but the value of the pension should be based on the earliest age for an unreduced pension, assuming continued employment up to retirement.

Recently, some rulings have used an "intermediate" retirement age. Others have relied on evidence as to the expected retirement age in the specific circumstances.

Since the lump-sum value may be significantly affected by the retirement age assumption, the implications of this assumption should be carefully considered. The enhanced early retirement values will normally be realized only if Mr. X continues future service under the plan until eligible for early retirement; wishes to retire early and is in a financial position to do so at the time. These may be affected by the consequences of marriage breakdown; accepts a lower total lifetime pension. Additional Basic pension will be earned for each additional year of service up to age 65. The weight given to the enhanced values should also give consideration to the possibility that Mr. X may voluntarily or involuntarily terminate employment for unforeseen reasons before qualifying for early retirement.

In the absence of agreement or clear evidence as to the expected retirement age, an intermediate retirement age assumption may make reasonable allowance for the possibility that the enhanced values will not be realized. Alternatively, the enhanced early retirement values could be reduced by a contingency discount.[25]

The value of Mr. X's Pension Asset would be highly dependent upon the applicable future retirement date. This is as much a legal issue as an actuarial matter. Any future retirement date is not known for certain. Retirement means an employee will forgo the often significant excess of income from employment over pension entitlements, and also forego the opportunity to obtain increased lifetime retirement income as a result of the combination of additional service (each year of service increases pension benefits), and additional higher average earnings. As such, many members, do not retire at the first opportunity to access an "unreduced" pension. On the other hand, many members may choose to take advantage of Plan terms and retire prior to age 65.

I suggest that the above possible retirement dates illustrate the range for the Pension Asset, the maximum value occurring only if Mr. X works to at least August 28, 2002 and retires at March 31, 2007, and the minimum value occurring if Mr. X maximizes his income and ultimate pension by working fully to Normal Retirement. Values for retirement at every intermediate date could be developed approximately by interpolation. One value which I suggest may be viewed as a fair and reasonable single value would be that developed by assuming employment to at least August 28, 2000 and retirement at or about September 30, 2009; namely, the average value of the extremes shown above.[26]

This suggests that averaging the values in reports reduce early retirement values.

The appropriate value of the pension asset would depend on the expected age of retirement. In different cases, the courts have favoured using the normal retirement age, using the earliest age that the plan member could receive an unreduced pension, or using an approach reflecting a compromise between these retirement dates. If the parties cannot reach an agreement then the time of retirement is a factual issue to be determined at trial, as any other issue, on the balance of probabilities.

The separation itself can alter the expected retirement date. In many cases, the separated plan member will not have the anticipated future financial resources that would permit retirement as early as had been previously assumed.

Younger plan members may have a greater probability of terminating employment rather than remaining in the plan until retirement. In that case, a compromise might be appropriate which considers the probability of terminating service before retirement and the probability of remaining with the employer (and in the plan) until retirement.

As an example, assume that there is a 50% probability that the plan member may terminate service and 50% probability that the plan member will retire from the plan. Then the pension asset might be calculated to be 50% of the commuted value (assuming actual termination of service) plus 50% of the value of the pension asset using the appropriate retirement age.[27]

This is another way to reduce the early retirement value but it would be difficult to apply.

One actuary develops values that provide full indexing before retirement and also develops values providing no indexing before retirement. He then suggests a discount for each assumed retirement age that is a percentage—usually 30 percent—of the difference between the fully indexed values and the non-indexed values. He suggests that a different method of discounting may be appropriate depending on the facts of the particular case.

SUMMARY

The values for retirement before normal retirement age should be reduced by a discount. The provision of a service discount is an appropriate method of doing this in a pension valuation, especially when the valuations produced have provided indexing before retirement. This assists the parties in coming to agreement on a particular value and reduces the need for lengthy negotiation.

Notes

1 (1993/1995) 15 O.R. (3d) 521 (Ont. Gen. Div.) 18 R.F.L. (4th) 218, (Ont. Ct. of Appeal).
2 (1999) S.C.J. No. 40, File No.: 26345, (1997) 31 R.F.L. (4th) 1 (Ont. C.A.), (1993) I.C.C.P.B. 8, 50 R.F.L. (3d) 120 (Ont. Ct. Gen. Div.) Court File No.: 32962-D.
3 (1990), C.F. 3.
4 (1996), 19 R.F.L. (4th) 454 (Ont. C.A.)
5 (1995) 26 O.R. (3d) 342 (Gen. Div.) 18 R.F.L. (4th) 362 (Ont. Gen. Div.) (July 12, 1996) Doc. 09174-91 (Ont. Gen. Div.).
6 (1995), 26 O.R. (3d) 342 (Gen. Div.) 18 R.F.L. (4th) 362 (Ont. Gen. Div.).
7 (1997), C.R.O. 699 File # CL 1169/90 before Pardu J.
8 (1993 & 1995) 15 O.R. (3d) 521 (Ont. Gen. Div.) 18 R.F.L. (4th) 218 (Ont. Crt of Appeal).
9 (1995) 11 R.F.L. (4th) 36 (Sask. Queen's Bench).
10 (1996) 23 R.F.L. (4th) 228.
11 (1983) 5 W.W.R. 406 22 MAN. R. (2d) 135.
12 (1991) 34 R.F.L. (3d) 387.
13 (1988) 13 R.F.L. (3d) 25.

14 (1989) 21 R.F.L. (3d) 383.

15 (1992), 44 R.F.L. (3d) 22, 99D L.R. (4th) 542, 12 O.R. (3d) 492 (Ont. Gen. Div.).

16 (1991) CarswellSask 497, 92 Sask. R. 68 (1991) W.D.F.L. 631.

17 (1990) CarswellOnt 281, 28 R.F.L. (3d) 86.

18 (1999) CarswellOnt 1473.

19 (1991) CarswellSask 85, 37 R.F.L. (3d) 433, 95 Sask. R. 258.

20 (1992) CarswellSask 428, 98 Sask. R. 311.

21 (1989) CarswellOnt 1328.

22 (1989) CarswellSask 431, 77 Sask. R. 171.

23 Mr. Ben Dibben of Eckler Partners Ltd.

24 Excerpt from an Eckler Partners Ltd. valuation report.

25 D'Alton Rudd and James Jeffery of Dilkes, Jeffrey and Associates, Inc. have included this wording in their valuation reports.

26 The preceding is an example of wording used by J.M. Norton of AON Consulting.

27 David Hart of Hart Actuarial Consulting.

Chapter 14

To Double Dip or Not to Double Dip, That is the Question

The Supreme Court of Canada issued their decision in *Boston v. Boston* in 2001. Many people have been waiting for this decision because of the double dipping concern. The Supreme Court of Canada's decision to the question stated above seems to be…maybe.

Concern about double dipping usually arises in the following way. On marriage breakdown the parties equalize the assets. The spouse with the pension—let's say the wife—must include the value of the future pension as part of her net family property. If the wife retains her pension, the husband must get other assets of the same value to equalize their net family properties. While the wife is still employed, she may be obliged to make spousal support payments to the husband. When she retires, however, and her pension comes into pay, the husband is making a double recovery if he continues to receive spousal support from the wife's pension income because he received assets equal to the capital value of the pension at the time of settlement. If support payments from the pension are maintained, he is collecting twice from the same source.

A question then arises. Is the wife entitled to reduce the support obligation to her former husband when she retires because her pension was already part of the agreed division of the matrimonial property?

Boston v. Boston[1]

Mr. and Mrs. Boston separated after a thirty-six-year marriage. By consent to judgement, in 1994, Shirley Boston received assets of approximately $370,000 (composed of a house and 168 acres worth $213,000, a car worth $2,000, and the balance in cash and RRSPs). Willis Boston received assets of approximately $385,000, which were composed almost entirely of his teachers' pension.

In addition, Mr. Boston agreed to pay Ms. Boston $3,200 per month in spousal support, indexed annually to the cost of living.

Mr. Boston retired in January 1997 and applied to have the amount of spousal support reduced, based on a change of circumstance. The motions judge reduced the support to $950 per month, not indexed.

The Court of Appeal disagreed and adjusted the support to $2,000 per month.

The Supreme Court of Canada heard the appeal in January 2001. At that time, Ms. Boston's assets were worth more than $493,000, and she had no debts. Mr. Boston's assets (other than his pension) exceeded his debts by $7,000. The Supreme Court of Canada listed the issues:

1. Is a retired payor spouse entitled to seek to reduce the support obligation to a former spouse on the basis that the pension now being received was previously considered in the distribution of matrimonial property?
2. Does the spouse who received assets in exchange for a share of the capitalized value of the other spouse's pension have an obligation to invest those assets in order to produce an income? If those assets are not invested to produce an income, should the court impute to the spouse an income based on what those assets could produce if invested and thereby reduce the spousal support obligation?

The court reviewed cases dealing with double dipping, including *Nantais v. Nantais*,[2] *Rintjema v. Rintjema*,[3] *Shadbolt v. Shadbolt*,[4] *Hutchison v. Hutchison*,[5] and *Campbell v. Campbell*.[6] They paid particular attention to *Shadbolt v. Shadbolt*, where Justice Czutrin recognized that pensions are different from other assets. Justice Czutrin said that a spouse who receives his pension entitlement as real capital under the Matrimonial Property Accounting must convert the capital to income when the other spouse retires, and live off capital, as the other is required to do. Then a court can compare the capital available at retirement and the income available from capital at retirement to decide whether a further adjustment is needed to promote inter spousal fairness.

The Supreme Court of Canada said,

> I agree with Czutrin J.'s reasons in *Shadbolt* and Professor McLeod's comments in annotation to that case. When a pension is dealt with by the lump-sum method, the pension-holding spouse (here the husband) must transfer real assets to the payee spouse (here the wife) in order to equalize matrimonial property. The wife can use these real assets immediately. Under a compensatory spousal support order or agreement, the wife has an obligation to use these assets in an income-producing way. She need not dedicate the equalization assets to investment immediately on receiving them; however, she must use them to generate income when the pension-holding spouse retires. [Mrs. Boston's support was mainly compensatory.] This requirement is based on the principle that, as far as it is reasonable, the payee spouse should attempt to generate economic self-sufficiency.
>
> However, where the payee spouse receives assets on equalization in exchange for a part of her former

spouse's pension entitlement, she must use those assets in a reasonable attempt to generate income at least by the time the pension starts to pay out. The reason for this requirement is clear. The payee spouse cannot save the assets that she receives upon equalization and choose instead to live on the liquidation of the payor spouse's pension when he retires. If she were permitted to do so, the payee spouse would accumulate an estate while the payor spouse's estate is liquidating.

When spousal support plays a compensatory role on marriage breakdown, it may be unreasonable to expect the payee spouse to generate investment income from the matrimonial home. As far as is practicable, the support payments should provide a level of income sufficient to maintain a lifestyle that is comparable to that enjoyed during the marriage. The ability to remain in the matrimonial home usually assists the payee spouse and the children in maintaining their previous lifestyle.

Each case depends on its own facts. Generally, the payee spouse would not be expected to sell or leave the matrimonial home, particularly if there are dependent children. However, in cases where the support order is based mostly on need as opposed to compensation, different considerations apply. It is not impossible to envisage circumstances where the value of the family home has become disproportionate to the means of the parties so that equity requires that it be sold and replaced appropriately. Such considerations do not arise in this appeal, as the support agreement was mainly compensatory.

To avoid double recovery, the court should, where practicable, focus on that portion of the payor's income and assets that have not been part of the equalization or division of matrimonial assets when the payee spouse's continuing need for support is shown. In this appeal, that would include the portion of the pension that was earned following the date of separation and not included in the equalization on net family property.

Despite these general rules, double recovery cannot always be avoided. In certain circumstances, a pension, which has previously been equalized, can also be viewed as a maintenance asset. Double recovery may be permitted where the payor spouse has the ability to pay, where the payee spouse has made a reasonable effort to use the equalized assets in an income-producing way and, despite this, an economic hardship from the marriage or its breakdown persists. Double recovery may also be permitted in spousal support orders/agreements based mainly on need as opposed to compensation.

Finally, if the payee spouse receives assets in exchange for a share of the capitalized value of the other spouse's pension and she does not invest those assets in an attempt to produce an income, the court should impute an income to the payee spouse based on what those assets could reasonably produce if invested.

The Supreme Court concluded that the motions judge had been reasonable in reducing the support to $950 per month. However, they did rule that this amount should be indexed to the cost of living.

No calculations were provided in the lower court, the court of appeal, or the Supreme Court of Canada that would explain how the decisions were arrived at. One should certainly not conclude that double dipping is never appropriate. The following would seem to summarize the conclusions of the Supreme Court:

1. The payee spouse should attempt to generate economic self-sufficiency.
2. Where the payee spouse receives assets on equalization, he must use those assets in a reasonable attempt to generate income at least by the time the pension starts to pay out.
3. The payee spouse cannot save the assets that he receives upon equalization and live on support payments from the payor spouse's pension.
4. It may be unreasonable to expect the payee spouse to generate investment income from the matrimonial home.
5. Where the support order is based on need as opposed to compensation, it may be reasonable to conclude that the family home has become dispropriationate to the means of the parties, and therefore the house should be sold.
6. To avoid double recovery, the court should focus on that portion of the payor's income and assets that have not been part of the equalization or division of matrimonial assets when the payee spouse's continuing need for support is shown. This would include the portion of the pension earned following the date of separation but not included in the equalization of Net Family Property.
7. In certain circumstances, a pension that has been equalized can be viewed as a maintenance asset. Double recovery may be permitted where the payor spouse has the ability to pay and where the payee spouse has made a reasonable effort to use the equalized assets in an income-producing way, yet economic hardship persists.

8. Double recovery may also be permitted in spousal support orders or agreements based mainly on need as opposed to compensation...

9. Finally, if the payee spouse receives assets in exchange for a share of the capitalized value of the other spouse's pension and does not invest those assets in an attempt to produce an income, the court should impute an income to the payee spouse based on what those assets could reasonably produce if invested.

Apparently there will continue to be some cases where double dipping is appropriate and somewhere it is not.

Notes

1   (2001) SCC 43. File No.: 27682.
2   (1995), 16 R.F.L. (4th) 201 (Ont. Ct. Gen. Div.).
3   (1996) O.J. No. 4717 (QL) (Gen. Div.).
4   (1997), 32 R.F.L. (4th) 253 (Ont. Ct. Gen. Div.).
5   (1998), 38 R.F.L. (4th) 377 (Ont. Ct. Gen. Div.).
6   (1998), 40 R.F.L. (4th) 462 (Ont. Ct. Gen. Div.).

Chapter 15

The Supreme Court of Canada and Best v. Best

The Supreme Court of Canada issued important decisions in the case of *Best v. Best*,[1] a marriage breakdown that happened more than eleven years earlier. In the process, it recognized that the treatment of pensions in the division of property on marriage breakdown raises many contentious and confusing issues and questions. This leading decision by Canada's highest court sets the rules for other pension valuations.

While the *Best* case is frequently cited because it deals with the question of value added versus pro rata, the Supreme Court of Canada discussed more than ten important issues. The judges' comments will be useful in considering some of these areas. However, their comments have also left many of these issues open to be decided in future cases. In this chapter I will discuss:

1. value added vs. pro rata
2. termination method or retirement method
3. vesting and vesting discount
4. retirement age to be assumed
5. subsequent events
6. "if and when" agreements
7. support and double dipping
8. costs.

VALUE ADDED OR PRO RATA

By now, I assume everyone realizes the consideration of value added versus pro rata arises only when a portion of the pension was earned before the marriage.

Some people say the value added method of valuing pensions recognizes that the value of the pension earned in the early years of employment is much lower than the value earned in later years. The pro rata method assumes that the pension is earned equally during each year of service.

The Supreme Court of Canada analyzed these two approaches very carefully. It considered and explained all aspects of each, and their effects on the determination of the portion of the value earned during the marriage. One important consideration, which had been raised in other cases, was the argument that the Family Law Act supported the value added method. This argument also suggested that the value added method must be used to be consistent with the method used to value other assets on marriage breakdown.

In the lower court decision, later upheld by the Ontario Court of Appeal, Justice Rutherford said, "I prefer the value added method for the valuation of Mr. Best's pension to the Pro rated method because the former is more consistent with the method of determining the value of other assets in the same exercise."

The Supreme Court pointed out that some cases had adopted the pro rata method, while others had adopted the Value added method. It ruled that it was *not* necessary that all assets be valued using the same method. Speaking for the court, Justice Major said:

> I am of the opinion that the Family Law Act, on its face, does not state any rule indicating a preference for the value added method over the pro rata method or vice versa. This legislative silence means that the appellant's defined benefit pension must be valued

according to the method that values the pension most equitably. The court should decide which valuation method most nearly describes how the defined benefit pension's value varied over time, with proper regard for the nature of the asset itself.

The Supreme Court of Canada was considering the method of valuing a defined benefit pension plan, not a defined contribution pension plan. Remember that Mr. Best's pension was a final average earnings plan and not a career earnings plan, a flat rate plan, or a contribution based plan. His pension benefit was equal to 2 percent of his final average earnings times his years of service.

Justice Major said,

> I have concluded that, absent special circumstances, a pro rata method of pension valuation best achieves the purpose of the Family Law Act, namely, the equitable division of assets between spouses.... I believe that the termination pro rata method produces a fairer valuation of defined benefit pensions for equalization purposes than the termination value added method. The pro rata method is not without flaws, nor will it inevitably be preferable to the value added method. Although cases may arise where other considerations will tilt the balance in favour of a different valuation method, the nature of defined benefit pensions indicates that, as a general rule, the pro rata method is preferable.

Although the Supreme Court of Canada ruled in favour of the pro rata method, it still left the door open for consideration of the value added method in special circumstances. It did not explain what these special circumstances might be.

We have seen many cases where the value added method cannot be used because it is impossible to obtain or estimate proper information at the date of marriage. We have also seen cases where the use of the pro rata method would not be fair.

The pro rata method was chosen by the Supreme Court of Canada in the belief that Mr. Best's pension was earned equally each year. Obviously in some cases this is not true. For example, tradespeople—electricians, plumbers—generally earn a pension based on the number of hours worked each year, to a certain maximum. Since these people are often out of work from time to time, their pension is not earned equally each year. The value added method may be more appropriate in such a case. Some other cases where value added may be more appropriate are:

- when it is a defined contribution plan..
- when it is a career earnings plan
- when the type of plan changed, for example from a defined contribution plan to a defined benefit plan
- when the member received a refund of contributions during the marriage and has not paid them back at the date of separation
- when the person worked for one employer at the date of marriage, changed employers during the marriage, and transferred the commuted value
- when the pension was not vested at the date of marriage
- when the member was employed before marriage but not a member of the pension plan, then joined the plan during the marriage and was allowed to count all his service including the period before joining the plan calculating the pension benefit.

In spite of the Supreme Court of Canada's decision in *Best v. Best*, there will be cases where the value added method is more appropriate than the pro rata method for valuing a pension on marriage breakdown.

TERMINATION METHOD OR RETIREMENT METHOD

Keep in mind that Mr. and Mrs. Best agreed the value of Mr. Best's pension should be based on the termination method and not the retirement method. They also agreed. when deciding the amount of pension benefit Mr. Best had earned, it should be assumed he had terminated employment at the date of separation. We're not sure they agreed about using the termination method when deciding on the assumed age of retirement. If literal termination of employment were assumed, Mr. Best would not qualify under the rule of ninety—age plus years of service equal ninety—until September 1992. If his future service were considered, he would qualify in June 1990. The second would be a much more valuable pension.

In most pension valuations, the value calculated under the termination method may not be the same as the amount the individual would receive if the pension were transferred to a locked in RRSP, for example, on literal termination of employment. The value determined by use of the termination method also may be quite different from the value determined under the Pension Benefits Division Act or by a pension administrator for termination of employment purposes. It is still important that the pension be valued by an experienced and qualified pension valuator.

Justice Major explained the termination method, the hybrid termination method, and the retirement method, and pointed out the confusion regarding the use of these terms.

In this case, the parties agreed on the termination method. Justice Major said,

> It is quite likely that a calculation which corresponds to a retirement method would have provided the fairest possible valuation of the defined benefit pension in this case. A retirement method could have much to recommend it, particularly given that a

pension's true value might change drastically after marriage due to changes in the benefit formula or substantial increases in salary. As I have suggested, there are compelling reasons to treat these changes as having an effect over the entire life of the defined benefit pension, not just at the time they occur....
[The retirement method] might be appropriate in a case where the employee spouse's final salaries and years of service are known with sufficient certainty.

The Supreme Court's comments could raise new disagreements about the value of many pensions—not just those that involve a pre-marriage period. One party might support of the termination method, the other argue for the retirement method. The values produced could be quite different.

VESTING

The Supreme Court pointed out that Mr. Best's pension was vested at both the date of marriage and at the date of separation. This was a part of its considerations when it concluded that the pro rata method was appropriate.

This leaves us wondering whether the pro rata method is appropriate when the pension has not vested at the date of marriage. In that case, should the value added method be used?

About the value of early retirement provisions, the Supreme Court said:

The respondent might argue that the option of retiring before age 65 with an unreduced pension is itself a benefit that increased the pension's value, and that the value of that benefit should be included in net family property because it accrued during the marriage. This argument fails because it effectively considers the pension's value to be unaffected by the early retirement provision until the employee actually begins to qualify for the early retirement benefit. Put another way, the respondent would have the Court consider the early retirement benefit to have a value of zero until the employee began to satisfy the "rule of 90" … Each year is of equal importance in determining the employee's satisfaction of the "rule of 90".

Not all pensions have a 90 Factor (also called a rule of 90). Some allow the member to retire on an unreduced pension, regardless of age, when they have accumulated thirty years of service. Using the termination method and the Supreme Court ruling in Best, such a pension should be valued ignoring future service. However, at the same time, the value of the early retirement provision should be recognized in the valuation. Apparently, there are two conflicting decisions in such a case, since it is usually impossible to recognize the value of the early retirement provision without considering future years of service. Perhaps the Supreme Court is saying it would be appropriate to value the early retirement provision to the extent that it had been earned only, and thereby discount the value of the pension by a service discount in order to leave out the portion of the value attributable to future service.

EARLY RETIREMENT PROVISIONS AND THE VESTING DISCOUNT

This is another area where the Supreme Court's gratuitous comments may have raised new arguments. The Supreme Court said:

The respondent might argue that the option of retiring before age 65 with an unreduced pension is in
itself a benefit that increased the pension's value, and
that the value of that benefit should be included in
net family property because it accrued during the
marriage. This argument fails because it effectively
considers the pension's value to be unaffected by the
early retirement provision until the employee actually begins to qualify for the early retirement benefit.
Put another way, the respondent would have the
court consider the early retirement benefit to have a
benefit of zero, until the employee began to satisfy
the rule of 90...Each year is of equal importance in
determining the employee's satisfaction of the rule of
90. Had the appellant not accumulated 20 years of
service prior to marriage, the early retirement benefit would not have vested if at all, until after the separation. Those early years of service were hardly less
important to the earning of the early retirement benefit than the years of service during the marriage.

The court explained the standards set by the Canadian Institute
of Actuaries require that early retirement provisions be recognized.
They also quoted from the Ontario Law Reform Commission report.

The Commission therefore recommends that the
proposed valuation regulations should provide that
where a pension plan contains a provision for an
early retirement benefit payable to a member on an
unreduced basis once certain vesting requirements
are met, such a benefit should be valued on the following basis. Vesting of the unreduced early retirement benefit should be assumed for the purposes of

pension valuation and a discount for the possibility
that plan membership will terminate prior to meeting the vesting requirements, should be applied.

The Supreme Court said, "The statements of the Canadian
Institute of Actuaries and the Ontario Law Reform Commission
support the view that early retirement benefits that are contingent
on years of service should not be viewed as obtaining value only
once they are vested. They are continuously earned over the course
of the employee's service."

The Supreme Court of Canada is supporting a view I have held
for some time. and one of the considerations I follow in valuing a pension. In my reports, I reduce the value based on early retirement by a
discount for the possibility that it may for many reasons not transpire.

On the other hand, if no future service accruals are considered,
as in *Best v. Best*, and if retirement age is based on service at the date
of separation, then the application of a service discount would not
be appropriate.

RETIREMENT DATE

The age at which it is assumed the member will retire often has
a substantial effect on the value of the pension for marriage breakdown purposes. In many cases the person retired after the date of
separation but before property matters had been settled. Should the
pension be valued based on the actual date of retirement? The
Supreme Court does not necessarily support this position.

Mr. Best retired after his appeal was submitted to the Ontario
Court of Appeal but before the Supreme Court of Canada considered the case. Mr. Best argued that his actual date of retirement should be used in the calculations, rather than some
assumed date.

The Supreme Court of Canada decided the actual date of retirement was a post-separation event that should be ignored. They agreed with the Ontario Court of Appeal decision in *Kennedy v. Kennedy.*[2] The date of retirement to assume should be based on the facts of the particular case and the member's state of mind at the date of separation.

The Supreme Court of Canada did not mention a mid-age value, as suggested by Justice Kurisko in the case of *Bascello v. Bascello.*[3]

The Supreme Court looked at circumstances and facts of the case, and considered the fact that Mr. and Mrs. Best had agreed on the termination method of valuing Mr. Best's pension. The court concluded that the age of retirement to assume must be the earliest date at which Mr. Best could receive an unreduced pension, and that future service should be ignored in the calculation.

SUBSEQUENT EVENTS

Mr. Best argued that his actual date of retirement should be used in calculating the value of his pension. The Supreme Court of Canada said:

> On October 3, 1997 the Court of Appeal dismissed the appellant's appeal. Charron, J.A. agreed on all points with the trial judge's reasoning regarding pension valuation. She added that, since the trial judge's reasons had been released, the Court of Appeal had decided in *Kennedy v. Kennedy* that a retirement date must be chosen "on a case by case basis upon consideration of all of the relevant evidence". Charron, J.A. concluded that Rutherford, J. had followed this rule by examining all of the evidence before him in choosing a probable retirement date of September 9,

1992.... Charron, J.A. also noted that using "hindsight" in choosing a retirement date for valuation
purposes would "introduce great uncertainty in the
litigation process" and "may well militate against the
early resolution of matrimonial disputes". Charron,
J.A. considered that post-separation events could be
relevant to determine "the probable age of retirement as contemplated by the pension plan holder"
on the date of separation. Conduct contemplated as
of the separation date, as well as the fact of separation itself, could also be relevant, but facts that were
unknown to or not contemplated by the pension
holder at separation could not.

After careful consideration, Justice Major said, "I therefore agree
with the Ontario Court of Appeal that under a termination method,
post-separation evidence should not be used in determining a likely
retirement date unless the evidence reflects facts that were within the
employee spouse's contemplation at the time of separation."

The Supreme Court pointed to three circumstances in which it
was proper to consider post-separation events and said that in using
a projected retirement method, "it might be fair to use hindsight
evidence in choosing the retirement age as well."

Justice Major said:

I do not believe that there was any reason to value
the pension on the date of marriage in light of an
assumption that the employee terminated employment on that date. That assumption ignored the
actual economic facts that occurred during the marriage. Namely that the appellant continued to work
continuously and eventually brought himself within
reach of retirement.

The Supreme Court indicated it might be appropriate to consider post-separation events in determining the amount of pension benefit to value:

> My conclusion that all the information available at the time of separation should be used in calculating the pension's value at separation and at marriage, ordinarily suggests that one should also consider post-separation information to the extent that it bears upon the benefit formula. For instance, it is now known for a fact, that the appellant retired at age 61, with 40.83 years of service. His best salaried years could also be ascertained with precision. It is quite likely that such a calculation, which essentially corresponds to a retirement method, would have provided the fairest possible valuation of the defined benefit pension in this case.

The Supreme Court of Canada said, "There was no error in valuing the pension as though the appellant terminated employment in 1988, even though in determining the spousal support the trial judge recognized that the appellant was still employed in 1993."

It seems odd to ignore post-separation events in determining the age of retirement to assume but consider post-separation events in determining the amount of benefit to include in the calculations. However, consideration of post-separation events is certainly appropriate in determinating the need for and the ability to pay support.

IF AND WHEN AGREEMENTS

The Supreme Court of Canada said:

Once the pension and all other assets have been tallied to produce the appellant's "net family property", the appellant is required to pay the respondent an amount equal to one-half of the difference between his and her net family properties. Section 9 of the Family Law Act allows a court to choose among several methods for payment of the equalization amount, including an order of immediate payment, the granting of security interest, an instalment scheme, postponement of payment, creation of a trust, and the transferral, partition or sale of property.

The lower court and the Ontario Court of Appeal decided it was appropriate to allow Mr. Best to pay the equalization amount over a ten-year period, as allowed by the Family Law Act.

The Supreme Court considered all complications involved in drafting an If and When agreement. They assumed that an If and When agreement would provide that Mrs. Best would receive a part of Mr. Best's pension only as long as payments were being made on his pension. They assumed that if Mr. Best died prematurely, Mrs. Best's payments would cease, although she may not have received the full equalization amount owing. They also assumed that there was a possibility Mrs. Best would continue to receive a part of Mr. Best's pension long after the equalization amount had been paid in full. They seemed to ignore the fact that the wording of the agreement and the provision of life insurance or other security could avoid these two possibilities.

The Supreme Court pointed out that the Family Law Act "allows a court to delay an equalization payment for up to 10 years, suggesting that the Ontario legislature did not object to continued ties after divorce as long as they were for a 'limited' time. Thus an If and When scheme might be the appropriate option where retirement was clearly imminent."

Justice Major concluded, "In light of the difficulties that seem to attend the drafting and administration of a fair 'If and When' order in Ontario, I do not believe that Rutherford, J. exceeded his discretion in choosing an instalment scheme for settlement of the appellant's equalization payment."

The Supreme Court concluded that an If and When settlement was allowed by the Family Law Act, and said this method might be appropriate when retirement and receipt of the pension payments are not far in the future.

SPOUSAL SUPPORT AND DOUBLE DIPPING

In the lower Court, Rutherford, J. ordered Mr. Best to pay $2,500 in monthly spousal support as long as he continued to draw a salary. Mr. Best argued that, because much of the pension had been subject to equalization as an asset, considering it as income for purposes of support would result in double dipping.

The Supreme Court said, "Cases and commentaries appear to be divided on the issue of whether a pension, once equalized as property, can also be treated as income from which the pension holding spouse may make support payments." The Supreme Court concluded that the trial judge did not err in valuing the pension as though the appellant terminated employment in 1988 while also recognizing that he was still employed in 1993. The court said it was appropriate for Justice Rutherford to order continuing support rather than limited support, and that since he was now retired, Mr. Best could apply for a variation of the support on the basis of change of circumstances.

The Supreme Court said in determining Mr. Best's ability to pay support, the trial judge had not considered his pension as income because Mr. Best had not yet retired. The lower court ordered support based on the fact that Mr. Best was drawing a salary at the time. Therefore, the order for support was upheld.

COSTS

The costs in the case were substantial, even at the lower court level. Although the respondent had made an offer of settlement that was more favourable than the judgement rendered, the judge in the lower court concluded that numerous factors detracted from the respondent's presumptive right to costs from the date of his settlement offer. He held that the respondent was entitled to recover half his costs to date.

The Ontario Court of Appeal awarded costs of the appeal to the respondent.

The Supreme Court of Canada said, "In light of the fact that the dispute was legitimate and complex, I do not believe that either party should recover costs from the other. The parties will therefore bear their own costs in all courts."

GENERAL COMMENTS

The Supreme Court of Canada has clarified that, absent special circumstances, in a case where there is a pre-marriage period, pro rating the value of the pension based on the number of years of service best achieves the purpose of the Family Law Act—namely, the equitable division of assets between spouses—when the case involves a final average earnings defined benefit pension plan.

The court said the retirement method might be more appropriate than the termination method when retirement was imminent or when enough information was available to use this method.

It opened the door to the deduction of a service discount to reduce the value of a pension when the value for early retirement is being considered.

Overall, the judges' comments and decisions may have raised more questions and problems than they solved. It is important, of course, to keep in mind that these decisions were based on the facts of this particular case and may not be valid in other cases.

The discussion and decisions in this Supreme Court of Canada case certainly make it clear that the valuing of pensions for the equalization of property on marriage breakdown is complicated and that it is never safe to settle property matters without having the pension properly valued. The case of *Best v. Best* thirteen learned judges to decide proper value. How can anyone ever hope to determine the proper value of a pension without considerable input from a qualified expert and a detailed proper valuation report?

Notes

1   (1999) S.C.J. No. 40, File No.: 26345, (1997) 31 R.F.L. (4th) 1 (Ont. C.A.), (1993) I.C.C.P.B. 8, 50 R.F.L. (3d) 120 (Ont. Ct. Gen. Div.) Court File No.: 32962-D.
2   (1996) 19 R.F.L. (4th) 454.
3   (1995) 18 R.F.L. (4th) 362.

Chapter 16

Retirement Age

Many court cases have tried to answer the question, What is the appropriate retirement age to assume? Some decisions were based on a person's statements of intention to retire early or late. Some ruled that, in the case they were examining, it was obvious the person could not afford to retire early. Still others automatically assumed the earliest date of unreduced pension. In this chapter, I will review more recent cases.

The courts have concluded that in every case, a judge consider the facts of the particular case and use them to determine the proper age of retirement to assume. It is not acceptable to choose a midpoint value (that is, the value that assumes a retirement age halfway between normal retirement age and the earliest age of unreduced pension) simply to avoid choosing an age based on the facts presented at trial.[1] Judges must choose the normal retirement age, the earliest date of unreduced pension, or some other age, based on the facts presented. In many cases judges choose the earliest date of unreduced pension. However, there is some confusion about how this date should be determined. Some pensions, such as teachers' pensions, allow the member to retire on a full or unreduced pension when his age and years of service added together total eighty-five. Other pensions, such as Ontario government pensions and auto workers' pensions, allow the member to retire after completing thirty years of service.

The 90 Factor (really the 85 Factor now) in teachers' pensions has been calculated differently in different cases. Justice Aitken explained this very well in a paper she delivered to a group of judges in Ottawa in April 1998. Should the pension be valued assuming the plan member quit working on the valuation date and, to reach the 85 Factor, only the increase in age of the member need be considered? Or should the pension valuator assume, in calculating when the 85 Factor will be reached, that the plan member continues to acquire years of service after the valuation date? In the latter case, the member can start to draw an unreduced pension twice as soon, and as a result the pension valuation will be higher.

STANDARDS

The standards set by the Canadian Institute of Actuaries in 1993 say,

> Accrued benefit enhancements and grow-in ancillary benefits (such as the right to unreduced early retirement subject to total age/service combinations, and/or bridging benefits) contingent only upon future service, to the extent accrued at the valuation date, must specifically be addressed°The phrase "must specifically be addressed" means that the actuary must present a separately identified value of such benefits, without any discount for possible future forfeiture.

There is no explanation of how this is to be accomplished or how the 85 Factor is to be calculated. However, the standards seem to say values should be produced that somehow recognize the value of being able to retire early.

Salib v. Cross

The case of *Salib v. Cross*[3] involved valuation reports prepared by two well-known actuaries. One assumed termination of employment as of the date of separation with no future service being considered in calculating the 90 Factor. The other produced values that took into consideration future service in determining the 90 Factor. Justice Chapnik says that if future service is considered in determining the 90 Factor, "the value of the pension as at the date of separation, assuming early retirement, would be substantially greater; and the husband would benefit from the wife's continued employment with the Board." Justice Chapnik adopted the first valuation approach. She was concerned that the other values did not include any provision for the possibility that Ms. Cross might terminate her employment before an age of retirement that took into account future service in determining the 90 Factor.

In reviewing the case, the Ontario Court of Appeal said,

> The second issue was the value of the respondent wife's pension. Two qualified actuaries presented the trial judge with reports; one of whom advocated what is referred to as the termination method of valuation and the other what is referred to as the retirement method. In adopting the former method as advocated by the respondent, the trial judge gave careful reasons as to why she felt it was the more appropriate method having regard to the particular facts of this case. In her own questioning of the appellant's actuary the trial judge demonstrated that she was fully alive to the significance of the issue and demonstrated an informed grasp of its complexities. We can find no reason for interfering with her treatment of the valuation of the respondent's pension.

The appeal court concluded that future service should not be considered in the calculation of the 90 Factor even though the actuaries didn't agree on this.

Best v. Best[4]

In the Ontario Court of Justice, General Division, Justice Rutherford pointed out that two valuation reports arrived at almost the same value for Mr. Best's pension at the date of separation. The judge said both values ignored future service in determining Mr. Best's 90 Factor. The Ontario Court of Appeal reviewed the case:

> In this case, both parties agreed that the "termination" method be used (as opposed to the "retirement" method). The termination method requires that the lump-sum value of the pension as at valuation date be calculated as if the employee had terminated employment on that date.
>
> By contrast, under the retirement method, the value of the pension is based on the assumption that the pension holder's employment will continue until retirement.

The Ontario Court of Appeal understood how the 90 Factor was being calculated. They concluded that future service should not be considered in calculating the 90 Factor.

The Supreme Court of Canada reviewed the decision: "Had the appellant terminated employment on the date of separation, February 1988, he would have qualified for early retirement under the 'rule of 90' by increase in age alone on September 9, 1992 at age 57.4. The assumption was that the appellant did not continue to earn pensionable service beyond February 1988. In choosing a probable retirement date of September 9, 1992, the trial Judge had to ignore the fact that the appellant was still working on the date of judgment. Charron J.A. concluded that Rutherford J. had followed this rule by examining all the evidence before him in choosing a probable retirement date of September 9, 1992."

The Supreme Court of Canada was satisfied the lower court and the appeal court understood and considered the matter carefully. Then they dealt with the calculation of the benefit earned:

> The "termination" method requires the actuary to determine the annual pension benefit by assuming the employee spouse stopped working on the date of separation. The "retirement" method requires the actuary to consider possible post-separation increases in the pension's value in order to determine as closely as possible what the pension benefit will actually be when the employee retires in the future.

The Supreme Court of Canada gave careful consideration to the retirement age that should be assumed: Retirement age is crucial to valuation because it determines both the length of the discounting period and also the length of time that the pension will last. Both factors materially affect a pension's present value on the date of separation. The presence of an early retirement provision such as the "rule of 90" will almost always be relevant to the choice of a likely retirement age. Determining when early retirement becomes available if at all, has produced several different approaches in Ontario. The trial Judge in this case assumed that the employee spouse terminated employment on the date of separation. That meant that the employee's years of service were frozen at that point, and the right to early retirement under the "rule of 90" could only be reached by virtue of the increase in the employee's age."

The Supreme Court of Canada pointed out that the parties did not challenge the decision of the lower court to consider the increase in age alone. "The termination method does not incorporate increases in the pension's value owing to events occurring after separation, such as post-separation years of service."

CONSIDERATION OF ACTUAL DATE OF RETIREMENT

If the actual date of retirement comes after the date of separation, there is a temptation to use the value based on the actual retirement date. This may not be appropriate. In *Best v. Best*, Mr. Best retired in 1996 and argued that the value should be based on this. The courts used the value for retirement in 1992. The Supreme Court of Canada said, "The result urged by the appellant would enable spouses with pensions to reduce the amount of their equalization payments, and profit from the length of divorce proceedings by delaying their retirement until after the close of all proceedings. We do not support a rule that could encourage that."

CONCLUSION

When the age of retirement cannot be agreed on, the decisions of the courts must be based on the evidence provided to them. The judge must be made aware of the method used to determine how the earliest date of unreduced pension has been calculated in the pension valuation. There must be careful consideration of whether future years of service should be considered in determining the retirement age. The courts have carefully considered this matter and have concluded that considering future service in the determination allows the non-member to share in the pension's increase in value beyond the date of separation. Whether future years of service are considered in determining the earliest date of unreduced pension can affect the value of the pension substantially in many cases. In an 90 Factor calculation, not counting future years of service would mean a later date of retirement, and therefore a lower value for the pension.

When a pension requires a certain length of service for early retirement, to ignore future years of service would mean that the normal age of retirement becomes the earliest date of unreduced pension. Again, this could reduce the value of the pension substantially.

Not recognizing future years of service would seem to offend the standards set by the Canadian Institute of Actuaries. Perhaps in future many valuation reports will show more values than before, and judges will be left to determine which value is right when they try to decide the appropriate age of retirement.

Normally, it is safe to assume literal termination of employment for the purpose of calculating the benefit earned. But assuming literal termination of employment for the purpose of determining the earliest date of unreduced pension may mean accepting the commuted value. This value often ignores early retirement provisions and indexing.

It seems quite clear that most problems with pension valuations exist because:

- pension valuations are complicated and not widely understood.
- coined phrases (termination method, hybrid method, retirement method) are used by different people to mean different things
- attempts are made to generalize and make rules that will apply to all pension valuations

Solutions include:

- more and better education about pension valuations for the people who must deal with the equalization of property on marriage breakdown.
- not using coined phrases; including full explanations
- developing new standards that deal with specifics rather than generalities

SUMMARY

The value of a definite age of retirement should be determined for equalization purposes. In some cases the decision will be whatever age is the earliest date of unreduced pension. Some considerations:

1. If the plan provides the opportunity to retire early on an unreduced pension, the pension should be valued accordingly. It should then be up to the member to prove he will not be able to take advantage of the early retirement provisions.
2. If the early retirement value is still being considered, it should be valued first, ignoring future years of service.
3. The report should provide a value that takes into consideration future years of service, and the value should be reduced to allow for the possibility that the person may leave before that age or retire after that age.

Notes

1   (1996) Court File No.: C12114 (Ont. C.A.), 19 R.F.L. (4t^h) 454 (Ont. C.A.).

4   *Ibid.*

Chapter 17

Dividing the Pension

INTRODUCTION

Each party to a separation or divorce lists all assets and liabilities to determine which party has the greater net value of property acquired during the marriage. To equalize net family propery, the party with the higher net value must transfer half the excess to the party with the lower value. While this may sound like a simple process, sometimes it is impossible to accomplish. For example, if one party has no net assets, and the only asset the other party has is a pension, what should be done?

When it is impossible to effect a lump sum payment or a transfer of assets from the payor to the payee to satisfy the equalization payment, the Ontario Family Law Act allows payment in installments over a period of up to ten years. This may not be acceptable in a situation where the payor cannot afford to make payments and the payee cannot afford to wait. This situation has brought about arrangements called "If and When" agreements, and the division of pension payments at source.

Even after you agree on the value of all assets, you and your spouse may find it impossible to equalize your assets by way of a lump sum payment or by one party transferring assets to the other. You can agree to split the pension payments when they are paid (if and when). Or you can divide the pension so you each have a pension. There are many problems with both approaches.

IF AND WHEN AGREEMENTS

Procedure

An "If and When" agreement or settlement comes into effect after the member retires. The pension payments are split between the two parties as each payment is received. Sometimes one person receives the payments for both parties and is required to send on a portion of each payment to the other party. Sometimes the pension administrator sends a separate cheque to each party. If an agreement cannot be reached between the parties, the Ontario Family Law Act makes provision for the courts to order the pension administrator to send one payment to each party when the pension is being paid. Both arrangements are fraught with possible problems. Both require careful consideration.

Problems

1. The debtor of the equalization amount may have no security to give for the unpaid balance. How can the non-member receive security for the unpaid liability in the event that the member dies before full payment is made? Some people suggest this can be avoided by the provision of life insurance. But be careful. Such insurance would require constant monitoring to ensure there is adequate coverage and that all premiums are paid on time.

2. Under the Ontario Pension Benefits Act, no payments can be made until the member retires. So the member controls when the non-member will start to receive payments.

3. If the member receives the total pension payments, he must include them in his income for income tax purposes. How is this income tax liability to be shared by the two parties?

4. It's simple to say that the pension payments must be split when they are paid. But how do you ensure that each party is treated fairly when you word the agreement? How do you ensure the requirements of the Family Law Act regarding court orders are adhered to? The wording is even more complicated when the pension provides for indexing.

5. What if the member terminates employment before reaching retirement age? The employee may accept a pension with payments starting at normal retirement age or they may transfer the funds from the pension plan to a locked-in RRSP or to the pension plan of a new employer. How is this to be covered in the separation agreement or court order?

6. What if the non-member dies before receiving the full amount owing to him? Should payments continue to his estate?

7. Once the parties have divorced, the non-member has no right to any information about the pension.

8. There are certain elections a member is allowed to make with regards to his pension. How do you ensure the member does not make elections detrimental to the non-member?

9. What happens if either party declares bankruptcy before full payments have been made?

10. There is some suggestion that an "If and When" arrangement may not be enforceable under the Pension Benefits Act.

Most of the problems with an If and When agreement were discussed in *Monger V. Monger*.[1] Mr. Monger was a school principal. His annual salary was $75,000, but he could not make the equalization payment, even if allowed ten years to pay it, because the liabilities of the couple (without the husband's pension) exceeded their assets. His pension was valued at $340,000. The wife was awarded support payments of $1,750 per month. The order further reduced Mr. Monger's ability to pay the equalization payment.

Justice Cusinato recognized the following problems and provided solutions:

Problem:

Should the non-member's share of the pension payments be calculated using the *Rutherford* formula? The formula is:

> Total number of years contributed to the plan up to the date of separation (during marriage)
>
> ————————————————————————
>
> 50% X Total number of years contributed by the pension holder to retirement. X Actual pension payments payable on retirement

Solution:

The judge concluded that to divide the payments on this basis would allow the non-member spouse to share in future salary increases and future pension plan enhancements. To avoid this he decided to use a formula developed in *Thompson v. Thompson.*[2]

> 1/2 times 2% times number of years of service (including any fraction thereof) to the valuation date, times the member's annual salary over the last 6 years (as provided in the contract) to the valuation date.

Comments:

Justice Cusinato's approach seems reasonable for use in all cases. Make sure the formula you use follows the formula set out in the pension plan for calculating the pension benefit at the date of separation. An adjustment is required for any service rendered prior to marriage or any refunds and paybacks of contributions. In addition, consideration must be given either to indexing the non-member's share of the benefit or requiring that annual interest is paid on the unpaid balance. An adjustment must also be made for any bridging benefit provided by the pension plan. This may mean using a different formula for before and after the member reaches age sixty-five.

Problem:

Should the non-member's share of the pension payments be indexed for inflation? Does this contravene Section 52(2) of the Pension Benefits Act? It would cause the non-member spouse to "become entitled to more than 50 per cent of the pension benefits, calculated in the prescribed manner, accrued by a member or former member during the period when the party and the member or former member were spouses."

Solution:

Justice Cusinato concluded that providing for indexing would not contravene the Pension Benefits Act.

Comments:

What if the indexing provisions in the plan, or the historical ad hoc indexing, are different at the date of separation from what they are at the date of retirement? Which do you apply?

If the indexing provisions of the particular plan have improved in the period between separation and retirement, the use of the provisions as they are at retirement would cause the non-member to share in post-separation improvements.

In his order, Justice Cusinato said that the benefit should be adjusted by the annual indexing factor provided under the teacher's pension plan both before and after retirement. The teachers' pension plan (and probably all other pension plans) does not make any provision for indexing before retirement unless the member terminates employment. Does this mean that the non-member's payments would not be indexed until after retirement?

A better approach might be to order the member spouse to make annual payments of the appropriate rate of annual interest on the unpaid amount.

Problem:

Since the non-member cannot collect any payments until the member decides to retire, the member can affect when the non-member's payments begin, and the total amount received, by not retiring on the assumed date of retirement.

Solution:

Justice Cusinato ordered that should Mr. Monger not retire on the date it was assumed he would retire, he must compensate his wife for her entitlement to the pension benefits payable. These payments must continue from the assumed date of retirement until actual retirement, at which time the administrator will be directed to divide the benefit at source.

Problem:

How to provide security to the non-member for the unpaid liability in the event that the member dies before retiring.

Solution:

The judge ordered that Mr. Monger, so long as he was employed by the London Board of Education, must designate Mrs. Monger as beneficiary of his school board group life insurance to the full extent of the proceeds of insurance.

Comments:

What if the amount of insurance becomes more than the amount owing to the non-member spouse?

Would this order be effective if the group life insurance provided that only a current spouse may be a beneficiary?

What if the group term life insurance ceases on termination of employment.

In the case of *Britton Estate v. Britton*,[3] an order made in matrimonial proceedings provided that the husband was to "maintain the [wife] as beneficiary of any insurance and/or other benefits to which she would be entitled under his company plan." The parties subsequently divorced. The husband named his common-law spouse (who later became his legal spouse) as the beneficiary under his pension plan and under a group term life insurance policy he had through his employment. At his death, the pension plan administrator paid the survivor benefits to the new spouse in accordance with the terms of the Pension Benefits Act, the company pension plan, and the designated beneficiary form filed by the husband. Justice Callon concluded that the employer was obliged to pay the survivor benefits to the second spouse and the life insurance company was obliged to pay the life insurance proceeds to her, as well. On appeal, it was ruled that only the life insurance would be paid to the first wife.

Some agreements or orders provide that the member must maintain a life insurance policy that names the non-member as the beneficiary. Such an arrangement would require constant monitoring on the part of the non-member to ensure adequate coverage and to ensure that all premiums were paid on time. And what if the member is not insurable?

Problem:

How to provide security for the non-member if the member dies after retirement but before any payments are made to the non-member, or before sufficient payments are made to repay the full amount of the liability. Mr. Monger's group term insurance ceased on his retirement.

Should the non-member continue to collect payments if the retired member dies before the full amount of the calculated liability is paid?

Should the non-member's estate continue to collect payments if the non-member dies before the full amount of the calculated liability is paid?

Solution:

The judge charged Mr. Monger's estate with the continuation of the benefit payment, to the extent of the available assets, until Mrs. Monger dies.

Comments:

Such a charge could cause the member's estate to be tied up for an inordinate length of time. It could be ineffective if the member dies with no assets other than his pension plan and if the death benefit is payable to his new spouse, as is required by law.

Problem:

A former spouse has no right to any information about the member's pension plan and cannot obtain any information without written authorization from the member.

Solution:

Judge Cusinato ordered Mr. Monger to deliver to Mrs. Monger copies of all communications between himself and the pension plan administrator.

Comments:

In addition, the plan member should provide an irrevocable direction to the administrator to provide the non-member with any information the non-member requests about the member's pension plan and to send copies to the non-member of all communications between the plan and the member, until such time as the non-member acknowledges she has been paid in full.

The member should also sign a release to allow the plan administrator to provide the non-member with any information she requests about the plan.

Problem:

Is there still a need to value the member's pension plan entitlements at the date of separation when it is obvious that payment of the equalization amount will be by way of an "If and When" settlement?

Solution:

Definitely.

Comment:

How else can you ensure that the non-member receives no more and no less than the amount to which he is entitled under the law? How else can you ensure that there is adequate security if the member dies prematurely?

Problem:

The member may make elections in connection with his pension that are detrimental to the non-member, for example, a higher survivor benefit for his new spouse that reduces his benefit to less than the amount to be paid to the non-member's previous spouse.

Solution:

Justice Cusinato said that Mr. Monger was Mrs. Monger's trustee for her interest in the pension plan benefits and pension payments. He ordered Mr. Monger not to make any election, designation, nomination or other direction under the pension plan that would in any way affect Mrs. Monger's share of the pension benefits without obtaining her approval.

Comment:

This could allow Mrs. Monger to control whether Mr. Monger terminates employment.

Problem:

The member's employment may be terminated, and he may be left with a deferred pension with no indexing. Or he may transfer his pension to a new plan.

Solution:

The agreement should provide that, when the member quits his current job, the non-member should have the right to deal with her share of the termination payment by electing to have her share paid according to any one of the options allowed on termination by the plan and applicable legislation.

Problem:

Any refunds that are repaid, or any service that is bought back, during the marriage period will fall into the value attributed to the husband, even if the service was rendered before the marriage.

Solution:

Ensure that refunds, repayments, and buybacks are considered carefully in valuation of the pension.

Problem:

What if the member becomes bankrupt before the non-member has received the full amount due to him?

Solution:

The agreement should state that if the member becomes bankrupt, the non-member is entitled to a judgement against the member for lump sum spousal support equal to the amount owing to her plus interest. The agreement should also say the non-member's entitlement should not be discharged by the bankruptcy.

GENERAL COMMENTS

In "If and When" agreements and orders, it's difficult to adequately protect the non-member spouse.

As Professor McLeod says in his comments on the Monger case:

> The problems are sufficiently great that an "if, as and when" division may be a lawsuit waiting to happen. In many cases it may be possible to provide the same benefits to the payee through support orders. Before counsel rush to force an "if, as and when" settlement, they should consider an order for periodic support or lump sum support payable in installments, which may be easier to enforce against a plan administrator and is more susceptible to change if the circumstances warrant it.

Generally speaking, divisions by way of agreement or court order and divisions under the Pension Benefits Division Act will be calculated based on the pro rata on service method. This may mean the non-member spouse will receive less than the amount he is entitled to by law, since it is not always appropriate to value the pension by the pro rata method. It is important to have a proper valuation prepared, and to make arrangements for the shortfall.

IF AND WHEN AGREEMENTS CHECKLIST

1. Has the pension been valued?
2. How are the payments to be split?
3. What about indexing?
4. What happens if there are major changes in the pension plan before retirement, for example, indexing?

5. When do split payments start?

6. When do split payments end?

7. How is income tax to be dealt with? What will happen if the parties are in different tax brackets?

8. Will there be interest on the unpaid balance?

9. What happens if the member declares bankruptcy?

10. What happens if the non-member declares bankruptcy?

11. What happens if the member dies first?

12. Has security been provided in the event of the member's early death?

13. What happens if the non-member dies first?

14. What happens if the member dies before retirement?

15. What happens if the member lives beyond normal life expectancy?

16. What if the member terminates employment before retirement?

17. How will the member's age of retirement be determined?

18. What happens if the member retires earlier than anticipated?

19. What happens if the member retires later than anticipated?

20. What happens if the member becomes disabled before retirement?

21. Has provision been made for splitting the pension into two pensions?

22. Who is to control any elections?

23. Will the non-member be supplied with copies of any correspondence between the member and the pension plan administrator?

24. Is the member to be allowed to buy back the pension from the non-member, and on what terms?

25. Has the agreement been approved by the pension administrator?

26. What happens if the pension administrator will not pay to the non-member the full amount agreed on?

27. What happens if the agreement is declared null and void?

SUGGESTED WORDING FOR AN IF AND WHEN AGREEMENT INVOLVING A TEACHER'S PENSION

(This is not to be construed as legal advice or a form to use in any particular case. It is a sample. A lawyer should draft any agreement.)

1. Non-Plan Member's Entitlement

The Plaintiff, _____, (hereinafter called "the Wife") shall be entitled to receive 50% of the value of the Defendant's, _____ (hereinafter called "the Husband") interest in the __Teachers'__ Pension Plan (hereinafter referred to as "the Plan") accrued after the date of marriage _____ (Date) to the valuation date _____(Date) and she has an interest in the Plan to the extent of her entitlement. The Husband's interest in the Plan is valued at as shown in the valuation report of _____ dated _____.

2. Payment of the Wife's Interest

The Wife shall receive her interest in the Plan in the following ways:

A) By the Wife receiving each month a portion of the Husband's pension benefits once those benefits are in pay, the quantum of the monthly payments to be calculated pursuant to paragraphs 3 and 4 of the Appendix.

B) By the Husband's interest in the Plan being severed into two shares, one for himself and one for the Wife pursuant to paragraph 7 of the Appendix.

3. Calculation of the Wife's Pension Entitlement

A) Commencing on the first anniversary date of (Date of Separation), the Wife's share of the pension shall be adjusted annually by the annual indexing factor provided under the Teachers' Pension Plan. The annual indexation shall be made before and after retirement.

B) Commencing on the first anniversary date of (Date of Separation), and each year thereafter until payment in full has been made, interest at the rate of 4.5 percent per annum will accumulate on the balance owing to the Wife.

4. Calculation of the Wife's Monthly Payments

The amount of the monthly payments to the Plaintiff are to be based upon the formulas set out immediately below and, for greater certainty, the amounts of these monthly payments shall be adjusted annually both before and after retirement:

i. Before the Husband reaches the age of sixty-five, the amount of the monthly payment is to be based on the following formula: 2% x (years of service during marriage) x (Average Salary) x 50%. The monthly payments will be _____ before indexation and interest.

ii. After the Husband reaches the age of sixty-five, the amounts of the monthly payments are to be reduced based on the following formula of 0.6% x (Years of Service During Marriage) x (Average Years Maximum Pensionable Earnings) x 50%, that is be _____ monthly. The monthly payments will be _____ before indexation and interest.

5. Method of Payment of Wife's Share of Pension

A) The Wife's share of the Husband's pension as calculated under paragraph X* of the Judgement and under paragraphs 1, 3, and 4 of this Appendix shall be payable in part by the Husband and in part by the plan Administrators. Commencing on (Date), or upon the date the Husband starts to receive a pension benefit under the Plan, whichever occurs first, the Husband shall direct the Administrator to pay each month directly to the Wife 50% of the Husband's pension benefits accrued between the date of marriage and the valuation date as calculated by the Administrator as the maximum amount the Administrator is able to pay to the Wife under the requirements of the Plan and applicable pension legislation, such payment not to exceed the payment owing to the Wife as calculated under paragraph X of the Judgement and paragraphs 1, 3, and 4 herein. These payments from the Administrator to the Wife shall cease upon the Husband's death or upon the Administrator being advised by the Wife or through a subsequent domestic contract or Court Order that all sums owing to the Wife in regard to the Husband's pension have been paid in full. Due to changes in legislation or otherwise, the Administrator from time to time may determine the maximum amount of the Husband's pension benefits payable to the Wife has changed. Whatever the case, the Administrator shall be authorized to pay the amount to which the wife is entitled under paragraph X of the Judgement and paragraphs 1, 3, and 4 herein.

B) When the Husband starts to receive a pension benefit under the Plan, the Administrator shall first deduct the monthly payment owed to the Wife from the total pension payable, and then pay the remaining balance to the Husband.

* X will be a number that corresponds with the appropriate paragraph in the individual's separation agreement or Judgement.

C) In the event that in any given month the monthly payment payable to the Wife calculated under paragraphs 3 and 4 herein (i.e. after indexation and interest) exceeds the amount that the Administrator will pay to her, the Husband shall, within ten days, personally pay the difference to the Wife.

D) If the husband should postpone retirement beyond age ___ (Assumed Age of Retirement), immediately upon his attaining ___ (Assumed Age of Retirement), he shall commence to pay the Wife and shall continue to pay her during each month thereafter until all sums owing to the wife from that date forward is the amount she would have received as her share of his pension benefits had he retired at age _____ (Assumed Age of Retirement). The monthly payments to be made by the husband shall include any indexing provisions under the Plan plus interest.

6. Taxation

A) Each party will receive his respective share of the Husband's pension benefits and pay tax at his individual income tax rate thereof. The Administrator shall make such source deductions, issue T4 forms for each of the parties based upon their respective receipts of pension benefits pursuant to the Judgement and this Appendix.

B) If the Administrator is unable or unwilling to issue separate T4 forms for each party, then the Wife shall indemnify the Husband and save him harmless from any tax liability attributable to her share of the Husband's pension and the benefits thereunder or payment under compensation equivalent to her share of the pension as provided herein, and there shall be an accounting annually to determine the amount of tax paid by the Husband, with respect to the Wife's share of the pension or equivalent compensation payments, which amount shall be payable by the Wife to the Husband forthwith upon determination and notice to the Wife.

Severing Pension

A) Whenever able to do so under the terms of the Plan and applicable pension legislation, the Husband shall sever his interest in the Plan into two parts, one for himself and one for the Wife, with the Wife's share being calculated in accordance with her interest as set out in paragraph X of the Judgement herein and in accordance with paragraphs 1, 3, and 4 of this Appendix.

B) Subject to the terms of the Plan and the relevant pension legislation, the Wife may, upon any such severance, direct the Administrator to transfer the commuted value of her pension into a Registered Retirement Savings Plan or other appropriate vehicle.

C) If the law at the time of the severance does not accord with the Parties' intentions or the intention of this Judgement and this Appendix, either of the parties may apply to the Court for a severance or Judgement in his or her favour in accordance with the intentions of the parties as set out in this Appendix and Judgement, namely to allow the Wife's share in the Husband's pension in accordance with the amount set out in paragraph X of the Judgement and paragraph 6 of this Appendix.

(D) Direction to the Administrator of the Plan

This paragraph constitutes an irrevocable direction from the Husband to the Administrator of the _____ Pension Plan to carry out all the applicable terms of this Judgement and Appendix. The Husband hereby authorizes the Wife to deliver to the Administrator a notarial copy of this Judgement and attached Appendix or a certified copy of any Order made in accordance with it.

Trust Provisions

   (I) Pension Elections, Designs by the Husband

        A) The Husband shall be a trustee for the Wife's interest in the Plan benefits and shall not do or omit to perform any act that would prejudice her interest. The Husband shall not make any election, designation, nomination or transfer under the Plan that would in any way affect the Wife's interest in the Plan, without first obtaining her written approval. Such approval not to be unreasonably withheld.

   (II) Communications and Information with Respect to Pension Plan

        (A) Between the Husband and the Wife

        The Husband shall deliver to the Wife copies of all communications between himself and the Administrator of the Plan with regard to the Husband's pension rights or any employment benefits derived for the Plan within ten days after such communication.

        (B) Between the Husband and the Pension Plan

        The Husband shall forthwith forward to the Administrator of the Plan a certified copy of this Judgement and Appendix and draw to the Administrator's attention the provisions of the Judgement and the Appendix with the Plan. The Husband will provide an irrevocable direction to the Administrator to:

(I) Provide the Wife with any information the Wife requests about the Husband's pension and;

(II) Send copies to the Wife of all communications between the Plan and the Husband;

(III) Pay directly to the Wife that portion of the Husband's pension plan as defined in the Judgement;

(IV) Carry out all of the applicable terms of this Judgement and Appendix. The Husband shall sign a release to the Plan in the form required by the Plan to allow the Plan to communicate with the Wife as to any communication between the Husband and the Plan and any information the Wife requests about the Plan.

(C) Between the Wife and the Pension Plan

The Administrator of the Plan shall upon request send directly to the Wife, copies of all communications sent to or by the Husband in connection with the Plan. The Administrator shall provide the Wife with any information she requests concerning the Plan. The Husband undertakes to provide the Administrator with his current mailing address from time to time for the purposes of this paragraph. The Wife shall supply to the Administrator such information as is required by him in order to allow the Administrator to deal with the Wife directly, including providing her date of birth, social insurance number, bank account and address.

9. Payment of Funds to Husband Subject to Notice

The Husband shall not accept funds from the Administrator other than monthly payments without first giving the Wife forty-five days notice of the proposed payment. Further, the Husband shall not transfer funds from the Plan to an RRSP without first giving the wife forty-five days notice of the proposed transfer or to another Pension Plan.

10. Protection by Administrator

Subject to the requirements of the Plan and applicable law, the Husband directs the Administrator to take all necessary steps to recognize and protect the Wife's interest in and claims to that portion of the Husband's pension under the Plan as provided herein.

11. Early Retirement

If the Husband should retire before he attains the age of ___(assumed retirement age) and receive a reduced pension under the Plan, he shall immediately pay the Wife a lump sum equal to the capitalized amount of the difference in benefits under the pension plan that the Wife will receive after the early retirement and the benefits under the Plan that she would have received had the Husband not taken retirement at a reduced pension.

12. Termination of Husband's Employment

In the event the Husband changes employment or his employment with the _____ is terminated, the Wife shall have the right to deal with her share of the termination payment by electing to have her share paid according to any one of the options allowed on termination by the Plan and applicable legislation.

13. In the Event of Wife Predeceasing Husband

If the Wife dies before she receives her interest in the Plan, her estate is entitled to her interest in the Husband's Plan. The Husband and/or the Administrator, as the case may be, will pay the

Wife's interest in the Husband's Plan to the Wife's estate in accordance with this Judgement and Appendix.

14. Life Insurance

Until such time as the Husband's Plan can be severed into two shares, one for the Husband and one for the Wife as set out herein or until such time as all sums owing to the Wife in regard to the Husband's pension have been paid in full, and notwithstanding an assignment in bankruptcy by the Husband, the following life insurance provisions will apply:

1. The Husband shall maintain in effect a policy of insurance on his life with a face amount of at least _____.
2. The Husband shall designate the Wife as the sole beneficiary of this life insurance policy and shall file the said designation with the principal office of the insurer in accordance with the provisions of the Insurance Act. The Husband shall give to the Wife a true copy of the said designation within fourteen days of this Judgement.
3. The Husband shall deliver to the Wife on or before January tenth of each year proof that the said policy remains in effect and that he has not transferred the said policy or borrowed against it or pledged it as security.
4. The Husband shall deliver to the Wife within fourteen days from the date when it is demanded proof that the policy is in good standing, the Wife having the right to demand this proof at reasonable times and from time to time.
5. If the Husband defaults in payment of any premium, the Wife may pay the premium and recover from the Husband the amount of the payment, together with all costs including solicitor and client costs together with any expenses that may be incurred in restoring the policy to good standing.

6. The Husband shall execute an authorization allowing the Wife to receive information directly from the Husband's insurer during such time as the Husband is obliged to maintain this life insurance coverage.

7. If the Husband is unable to maintain or obtain life insurance coverage on his life with a face amount of at least _____ then he shall be obliged to provide the Wife with comparable security of an equal amount in a form satisfactory to the Wife and failing agreement, as the Court orders. For greater certainty, such security may include the Husband irrevocably designating the Wife as beneficiary of the following:

    (I) The supplementary death benefit under the Plan;

    (II) If at the time of the Husband's death, there are no survivors who are eligible for continuing benefits, the greater of the return of the Plan contributions with interest or 5 years worth of pension payments;

    (III) The death benefit payable under the Canada Pension Plan;

    (IV) A return of the supplementary retirement benefits contributions if there are no eligible survivors following the Husband's death;

    (V) Any other benefits under the Plan or the Canada Pension Plan for which the Husband may designate a beneficiary.

8. If the Husband dies without having in effect the required amount of insurance coverage under this paragraph, and without having provided the Wife with alternate security satisfactory to the Wife, there shall be a first charge against the Husband's estate in favour of the Wife for the sum total owing to the wife.

    (I) The life insurance provisions under this Judgement and Appendix are intended to survive an assignment in bankruptcy by the Husband or subsequent discharge. Accordingly, in the event of an assignment in bankruptcy by the Husband or subsequent discharge, these provisions shall be deemed valid and enforceable until such time as the Husband obtains a declaration that they are void and null. The Husband shall be responsible for the Wife's solicitor and client costs in litigating this matter in any event of the cause.

15. Bankruptcy

If the Husband becomes bankrupt prior to the severance of the Plan or prior to all sums owing to the Wife in regard to the Husband's pension have been paid in full, this Judgement and Appendix shall be deemed an assignment in favour of the Wife on an interest in moneys payable under a pension plan pursuant to s. 65 of the Pension Benefits Act. In the event that the Wife, notwithstanding the aforesaid assignment, is not a secured creditor pursuant to the Bankruptcy Act, as amended from time to time, the Wife shall be deemed to have been entitled as of the date of the Judgement to a lump sum maintenance payment from the Husband equal to one-half of the after tax value of the Husband's pension as of the valuation date as calculated under paragraph X of the Judgement and paragraphs 1, 3 and 4 of this Appendix less any necessary adjustments required as a result of any partial payments made to the Wife herein. This entitlement to a further Judgement for lump sum support shall be in lieu of the Wife's entitlement to an interest in the Husband's pension. The Wife shall be entitled to a further Judgement as of the date of this Judgment for the lump sum support payment referred to in this paragraph. The entitlement of the Wife to the lump sum support payment under this paragraph shall not be discharged by the Husband's bankruptcy or subsequent discharge but shall be an obligation of the Husband that survives the bankruptcy and discharge. The lump sum support obligation shall not be subject to variation for any reason whatsoever, regardless of any material change in circumstances of either of the parties following the date of this Judgement.

16. Alteration

A. If the Administrator of the Plan requires any minor alterations to this Judgement or Appendix dealing with the Plan in order to effect the division as intended by this Judgement, the Parties shall consent to any necessary changes thereto.

B. If the Administrator requires that any division of the pension be pursuant to a Court Order or Judgement the Husband agrees to take all necessary steps to obtain the Court Order or Judgement and the Husband agrees that he shall be solely responsible for the legal costs in obtaining such a Court Order or Judgement.

C. This Judgement is intended to conform to those provisions of the Plan, which might affect the perceived ability of the Plan Administrator to divide the pension at source each month during the Husband's lifetime, and particularly Section 51 and Regulation 56 of the Ontario Pension Benefits Act. In the event that a minor change in the amounts or procedures defined in this Judgement is requested by the Plan Administrator, then approval of that change will be given forthwith in the form required by the Administrator.

D. If for any reason the method of equalizing the pension benefits as set out herein is held to be ineffective due to any legal or other prohibition, then notwithstanding any limitation period, the division of the pension shall be renegotiated based on the principles as set out in this Judgement and Appendix.

17. Pension Paragraph Void/Dispute Resolution

A) The power to make further orders as to the pension and any benefits thereunder shall be reserved to the Court. If for any reason the Parties are unable to satisfy the Wife's entitlement under the Judgement and Appendix herein, that entitlement shall be satisfied in such other manner as agreed to between them, ordered by the Court or, failing jurisdiction in any Court, by arbitration. This clause shall constitute an agreement to arbitrate pursuant to the Arbitration Act, as amended from time to time.

B) This method of payment is called the "If and When" division of the pension. There may be questions concerning the validity and enforceability of the "if and when" pension provisions in this Judgement and Appendix. Consequently if at some time in the future, the "if and when" provisions in this Judgement and Appendix are found to be unenforceable or void, the Wife shall be entitled to a Judgement against the Husband at that time for an equalization payment equal to one-half of the after-tax value of the Husband's pension as of the valuation date as calculated herein plus interest until the date of payment. The Court shall have the jurisdiction to determine: (1) the appropriate deduction from the capitalization amount for any payments already made by the Husband to the Wife on account of his pension entitlement; (2) the amount of pre-judgement and post-judgement interest from the valuation date to the date of payment; and (3) the method by which the said equalization payment will be satisfied. Both parties shall be entitled to present evidence to the Court on these issues.

18. Waiving of the Time Limit

In the event that either party brings an application pursuant to paragraph (A) or (B) above, the parties shall be deemed to have waived the application of any limitation period under the Family Law Act and the Divorce Act or any other legislation.

19. Court Jurisdiction

The power to make further orders as to the pension and any benefits thereunder, including security, shall be reserved to the Ontario Court (General Division) in _____(City) or to the jurisdiction in which the Wife resides at that time.

20. Pension Valuator/Accountant

Should a valuation of the Husband's pension or of the Wife's interest in his pension be required at any time in the future, the parties shall jointly choose and retain a qualified pension valuator to do the calculations. Similarly, should it become appropriate for the parties to retain an accountant to resolve matters arising out of the Judgement and this Appendix, the parties shall jointly choose and retain a qualified accountant to perform the necessary calculations. Failing agreement by the parties, the dispute resolution provisions hereafter set out shall apply.

21. Pension Benefits

For greater certainty, the words "pension benefits," "pension," and "pension rights" when used in this Judgement and Appendix shall include but not be limited to the monthly pension benefits payable, any lump sum payable, and any other amount or amounts payable as a result of the Husband's membership in the Plan.

Valuation

Even if arrangements are made to split the pension payments as they are paid, still it will be necessary to have the pension valued at the date of separation in order to ensure that each party will receive the proper amount.

Dividing Public Sector Pensions

The spouse who has the pension may attempt to avoid the cost of obtaining a valuation report. He might also want to avoid the ensuing arguments over the value; such arguments could delay the divorce and increase legal fees. The member or his lawyer might suggest that the pension be divided under the provisions of applicable pension legislation when the circumstances allow it.

The Ontario Pension Benefits Act, the Federal Pension Benefits Standards Act, and the Pension Benefits Division Act all provide for splitting the member's pension rights and transferring a part of such rights under the pension plan to the spouse on marriage breakdown. These acts provide for the transfer of the commuted value of the spouse's rights to an RRSP or other retirement vehicle for the spouse. Under the Ontario Pension Benefits Act, such a transfer cannot take place until the member terminates employment. Most lump sum transfers to an RRSP from a pension plan involve plans regulated by the Pension Benefits Standards Act and the Pension Benefits Division Act; both allow immediate transfer at any time after the valuation date.

The Pension Benefits Division Act applies only to certain pensions created under the following federal statutes: Public Service Superannuation Act, Canadian Forces Superannuation Act, Defense Services Pension Continuation Act, Royal Canadian Mounted Police Superannuation Act, Royal Canadian Mounted Police Pension Continuation Act, Diplomatic Service (Special)

Superannuation Act, Lieutenant Governor's Superannuation Act, Governor's General Act, Members of Parliament Retirement Allowance Act, and Special Retirement Arrangements Act. It has no effect whatsoever on any other pensions. It does not apply to provincially regulated pension plans.

The Pension Benefits Division Act allows for the division of pension benefits between a pension member and a spouse or former spouse. The purpose of the act is to assist in the division of the value of certain federal pensions, but only to the extent that the federal government is prepared to do so. An application for division of the pension must be made in writing and must be accompanied by a copy of any court order or separation agreement that provides for the division of the pension benefits. The pension benefits to be divided are those that have accrued to the member during "the period subject to division." This period can be determined by a court order or by a spousal agreement specifying the period. In the absence of a court order or spousal agreement the minister will determine the period. Usually "the period subject to division" will be the period between the date of marriage and the date of separation. Often the period established by the minister will to be greater or less than the proper period. This can be a problem.

The division will be accomplished by transferring half the termination value of the pension benefits accrued during the "period subject to division" to the spouse's pension, to a locked in RRSP for the spouse, or to a financial institution to purchase a life annuity for the spouse. The plan administrator will determine what half the value of the pension benefit is, based on the guidelines included in the regulations. Another provision allows the court or the individuals involved to determine the lump sum amount to be transferred, as long as the amount stipulated in the court order or agreement is less than the amount that would otherwise be transferred as calculated by the plan administrator.

There are three separate steps in the Pension Benefits Division process:

1. Submit a request for information on pension benefits division. You will be told the approximate allowable amount of the division and an explanation of what went into the calculations.
2. Fill in and return the application for the pension benefits division. At this point the member has the opportunity to object to the division.
3. Once the division is approved, the value of benefits allowable for the period subject to division is transferred into the applicant's chosen retirement vehicle. The member's pension benefits are then reduced accordingly.

When is the Pension Benefits Division Act useful? Let's say Mr. & Mrs. Brown have separated and wish to equalize the value of their assets acquired during the marriage. They have no liabilities. Mr. Brown is a member of the Canadian Forces. Their house is registered in Mrs. Brown's name and Mr. Brown has his pension. They have no other assets. The equalization amount is calculated as follows:

Assets-	Mr. Brown Pension	$200,000.00
	Mrs. Brown Matrimonial Residence	$100,000.00
Difference		$100,000.00

Mr. Brown's assets acquired during the marriage are worth $100,000 more than the assets acquired by Mrs. Brown during the marriage. Mr. Brown must transfer $50,000 worth of assets to Mrs. Brown so that they both end up with assets worth $150,000.

Mr. Brown transfers $50,000 worth of his pension to an RRSP for Mrs. Brown. This equalizes their property. Mr. Brown's pension is reduced accordingly.

The amount calculated by the pension plan administrator as available for transfer under the Pension Benefits Division Act will rarely be the proper value for equalization on marriage breakdown. There are a number of reasons for this.

1. The value calculated under the Pension Benefits Division Act is based on the Canadian Institute of Actuaries' recommendations for the computation of transfer values from registered pension plans. These recommendations were not intended to be used to divide the value of a pension equally and fairly between two parties. The purpose of these recommendations is to provide a minimum value of a plan member's pension rights for transfer purposes on termination of employment. The goal is to protect the pension fund as well as the member whose pension rights are being transferred out. The standard of practice for marriage breakdown computations has an entirely different focus, and will usually produce a different value.

2. The economic assumptions stipulated in the recommendation for the computation of transfer values are different from those stipulated in the Standard of Practice for marriage breakdown computations.

3. In Ontario, under the Standard of Practice for marriage breakdown computations, the portion of the value of the pension that was earned during the marriage might be determined using the value added method. Under the Pension Benefits Division Act, the pro rata method is stipulated. These two methods can produce vastly different results.

4. Under the Ontario Family Law Act, pension benefits are valued at the date of marriage and again at the date of separation to determine the value for marriage breakdown purposes. Under the Pension Benefits Division Act regulations, pension rights are valued at the day the calculations are being performed. The value earned during the marriage is

determined by the pro rata method. Part of the post-separation value may be pro rated to the marriage period.

5. The mortality tables used under the Pension Benefits
   Division Act are determined by experience with the specific
   plan membership plus a projection for improvements in mortality. Under the Standard of Practice on marriage breakdown, the 1983 Group Annuity Mortality Tables are used.
   These are general mortality tables for the working population, which include no projection for improvements. Under
   the Standard of Practice and case law, the impaired health of
   a plan member can result in different mortality assumptions
   being applied. This is specifically prohibited in the regulations to the Pension Benefits Division Act.

6. Under the Ontario Family Law Act, the assumption of
   which date a pension plan member will commence to
   receive a pension (the assumed retirement date) is a question of fact in every case. Under the Pension Benefits
   Division Act, plan experience determines the assumed
   retirement date based on the age, sex, and years of service of
   the member. A different retirement date can mean an
   entirely different value for the pension.

7. The maximum transferable amount under the Pension
   Benefits Division Act is given in before-tax dollars.
   Normal valuations of pensions provide the values in after-
   tax dollars so they can be compared with the after-tax value
   of other assets and included in the required Net Family
   Property Statement.

Justice Metivier discussed the value determined under the
Pension Benefits Division Act in the case of *Schaeffer v. Schaeffer*.[4]

There was some evidence led on the value, which is
determined by the Pension Benefits Division Act.

Mr. Woods stated, and I agree, that the Pension Benefit Division Act value is one, which is generally totally unreliable as an accurate valuation for specific individuals for purposes of the Family Law Act. Appealing though it may be to rely on a quick and easy solution to these difficulties of valuation, the Act remains merely a mechanism for transferring monies out of the plan. While the Pension Benefits Division Act provides for its own method of valuing pensions it does so for the Federal Government's own specific purposes. These include maintaining the integrity of the plan, benefiting the members as a whole and again only with a view to a mechanism for transferring out certain monies. These methods however, have nothing to do with provincial laws relating to property rights and the disposition of those as between former spouses. In the Canada Gazette Part 2, Volume 128 Number 21 the regulations to the Pension Benefits Division Act are followed by a regulatory impact analysis statement. Of interest is the following paragraph. "It should be noted that the purpose of the Act and the Regulations is to provide a mechanism for making payments out of the pension funds, not to fix the value of the pension as between spouses and property settlements made upon the breakdown of their relationship."

With the difference between transfer value and marriage breakdown value, different discount rates used in the calculations, value added method versus pro rata method, a different period for the earnings of the pension benefit, different mortality tables, a different assumed retirement date and either a proper allowance for income taxes or no allowance, it is not surprising that the value determined under the Pension Benefits Division Act normally will be different than the proper value for marriage breakdown purposes. These differences can result in the Pension Benefits Division Act valuation being significantly greater or lesser than the proper value for marriage breakdown purposes. Some cases give an idea of how these values can differ.

Mr. David was born in April 1952. He enrolled in the Canadian Forces in May 1972. He was married in September 1987 and separated in November 1995. He obtained a letter from National Defense headquarters stating, "[T]he amount that would be paid to your former spouse, as a result of the division of your pension entitlement under the Canadian Forces Superannuation Act for the cohabitation period, is $40,440.63." We acted for Mrs. David, and calculated that the proper value of Mr. David's pension for the portion earned during the marriage was $119,300. Mrs. David's share of the pension should have been $59,650.

In another case, Mr. Philip was born in 1944, joined the Canadian Forces in 1962, married in 1968, separated in 1992, and retired in 1996, although he had already qualified for retirement on an unreduced pension at the date of separation. Counsel for the spouse had a valuation report prepared, which produced after-tax values ranging from $145,000 to $292,000. They also had a letter from the actuary stating that, based on the Pension Benefits Division Act, "The capitalized value of pension entitlements accrued during the member's whole service is $307,922 (before tax allowance)." Counsel for the spouse included the last figure in the financial statement for the member, and insisted it must be the proper value since it was the value established by the Pension Benefits Division Act and was the amount available for transfer. We were acting for the member and were able to prove a value of $170,650, thereby reducing his assets by $130,000.

Whether you are the member or the spouse, obtain a valuation of the pension even when the benefits are being divided under the Pension Benefits Division Act.

MISUNDERSTANDINGS AND MISUSE OF THE PENSION BENEFITS DIVISION ACT

When a federal government pension is being considered on marriage breakdown, the Pension Benefits Division Act allows for a mechanism to divide, at source, pensions created under a specific group of federal statutes. The act does not attempt to deal with the issue of entitlement to share the value of a pension following separation; that matter is dealt with under the Family Law Act of Ontario.

Public Works and Government Services Canada issues two reports indicating the value of the member's pension. The pension calculation report shows a value based on the full service pension from enrollment date to separation date. The pension benefit report shows values based only on the period subject to division. If you are presented with a pension calculation report and there is a pre-marriage period, the report describes the value of the pension for the full service, not just for the period of cohabitation.

Regulations under the PBDA establish the maximum amount the federal government is prepared to transfer out of its pension fund for the benefit of the spouse of the plan member. This amount is known as the Maximum Transferable Amount (MTA). Some people think this amount is the value of the pension for marriage breakdown purposes. In reality, the MTA is the maximum amount that could be transferred to the spouse's retirement savings vehicle. When a member is non-vested, the MTA is half the amount contributed by the member during the period subject to division, plus interest. If the member is vested, the MTA is half the value of the member's pension entitlement for the period subject to division. For the purpose of managing its pension funds and protecting the interest of its plan members, the federal government is setting as to what can be transferred out to a spouse's retirement vehicle.

The valuation guidelines are set out in the regulations of the PBDA, and they differ from the guidelines in the Canadian Institute of Actuaries' "Standard of Practice For the Computation of the Capitalized Value of Pension Entitlements on Marriage Breakdown for Purposes of Lump-Sum Equalization Payments."

In cases where the value calculated using guidelines set forth in the standards produces values greater than half the MTA, the allowable amount under the PBDA can be used to satisfy a portion of the equalization amount; the remainder must be satisfied through other means.

We recently valued a Canadian Forces pension. We were given two quotes for the MTA, calculated a year and a half apart by Canadian Forces. The date of separation in each case was the same. The second MTA was $6,000 higher than the first. The difference is partly because the Canadian Forces adds interest from the date of valuation to the date of calculation. The value we calculated for marriage breakdown purposes was almost $10,000 lower than the higher of these amounts.

In our experience, the values that should be used for family law purposes are lower than those calculated by the federal government for PBDA purposes. Here are some examples:

Family Law	Value PBDA
$ 137, 513	$ 182, 868
$ 209, 596	$ 267, 442
$ 17, 377	$ 18, 797
$ 104, 496	$ 106, 605
$ 114, 137	$ 120, 257
$ 50, 236	$ 75, 842
$ 75, 000	$ 95, 970

In *Woodley v. Woodley*,[5] the judge accepted the evidence of an actuary as to the capitalized value of the husband's Canadian Forces pension on the valuation date. He ordered an equalization payment to be made by the husband to the wife, in gross, before-tax dollars, based on the actuarial valuation. He stipulated that the payment would be satisfied in whole or in part through a transfer under the PBDA. If the MTA was less than the equalization payment, the husband had to make up the shortfall less 26 per cent for income taxes.

The Pension Benefits Division Act allows the mechanism to divide the pension. The method of division must be addressed.

Sheryl Smolkin, director of the Canadian Research and Information Centre, spoke at the Pensions, Benefits and Family Law Conference, November 20, 1998. "[The] only method of settlement provided for under the PBDA is the transfer of a lump sum amount not exceeding 50 per cent of the value of the pension benefits that have accrued to the member during the period subject to division, as determined under the PBDA Regulations, to another pension plan selected by the non-member spouse, if the pension plan so permits; a locked-in RRSP; or a financial institution for the purchase of an immediate or deferred life annuity. If an immediate annuity is chosen, the periodic payments must commence within one year of its purchase."

Funds cannot be released as cash in most instances. If money is transferred from the pension fund to an immediate life annuity, the income from the life annuity is considered as income to the spouse, thereby reducing the amount of support required.

If you are the member and are settling the equalization payment by way of a transfer under the PBDA, you may wish to reduce any support claim. Then you should suggest a transfer to a financial institution for the purchase of an immediate annuity to the spouse.

If you are the non-member spouse, you might argue that the transfer should be to a locked-in RRSP so you can collect a pension some day. This would not reduce your need for support.

WHY NOT THE PENSION BENEFITS DIVISION ACT VALUE?

Should the MTA be used in calculating the equalization amount. Our answer to this question is that it depends on three things:

1. Do you care whether you are using the correct value for marriage breakdown purposes?
2. Are you concerned that you may be sued for negligence or have the separation agreement declared null and void because you have used the wrong value for the pension?
3. How will you determine the proper income tax allowance when it could range from 0% to as high as 45%?

Many judges recognize that the MTA may not be the proper value for marriage breakdown purposes.[6] As well, the MTA may be lower or higher than the proper value. There are different reasons for this.

- The sex of the particular individual is ignored, and the calculations are based on a combination of male and female life expectancies.
- The discount rate used in the present value calculation is appropriate for the date the calculations are being performed, and may be too high or too low for the date of separation.
- It assumes an arbitrary date of retirement.
- The calculations are based on the Recommendations for the Computation of Transfer Values from Registered Pension Plans established by the Canadian Institute of Actuaries, and not the standards for valuing pensions on marriage breakdown.
- The principal of paramountcy does not apply.[7]
- The minister determines the period subject to division, which may be different than the marriage period determined by the parties involved.

- It may ignore the value of early retirement provisions.
- The reasoning behind the calculations is to minimize the amount that is transferred out of the pension fund.
- If the member has already retired, the MTA will have been reduced by pension payments already made.
- No income tax allowance has been deducted. (Unless both parties will be in the same tax bracket after retirement, income tax cannot be ignored.)
- It usually includes interest from the date of separation to the date the calculations are completed.
- The value of the post separation improvements in the pension plan may have been included.
- Reduced life expectancy is ignored.

The following is a list of valuations in which we have been involved in where we compared the MTA to the proper value. The range of error in the MTA value was from overstating the value by $77,360.44 to understating the value by $29,156.56. The percentage of error ranged from understating the value at a 4.83% of error to overstating the value at 103% of error. As you will note, in almost all cases, the MTA value was greater than the family law value.

NRA	Midpoint	Earliest	MTA NRA	% Error	% Error Midpoint	% Error Earliest
54, 822.00	68, 398.50	84, 404.00	80, 329.99	-46.53%	-17.44%	4.83%
28, 489.50	33, 888.50	40, 898.00	51, 702.89	-81.48%	-52.57%	-26.42%
30, 142.00	18, 343.00	22, 373.00	37, 234.51	-23.53%	-102.99%	-66.43%
36, 196.00	44, 296.00	53, 877.50	67, 471.06	-86.40%	-52.32%	-25.23%
32, 741.50	35, 190.00	37, 864.50	40, 480.80	-23.64%	-15.03%	-6.91%
205, 961.00			211, 993.95	-2.93%		
54, 385.00	67, 287.50	82, 186.50	72, 377.07	-33.08%	-7.56%	11.94%
18, 941.50	23, 102.50	28, 616.00	30, 374.99	-60.36%	-31.48%	-6.15%
107, 598.50	136, 077.00	214, 115.50	184, 958.94	-71.90%	-35.92%	13.62%
64, 786.00	76, 012.50	92, 572.00	105, 478.74	-62.81%	-38.76%	-13.94%
63, 695.00	78, 036.50	97, 668.00	111, 835.49	-75.58%	-43.31%	-14.51%
51, 267.00	61, 689.00	76, 621.50	93, 133.63	-81.66%	-50.97%	-21.55%
41, 909.50	47, 702.50	55, 942.00	57, 590.56	-37.42%	-20.73%	-2.95%
24, 909.50	27, 409.00	30, 959.00	37, 327.28	-53.42%	-36.19%	-20.57%
38, 554.00	45, 048.00	54, 090.50	61, 427.96	-59.33%	-36.36%	-13.57%

The purpose of the Pension Benefits Division Act is to allow a means of settling the equalization payment. It was not intended to be a means of valuing the pension for purposes of completing the Net Family Property statement.

Settling the equalization of property on marriage breakdown using the value calculated according to the Pension Benefits Division Act probably will cost one of the parties thousands of dollars.

DIVIDING CERTAIN PRIVATE SECTOR PENSIONS

The Pension Benefits Standards Act is federal and applies to private sector pension plans in, for example, banks, airlines, the CNR and CBC. For a complete list see the Appendix.

Pursuant to a court order or the request of a member, a pension plan covered by the Pension Benefits Standards Act may assign all or part of the pension benefit, benefit credit, or other benefit under the plan to the member's spouse, effective on divorce, annulment, or separation. When the division is made, the spouse is deemed to have been a member of the pension plan for the purposes of the Pension Benefits Standards Act. According to the Act, the plan administrator must divide and administer the pension benefit in a prescribed manner in accordance with the court order or agreement once all appeals have been exhausted. For the purposes of the division, the non-member spouse is treated like a member who has terminated employment. The non-member spouse may transfer the credits into another pension plan or locked-in RRSP, or to a life insurance company for the purchase of an immediate or deferred life annuity. The legislation gives both the member and the spouse a right to information about the plan.

The non-member spouse may choose a deferred pension in the same plan. In this case the division results in a complete separation of the interest of the spouse as of the effective date of the division.

When the non-member spouse elects a deferred pension, as soon as he reaches pensionable age under the plan, he is treated like a former member and is entitled to a pension based on the member's period of employment and salary at the time of division. The act also provides for the division of a pension that is already being paid.

There have been some unusual decisions in court cases dealing with divisions under the Pension Benefits Standards Act, especially in cases where it is difficult to determine whether a federal or provincial pension act applies.

Air Canada has a document called "Administrative Policy On The Distribution of Benefits under The Air Canada Pension Plan Upon Separation, Divorce or Annulment of Marriage." This document explains the plan's policies and restrictions very well. Most companies will have a similar document. If your spouse suggests dividing the pension, be sure to read and understand this document.

> The Bank of Nova Scotia issued the following memo in 1998:
>
> The Scotiabank Pension Plan is governed by the Pension Benefit Standards Act 1985.
>
> This Act requires the Plan Administrator to be responsible for valuing assigned pension benefits disbursed from the Plan, and for calculating the residual pension benefits due to members, subsequent to any partial assignment of pensions, as mandated by marriage breakdown agreements or court orders.
>
> Under the legislation, these value determinations must be made as of the effective date of the assignment of, or agreement on, the division of pension benefits, and these determinations are required only if pension benefits under the Plan are to be divided, i.e., not when alternative settlements are made in respect of pension assets.

There is no specified basis, under either provincial property law or in the Pension Benefit Standards Act 1985, as to how pension benefit values may be determined for *purposes of valuing family property*. Nor does the Bank have any legal responsibility, under pension benefits legislation, to determine a value for this purpose.

We are able, however, to provide a calculation of the amount of *pension benefit* earned during the period of the marriage, to plan members who are working out a division of family property. For purposes of these determinations, we assume termination at the date of marriage breakdown, and we quote the *monthly pension* earned to that date and payable at Normal Retirement Date.

In addition, we are able to provide a commuted value of the quoted monthly pension. However, this value will be calculated based on the interest and mortality assumptions used in determining minimum transfer values on termination of employment. This amount represents the maximum amount that can be assigned to a spouse, under any agreement.

To minimize the complexity of the agreement wording that would otherwise be required, we would urge members and their spouses to ultimately describe the agreed upon split of the Scotiabank Pension in terms relative to the *commuted value* of the member's pension. If the agreement is described in terms of amount of pension to be assigned, complete details of such pension must also be given including: the amount of pension, the pension commencement date/age and what, if any, benefits are payable on death before or after pension commencement. Also, if the pension assignment is contingent on certain future events, each event, and the disposition of the assigned benefits on the occurrence of each event, must be defined in detail, in order to ensure that all parties, including the Plan Administrator, will be able to understand what has been agreed to.

Note that a member's spouse, in a marriage breakdown situation, cannot revoke an entitlement to the death benefit payable as a result on any residual pension benefit to the member, if a member is still legally married at the time of death and was not, in an eligible common-law relationship, at the time.

We have enclosed the Commuted Value Release form for your signature.

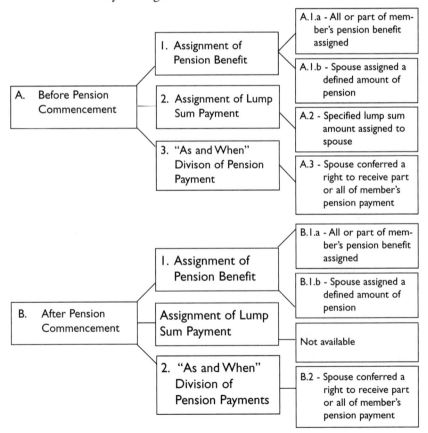

SCOTIABANK PENSION PLAN
COMMUTED VALUE REQUEST

I, _____am requesting Scotiabank to provide me with the commuted value of my pension entitlement in the Scotiabank Pension Plan accrued as at _____.

I understand that:

1. This value is strictly a calculation of the amount that would have been transferable to my RRSP had I terminated employment on the date indicated above. I understand that this value is not necessarily an appropriate value to attach to the pension asset for purposes of marriage breakdown.

2. I have been advised the merit of seeking advice from an independent actuary. Because of the many assumptions employed in the calculation of this value, it is most likely that an independent actuary would arrive at a different value than the one being provided to me. The value that will be provided by Scotiabank could be higher or lower, than the value that an independent actuary might produce.

3. The value provided to me will reflect the pension accrued during the period of marriage only and will not address the impact of taxation on amounts payable.

4. Scotiabank cannot provide an opinion about the fairness of the figure, nor attest to the appropriateness of the value for marriage breakdown purposes in any court action relating to the marriage breakdown, should one arise.

Employee Name & # _____

Signature _____

Date _____

DIVISION OF OTHER PRIVATE SECTOR PENSIONS

The Ontario Pension Benefits Act provides that pension payments may be divided at source pursuant to an agreement or a court order. Such an arrangement is valid only if it is clear that the non-member may not, under any circumstances, receive more than half the value accrued during the marriage. The act does not make any provision for payments to be made to the non-member before the member retires or after the member dies.

Some provinces provide for dividing a pension into two separate pensions—one for each party—on marriage breakdown, or for payment of a lump sum before the member retires.

- Alberta
- British Columbia
- Manitoba
- Newfoundland
- Nova Scotia
- Saskatchewan

TEACHERS' PENSIONS AND MARRIAGE BREAKDOWN

Stephanie Wood, legal council to the Ontario Teachers' Pension Plan Board, explained Ontario teachers' pensions and marriage breakdown.

1. Introduction
The following information will be of interest to family law practitioners acting on behalf of members of the Ontario Teachers' Pension Plan or their spouses or former spouses with respect to negotiation of a separation agreement or proceedings under the *Family Law Act*[8] or the *Divorce Act*[9]. I will briefly out-

line the statutory framework governing the division of pension payments at source upon marriage breakdown as well as provide a general description of spousal survivor benefits under the Ontario Teachers' Pension Plan.

My comments herein are general comments only, intended to raise awareness of these issues among family law practitioners and should not be relied upon as legal advice or as binding on the Ontario Teachers' Pension Plan Board. Counsel acting in these matters should contact the Board with any specific questions they may have and should obtain confirmation from the Board with respect to their clients' entitlements under the pension plan. Entitlement to spousal survivor benefits in particular can vary according to several factors, including the exact date on which the member of the pension plan ceased employment in education, which in turn determines the applicable version of the plan terms. Furthermore, under a defined benefit pension plan such as the Ontario Teachers' Pension Plan, members of the plan have little scope for designating a beneficiary of survivor benefits under the plan and any lawyer acting for a member of the pension plan or his or her spouse should obtain information from the Board on the issue of entitlement to survivor benefits before finalizing any agreement or order that purports to deal with survivor benefits under the pension plan.

2. Background — The Ontario Teachers' Pension Plan

The Ontario Teachers' Pension Plan is the largest single invested pension plan in Canada with total assets exceeding $35 billion. The plan's contributing membership consists of approximately 160,000 elementary and secondary school teachers and others employed in education in Ontario. The plan pays pensions to more than 49,000 retired teachers and their survivors. For many members of the pension plan, their pension benefit will be the most valuable single item of property to be included in the calculation of net family property in the event of marriage breakdown.

The Ontario Teachers' Pension Plan is a defined benefit pension plan administered by the Ontario Teachers' Pension Plan Board in accordance with the *Teachers' Pension Act[10]*, the *Pension Benefits Act[11]* and the *Income Tax Act[12]*. The current text of the pension plan is set out in Schedule 1 to the *Teachers' Pension Act* as adopted by the plan sponsors. The language of particular provisions in Schedule 1 has been amended from time to time by the co-sponsors of the plan. Earlier versions of the plan text are set out in the *Teachers' Superannuation Act, 1986[13]* and the *Teachers' Superannuation Act, 1980[14]*.

The Ontario government (through the Minister of Education and Training) and the Ontario Teachers' Federation (through its executive) are the joint sponsors of the pension plan. Together these two sponsoring partners are responsible for the design of the pension plan and the level of benefits. Under the terms of an agreement signed by the partners and effective January 1, 1992, a six-member partners' committee is responsible for changes in plan design such as benefit levels and contribution rates. The Board is responsible for administering the terms of the pension plan as set by the partners.

3. Pensions and Marriage Breakdown
(a) Equalization

Pensions are "property" as defined in Section 4 of the *Family Law Act* and therefore must be valued and taken into account when calculating a spouse's net family property under the Act. The Board does not value the member's pension benefits for the purpose of calculating net family property under the *Family Law Act*. An actuary should be consulted for this purpose.

In order to satisfy an equalization claim, some members will agree to split their pension payments with their spouse or former spouse when they begin to receive them. Under the *Pension Benefits Act*, the Board may divide pension payments in accordance with a domestic contract as defined in the *Family Law Act* or in accordance with a court order made under the *Family Law Act*.

Under Subsection 65 (1) of the *Pension Benefits Act*, "every transaction that purports to assign, charge, anticipate or give as security money payable under a pension plan is void." Subsection 65 (3) then goes on to provide that this general prohibition on assignment does not apply to prevent the assignment of an interest in money payable under a pension plan by an order under the *Family Law Act* or by a domestic contract as defined in Part IV of the *Family Law Act*. It is this provision in the *Pension Benefits Act* that allows a member of the pension plan to assign to his or her spouse a share of the member's pension payments.

In order to divide a member's pension payments with a spouse or former spouse the Board requires a copy of the separation agreement or court order in which a share of the member's pension benefits is assigned to the spouse. This agreement or order should be certified to be a true copy of the original agreement or order. The Board also requires the member's direction to divide his or her pension payments and make the payments to his or her spouse or former spouse in accordance with the agreement or order. It is the Board's usual practice if it has not already received this direction to ask the member for the direction at the time he or she applies for a pension. As well the Board will need the name, address and telephone number of the non-member spouse so that Board staff can contact the non-member spouse to arrange for payment of his or her share of the pension payments. The Board pays pension payments by direct deposit to the financial institution account designated by the recipient.

Subsection 51 (1) of the *Pension Benefits Act* provides that a domestic contract as defined in Part IV of the *Family Law Act* or an order under Part 1 of the *Family Law Act* is not effective to require payment of a pension benefit before the earlier of the date on which payment of the pension benefit commences or the normal retirement date of the relevant member or former member. Accordingly, the Board cannot divide pension payments between spouses until the member's pension begins.

Section 51 (2) of the *Pension Benefits Act* limits the amount of a pension that the Board can pay to a non-member spouse:

A domestic contract or an order mention in subsection (1) is not effective to cause a party

to the domestic contract or order to become
entitled to more than 50 per cent of the pension benefits, calculated in the prescribed
manner, accrued by a member or former
member during the period when the party and
the member or former member were spouses.

Under section 51 (2) a spouse cannot receive
payment reflecting more than 50 per cent of the pension benefits accrued during the spousal period.
Section 56 of the Regulations made under the
Pension Benefits Act requires that the pension benefits
be calculated as if the member had terminated membership in the pension plan on the valuation date:

> For purposes of subsection 51 (2) of the Act,
> the pension benefits accrued during the peri-
> od a member had a spouse shall be deter-
> mined as if the member terminated employ-
> ment at the valuation date in accordance with
> the terms of the plan at the date and without
> consideration of future benefits, salary or
> changes to the plan but with consideration for
> the possibility of future vesting.

The Board calculates this section 51 (2) limit
amount based on the termination method and then
compares this amount with the amount yielded by
the formula or percentage agreed to by the parties in
their agreement or court order. The Board will pay
the lesser of these amounts to the non-member
spouse each month. The Board will provide counsel
for the member and/or counsel for the member's

spouse with this section 51 (2) limit figure upon receipt of written consent from the member authorizing the Board to release his or her pension information to the party requesting it.

When making these divided pension payments, the Board automatically takes tax off of each spouse's pension payments after division in accordance with their individual rates. The monthly pension payments that both spouses receive from the Board will already have the appropriate income tax deducted.

Under the terms of the pension plan, members' pensions are automatically adjusted for inflation each year going forward in accordance with the inflation adjustment mechanism under the plan. If the agreement or court order so provides both the member's share of the pension *and* the spouse's share of the pension will be adjusted for inflation each year going forward in accordance with the inflation adjustment mechanism under the plan.

Under the terms of the pension plan, members' pensions are automatically reduced, using a formula set out in the pension plan, when the member reaches age 65 in order to reflect Canada Pension Plan integration. Accordingly, the member's share of the pension and the spouse's share of the pension will both automatically be lowered when the member reaches age 65.

Unless the agreement or court order expressly states that the pension payment to the non-member spouse are to revert to the member upon the death of the spouse, the Board will have to continue to make the payments as assigned to the spouse's estate until the pension ends with the member's death.

The member's pension, and accordingly the share of that pension being paid to the spouse, ends with the member's death.

(b) Options on Termination of Membership

A significant departure from the scheme for the division of pension benefits outlined above occurs where a member terminates employment in education, thereby ceasing to be a member of the pension plan, before his or her pension begins.

Subsection 51 (5) of the *Pension Benefits Act* provides as follows:

> A spouse on whose behalf a certified copy of a domestic contract or order mentioned in subsection (1) is given to the administrator of a pension plan has the same entitlement, on termination of employment by the member or former member, to any option available in respect of the spouse's interest in the pension benefits as the member or former member named in the domestic contract has in respect to his or her pension benefits.

Lawyers acting on behalf of non-member spouses should realize that although the Board cannot begin to divide pension payments between the spouses until the member's pension begins, subsection 51 (5) addresses the possibility of the member terminating employment before his or her pension begins. Because of this possibility, there is an advantage to sending a copy of the domestic contract or court order to the Board as soon as it is executed. If a member of the plan terminates his or her employment in education, and thereby ceases to be a member of the pension plan he or she may be entitled to certain options on termination such as the transfer of a lump sum amount out of the pension fund and into an RRSP. If the administrator has not received a copy of the domestic contract or court order then it will not be able to consider the non-member spouse's interest in the pension benefits should the member terminate his or her membership in the plan.

(c) Support
Subsection 66 (1) of the *Pension Benefits Act* provides that money payable under a pension plan is exempt from execution, seizure or attachment. However, subsection 66 (4) provides that deposits subsection (1), payments under a pension are subject to execution, seizure or attachment in satisfaction of an order to support enforceable in Ontario to a maximum of one-half the money payable.

In response to a notice of Support Deduction from the Family Support Plan in accordance with the provisions of the *Family Support Plan Act*, the Board will deduct and remit to the Family Support Plan an amount from each monthly amount payable to the member.

It is the Board's position that subsection 51(2) and subsection 66 (4) of the *Pensions Benefit Act* are not mutually exclusive. Division of the pension payments resulting from an assignment for the purposes of paying an equalization claim and attachment of the payments under the pension plan in satisfaction of an order for support have separate statutory bases in the *Pension Benefits Act* and separate statutory limits as to the amount that can be assigned or attached. Accordingly, it is possible for a non-member spouse to receive both divided pension payments under a separation agreement or court order up to the subsection 51 (2) limit of 50 per cent of the benefits accrued during the spousal period as well as an amount of monthly support taken from the member's pension under a Notice of Support Deduction.

(d) Spousal Survivor Benefits

(i) Members Who Cease Employment in Education After December 31, 1989

Under the current terms of the pension plan, applicable to members who cease employment in education after December 31, 1989, if a member of the pension plan dies *before beginning his or her pension*, the spouse of the member on the date of death is entitled to a pre-retirement spousal death benefit (which may be a lump sum and/or a survivor pension) provided the member and the spouse were not living separate and apart on the date of death. Separation before the date of death will disentitle a spouse from receiving pre-retirement spousal death benefits under the plan.

Under the current terms of the pension plan, applicable to members who cease employment in education after *December 31, 1989*, if a member of the pension plan dies *after beginning his or her pension*, the spouse of the member on the date the first installment of the pension was due is entitled to a survivor pension, provided the member and the spouse were not living separate and apart on the date the first installment of the pension was due. Note that under the current terms of the pension plan, separation before the first installment date will disentitle a spouse from receiving a spousal survivor pension under the plan but separation, or even divorce, after the first installment date does not.

The definition of "spouse" under the current terms of the pension plan is the definition of spouse set out in section 1 of the *Pension Benefits Act*. In that Act, spouse is defined as:

Either of a man and woman who
    (a) are married to each other, or
    (b) are not married to each other and are living together in a conjugal relationship.
      (i) continuously for a period not less than three years, or
      (ii) in a relationship of some permanence, if they are the natural or adoptive parents of a child.

The Ontario Teachers' Pension Plan is a defined benefit pension plan and accordingly there is little scope for designating a beneficiary of survivor benefits under the plan. In the pre-retirement period, it is possible for a member to designate a beneficiary of pre-retirement survivor benefits under the plan only where the member does not have a spouse or dependent children entitled to a benefit payable on his or her death. If a beneficiary has been so designated the benefit payable to that beneficiary is a lump sum payment equal to the commuted value or the deferred pension to which the member was entitled for credited service for employment on or after January 1, 1987.

For members who die after beginning a pension, a designated beneficiary is only entitled to receive a beneficiary's pension if the member does not have a spouse entitled to a survivor pension or a dependent child entitled to a child's pension and if the beneficiary is a dependent as defined under the survivor benefit provisions for registered pension plan prescribed under the *Income Tax Act* (This definition does not include a former spouse).

(i) Members Who Ceased Employment in Education on or Before December 31, 1989.

In very general terms, under earlier versions of the pension plan, spousal status and therefore entitlement to spousal survivor benefits is determined as of the date of death in both the pre and post-retirement scenarios. The spouse of the member on the date of death is entitled to a survivor benefit as long as the member and the spouse were spouses before the member's last day of employment in education. The spouse will be entitled even if the member and the spouse were separated on the date of death. The spouse will not be entitled if the member and the spouse were divorced before the date of death. In addition, survivor benefits for those members who ceased employment in education between December 31, 1987 and December 31, 1989 are governed by both the *Teachers' Superannuation Act, 1983* and the *Pension Benefits Act*. The *Pension Benefits Act* provisions are similar to the current pension plan as described above.

Again, lawyers drafting agreements that purport to deal with survivor benefits under the plan should obtain information from the Board on the issue of entitlement to survivor benefits in each individual case. This entitlement can vary according to several factors.

4. Conclusion

It is hoped that the above information will serve as a helpful starting point for family law practitioners acting on behalf of members of the Ontario Teachers' Pension Plan or their spouses of former spouses. Further and more specific information should be obtained by contacting the Board directly.

Notes

1   (1994), 8 R.F.L. (4th) 157, Ont. Ct. of Justice, Gen. Div.).

2   (1987) 62 O.R. (2d) 425, Ont. H.C.

3   (1993) O.J. No. 2814 (Gen. Div.).

4   (1996) Court File No.: 47942/94.

5   (1994) (Ont. Gen. Div.).

6   See, for example *McNutt v. McNutt* (2000), 5. R.F.L. (5th) 90 (Ont. S.C.J.) and *Shafer v. Shafer* (1996) 25 R.F.L. (4th) 410 (O.T.C.) affirmed (1998), 37 R.F.L. (4th) 104 (Ont. C.A.) and *Lockyer v. Lockyer* (2000) 10 R.F.L. (5th) 318 (Ont. S.C.J.).

7   *McNutt v. McNutt* (2000) 5 R.F.L. (5th) 90 (Ont. S.C.J.).

8   R.S.O. 1990.c.F.3.

9   R.S.C. 1985 (2nd Supp.) c.3.

10 R.S.O. 1990, c.T.1.

11 R.S.O. 1990, c.P.8.

12 R.S.C. 1985 (5th Supp.), c.1.

13 S.O. 1983, c. 84.

14 R.S.O. 1980. c. 494.

Chapter 18

Disability Benefits

INTRODUCTION

Should a disability benefit be included in the equalization of net family property on marriage breakdown? The answer to this question will depend on the answers to three distinct questions:

1. Is it property?
2. Is it exempt?
3. Would it be unconscionable to include the value in the accounting?

The answer to these questions depends on what type of disability benefit is being considered. The different types are:

- part of a normal retirement pension plan
- from an employer sponsored disability plan
- Workplace Safety and Insurance Board (formerly Worker's Compensation Board) payments
- Canada Pension Plan disability benefits
- payments from a privately owned disability insurance policy
- payments from an accident and sickness insurance policy
- disability payments under a life insurance policy.

As well, provincial family law must be considered. There are reported court cases in Ontario, Alberta, British Columbia, Nova

Scotia, Saskatchewan, and Manitoba. In this chapter we deal with decisions under the Ontario Family Law Act.

Is it Property?

The definition of property in the Ontario Family Law Act is all-inclusive and it is difficult to imagine something that is not property. The only example that comes to mind is a person's career. Since the definition of property is all-inclusive, disability benefits would be considered property. Two cases that have clarified this point.

In *Brinkos v. Brinkos*,[1] Mrs. Brinkos transferred gifted property to a trust. She was the beneficiary of all the income, and the trustees had the right to encroach on capital for her benefit. Mrs. Brinkos argued that her right to future income from this trust was not property, and that her interest in the trust could not be property because, by its terms, it was incapable of being transferred. The trial judge agreed with her. However, the Court of Appeal reversed the decision. The court quoted the definition of property from Jowitt's Dictionary of English Law:

> In its largest sense property signifies things and rights considered as having a money value, especially with reference to transfer or succession, and to their capacity of being injured. Property includes not only ownership, estates and interests in corporeal things, but also rights such as trademarks, copyrights, patents and rights *in personam* capable of transfer or transmission, such as debts.

The court went on to say,

> Jowitt cannot have intended to exclude from property anything rendered inalienable by choice or agreement. The last three lines of his definition must be taken to mean that the item under consideration be intrinsically capable of transfer. This would exclude personal income because it is inseparable from the personal effort required to attract it; it does not exclude a vested entitlement to income even though it is not marketable. This remains property without a market value, but with a very real value to the owner.

The court decided the present value of future income from the trust was property. In the same way, the right to future disability income payments are property.

Some people argue that a future stream of income should be used only to determine ability to pay support, and that to include future income in property could lead to double dipping.

The Supreme Court of Canada dealt with the question in the case of *Clarke v. Clarke.*[2] They ruled that a pension in pay was property. (Double dipping was not a consideration in this case.)

In most reported court cases, disability benefits were determined to be property.

Is It Excluded Property?

Since the legislators were careful to ensure that everything is to be included in the definition of property, it follows that nothing is to be exempt unless it accords perfectly with the definition of excluded property.

Section 4(2) of the Ontario Family Law Act says,

The value of the following property that a spouse owns on the valuation date does not form part of the spouse's net family property:

1. Property, other than a matrimonial home, that was acquired by gift or inheritance from a third person after the date of the marriage.
2. Income from property referred to in paragraph 1, if the donor or testator has expressly stated that it is to be excluded from the spouse's net family property.
3. Damages or a right to damages for personal injuries, nervous shock, mental distress or loss of guidance, care and companionship, or the part of a settlement that represents those damages.
4. Proceeds or a right to proceeds of a life insurance policy as defined in the Insurance Act, that are payable on the death of the life insured.
5. Property, other than a matrimonial home, into which property referred to in paragraphs 1 to 4 can be traced.
6. Property that the spouses have agreed by a domestic contract is not to be included in the spouse's net family property.

Section 4(3) places the onus of proving an exclusion under section 4(2) "on the person claiming it."

Whether the value of the disability benefit may be excluded from the Net Family Property Statement as exempt property will depend on whether it meets one of these definitions. Some disability benefits will be excluded property, and some will not.

REASONS FOR INCLUDING

Justice Quinn pointed out that the case of *Mead v. Mead*[3] dealt with the definition of life insurance in the *Insurance Act*.[4] In that case, under section 1(16) of the Insurance Act, disability insurance was considered to be life insurance. The judge said,

> Since the drafters of the *Family Law Act* went to some pains to exclude, from net family property calculations, life insurance payable in the event of death but were silent as to life insurance payable in the event of disability, it might be said, with at least some justification, that what is not excluded must be included.

Disability payments from a life insurance policy as defined in the *Insurance Act* are not excluded property because they are not payable on death.

In the case of *Snjaric v. Snjaric*,[5] Justice Aston dealt with disability payments under the Workers' Compensation Act and the Canada Pension Plan Act. He said,

> Workers' Compensation benefits...are a direct substitution for a person's common-law right to claim damages. I think that is an important distinction; in fact, more important than whether the notion of damages depends upon fault or no fault. Canada Pension benefits or private disability insurance benefits (as in *Iurincic*) may be payable to a person based on illness. But Workers' Compensation benefits are only payable in relation to an injury sustained at the workplace, which might otherwise sustain a claim for damages, but for the *Workers' Compensation Act*.

> Canada Pension benefits, on the other hand, are not paid as a substitute for any right to claim damages. Such benefits are not excluded under section 4(2) 3 and must be included in the spouse's net family property calculation.... Canada Pension Plan disability payments and Workers' Compensation benefits in pay at the date of separation represent a future income stream, not dependent upon personal services and are, therefore, "property" within the meaning of section 4 (1) of the *Family Law Act*. Canada Pension Plan disability payments do not constitute "damages or a right to damages" and should not be excluded from net family property because they are "akin to damages," however equitable the result.

In *Birce v. Birce*,[6] Justice Rutherford had some reservation about including the value of Canada Pension Plan disability benefits but concluded, based on the analysis in *Snjaric v. Snjaric*,[7] that the value of the benefits should be considered as property. Disability benefits that are not damages—that is, benefits based on sickness or inability to work—should not be exempt.

REASONS FOR EXCLUDING

In *Balcombe v. Balcombe*,[8] the trial judge found that the disability pension payable to Mrs. Balcombe was excluded property under Section 4(2) 3 of the *Family Law Act*. Divisional Court upheld this decision: "In our view, the essence of the matter is that the yearly payment of $3,198.60 received by the wife ... is not a payment from a 'retirement pension plan' but payment from a plan that is predominantly a 'disability pension plan' and, therefore, qualifies as 'excluded property' within the provisions of s. 4(2) 3 of the Act."

In *Fahner v. Fahner,*[9] Mrs. Fahner received a lump sum CPP disability benefit and continued to receive disability benefits. No one questioned the monthly payments. In deciding that the lump sum amount was exempt, Justice Gordon explained that the disability payment was composed of two parts, a flat rate plus a percentage of retirement pension. He said, "The calculation does not, in my view, establish the funds as being paid for loss of earnings but rather to reflect compensation for the disability." He did not discuss whether the payment constituted damages.

The Ontario Supreme, High Court of Justice heard the case of *Kelly v. Kelly.*[10] Justice Kerr said,

> Notwithstanding the method of calculation of the compensation, it does not appear that the compensation payable is actually paid as loss of earnings as opposed to compensation for the injury itself. Rather it appears to be paid as compensation for a reduced earning capacity. As such, it is clearly damages for personal injuries. In this respect I adopt the reasoning of McKinnon L.J.S.C. in *Young v. Young.*[11]

Justice Kerr defined damages as, "The value estimated in money of something lost or withheld; the sum of money claimed or adjudged to be paid in compensation for loss or injury sustained." He excluded the Workers' Compensation disability payments becaise they were exempt property.

In *Vanderaa v. Vanderaa,*[12] the payments were found not to be fault-based. Justice Leitch said,

> In this case the [husband's] disability pension cannot be considered tantamount to a retirement pension. The disability pension is not the hybrid disability/ retirement pension considered in

McTaggart. This pension is like the type of pension considered in *Pallister* and *Balcombe.* The benefits paid to the [husband] are paid to compensate him for his disability. The benefits are not paid because of years of service rendered to his former employer. [The husband's] right to these disability benefits is within the very broad definition of 'property' set out in s. 4(1) of the *Family Law Act.* However, I would exclude the value of these benefits from the [husband's] net family property pursuant to s. 4(2) para.3 of the *Family Law Act,* having classified them as compensation for personal injury.

Justice Leitch held that all compensation for personal injury is exempt whether it is fault related or tort related.

In *Brignolio v. Brignolio,*[13] Justice Quinn said:

It was held that the disability pension was property but it was excluded under s. 4(2) 3. Poupore J. concluded that a disability pension which was subject to termination (that is, upon a finding that the disability is no longer total and permanent) is a true disability pension and such a pension is excluded property under the *Family Law Act.*

In *MacDonnell v. MacDonnell,*[14] Justice Roscoe seems to have concluded that the CPP disability pension should not be included in the equalization of assets because the splitting of CPP credits is available under the Canada Pension Plan Act. In *Czemeres v. Czemeres,*[15] Justice Hunter reached the same conclusion. Apparently they were not told that part of the disability benefit could not be equalized under the Canada Pension Plan Act.

The Ontario legislators have chosen to consider "damages" as excluded property in section 4(2) 3. They could have limited the exclusion to damages that are tort based, but they did not. The courts seem to have given "damages" a wide definition.

PARTIALLY INCLUDED AND PARTIALLY EXCLUDED

For disability benefits to be excluded under s. 4(2) 3, they must be "damages or a right to damages for personal injuries, nervous shock, mental distress or loss of guidance, care and companionship, or the part of a settlement that represents those damages."

The case of *Shaver v. Shaver*[16] considered the matter of excluded property. Mr. Shaver was in an automobile accident and received a lump sum disability payment. The amount was composed of general damages and lost future wages. However, the lost wages were reduced by disability benefits received from another source. In considering section 4(2), paragraph 3, Justice Mendes da Costa said,

> The legislative purpose is to permit spouses to retain for their own purposes property which is "completely personal" to them, and to which they are entitled for the purpose of replacing "some aspect of their enjoyment of life which cannot be truly shared with any other individual, no matter how close the relationship.

Citing *Mittler v. Mittler*,[17] Justice da Costa said, "Lost wages and disability benefits do not satisfy the statutory test, and the value that qualified for exclusion was the general damage award of $25,000, which, I understand, was compensation for pain and suffering."

The court considered each part of the payment separately, then decided that the payment for pain and suffering qualified as damages and was thus excluded under section 4(2), paragraph 3, of the Ontario Family Law Act. The payment for lost future wages did not qualify and was included.

In *Iurincic v. Iurincic*,[18] Jusitce Quinn reviewed the jurisprudence and discussed whether the disability pension was property, whether it was excluded, and whether it would be unconscionable to include it in the equalization. Justice Quinn took his definition of damages from *The Dictionary of Canadian Law*[19]: "Pecuniary compensation for a wrong, either a breach of contract or a tort." The judge reviewed *McTaggart v. McTaggart*[20] and said,

> I concur with the result in *McTaggart*. However, I would not have found it necessary to enter into an in-depth analysis of the disability pension. Whether it was funded by the employer or was geared to Mr. McTaggart's level of income or years of service is not relevant, in my opinion, on the issue of whether the pension is property under s. 4(1) or excluded as "damages" under s. 4 (2) 3…. In most, if not all, of the cases where a disability pension has been found to be excluded property, it has been because the pension was seen as damages or the equivalent of damages under s. 4(2) 3…. the definition of damages adopted by the Court in *Kelly v. Kelly, supra*, and by subsequent courts, omits what I regard as the essence of damages— the element of fault or of wrongdoing. In my view, the language of s. 4(2) 3, all of it, bespeaks fault-based or tort-based compensation.

Justice Quinn decided Mr. Iurinic's disability benefits were not excluded property.

Whether the value of disability benefits is exempt property or excluded property depends entirely on what definition of "damages" is applied. What exactly is meant by "damages"?

DEFINITIONS

The term "damages" is defined differently in different dictionaries.

Black's Law Dictionary defines damages as, "A pecuniary compensation or indemnity, which may be recovered in the courts by any person who has suffered loss, detriment, or injury, whether to his person, property, or rights, through the unlawful act or omission or negligence of another". The Canadian Oxford Dictionary says that damages are a sum of money claimed or awarded in compensation for a loss or an injury. Webster's Dictionary of Law says:

Damage is derived from an old French word "Dam" meaning injury, harm, or from the Latin word "Damnum", which means financial loss or fine. Damages has the following possible meanings:

1. Loss or harm resulting from injury to person, property or reputation.
2. Damages means damages deemed to compensate the injured party for losses sustained as a direct result of the injury suffered. This is also called compensatory damages.
3. Direct damages means damages for a loss that is an immediate natural and foreseeable result of the wrongful act.
4. Expectation damages or expectancy damages means damages recoverable for breach of contract and designed to put the injured party in the position he or she would have been in had the contract been completed.
5. General damages means damages for losses (such as pain and suffering, inconvenience, or loss of lifestyle) whose monetary values are difficult to assign.

The compact edition of the Oxford English Dictionary defines damages as, "the value estimate in money of something lost or withheld; the sum of money claimed or adjudged to be paid in compensation for loss or injury sustained."

The Dictionary of Canadian Law defines damages as, "Pecuniary compensation for a wrong, either a breach of contract or a tort."

Perhaps Justice Quinn was right when he said damages must be fault based or tort based. If the disability is due to illness that was not fault based, it may not qualify as damages. Disability payments for pain and suffering or for inability to work may not be exempt property if they are not fault based. Would it be unconscionable to include the value of the benefits in a spouse's net family property?

On the other hand, some of the definitions imply that disability payments could be damages even though they are not fault based. Then there would be no need to prove them unconscionable.

Dictionary definitions can never replace court decisions. Most case law that deals with the point indicates the value of payments for pain or suffering is exempt property, fault related or not

The Newfoundland Marital Property Act provides an exemption for "personal injury awards, except the portion of the award that represents compensation for economic loss." This does not require a third-party fault, but would not exempt payment for loss of future income or loss of ability to earn income.

The Alberta Matrimonial Property Act makes it clear that the damages must be "damages in tort."

The British Columbia Family Relations Act says that a, "disability pension means a benefit paid to a member under a plan as a consequence of a member's disability," There is no mention of damages or fault. However, the British Columbia act includes all pensions as property and does not provide any exemptions.

The Saskatchewan Matrimonial Property Act says,

(3) Subject to subsection (4), matrimonial property, other than a matrimonial home or household goods, is exempt from distribution pursuant to this Part where that property is:

a) an award or settlement of damages in tort in favour of a spouse, unless the award or settlement is compensation for a loss to both spouses;

b) money paid or payable pursuant to an insurance policy that is not paid or payable with respect to property, unless the proceeds are compensation for a loss to both spouses.

The Nova Scotia Matrimonial Property Act provides an exemption for "an award or settlement of damages in court in favour of one spouse."

The Manitoba Matrimonial Property Act says, "This Act does not apply to the proceeds of any damage award or settlement or insurance claim made in favour of a spouse for personal injury, or disability, except to the extent that the proceeds are compensation for loss to both spouses." However, "rights under a life insurance policy" and "rights under an accident and sickness insurance policy" are included in family assets. The excluded damages need not be fault based.

When can damages be exempt? First, if the amount is being received for loss or damage that is so personal that only the party receiving the benefit was affected by the loss. This would include pain and suffering, loss of a limb, or loss of sight. It could also include disability benefits paid for the loss of the ability to work and earn money. The Ontario Family Law Act does not make the exemption provision clear, and the Canada Pension Plan Act does not state what the payments are for. The court decisions that allow an exemption seem to be based on this logic. There does not seem to be any logic to limiting the exemption to damages that are fault related or tort related. Justice McKinlay probably said it best in *Mittler v. Mittler*[21] :

In reaching the conclusion that those two amounts may be deducted as property owned on the date of marriage, I have considered what appears to be the policy of the legislature in excluding damages or the right to damages from the calculation of net family property. The purpose can only be to permit spouses to retain for their own purposes property which is completely personal to them, and to which they are entitled for the purpose of replacing some aspect of their enjoyment of life which cannot be truly shared with any other individual, no matter how close the relationship.

UNCONSCIONABLE

Section 5(6) of the Ontario Family Law Act provides for unequal division of assets when equal division would be unconscionable. The exact provision of subsection (6) is as follows:

Variation of share—The Court may award a spouse an amount that is more or less than half the difference between the net family properties if the Court is of the opinion that equalizing the net family properties would be unconscionable, having regard to.

a) A spouse's failure to disclose to the other spouse debts or other liabilities existing at the date of the marriage;
b) The fact that debts or other liabilities claimed in reduction of a spouse's net family property were incurred recklessly or in bad faith;
c) The part of a spouse's net family property that consists of gifts made by the other spouse;

d) A spouse's intentional or reckless depletion of his or her net family property;

e) The fact that the amount a spouse would otherwise receive under subsection (1), (2) or (3) is disproportionately large in relation to a period of cohabitation that is less than five years;

f) The fact that one spouse has incurred a disproportionately larger amount of debts or other liabilities than the other spouse for the support of the family;

g) A written agreement between the spouses that is not a domestic contract; or

h) Any other circumstance relating to the acquisition, disposition, preservation, maintenance or improvement of property.

Black's Law Dictionary says, "An unconscionable bargain or contract is one which no man in his senses, not under delusion, would make, on the one hand, and which no fair and honest man would accept, on the other".... "Unconscionable conduct [is] conduct that is monstrously harsh and shocking to the conscience." "Unconscious" means, "not possessed of mind."

Webster's Dictionary of Law defines "unconscionable" as "unreasonably unfair to one party, marked by oppression or otherwise unacceptably offensive to public policy." Compare this to the definition of "conscionable": "guided by conscience, characterized by fairness and justice."

In the American Heritage Dictionary, "unconscionable" means "not restrained by conscience; unscrupulous; beyond prudence or reason; excessive". Hutchinson's Dictionary of Difficult Words defines unconscionable as "unreasonable; against the conscience." Roget provides synonyms: "beyond all reason; obscene; outrageous; preposterous; ridiculous; shocking; unreasonable; lacking scruples or principles; ruthless; unethical; unprincipled; unscrupulous."

The case of *Grant-Hose v. Grant-Hose*[22] was heard by the Ontario Unified Family Court. Justice Mendes da Costa considered whether a matter was unconscionable. "What is required are circumstances such as to shock the conscience of the Court, whereby the party seeking redress has been placed in a position so unfair as to cry out for relief."

In *Shaver v. Shaver*,[23] Judge da Costa said, "Unequal division may be ordered where to do otherwise would be 'patently unfair' or 'inordinately inequitable.'"

In *Brinkos v. Brinkos*,[24] the Court of Appeal said,

> The husband's record of performance within the marriage and beyond does not say much to commend him and, in fact, if this were a matter of pure discretion, it would be easy to deny him any recovery. However, none of the provisions of s. 5(6) (a) to (g) apply to the circumstances and I cannot bring myself to think that the language of para. (h) raises relevant considerations which could make this payment unconscionable.

In *Fahner v. Fahner*,[25] Justice Gordon concluded that the CPP payment was exempt under section 4(3) of the Family Law Act. He said, "It might well be exempt as unconscionable under s. 5(6)(h)." But he did not explain why.

In *Iurincic v. Iurincic*,[26] Justice Quinn said, "The husband did not raise or argue the issue of unconscionability. Nonetheless, I volunteer my view that it would not be unconscionable, in the circumstances of this case, to fully include his disability pension in the equalization process."

In *Snjaric v. Snjaric*,[27] Justice Aston concluded that, because of the small amount involved, the idea of unconscionability need not be considered. In *MacDonnell v. MacDonnell*,[28] Justice Roscoe said he agreed with Professor Bissett-Johnson that disability insurance should be exempted from matrimonial assets because it would be unfair to the disabled spouse to include it. He did not give reasons.

Justice Kerr gave this opinion:

> While it is not necessary to my decision in view of the above finding, I am of the view that there is another ground upon which I would be prepared to give relief to the petitioner. Section 5(6) of the Family Law Act allows me to award to the spouse an amount that is more or less than half the difference between the net family properties if I am of the opinion that equalizing the net family property would be unconscionable having regard to the various types of situations described thereunder.
>
> It is my opinion that s. 5(6)(h) applies to this case and that the circumstances relating to the acquisition and preservation of this particular asset are such that it would be unconscionable for me to award any sum whatsoever to the respondent by way of equalization of this particular asset. It was the petitioner who suffered and continues to suffer the disability with the attendant pain, and her efforts and hers alone which led to the acquisition of the award. By virtue of her having pursued her remedies through the appeal process over many years, without assistance or encouragement of the respondent, she has been able to realize a small monthly compensation payment. This small payment has reduced her dependence upon the respondent and is reflected in the amount of support payment which he is obliged to make to her for the future. It would be unconscionable to take from her any portion of that award up to the valuation date.

In an unreported case, *Artus v. Artus*,[29] the plaintiff's disability benefits came from injuries incurred before his marriage. Justice Errico said the interest was a family asset but, considering the duration of the marriage, the date when the disability was suffered, and the plaintiff's need for his pension due to his disability, it would be unfair for the pension to go to anyone but the disabled plaintiff.

Obviously, making a decision of "unconscionable" would require unusual circumstances. The fact that the equalization calculation includes the value of a disability benefit would not be sufficient. If there are other assets and the other party is in need, it would clearly not be unconscionable to include the value of the disability benefits in the calculation of Net Family Property.

CANADA PENSION PLAN

The Canada Pension Plan was established in 1966 to provide a retirement pension for everyone who is employed or has self-employment earnings. The retirement pension is payable for life from age sixty-five, but reduced payments may start as early as age sixty. The amount of retirement pension an individual receives is based on his accumulated credits and on the number of years he has contributed. Each person's contributions are based on his annual earnings. The accumulated CPP credits are subject to equalization between spouses on marriage breakdown.

The Canada Pension Plan also provides a disability pension, payable to CPP participants who are "unable to work due to a severe prolonged and permanent and/or long-term physical or mental disability." Disability pensions are payable up to age sixty-five, when they are converted to retirement pensions, or until the person recovers from the disability. The monthly benefit is composed of two parts. First, a flat rate portion provides the same amount of payment to everyone who qualifies. The second portion is equal to 75 percent of the CPP retirement pension the disabled applicant would receive at age sixty-five. When a disabled person turns sixty-five, the flat rate portion of his disability benefit ceases, and the portion based on accumulated pension credits is recalculated. There is no doubt that the right to receive these benefits is property. Whether part of the disability benefit is excluded property will depend on whether it meets the definition of damages under section 4(2) 3 of the Ontario Family Law Act.

The case of *Canada (Ministry of National Health & Welfare) v. Blackwood*[30] clarified the point that the Ministry of National Health & Welfare may divide the unadjusted pensionable earnings of the parties in accordance with the provisions of the Canada Pension Plan, notwithstanding an agreement or divorce judgement to the contrary. Thus the sharing of normal Canada Pension Plan benefits is dealt with under the Pension Plan Act and not under the Family Law Act of Ontario. This equalization of unadjusted pensionable earnings applies only to the retirement portion of a disability pension. It does not apply to the flat rate portion. Only the disabled person may receive any part of the flat rate portion of the disability benefit.

Since the flat rate portion of the disability benefit is the same amount for everyone who qualifies, and since it is not related to earnings, and since only the disabled person may receive any part of it, there seems to be good argument that at least the flat rate portion of the disability benefit is for damages and should qualify as excluded property. In some cases this would be true only if you accept the court decisions that indicate damages need not be fault related or tort related.

The value of the portion of the CPP Disability Benefit based on accumulated pension credits should not be included as property because of something called "the law of paramountcy." These credits are equalized between the parties on marriage breakdown by the Canada Pension Plan, and this part of the value should not be included in the sharing of property under provincial laws (except perhaps in provinces that allow the parties to opt out of the CPP provision to split credits).

The cases of *Fahner* and *Shaver* determined that Canada Pension Plan Disability Benefits were exempt. However, the cases of *Birce* and *Snjaric* determined they were not exempt, as they did not meet the definition of damages. In *Fahner* it was said that it might be unconscionable. In *Shaver* it was said that unconscionableness was not proven. Most cases did not differentiate between the two parts of the CPP disability benefit.

The only cases that recognized the *Canada Pension Plan Act* would override the provincial legislation were a Saskatchewan case, *Czemeres*, and a Nova Scotia case, *MacDonnell*.

WORKERS' SAFETY AND INSURANCE BOARD (WORKERS' COMPENSATION BOARD)

As explained in *Division of Pensions*,[31]

> Each province and territory in Canada has legislation to provide compensation to a worker or a worker's family where injury to the worker or death of the worker results from employment. The employer pays premiums based on an industrial and company assessment rate. The worker's compensation program replaces the worker's right of legal action against the employer for injuries or death arising from employment.
>
> Worker's compensation benefits include those for temporary disability, permanent disability, health care benefits and spousal and dependants' benefits.
>
> Generally, worker's compensation benefits have been held not to be matrimonial property, or not to

be property for the purposes of equalization under a
matrimonial property statute. The actual character-
ization of the benefits payable will depend in part on
the provisions in the relevant worker's compensation statute under which the benefit arises.

The Ontario Worker's Compensation Board Act Section 42 (for
injuries or accidents before January 1, 1998) provides that, "A worker who suffers permanent impairment as a result of an injury is entitled to receive compensation for non-economic loss in addition to any
other benefit receivable under this Act." Worker's Safety and
Insurance Board Act Section 46 (for injuries or accidents after January
1, 1998) provides that, "If a worker's injury results in permanent
impairment, the worker is entitled to compensation under this section
for his or her non-economic loss." Neither act defines "non-economic loss." The amount paid has no relationship to the worker's previous or future earnings and is obviously payment for the existing and
anticipated consequences of the injury or for pain and suffering.

Section 43 of the Worker's Compensation Board Act provides
compensation for future loss of earnings arising from the injury.
When the worker reaches sixty-five, this compensation ceases and
he receives a retirement pension.

Section 16 of the Worker's Compensation Board Act provides
that, "The provisions of this Part are in lieu of all rights and rights
of action, statutory or otherwise, to which a worker or the members
of his or her family are or may be entitled against the employer of
such worker, or any executive officer thereof, for or by reason of any
accident happening to the worker," while the worker was in the
employment of the employer. Section 16 clearly says the employee
has no action against the employer for such injury.

The payments from the Workers' Safety and Insurance Board
for non-economic loss must be for pain and suffering and possibly
for the loss of the ability to earn income. These are personal con-

siderations, and therefore might be classified as exempt property or perhaps unconscionable.

The payments under either section of the act are in lieu of all rights to claim damages.

In the case of *Arvelin v. Arvelin*,[32] Justice Wright said,

> Are these benefits excluded? If we proceed on the basis that Section 4(2) 3 of the *Family Law Act* applies only to "general" damages (for pain and suffering) and not to "special" damages (for loss of income) then we must determine whether the Workers' Compensation payments fall within the former or latter classification. According to Exhibit 30 these payments were made as temporary total disability benefits. Temporary total disability benefits are paid under Section 37 of the *Workers' Compensation Act*. Payments under that section are based on 90% of the loss of net average earnings. These payments were intended as income replacement and are not excluded.

He required that the value of the Workers' Compensation Act disability benefits be included. Justice Wright did not consider whether this would be unconscionable.

In *Buske v. Buske*,[33] *Kelly v. Kelly*,[34] *Snjaric v. Snjaric*,[35] and *Yee v. Yee*,[36] judges decided the Workers' Compensation Board benefits qualified as damages and were exempt property.

In *Kelly v. Kelly*, Justice Kerr held the benefits to be excluded by virtue of section 4(2) 3 of the Family Law Act:

> While it is not necessary to my decision in view of the above finding, I am of the view that there is another ground upon which I would be prepared to give relief to the petitioner. Section 5(6) of the

Family Law Act allows me to award to the spouse an amount that is more or less than half the difference between the net family properties if I am of the opinion that equalizing the net family property would be unconscionable having regard to the various types of situations described thereunder.

It is my opinion that s. 5(6) (*h*) applies to this case and that the circumstances relating to the acquisition and preservation of this particular asset are such that it would be unconscionable for me to award any sum whatsoever to the respondent by way of equalization of this particular asset. It was the petitioner who suffered and continues to suffer the disability with the attendant pain, and her efforts and hers alone which led to the acquisition of the award. By virtue of her having pursued her remedies through the appeal process over many years, without assistance or encouragement of the respondent, she has been able to realize a small monthly compensation payment. This small payment has reduced her dependence upon the respondent and is reflected in the amount of support payment which he is obliged to make to her for the future. It would be unconscionable to take from her any portion of that award up to the valuation date.

OTHER DISABILITY BENEFITS

In *McTaggart v. McTaggart*,[37] Mr. McTaggart was receiving disability benefits from a retirement pension plan. Justice Huneault said,

After 25 years of employment with Inco, the respondent's various heart ailments rendered him physically unable to continue working.

The Inco pension plan is fully funded by the employer. Under this plan, an employee can become eligible for retirement benefits in a number of ways:

12 (a) normal service retirement
13 (b) early service retirement
14 (c) 30-year early service retirement
15 (d) late service retirement
16 (e) disability retirement.

In view of his age and years of service, the respondent's only option was to seek a disability retirement pension based on his total and permanent disability as defined in the plan.... In the case at bar, it is clear from the Inco Pension Plan Manual (Exhibit 5) that the disability benefits paid to the respondent are part and parcel of an overall employee pension benefit plan totally funded by the company. The witness, Terry Duncan, supervisor of benefits for Inco, has testified that the benefits received by the respondent represent a level of income earned by the employee for services rendered. It is clearly, therefore, a benefit related to services rendered to the company and not as compensation for his disability. By no stretch of the imagination can it be considered as "damages" and thereby excluded under the Act.

Justice Quinn dealt with the same question in *Iurincic v. Iurincic*.[38] He began his decision by saying, "I confess that there is one word which, given the choice, I would prefer not to hear in a matrimonial proceeding: 'pension'." The husband had a back injury and qualified for a disability pension from OMERS. The disability calculations took into account the husband's pensionable earnings and the number of years of credited service. When he retired, the disability pension would be replaced by a retirement pension. Justice Quinn disagreed with the decision in *Kelly v. Kelly*. In his opinion, damages must include the element of fault or wrongdoing. After a lengthy explanation of each case, the judge said:

> I fail to see how there can be any doubt that the disability pension is property. Apart from adding words such as, "everything under the sun", it is difficult to imagine how s.4 (1) could be drafted with a broader compass.
>
> In most, if not all, of the cases where a disability pension has been found to be excluded property, it has been because the pension was seen as damages or the equivalent of damages under s. 4(2) 3. As I explained earlier, the definition of damages adopted by the court in *Kelly v. Kelly, supra,* and by subsequent courts, omits what I regard as the essence of damages; the element of fault or of wrongdoing. In my view, the language of s. 4(2) 3 bespeaks fault-based or tort-based compensation. Consequently, benefits paid under workers' compensation legislation for work-related injuries would not be caught by s. 4(2) 2 since such legislation is not fault-based; it provides benefits regardless of fault or wrongdoing and in lieu of a worker's right to sue for damages. It is noteworthy that the words "illness" or "sickness" do not appear in s. 4(2) 3 and, in my opinion, neither is commonly thought of as being a personal injury.

In the result, the disability pension being received by the husband is not excluded property under s. 4(2).

The husband did not raise or argue the issue of unconscionability. Nonetheless, I volunteer my view that it would not be unconscionable, in the circumstances of this case, to fully include his disability pension in the equalization process.

In *Vanderaa v. Vanderaa*,[39] both spouses were in a motor vehicle accident before they sepaprated. Both settled their actions for damages after they separated. Justice Leitch said,

The cause of action which resulted in the settlements in favour of the petitioner and respondent existed prior to the date of separation and accordingly, the settlement monies are property within the definition of property set out in s. 4(1) of the Act. There is no question that the amounts received by the petitioner and the respondent as general damages are excluded property with the meaning of s. 4(2) para.3 of the Act as those amounts clearly represent compensation for personal injuries…

The contentious issue in this trial is the extent, if any, to which the settlements for past wage loss and for future loss of income should be excluded….

In my view there is a distinction between compensation for retraining, rehabilitation or loss of competitive advantage and damages resulting from a measurable wage loss. The first category of damages is personal and is of the nature meant to be excluded by para.3 of s. 4(2) and the latter category of damages is not in the words of *Mittler v. Mittler* completely personal to the recipient and for the purpose of replacing some aspect of their enjoyment of life which cannot be truly shared with any other individual no matter how close their relationship

Compensation for a wage loss which accrued during a period prior to the date of separation is sharable property. Such damages are not paid for the injury itself and are paid to replace lost wages and, in essence, are income replacement and should be shareable to the extent that they replace income that would have been earned but for injuries sustained prior to the date of separation... A party's right to claim lost income is a property right and therefore the value of this property right as at the valuation date should be included in net family property. This interpretation provides a logical result because damages that compensate for sharable property ought to be shared and included in the calculation of net family property. However, the value of the right to claim lost income as at the valuation date would not include the amount of damages paid to replace lost wages which would have been earned after the date of separation. This also provides a reasonable result because these monies would not have been shared in any event and should be excluded from the calculation of net family property as at the valuation date. Similarly, I find that these *settlements for future wage loss are within the category of damages* that are completely personal to the parties and are therefore excluded from their net family property pursuant to para. 3 of s. 4(2) of the Act (emphasis added).

Mr. Vanderaa was also receiving benefits under a long-term disability plan provided by his employer. Justice Leitch said,

In this case the respondent's disability pension cannot be considered tantamount to a retirement pension. The disability pension is not the hybrid disability/retirement pension considered by the court in *McTaggart*. This pension is like the type of pension considered in *Pallister* and *Balcombe*. The benefits paid to the respondent are paid to compensate him for his disability. The benefits are not paid because of years of service rendered to his former employer…. The respondent's right to these disability benefits is within the very broad definition of "property" set out in s. 4(1) of the *Family Law Act*. However, I would exclude the value of these benefits from the respondent's net family property pursuant to s. 4(2) para. 3 of the *Family Law Act*, having classified them as compensation for personal injury.

SUMMARY

It is clear that the right to receive disability benefits is property as defined in provincial legislation, regardless of the source or reasons for the payments. However, disability benefits may qualify as exempt property. They clearly qualify if they are damages that are fault related.

The source of the payments does not determine whether they are exempt. It should not matter whether the payments are tort related or not, whether they are for lost wages or future lost wages. The determining factor is, are they damages?

Benefits for personal pain and suffering or loss of ability to earn income should qualify as damages and should be exempt.

If the disability benefits are not exempt property, it might be unconscionable to include their value in the equalization of assets.

All this is true, regardless of the type of disability benefit being considered unless the benefit is paid from a Canada Pension Plan related to accumulated pension credits. Such CPP benefits should be excluded since they are dealt with under the Canada Pension Plan, a federal statute.

As with so many aspects of the law, the decision will invariably depend on the facts of the particular case.

Notes

1   (1989) CarswellOnt 252, 20 R.F.L. (3d) 445, 69 O.R. (2d) 225, 60 D.L.R. (4th) 556, 33 O.A.C. 295, 34 E.T.R. 55.
2   (1990) CarswellNS 49, 28 R.F.L. (3d) 113, 73 D.L.R. (4th) 1, 113 N.R. 321, [1990] 2 S.C.R. 795, 101 N.S.R. (2d) 1, 275 A.P.R. 1.
3   (1990), 31 R.F.L. (3d) 101 (Ont. Gen. Div.).
4   R.S.O. 1980, c. 218 (now R.S.O. 1990, c. I.8, s.1.).
5   (1999) CarswellOnt 1073, C.E.B. & P.G.R. 8357 (headnote only).
6   (2000) CarswellOnt 1635 and 2922.
7   (1999) CarswellOnt. 1073, C.E.B. & P.G.R. 8357 (Ont. Gen. Div.).
8   (1990) CarswellOnt 322, 30 R.F.L. (3d) 177, 42 O.A.C. 150.
9   (1994) CanRepOnt 2036.
10 *Kelly v. Kelly* (1987) CanRepOnt 329, 8 R.F.L. (3d) 212.
11 *Young v. Young* (1986), 5 R.F.L. (3d) 337 at 344 (B.C.S.C.).
12 *Vanderaa v. Vanderaa* (1995), 18 R.F.L. (4th) 393 (Ont. Gen. Div.)
13 *Brignolio v. Brignolio* (March 6, 1997), Doc. Sudbury D-12, 180/94 (Ont. Gen. Div.).
14 *MacDonnell v. MacDonnell* (1991) CanRepNs 55, 33 R.F.L. (3d) 52, 103 N.S.R. (2d) 435, 282 A.P.R. 435.
15 (1991) CanRep Sask 53, 32 R.F.L. (3d) 243, 92 Sask. R. 1.
16 (1991) Carswell Ont 346, 37 R.F.L. (3d) 117.

17 (1988), 17 R.F.L. (3d) 113 (Ont. H.C.) at p. 145.
18 (1998) CarswellOnt 2263, 40 R.F.L. (4th) 258.
19 (Scarborough: Carswell, 1990), p. 250.
20 (1993), 50 R.F.L. (3d) 110 (Ont. Gen. Div.).
21 (1988) 17 R.F.L. (3d) 113.
22 (1991) 32 R.F.L. (3d) 26 (Ont. U.F.C.).
23 (1991) CarswellOnt 346, 37 R.F.L. (3d) 117.
24 (1989) 69 O.R. (2d) 798, 61 D.L.R. (4th) 766 (Ont. C.A.).
25 (1994) CanRepOnt 2036.
26 (1998) CarswellOnt 2263, 40 R.F.L. (4th) 258.
27 (1999) CarswellOnt 1073, C.E.B. & P.G.R. 8357 (headnote only).
28 (1991) CanRepNS 55, 33 R.F.L. (3d) 52, 103 N.S.R. (2d) 435, 282 A.P.R. 435.
29 (1985) W.D.F.L. 827 (BC S.C.).
30 (1993) CarswellNat 11, 3 R.F.L. (4th) 337, 169 N.R. 236, C.E.B. & P.G.R. 8184 (FED.C.A.).
31 By Pask & Hask, 1995, Release 1.
32 (1996) CanRepOnt 394, 20 R.F.L. (4th) 87.
33 (1988) CanRepOnt 210, 12 R.F.L. (3d) 388, 63 O.R. (3d) 749.
34 (1987) CanRepOnt 329, 8 R.F.L. (3d) 212.
35 (1999) CarswellOnt 1073, C.E.B. & P.G.R. 8357.
36 (1990) CanRepOnt 236, 25 R.F.L. (3d) 366.
37 (1993) CarswellOnt 366, 50 R.F.L. (3d) 110.
38 (1998) CarswellOnt 2263, 40 R.F.L. (4th) 258.
39 (1995) CarswellOnt 685, 18 R.F.L. (4th) 393.

Chapter 19

Other Employment Related Assets

INTRODUCTION

There are many assets you may have that should be included in the Net Family Property statement. There are some employment related assets you or your spouse may not think of, or perhaps your spouse may try to hide some assets from you.

In a recent case, the lawyer for the vice president of a large public company submitted his pension valuation to his spouse. The spouse's lawyer asked us to review the pension valuation to determine if it was fair to his client. We found the pension valuation report biased; it grossly understated the value of the pension for marriage breakdown purposes. We had a difficult time coming to this conclusion because the vice-president was not co-operative in providing information, and he instructed his staff not to answer our questions. We couldn't get information from the employee benefits department and had to collect information through other means. In the process we discovered that the spouse had not disclosed all employment related assets. We were able to obtain information about all the assets and place a value on them. We gained $50,000 for our client.

Another case involved an accountant who had retired from a large national firm. He said the payments he was receiving from his retirement arrangement were not a pension. While we agreed that he was not collecting a pension, we were able to prove that his retirement arrangement was property. It had a value in excess of $500,000.

There are various employment related assets you can expect to see on your spouse's net family property statement.

SICK LEAVE GRATUITY

Most teachers receive an amount, on retirement, to compensate or reward them for the fact that they were not absent from work as much as they were legally allowed to be. This special payment is generally covered by an agreement between the employee and the employer. It could be a part of a collective agreement. The agreement generally provides that the employee is allowed a certain number of sick days each year. Any sick days not used are accumulated until retirement. At that time the employee has a choice of taking the accumulated time off or taking a lump sum payment. The lump sum is generally calculated as the employee's daily pay rate at the time of retirement times the total accumulated sick leave days not taken (to a maximum number of days) divided by two. A teacher can receive up to six months' salary.

The sick leave gratuity is a contractual future interest in a sum of money, and therefore it is property under the Family Law Act. The possibility of receiving it on retirement causes it to be of value. There are sometimes problems in valuing this asset. Often the value accrued during the marriage ranges from $10,000 to $25,000. A princely sum indeed to be added to your spouse's assets, if he happens to be a teacher or other employee accruing this benefit.

TERMINATION PAYMENT

The Ontario Public Service Act establishes that Ontario government employees have a right to a "termination payment" on retirement, death, or release from employment. This payment is based on the pay rate and the service accumulated while the employee worked for the Ontario government. The payment is a right. It is calculated based on past service, so it is obviously an asset that must be accounted for on separation or divorce. If your spouse is an employee of the Ontario government, make sure this asset is included in the Net Family Property statement.

SEVERANCE PAY OR RETIREMENT ALLOWANCE

The master agreement between the Treasury Board and the Public Service Alliance of Canada provides for payment of severance pay to members of the alliance on retirement, layoff, resignation, or death. The payment is based on salary and years of service. The payment is pursuant to a legal contract and is granted for past service. Most case law has determined this to be a family asset.

In *Valenti v. Valenti*,[1] Mrs. Valenti was a federal government employee. Justice Metivier said:

> The severance pay was received during the marriage and no evidence was tendered as to whether all, or only part of this amount, was part of the inducement to leave known as the buy-out or was true severance and part of the terms of the wife's employment contract. The wife requests that a Pro-Rata treatment be accorded to her severance since part of it was earned pre-marriage. The husband says there is no evidence that these rights to severance were in existence pre-marriage. I agree with the husband's position. In the absence of any other evidence the source of this asset or its use is irrelevant. It is simply valued as at the date of separation.

CASH BONUS

Ontario Hydro's employee handbook says, "[An] employee who has completed ten years of continuous employment shall be given, on retirement, a cash bonus equal to one month's pay." This asset must be included in the Net Family Property statement.

RETIREMENT LEAVE OR SEVERANCE PAY

The booklet *After the Gold Watch*, published by the Royal Canadian Mounted Police, says:

> Upon your discharge from the force you may be entitled to a severance benefit of either pension retirement leave or severance pay depending on your length of service. The amount of your benefit is determined by a formula based on the number of completed years of service multiplied by 1 or 1/2 week's pay. Depending on the date you joined the force you may have the choice of receiving retirement leave or severance pay. If you joined prior to January 1, 1970 you may receive your entitlement as either severance pay or retirement leave or a combination of the two. If, however, you joined after January 1, 1970 you are entitled only to severance pay.

In one court case, this was not a shareable asset because it does not accrue until an employee leaves his employer. (This was probably a bad decision.) The asset should be valued and included in the equalization calculation.

In *Schaeffer v. Schaeffer*,[2] Patrick Schaeffer retired from the RCMP and received one month's pay in lieu of leave. Justice

Metivier decided this was an asset at the date of separation. Mr. Schaeffer also received severance pay of $35,000 when he retired. Justice Metivier apportioned this on a pro rata basis and said the portion earned during the marriage was an asset to be included.

LIEU TIME

Police officers often are required to attend at court outside their normal hours of work. Usually they are not paid overtime for these hours; instead, they can accumulate the time and take equivalent time off at their convenience. This is referred to as "lieu time." They can also accumulate lieu time for working statutory holidays. Any lieu time accumulated at the date of separation should be valued and included in the officer's assets.

PAID ABSENCE

Bell Canada's general circular Number 204-1 Section 7 says:

> [Paid] absence prior to pension (PAPP) is a privilege not a right, which is granted primarily in recognition of long service. In some instances it may assist management in retiring an employee at the proper time to the satisfaction of both the employee and the company. In general it is expected that the maximum period will be authorized. However, when the employee is being retired because of serious and willful misconduct no absence with pay should be authorized.

Such a payments would qualify as payment for past service, but it could be argued the payment is not a family asset because:

1. the employee has no legal right to receive it.
2. it is payable only on retirement, not on resignation or death.
3. the right to payment arises only after it is authorized. It may be paid evan as an incentive to retire early or as a replacement for future lost income.

SECURITY RESERVE FUND

In addition to its pension, INCO has a security reserve fund plan for salaried employees. Members of the plan are allowed to contribute from 2 percent to 6 percent of their base salary. INCO adds between 50 percent and 100 percent of the member's contributions, depending on the member's age and years of service. The member is allowed to make additional voluntary contributions that are not matched by the company. All contributions are invested. It is intended that they be held until the member retires. However, there is provision for withdrawals before retirement. Such funds can be substantial. INO's booklet says, "Believe it or not, your Security Reserve Fund Plan could be worth more than your house by the time you retire." There is an example: a member joins the plan at age thirty-five and contributes 4 percent of his salary to the plan each year. If his annual base salary is $50,000, the fund could be worth $200,000 when he retires. This is another asset to be valued on marriage breakdown.

SHARE PURCHASE PLAN

General Motors has a stock purchase plan for salaried employees. The company matches the employee's contributions to the plan. The money is invested in shares of General Motors and in Government of Canada bonds.

PROFIT SHARING PLAN

Like many companies, Canadian Tire has a profit sharing plan for employees. These funds are often invested in shares of the employer. The value of interest at the date of separation should be included in the assets.

STOCK OPTION PLAN

Some companies, for example A & P, have a stock option plan (sometimes called "stock rights.") Generally, it is executives who participate in these plans. Under the terms of the plan, the executive is given rights to buy shares of the company at a certain price after a certain date. If the price is less than the value of the stock at the date of separation, this asset should also be valued and included in the financial statement.

SABBATICAL

Another employment related benefit that may be an asset is the sabbatical leave, enjoyed by university professors, teachers, and others. Some universities provide a one-year sabbatical every seven years. Like sick leave gratuity or paid vacation, this asset accrues evenly over the seven years. If your date of separation is just before your sabbatical, an argument can be made that the salary received on sabbatical was earned during the marriage. Depending on the timing of the sabbatical, there could be a value equivalent to an entire year's after-tax income.

OTHER

No matter who you work for, you probably have an accrued benefit under the Canada Pension Plan. While this asset is not included in the equalization calculation, it should not be forgotten. Canada Pension Plan will equalize this benefit for a couple who have divorced. Of course, for this to happen, you must inform CPP of your divorce.

Paid vacation is a right given to employees by the Employment Standards Act. The act provides that an employee must be given a vacation with pay upon completion of each twelve-month period of employment. Most long-time employees also qualify for additional vacation time. Is vacation entitlement accrued to the date of separation a part of the income package? Does it represent time that could be taken away from work (not cash payable), and is it therefore not subject to equalization on marriage breakdown? The value of accrued vacation pay should be included in the equalization calculation.

An RRSP—a personal RRSP or a group RRSP provided by an employer—is an asset to be counted in the equalization process.

Until recently, pensions were not portable. They are now. With changes of employment, you may have earned a deferred pension from a previous employer. This would be a separate asset to be valued.

Other assets to watch for:

- A & P: stock options
- Air Canada: top-up pension plan
- All Employers: accrued vacation pay
- Apple Computers: stock options
- Bell Canada: group RRSP
- Bristol Myers: stock options
- Canadian Forces: paid leave, retiring allowance
- Canadian Pacific Railway: stock options, senior executives incentive plan

- Canadian Tire: profit sharing plan
- Dow Chemical: deferred profit sharing plan, employee profit sharing plan, group RRSP
- Dofasco: employees savings and profit-sharing fund, deferred profit-sharing plan, group RRSP
- Federal government employees: severance pay, sick leave gratuity
- Firefighters: sick leave gratuity
- General Motors salaried employees: stock purchase plan
- IBM: stock options
- INCO: incentive plan, savings plan, stock options, security reserve fund, share award plan
- Joseph Seagrams: stock options
- Moore Corporation: employees' savings plan
- Municipal employees: sick leave gratuity
- Northern Telecom: employees' savings plan, stock options, retirement allowance plan
- Police officers: lieu time, sick leave gratuity
- Provincial government employees: retiring allowance
- Royal Bank: post-retirement life insurance, group health and dental insurance
- Royal Canadian Mounted Police: retirement leave, severance pay
- Scotiabank: retirement allowance, share purchase plan
- Sears: profit sharing plan, profit sharing retirement fund, associate savings plan
- Stelco: 15 weeks retirement vacation
- Teachers: sick leave gratuity
- Universities: retiring allowance
- WCI / Frigidaire: employees' savings plan

Workers' Compensation Payments

In the case of *Arvelin v. Arvelin*,[3] Jusitce Wright concluded that payments made as temporary total disability benefits under Section 37 of the Worker's Compensation Act are intended as income replacement, and therefore they are not excluded from family property.

In *Buske v. Buske*,[4] a case that involved payments for non-economic loss (pain and sufferings) under Section 42 of the Worker's Compensation Act, the payments were excluded because they were damages for personal injuries.

Sundry

Many companies have employment related assets—executive pension plans, group RRSPs, air miles, medical benefits that continue beyond retirement. Make sure you check into all of these.

Notes

1   (1996) 21 R.F.L. (4th) Page 246 (Ont. Ct. Gen. Div.).
2   (1996) Court File No. 47942/94.
3   (1996) 20 R.F.L. (4th) 98.
4   (1988) 12. R.F.L. (3d) 388 (Dist. Ct.).

Chapter 20

Accrued Sick Leave Gratuity

INTRODUCTION

Most teachers receive an amount on retirement to compensate or reward them because they were not absent from work as much as they were legally allowed to be. The special payment is generally covered by an agreement between the employee and the employer. It could be a part of their collective agreement.

Usually, the agreement gives the employee a certain number of sick days each year. Any sick days not used are accumulated until retirement. At that time the employee often has a choice: he can take the accumulated time off, or he can accept a payment of a lump sum. The lump sum is sometimes calculated as the employee's daily pay rate at the time of retirement, times the total accumulated sick leave days not taken (to a maximum number of days), divided by two. The lump sum payment can be as much as six months' salary.

CASE LAW

There are several reported cases.

Gasparetto v. Gasparetto[1]

Mr. Gasparetto worked as a teacher for the Department of National Defense and was entitled to a discretionary early retirement incentive and a retirement gratuity based on accumulated sick leave credits. The credits were his entitlement as part of the collective agreement.

Justice Campbell considered both incentives.

> [There] is no present right to any payment and no vested or contingent interest in any future payment. That being the case, the early retirement incentive plan is not property within the meaning of s. 4 (1) (a) or (c) of the Family Law Act. He seems to have decided this because in this case the payment was discretionary. The retirement gratuity is another matter. It is provided as an entitlement in the collective agreement and does not depend on the discretion of the board or the Department of National Defense. It is an entitlement as of right, on retirement, to a certain proportion of annual salary depending on number of years of service and remaining accumulated sick leave credits. It does not depend on any contributions by the board or the employee. Although it is called a gratuity it is not a gratuity but a payment as of right based on the collective agreement. It is a future interest in a sum of money and is therefore property within the meaning of the Act.

Alger v. Alger[2]

Mr. Alger was a schoolteacher. Under the terms of his collective agreement he had the right to receive a sick leave gratuity payment on retirement. Justice McDermid determined that this was property as defined by Section 4(1) of the Ontario Family Law Act, and referred to the case of *Gasparetto v. Gasparetto*. Opposing counsel suggested discounts for several contingencies, including the possibility that Mr. Alger might terminate employment or transfer to another school board before retirement, that he might use up the sick credits before retirement, and that the benefit could be eliminated from the collective agreement. The judge did not allow the discounts.

Justice McDermid also considered the possibility that, when he retired, Mr. Alger might roll the sick leave gratuity into an RRSP, thus not paying immediate income tax on it. The judge said, "However, since the discount for income tax was not opposed in principle, I permit it."

Hilderley v. Hilderley[3]

Mr. Hilderley was a school principal. In considering the matter, Justice Osborne said:

> The Oxford Board of Education has a sick leave plan from which the defendant can accumulate 20 days sick leave each year to a maximum of 240 days. Upon retirement the defendant is entitled, if eligible, to be paid one half his last year's salary. Eligibility depends on the defendant having earned at least 200 sick leave days. The defendant must have been employed for 20 years and the beneficiary of the sick leave plan to be eligible, must be eligible for and receive pension benefits within the prescribed time. Mr. Clayton, for Mr. Hilderley, takes the position that, on the valuation date, the defendant was not eligible for pension and that the right to the sick leave gratuity had not crystallized to the point so as to permit the right to be viewed as property under the Family Law Act.

It seems to me the observations of Campbell J. in Gasparetto apply to the retirement gratuity issue in this case. Although Mr. Hilderley's access to the retirement gratuity had not crystallized on 9th, July 1987, the defendant's future access to the gratuity was something, which on the evidence had an economic value as of July 1987 and was property as defined in the Family Law Act. There were some obvious contingencies. The defendant had to work to a point where he could retire on full pension. At the valuation date, that time would arrive when the defendant was 62. The evidence now discloses, as I have said, that the defendant has access to retirement at age 55. The defendant has to in fact have 200 sick leave days as of the time he is otherwise eligible for this retirement gratuity. Illness in the period between the valuation date and retirement would compromise the benefit accruing to the plaintiff. The benefit must still exist on retirement. Mr. Clayton dealt with this in cross-examination and fairly conceded in argument that although this is a contingency, it is a modest one. No doubt the collective agreement could be changed. I agree with that in the real world, that as related to Mr. Hilderley, that is unlikely. As I mentioned earlier in another context, the defendant might change jobs. That would severely compromise, if not eliminate, the defendant's access to the sick leave gratuity.

The actuaries are not far apart on the gross value of the retirement gratuity. The value according to Mr. Rudd was about $15,000. Tax would reduce that to $11,000. Mr. Aseltine for the defen-

dant set his approach out in Ex.13. I agree generally with Mr. Aseltine's approach as set out in Ex. 13,
particularly at pp. 4 and 5.

It seems to me that if it is assumed that the gratuity will not be taxed that assumption obviously
will increase the value of the gratuity. If the gratuity
could be rolled over into an RRSP, tax will at least
be deferred. If it cannot be rolled over, the gratuity
will be viewed as income in Mr. Hilderley's hands
when it is received.

There is a provision for the gratuity to be paid
in two taxation years, thus potentially reducing
the impact of income tax. In these circumstances,
that benefit is marginal, but I would think particularly if Mr. Hilderley were to retire on full pension, as he said he intended to do at age 55, and if
he were to obtain other employment, the gratuity
would then be taxed at Mr. Hilderley's marginal
rate, if it were viewed for purposes of this analysis as his last income.

In the circumstances, having in mind the taxation uncertainty, which I view as something akin to
a contingency, I assess the value of the sick leave
gratuity at $13,000.

Justice Osborne recognized that the accrued sick leave gratuity is subject to equalization. However, he refused to allow a
deduction for contingencies because there was little chance of
Mr. Hilderley not collecting the money. He cut the income tax
allowance in half, because the rate of tax Mr. Hilderley would pay
was uncertain.

Rickett v. Rickett[4]

Mr. Rickett was a schoolteacher who would have to work to retirement age to collect sick leave gratuity. Justice Granger concluded that placing a value on the sick leave gratuity would be allowing Mrs. Rickett to benefit from Mr. Rickett's employment after the separation of the couple.

The judge stuck to a strict interpretation of the phrase "termination method." He seems to be alone in this; later cases allow for valuations that consider the early retirement provisions of a pension even though the person must continue employment to qualify for early retirement. The current Standards of Practice of the Canadian Institute of Actuaries require that the early retirement provisions be valued even though the requirements for early retirement may not have been met. If Justice Granger's view holds, the sick leave gratuity has no value until the day a person retires. The entire value of the sick leave gratuity is earned on retirement day. This is not a reasonable view.

Deroo v. Deroo[5]

This case does not involve sick leave gratuity, but Justice Misener's comments are useful. He considers Hilderley, applies Alger, but does not follow Rickett. He says,

> Although I am not at all sure how Osborne J. arrived at the valuation he did in *Hilderley*, I think that the views he expresses in that case on this issue are correct. I think that Judge McDermid has adopted the right approach (in *Alger*). He considers Section 52 of the regulations under the Pension Benefits Act (even though they don't apply). He goes on to say, "It follows

that if in fact the pension benefits acquired up to valuation date become payable at age 55 if the employee
continues in his present employment up to that age,
the valuation of the pension benefits must be made on
the basis that they will in fact become so payable."

Many cases have followed this principle in deciding to accept the
value of a pension based on the earliest date of unreduced pension.
The same principle should apply to accrued sick leave gratuity.

Belyea v. Belyea[6]

This case did not involve sick leave gratuity, but the principles are the
same. Justice Guerette considers numerous reported cases and says:

To cut off the benefits as at the date of separation
without making allowances for considerations arising beyond that date is no more realistic than dividing the marital home by ordering carpenters to saw
it down the middle. All these assets have fundamental characters, which must be taken into account
when a division of marital property is effected.

Cliche v. Cliche[7]

The Ontario Court of Appeal supported the reasoning in *Hilderley*
and *Alger*. The court concluded that Mr. Cliche's accumulated sick
leave credits should have been considered a property interest. They
ruled that the payment be shared when it is received.

McIntosh v. McIntosh[8]

For purposes of calculating the equalization payment, Justice Forestell included the value of Mr. McIntosh's accumulated hours of sick leave at separation as property. He did not allow further discounts for contingencies that could arise between separation and retirement, when the sick leave gratuity would be paid, because:

1. the husband's income would increase between the date of separation and the date of retirement, and the banked sick leave would therefore increase in value,
2. the contingency of an early death would be compensated for through term insurance, and
3. any other contingency that could reduce the value of the banked sick leave would be within the control of the husband in any event.

Tanouye v. Tanouye[9]

Mr. and Mrs. Tanouye separated in 1991, and their case was heard in 1994. In January 1990, Mr. Tanouye retired and received $14,400 for accumulated sick pay. He rolled the payment into an RRSP. He agreed the payment was an asset in the equalization calculation, but sought to have it reduced, on a pro rata basis, for the portion earned before the marriage. The court refused any deduction, since no evidence was presented to support the value of the asset at the date of marriage.

Levac-Vicev v. Vicev[10]

Mrs. Levac-Vicev, a schoolteacher, had accumulated sick leave at the valuation date. However, under the terms of her contract with the school board in effect on the valuation date, there was no provision for payment of compensation in lieu of sick leave still unused at the time of the teacher's retirement. After the couple separated, but before the trial, a new contract between the school board and the teachers came into effect. The new contract allowed for the payment of compensation for unused sick leave benefits accumulated during a certain period. Some of that time came before the valuation date. The new contract was not known on the valuation date, and it was possible the new benefit could be withdrawn in subsequent contracts, so Judge Doyle excluded the sick leave benefits from the equalization of assets. I agree with the decision because there was no property of any value in connection with the accumulated sick days at the date of separation. The withdrawal of the plan in a subsequent contract would be a post separation event that should not be considered.

Ramsay v. Ramsay[11]

Justice Halvorson, determined that accrued sick leave credits were property if the employee was contractually entitled to the benefit, even though the benefit was not payable until retirement.

Offet v. Offet[12]

Justice Wiemer explained that in *Ramsay v. Ramsay* Justice Halverson regarded the value of unused sick leave as divisible matrimonial property. He added that the right to the benefit must be shown to have existed at the date of the application, and its values must be calculable. He noted that in the case of *Offet v. Offet*, there was no evidence to show how much unused sick leave Mr. Offet had accumulated at the date of division. He also noted that the sick leave had no crystallized value on that date, and that Mr. Offet could not have insisted upon payment for it. The judge concluded that, if Mr. Offet had continued work, he probably would have used up the sick leave. According to the judge, the unused sick leave credits of a person in employment are akin to expectation of the payment of future salary. He said the unused sick leave credits have no realizable value unless the employment ceases before the credits are exhausted. He decided they have no value in marriage breakdown. He had little alternative, because no evidence was provided regarding the value, if any, of the possible asset.

Sousa v. Sousa[13]

Judge Metivier ruled that the teachers' accrued sick leave gratuity was to be included in the equalization calculation. He chose to ignore the actuary's present value calculation, and valued the gratuity at the current value at the date of separation. He reduced the income tax allowance, because he assumed that half the gratuity would be rolled into an RRSP and thus not attract tax. His reasons for ignoring the actuary's report are not clear.

Leavoy v. Leavoy[14]

The Ontario Court of Appeal upheld a lower court decision to include the value of Mr. Leavoy's accrued sick leave gratuity and refused to allow him a contingency discount because he had no evidence to support such a discount.

CONCLUSIONS

Sick leave gratuity is a contractual future interest in a sum of money, and there is no doubt it is property under the Family Law Act. The possibility of receiving it on retirement causes it to be of value. Any problems seem to be in connection with valuing the asset.

The method of valuation should be based on the terms of the particular sick leave gratuity plan. If the money cannot be received until retirement, the value should be present valued. Income tax allowance should be deducted. There may be a need for a contingency discount.

There are arguments for and against placing any value on this asset.

ARGUMENTS

Sick Leave Gratuity as an Asset

1. It is an entitlement under a collective agreement (or other contract).
2. It is a future interest in a sum of money and is therefore property within the meaning of the Ontario Family Law Act.
3. It is earned equally over the years, not suddenly when the person retires and receives it.
4. If the person uses up accumulated sick leave credits, or terminates employment between the date of separation and the date of retirement, these are post-separation events and should not be considered with hindsight.
5. If the program ceases, that is also a post-separation event and in all likelihood earned benefits would be grandfathered and would not be wiped out.

Cases Supporting Sick Leave Gratuity as an Asset

- *Alger v. Alger* (1989) 21 R.F.L. (3d) 211 (Ont. H.C.)
- *Bellemare v. Bellemare* (1990) CarswellNS 50, 28 R.F.L. (3d) 165, 98 N.S.R. (2d) 140, 263 A.P.R. 140 (N.S.S.C.)
- *Belyea v. Belyea* (1990) 30 R.F.L. (3d) 407 (N.B.)
- *Cliché v. Cliché* (1991) 36 R.F.L. (3d) 297 (ON C.A.)
- *Deroo v. Deroo* (1990) 28 R.F.L. (3d) 86 (ON Supreme Ct. H.C.J.)
- *Gasparetto v. Gasparetto* (1988) 15 R.F.L. (3d) 401 (ON. H.C.J.)
- *Hartnett v. Hartnett* (2000) CarswellOnt 3688
- *Henry v. Henry* (1992) CarswellBC 1218
- *Hilderley v. Hilderley* (1989) 21 R.F.L. (3d) 383 (ON H.C.J.)
- *Hutchison v. Hutchison* (1992) CarswellOnt 1544
- *Leavoy v. Leavoy* (2000) CarswellOnt 3185, Docket CA 31154 (Ont. Ct. of Appeal)
- *McIntosh v. McIntosh* (1993) O.J. No. 3020 (ON. Gen. Div.) 1994 W.D.F.L. 240
- *Ostapyk v. Ostapyk* (1993) CarswellOnt 1687
- *Ramsay v. Ramsay* (1994) S.J. No. 49 (Q.B.)
- *Sousa v. Sousa* (1998) Ottawa Doc. No. 51085/95 and 27702/95 (Ont. Gen. Div.)
- *Stapleton v. Stapleton* (1990) CarswellNB 80, 112 N.B.R. (2d) 181, A.P.R. 181
- *Tanouye v. Tanouye* (1996) 10 R.F.L. (4th) 135 (SK C.A.)
- *Woodman v. Duremo* (1995) W.D.F.L. 1785 (ON Gen. Div.), (1997) W.D.F.L. 063 (Ont. C.A.)
- *Yaschuk v. Logan* (1992) CarswellNS 64, 39 R.F.L. (3d) 417, 110 N.S.R. (2d) 278, 299 A.P.R. 278

Arguments Against Sick Leave Gratuity Being An Asset

1. The person may use up the sick leave credits or terminate employment before retirement, and therefore never receive the amount.
2. In the light of current cutbacks in education costs, the program may be cancelled.

These are post separation events and should not be considered.

Cases Against Sick Leave Gratuity Being an Asset

*   *Levac-Vicev v. Vicev* (1994) O.J. No. 17 Action No. 43152/92, Doyle J. W.D.F.L. 352, (Ont. Gen. Div.)
*   *Offet v. Offet* (1995) 17 R.F.L. (4ᵗʰ) 352 (SK Ct. Q.B.)
*   *Rickett v. Rickett* (1990) 25 R.F.L. (3d) 188, 72 O.R. (2d) 321, 67 D.L.R. (4ᵗʰ) 103 (ON. H.C.J.)

Notes

1   (1988) 15 R.F.L. (3d) 401 (Ont. H.C.J.).
2   (1989) 21 R.F.L. (3d) 211 (Ont. Supreme Court).
3   (1989) 21 R.F.L. (3d) 383 (Ont. High Court).
4   (1990) 25 R.F.L. (3d) 188 (Ont. Supreme Court).
5   (1990) 28 R.F.L. (3d) 86 (Ont. Supreme Court).
6   (1991) 30 R.F.L. (3d) 414 (N.B.).
7   (1991) 36 R.F.L. (3d) 297 (Ont. C.A.).
8   (1993) O.J. # 3020 (Gen. Div.).
9   (1994) 10 R.F.L. (4ᵗʰ) 135 (Sask. C.A.).

10 (1994) O.J. No. 17 (Gen. Div.).

11 (1994) 1 R.F.L. (4th) 447, 3 W.W.R. 562, 2 C.C.P.B. 120, 111 D.L.R. (4th) 312, 119 Sask. R. 81 (Q.B.).

12 (1995) 17 R.F.L. (4th) 357 (Sask. Ct. Q.B.).

13 (1998) Ottawa Doc. No. 51085/95 and 27702/95 (Ont. Gen. Div.).

14 (2000) CarswellOnt 3185, Docket CAC 31154 (Ont. Ct. of Appeal).

Chapter 21

Divorce Support and Other Helpful Organizations

INTRODUCTION

Sixty-four percent of all divorced women eventually remarry. Unfortunately, one in four women who divorce and remarry will get divorced again. The statistics are nearly the same for men. How can you stop yourself from making the same relationship mistakes over and over?

A support or therapy group can be the ideal place for you to explore inexpensively what went wrong with your marriage … How do you know a group is right for you? Well, you won't know until you go!

CHOOSING A DIVORCE SUPPORT GROUP

When your marriage breaks up and you find yourself in uncharted emotional waters, where can you turn for help?

A self-help group can be a group of people getting together to share information. It can be led by a trained facilitator or managed by members of the group. A self-help group is a forum for people who have been there to get together, share experiences, solve problems, and share resources. Participating in such a group can help you regain your emotional center.

How do you find a group? A recommendation is always a good starting place. Ask your doctor, spiritual counsellor, or social worker for recommendations. A check through the Yellow Pages can yield some choices.

Figuring out which is the right group for your needs can be a challenge. Here are some questions to ask yourself when choosing a self-help group:

1. What are you looking for in a group? Emotional support? Information about being divorced? Information about how to get the help you need? Access to services? People you can relate to?
2. Is there a contact person from the group who can respond to your inquiries and who can send you information before you attend a meeting?
3. Does the group have any requirements for attending?
4. Is the meeting place accessible to you? Is there public transportation, wheelchair access, an interpreter?
5. Are you comfortable with the general makeup of the group—age, gender, religious affiliation?
6. Do you feel safe after a few visits?
7. Is the group open to individual participation?
8. Do members reach out to each other—including you—beyond meetings?
9. Do meeting facilitators have sufficient skills? Is there enough clarity in the meeting format to meet your needs?

You may need a counsellor for yourself or for your children, or a chiropractor or massage therapist to help ease the stress, or a financial consultant to help put you on the road to a brighter post-divorce future.

This section lists self-help organizations, programs, workshops, and support services. Some groups offer sliding scale fees or ask for a small donation. Some may be free. Some have fixed fees. Call them for more information. We are not endorsing any group on the list.

INTERNATIONAL

Beginning Experience
phone 313-965-5110
Provides support and programs for separated, widowed, and divorced people

Child Quest International
phone 408-287-4673
24-hour sighting line 888 818-4673
An organization devoted to the protection and recovery of missing children

The Grief Recovery Institute
Grief recovery outreach program. A 12 week program, facilitated by grief recovery specialists, Certified by the Grief Recovery Institute. Helps willing participants complete the pain caused by death, divorce and other losses. Some programs are fee based, some are sponsored. Call 800-334-7606 for information and referrals. All states; many communities

National Sleep Foundation
729 Fifteenth St. NW, Fourth Floor
Washington, D.C. 20005
phone 888-NSF-SLEEP
website www.sleepfoundation.org

Call or check out the website for information about local NSAW activities or to learn more about how to get a good night's sleep

North American Conference of
Separated and Divorced Catholics
phone 541-893-6089, 541-893-6089
Addresses the religious, emotional, financial, and parenting issues relating to separation, divorce, and remarriage

Parents without Partners
website www.parentswithoutpartners.org
Parents without Partners is an international, non-profit, educational organization of custodial and non-custodial parents: widowed, divorced, separated, or never married. Its objective it to provide understanding and mutual support to single parents and help them deal with the problems of raising children in a one-parent household.

Retrouvaille International
phone 800-470-2230
A program for couples in troubled marriages, separated individuals, and those who want their previous marriage to work again.

Meet Me Online
A safe way of meeting someone. This website screens all its members by conducting individual background checks.

SUPPORT ON THE WEB

Child Cybersearch Canada
www.childcybersearch.org

Dedicated to finding missing children, this site also offers a list of child-approved sites.

Credit Counseling Service

www.creditcanada.com

This site provides information about financial counselling, seminars, and workshops.

DADS Canada

www.dadscanada.com

Non-profit paralegal service using lawyers, accountants, doctors, and social workers to help non-custodial parents receive fair treatment in court.

Divorce As Friends

www.divorceasfriends.com

This site offers help with letting go, healing, resolving issues, and ending the conflict.

Infidelity

www.infidelity.com

Provides information, expert advice, education, and opportunities to help you rebuild your life after your spouse has been unfaithful.

Single Mothers

www.singlemomz.com

Connect with other single moms facing divorce, child support, custody battles, money problems, and job-related issues.

Smart Divorce

www.smartdivorce.com

A divorce learning center providing practical solutions to divorce challenges.

NATIONAL

The Canadian Bar Association
902-50 O'Connor Street, Ottawa, On K1P 6L2
phone 613-237-2925, 613-237-1988
toll free 800-267-8860 fax: 613-237-0185
website www.cba.org e-mail: info@cba.org

National Shared Parenting Association
phone 888-543-2339
Contact Danny Guspie
e-mail doppler@total.net

MEDIATION ORGANIZATIONS

Arbitration & Mediation Institute of Canada Inc.
Institut d'Arbitrage et de Médiation du Canada Inc.
232 – 329 March Road. Box 11, Kanata, ON K2K 2E1
phone 877-475-4353, 613-599-0878 fax 613-599-7027
website www.amic.org e-mail amic@igs.net

Family Mediation Canada (FMC)
528 Victoria Street North Kitchener, Ontario N2H 5G1 phone
519-585-3118 fax: 519-585-3121
website www.fmc.ca e-mail fmc@web.net

ALBERTA
Family Lawyers

The Canadian Bar Association
2610-10104 103rd Avenue Edmonton, AB T5J 0H8

phone 403-428-1230 fax 403-426-6803

Mediation

Alberta Family Mediation Society
P.O. Box 405, 918—16 th Avenue N.W., Calgary
AB T2M 0K3 phone 403-233-9027 fax 403-262-2633

Alberta Arbitration & Mediation Society
110 Law Centre, University of Alberta, Edmonton, AB T6G
2H5 phone 780-433-4881, fax 780-433-9024

BRITISH COLUMBIA
Counselling, Therapy

British Columbia Association of Marriage & Family Therapy
207-1168 Hamilton Street, Vancouver, BC V6B 2S2 phone
604-687-6131 website www.familyforum.com/bcamft

Family Lawyers

The Canadian Bar Association
10th Floor, 845 Cambie Street, Vancouver BC V6B 5T3
phone 604-687-3404 fax 604-669-9601, website www.bccba.org
e-mail cba@bccba.org

Mediation

British Columbia Arbitration & Mediation Institute
1628 West 7th Avenue, Vancouver, BC V6J 1S5
Phone 604-736-6614, Fax 604-736-6225
website www.amibc.org, e-mail info@amibc.org

British Columbia Arbitration &
Mediation Institute, Vancouver Island Branch
    c/o 177 Hampshire Road
    Victoria, BC V8R 5T7
    phone 250-592-7700 fax 250-592-7700

British Columbia Arbitration &
Mediation Institute, Interior Branch
    c/o Grant Thorton, 247 Lawrence Avenue
    Kelowna, BC V1Y 6L2 phone 250-762-4434 fax 250-762-8896

Mediation Development Association of BC
    Suite 6, 704 Sixth Street
    New Westminister, BC V3L 3C5
    phone 604-524-4552 fax 800-663-7053

MANITOBA
Family Lawyers

The Canadian Bar Association
    105, 400 St. Mary Avenue, Winnipeg, MB R3C 4K5
    phone 204-944-1491 fax 204-947-1035
    e-mail cba_mba@pcs.mb.ca

Mediation

Family Mediation Manitoba
    P.O. Box 2369, Winnipeg, MB R3C 4A6 phone 204-989-5330
    Fax 204-694-7555 e-mail president@fmm.winnipeg.mb.ca

Arbitration & Mediation Institute of Manitoba Inc.
    c/o 45 Galinee Bay, Winnipeg, MB R3K 0R9

phone 204-783-0529 fax 204-897-7091

NEW BRUNSWICK
Family Lawyers

The Canadian Bar Association
204-113 Regent Street, Fredericton, NB E3B 3Z2
phone 506-452-7818 fax 506-459-7959

Mediation

Family Mediation New Brunswick
P.O. Box 20010, Saint John, NB E2L 5B2
phone 506-658-2400

NEWFOUNDLAND
Family Lawyers

The Canadian Bar Association
215 Water Street, 5th Floor, St. John's, NF A1C 5M3 phone
709-579-5783 fax 709-726-4166 e-mail cbanfld@thezone.net

Mediation Newfoundland & Labrador
c/o Unified Family Court, 21 Kings Bridge Road,
St. John, NF A1C 3K4
phone 709-729-2258 fax 709-729-0784

NORTH WEST TERRITORIES
Family Lawyers

The Canadian Bar Association
P.O. Box 1985, 4918 50th Street, Yellowknife, NT X1A 2P5
Phone 867-669-7739, fax 867-873-6344
e-mail: cbanwt@lawsociety.nt.ca

Mediation

Family Mediation Association of the Northwest Territories
c/o Robert O'Rourke, P.O. Box 1806,
Yellowknife, NT X1A 2P4
phone 403-873-4283

NOVA SCOTIA
Counselling, Therapy

Nova Scotia Family Service Association
6080 Young Street, Suite 509, Halifax, NS B3K 5L2
phone 902-420-1980 fax 902-423-9830
website www.chebucto.ns.ca

Mariner & Mariner Counselling
Suite 218, Halifax Professional Centre,
5991 Spring Garden Road, Halifax, NS B3H 1Y6
phone 902-496-5656 fax 902-454-4857

Family Service Association
Halifax Regional Municipality, 6080 Young Street, Suite 509,
Halifax, NS B3K 5L2 hone 902-420-1980 fax 902-423-9830
website www.chebucto.ns.ca

Divorce Support and Other Helpful Organizations

Family Lawyers

The Canadian Bar Association
526-1657 Barrington Street, Halifax, NS B3J 2A1
phone 902-422-1905 fax 902-423-0475 cbans@istar.ca

Nova Scotia Association of Women and the Law
c/o Beaton, Derrik and Ring, Artillery Place,
Suite 100, Halifax, NS
phone 902-422-7411

Dalhousie Legal Aid Services
2209 Gottingen Street, Halifax, NS
phone 902-423-8105 fax 902-422-8067

Mediation

Atlantic Provinces Arbitration & Mediation Institute
c/o Box 84, Hubbards, NS B0J 1T0 phone 902-857-9445
fax 902-857-9445 e-mail norcan@ns.sympatico.ca

Family Mediation Nova Scotia
P.O. Box 3154, South Halifax, NS B3J 3H5

ONTARIO
Counselling

Community Counselling Centre
2026 Caroline Street, Burlington, ON L7R 1L2
phone 905-639-2261.
151 York Boulevard, Hamilton, ON L8R 3L4
phone 905-528-0065 Contact Rev. Dr. Trent Walker

369

Core Belief Engineering
Phone 888-361-9466 Contact Sharon Roach

Court Support and Counselling Services
Phone 416-789-9793

Etobicoke Family Life Education Council (EFLEC)
Phone: 416-255-8969, e-mail eflecdir@volnetmmp.net
Contact Jean Shakespeare

Families in Transition
2 Carleton Street, Suite 917, Toronto, ON M5B 1J3
phone 416-585-9151

The George Hull Centre for Children and Families
phone 416-622-8833

Haley & Associates
522 Eglinton Avenue East, Toronto, ON M4P 1N6
phone 416-487-0791 e-mail: psych@ican.net

Hoffman Quadrinity Process
phone 800-741-3449

Interval House of Hamilton-Wentworth
phone 905-547-8485 crisis line 905-547-8484
e-mail interval@netcom.ca

Jewish Family & Child Service
Phone 905-882-2331 contact Elinor Gertner,
website www.toronto.com/jfcs e-mail info@jfandcs.com

K.I.D.S. First
phone 905-731-4046

The Louise Hay Program
phone 416-504-6912 contact Catherine Wood
e-mail cwood@axxent.ca

Parenting For Today
Phone 416-225-6381 contact Risa Mlotek e-mail hej@idirect.com

Peel Counselling + Consulting Services
phone 905-567-8858 contact Debra Rodrigues
e-mail drodrigues@globalserve.net

Toronto Fathers' Resources
24 hour hotline 416-861-0626 e-mail: doppler@total.net

The Women's Centre of Hamilton-Wentworth
phone 905-522-0127 website cdnx.netinc.ca/~wchw
e-mail: womenscentre@on.aibn.com

Courses, Seminars

A Different Road
phone 905-873-3033 contact Barb Lyons
website www.adirrentroad.com

Divorce & Separation Seminars
phone 416-283-3305, 905-338-9879 contact: David Whealy

Self-Help Resource of Greater Toronto
phone 416-487-4355 website www.selfhelp.on.ca
e-mail shrc@selfhelp.on.ca

Parents, Children

Fathers Are Capable Too

3044 Bloor Street West, Suite 205, Toronto, ON M8X 2Y8
phone 416-410-FACT (3228) website www.fact.on.ca

Parents Without Partners

phone 416-463-9355 website: www.parentswithoutpartners.org

Rainbows

17 Theresa Street, Barrie, ON L4M 1J5
phone 877-403-2733, 705-726-7407, fax 705-726-5805
contact Thelma Cockburn website www.rainbows.org
email rainbowscanada@home.com

Support Groups

The Life Skills

phone, fax 416-494-8369 contact Eleanor or Sandra Third
e-mail: el3rd@interlog.com

New Beginnings

3377 Batview, Willowdale, ON M2M 3S4
phone 416-222-1101, ext. 107 or 258

New Directions

phone 416-487-5317 website www.newdirections.ca
e-mail newdirections@newdirections.ca

Parent Education & Resource Centre

phone 905-882-7690 contact Sara Dimerman,
e-mail dimerman@pathcom.com

Scarborough Women's Centre
2100 Ellesmere Road, Suite 245, Scarborough, ON M1H 3B7
phone 416-439-7111 fax 416-439-6999
website: www3.simpatico.ca/scar.wom.ctr
e-mail scar.wom.ctr@sympatico.ca

Family Counselling Services

OAMFT
1-800-267-2638 website www.oamft.on.ca

PRINCE EDWARD ISLAND
Family Lawyers

The Canadian Bar Association
93 Pownal Street, Charlottetown, PE C1A 3W4
phone 902-566-1590 Fax 902-566-3352 e-mail cbapei@isn.net

Mediation

Mediation PEI
c/o 166 Fitzroy Street, Charlottetown, PE C1A 1S1
phone 902-628-2257 fax 902-368-2715

QUEBEC
Family Lawyers

The Canadian Bar Association
445, Boulevard Saint-Laurent, Bureau 410,
Montreal, QC, H2Y 2Y7
phone 514-393-9600 fax 514-393-3350 e-mail: info@abcqc.qc.ca

Maison du Barreau
3445, Boulevard Saint-Laurent, Montreal, QC H2Y 3T8
phone 514-954-3420 website: www.barreau.qc.ca

Support Groups

Spa Montreal
phone 514-364-0260

Mediation

Resoulution de Conflit
phone 514-279-6078 fax: 279-5302
e-mail dianeleblanc@videotron.ca contact: Diane Leblanc

Association de Mediation Familiale du Quebec
6896 Somerled, Montreal, PQ, H4V 1V1
phone 514-866-6769, 800-667-7559 fax 514-487-6360

Institut d'Arbitrage et de Mediation du Quebec
P.O. Box 5455, Station B, Montreal, PQ, H4V 1V1
phone 514-237-5678 fax 514-205-5344
e-mail lacouture@huisclos.com

SASKATCHEWAN
Family Lawyers

The Canadian Bar Association
411-105 21st Street East, Saskatoon, SK, S7K 0B3
phone 306-244-3898 fax 306-652-3977
e-mail cdn.bar@sk.sympatico.ca

Mediation

Arbitration & Mediation Institute of Saskatchewan
134 Chan Cres. Saskatoon, SK, S7K 5N8 phone: 306-934-3450
fax 306-955-1239 website www.saskstar.sk.ca/amis
e-mail r.graham@sk.sympatico.ca

Mediation Saskatchewan
P.O. Box 3765, Regina, SK S4P 3N8 phone 306-565-3939

YUKON
Family Lawyers

The Canadian Bar Association
101 Finch Crescent, Whitehorse, YT, Y1A 5L5
phone 867-393-4700 fax 867-393-4764

Mediation

Mediation Yukon Society
P.O. Box 31102, 211 Main Street, Whitehorse, YT Y1A 5P7
phone 403-667-7910 fax 403-667-7910

Chapter 22

Real Estate Appraisals

INTRODUCTION

You or your spouse may own real estate. You need to have it valued in the Net Family Property statement. The real estate may be your principal residence; it may be a cottage. It may be a farm, investment, or business property. It does not make sense to undervalue your real estate. This will merely prolong proceedings, delay the divorce and also increase the legal fees and other costs. All real estate should be appraised by a qualified appraiser.

1. Four methods are used in appraising real estate:
   the comparison method, used to appraise a residence, cottage, industrial property, commercial property, or farm,
2. Replacement cost approach, used to value a residence, cottage, industrial property, commercial property, or farm,
3. income approach, used mainly in valuing investment property,
4. net value method, used in valuing land being held for future development.

COMPARISON METHOD

In this method, your property is compared to similar properties that have sold recently. Real estate is worth what a knowledgeable buyer will pay and what a willing vendor will accept. Make sure the physical and geographic attributes of the properties chosen for comparison are similar; as well, make sure the terms of sale were not unusual—for example, a low down payment with a high mortgage taken back.

Finally, you may need to adjust for differences in geographic area or special attributes, for example a garage or a fireplace.

The comparison works only if you look at recent sales of similar properties. Properties that are listed but have not sold do not give useful information.

REPLACEMENT COST APPROACH

The appraiser determines the square footage of the building and multiplies it by the current cost per square foot of constructing such a building. He adjusts for anything unusual in the particular property and for any physical depreciation. Then he adds the value of the land (usually determined by the comparison method).

INCOME APPROACH

For an investment property, the appraiser attempts to locate comparable sales and to determine the replacement cost. However, the main measure of the value of an investment or income property is the net income it is earning or could earn.

The first step is to ascertain the gross rental income being earned and the gross income that could be earned, taking into account existing leases.

Next, the appraiser looks at all the expenses the landlord must pay—municipal taxes, insurance, repairs, maintenance. He looks at past bills and updates them. He includes such things as services that have been provided by the owner, as well as interest cost on borrowed money.

The next step is to calculate the sustainable net income for the property. The appraiser deducts the calculated expenses from the obtainable gross rental income, then deducts a vacancy allowance. The net income is multiplied by a factor that accounts for the rate of return available on other investments and the risk involved in this particular investment property.

NET VALUE

For vacant land being held for future development, the net value method is used. Determine the expected sale price of the developed land. Deduct the estimated development costs, carrying costs, and selling costs, as well as a reasonable profit for the owner based on risk and the amount of funds tied up. This leaves a net value for the raw land.

FOR A HIGHER VALUE

Before the appraiser inspects the property, make sure the house is in presentable condition, with all floors vacuumed or washed and waxed, everything neat and tidy, the grass cut, and any minor repairs completed.

Point out all special features that add value to your property. Provide the appraiser with details of similar properties that sold recently at a high price.

If it's an income property, make sure all income is disclosed. Point out any expenses that were non-recurring.

FOR A LOWER VALUE

Make sure the property is unkempt and doesn't show well when the appraiser arrives. Ensure that all expenses and necessary repairs are disclosed to the appraiser. Point out any major flaws of the property. Provide details of any recent sales of similar property where you know the price was low.

SUMMARY

The valuing of real estate is a complicated matter. There is no easy rule of thumb. The value must be determined by a competent real estate appraiser who has experience in appraising the particular kind of property. A one-page letter of opinion prepared by your friend the real estate agent will not suffice.

The best approach is for both parties to agree on an appraiser and talk to him. If this is not possible, then get a second opinion from another appraiser.

REAL ESTATE APPRAISERS

The Appraisal Institute of Canada, founded in 1938, is a national professional institute of real estate appraisers dedicated to high standards for members of the appraisal profession. You can recognize a qualified member of the Institute by the designation AACI or CRA.

AACI (Accredited Appraiser Canadian Institute) designates fully accredited membership in the institute and may be used by the holder in connection with the appraisal of a wide range of real property.

CRA (Canadian Residential Appraiser) designates individuals qualified in the appraisal and valuation of individual undeveloped residential dwelling sights and dwellings containing not more than four self-contained family housing units.

The Appraisal Institute membership, more than six thousand, is governed by a code of ethics, rules of professional conduct, and standards of professional practice that establish a minimum standard of performance in appraisal assignments. Provision is made for the continuing professional development of members through seminars and conferences. Chapters located in all major cities in Canada conduct regular educational meetings, which provide forums for discussion. Members must complete a rigorous course of studies in all aspects of real estate valuation before they are granted the use of either designation.

For further information contact the Appraisal Institute of Canada, 1111 Portage Avenue, Winnipeg, Manitoba, R3G 0S8, telephone (204) 783-2224, fax (204) 783-5575, e-mail aicanada @ escape.ca

APPRAISAL DEGREES

Real estate appraisal degrees you may see:
AACI, Accredited Appraiser Canadian Institute, Appraisal Institute of Canada
ARA, Accredited Rural Appraiser, American Society of Farm Managers and Rural Appraisers
CRA,Canadian Residential Appraiser,Appraisal Institute of Canada
DAR, Designated Appraiser (Residential), Canadian National Association of Real Estate Appraisers
FRICS, Fellow of the Royal Institution of Chartered Royal Institution of Chartered Surveyors, Surveyors (U.K.)
MAI, Member of the Appraisal Institute, Appraisal Institute (USA)
MVA, Market Value Appraiser, Residential, Canadian Real Estate Association
The appendix also lists qualified appraisers.

Chapter 23

Business Valuations

INTRODUCTION

If one or both of you own a business or an interest in a business, the business must be valued for inclusion in the equalization of net family property.

Many people think a business can be valued by reference to the net profit shown on the financial statement. An argument then ensues—should it be six times earnings or eight times earnings. Then you agree on seven times earnings. If this approach does arrive at a reasonably fair value for the business, it is probably a coincidence.

There are many reasons a simple multiple times the profit shown on the financial statement is not a fair indication of the value of a business. For example, the financial statement may include unusual income or expenses that will not recur again. In many privately held businesses, the wages paid to the owner and his family may not be a fair measure of their contribution to the success of the business.

Hire a competent, experienced business valuator to value your business. There are four possible approaches to use in valuing a business.

COMPARISON APPROACH

The fair market value of an asset is what a knowledgeable buyer will pay to a willing vendor. One good way to establish the value of a business is to compare recent sales of similar privately held businesses. There are two reasons this approach is rarely used.

First, it is very difficult to find a recent sale of a business that is similar enough to the business that is being valued.

Second, even if you can find the recent sale of a comparable business, the information regarding income, expenses, and terms and price of sale are usually confidential. With real estate sales, the terms and sale price of a property are available at the registry office that holds the transfer of title. However, this is not true with the sale of a business. A competent business valuator will have accumulated information from experience and will subscribe to a professional service that provides general information regarding sales of businesses.

LIQUIDATION VALUE (ASSET APPROACH)

Another approach to valuing a business is to estimate how much would be realized from the sale or liquidation of each asset separately. You may need other appraisers, for example, a real estate appraiser.

This approach is appropriate only for some businesses. It generally does not recognize the goodwill value of the business as a going concern.

NET INCOME METHOD (INVESTMENT APPROACH)

The value of a business can be established based on a multiple of net income or cash flow. This usually requires making adjustments to the profit shown on the financial statement to arrive at true maintainable net income. Be very careful which multiple you use.

The first step is to examine the gross revenue and establish what portion of it can be expected to continue into the future. Consider the possibility of loss of a few of the largest customers, and the ease with which someone may set up a competing business and take customers away.

Next, review each expense claimed by the business and establish how these expenses can be expected to continue into the future. Consider wages to the owner and his family, promotion, and financing costs.

Third, determine the maintainable pre-tax net income by deducting the adjusted expenses from the expected gross revenue. This gives you a net profit that can be expected from the business if you make no changes in the operations. Don't forecast increased revenue or reduced expenses.

Fourth, consider adjusted historic net incomes over a period of years. Do they represent future operating profit prospects? It is anticipated profits that determine the value.

Remember to consider redundant assets.

Once you have the future maintainable net income, the business valuator establishes the multiple to apply to the net income based on the return that can be obtained on other investments and the amount of risk involved.

SPECIAL CASES

Valuators use rough rules of thumb to value some businesses. For example, the value of a general insurance agency or a public accounting practice often is determined by reference to gross income: in both businesses, the owner can expect his clients to come back every year.

Remember, though, the most important consideration in the valuation of a business is the real net income that can be earned. Rules of thumb should be used with caution.

ADJUSTMENTS

There are many potential adjustments to consider.

1. Is the goodwill of the business based on personal goodwill (such as for a lawyer or a doctor)?
2. Is the goodwill really goodwill of a good location and if so, is the real estate owned or tied up on a long-term lease?
3. Is there a possible special buyer who would be prepared to pay more than the determined value?
4. If the business is not owned 100 percent or controlled more than 50 percent, should there be a reduction for the minority interest?
5. Are there redundant assets, for example, equipment that is no longer efficient?

SUMMARY

Experienced business valuators normally charge by the hour. If the valuation is a simple matter, the cost will not be very high. Find out the valuator's hourly rate, and get a written estimate of the total fee. Make sure all the information he uses is accurate.

FOR A HIGHER VALUE

Provide any information you can get about similar businesses that sold for a high price.

Make sure you can justify any unreported income the business may have had.

Be prepared to justify a low salary from the business so the net profit will be higher.

Tell the the business valuator about any expenses you claimed for income tax purposes that were actually more of a personal nature or not important to business operations.

Tell him about the low risk of loss in the business, and how well the business could carry on with only one owner.

FOR A LOWER VALUE

Provide any information about a similar business that sold for a low price.

Be prepared to justify a high salary for yourself, so the net profit after your salary is lower.

Point out any business expenses that were paid personally, and any business use of personal assets that do not appear on the company's balance sheet.

Point to any indications that you could lose customers or incur major expenses in the future.

Explain why the business could not operate profitably without you.

BUSINESS VALUATORS

Before 1970, most business valuations were completed by trust officers, by estate or divorce lawyers, by corporate investment dealers, or by accountants. In response to the federal capital gains tax in 1971, the Canadian Association of Business Valuators was formed as a federally chartered non-profit professional association consisting of twenty-nine experienced valuators. The organization grew quickly. In the next fifteen years they established a code of ethics, rules of professional conduct, a professional accreditation program, and a program of national conferences and regional workshops.

In 1985 the Canadian Association of Business Valuators became the Canadian Institute of Chartered Business Valuators. The institute is the largest professional business valuation organization in Canada. It trains and certifies individuals in business valuation and litigation support. It continues to develop and update education programs, develop and issue valuation practice standards and force adherence by its members to its code of ethics and practice standards. Through conferences, workshops, and publications, it provides continuing education to its members.

To obtain the designation Chartered Business Valuator (CBV; in French, EEE), an individual must complete a course of studies and meet certain practical experience requirements. A chartered business valuator is an independent trained certified professional who uses a wide variety of methods and techniques to determine the value of a business. A business valuation is a logical, carefully crafted analysis that takes into account all financial management, business, and economic factors, including considered judgement on future earning streams. The valuator must bring broad expertise and good judgement to his work.

As of August 2001 the Canadian Institute of Chartered Business Valuators had 850 members.

For information, contact

Canadian Institute of Chartered Business Valuators,
277 Wellington Street West, 5th Floor,
Toronto, Ontario, M5V 3H2
telephone (416) 204-3396.

The appendix contains a list of chartered business valuators.

Chapter 24

Pension Entitlements and Equalization Entitlements on Bankruptcy

INTRODUCTION

On bankruptcy, do a person's pension plan entitlements enter into the equalization calculation? The Pension Benefits Standards Act (Canada) and the Pension Benefits Act (Ontario) provide that no pension benefit may be assigned, charged, anticipated, or given as security. They are exempt from execution, seizure, and attachment. The acts make it impossible for a bankruptcy trustee to seize or otherwise deal with a bankrupt's pension plan entitlements. Thus a person's pension plan is not affected when he declares bankruptcy. It is an asset that is shareable on marriage breakdown if the bankruptcy occurred before the the separation. Of course, if the separation occurred before the bankruptcy, it could be argued that the debt created by the equalization has been extinguished by the bankruptcy. We will explain this in more detail.

In Ontario, the timing of the bankruptcy, the discharge, and the date of separation can be extremely important. On separation, each party to the marriage is required to value and list his assets and liabilities. The Family Law Act requires the spouse with the higher value of net assets to make an equalization payment equal to half the difference to the spouse with the lower value of net assets. On separation, the equalization requirement creates a liability for one party and an asset for the other.

The act of declaring bankruptcy, and the subsequent discharge therefrom, wipes out all a person's assets and liabilities except for the pension plan and a few other assets.

Some examples will show what happens.

EXAMPLES:

Mr. A has a pension, and his net assets for equalization purposes are higher in value than the net assets of Mrs. A, who has no pension. Mr. A declares bankruptcy, then separates from Mrs. A. The act of declaring bankruptcy wipes out all Mr. A's assets and liabilities except for his pension. His separation from Mrs. A. creates an equalization liability for him and an asset for her. All Mr. A's liabilities were wiped out by the bankruptcy, leaving him with only his pension, and therefore his net assets may be higher. Mrs. A. will be able to recover the equalization payment from Mr. A in this example.

What if Mr. A declares bankruptcy *before* the separation? This could wipe out Mrs. A's equalization right, because Mr. A's liabilities are extinguished on the bankruptcy—before the equalization payment is made.

Let's look at Mrs. A's position in the situation. Mr. A. declares bankruptcy, then separates from Mrs. A. Let's assume Mrs. A also declares bankruptcy before the separation. The equalization payment requirement arises on the date of separation, and Mrs. A has declared bankruptcy before that time. So she should still have her equalization rights.

Now assume Mr. A declares bankruptcy, then later Mr. and Mrs. A. separate. After that, but before the equalization, Mrs. A declares bankruptcy. Mrs. A's right to the equalization payment would pass to her trustee and her creditors.

A good guide to such problems is Robert A. Klotz's *Bankruptcy and Family Law*. As well, read the reported court case of Charlotte Maureen Balyk and Steven Andrew Theodore Balyk.[1] The judge does an excellent job of explaining the relationship between the Family Law Act and the Bankruptcy Act. Justice Wright said:

> The parties separated in March of 1989. These proceedings were initiated in, I believe, February of 1990. The husband made an assignment in bankruptcy on June 29th, 1993. At the present time he is undischarged but his discharge is scheduled for March 29, 1994, a date which is approximately two and one half weeks hence. In effect, there is little property. In effect, the parties, having realized this, have proceeded on the basis that the debts of the husband and his other contingent liabilities, as defined in the *Family Law Act*, equal his other property, and that we should approach the equalization on the basis that the husband has one asset, that is, his pension, and no liabilities, and that the wife has no property or no assets and no liabilities. In effect, the parties say, let us treat the husband's pension as though it were the only asset for equalization purposes and proceed. Doing this, the parties agree that the pension value itself is some $8,300, which, under this scheme, would mean that the wife has an entitlement of $4,150.
>
> What makes this case extremely important for the people of Ontario is the fact that the husband makes two submissions. In the first place, he submits that all proceedings against the bankrupt are stayed by virtue of section 69.4 of the *Bankruptcy Act*, and that until the wife obtains leave of this court sitting in bankruptcy to proceed, her claim against him in this respect is stayed. The second point made by the husband is that the wife has no claim against the husband other than a claim for a simple debt based upon an

amount determined by the process of equalization. As such, she has a claim provable in bankruptcy and that her remedy simply is to make a claim in bankruptcy and take a share of whatever dividends may be declared by the trustee.

The wife submits that she is in the position of a secured creditor and that she is entitled to proceed without reference to the bankruptcy court. She submits that she has an interest in this pension and that she is in the same position as a secured creditor who is entitled to proceed to enforce his or her security without reference to the trustee in bankruptcy. The wife submits that she differs from an ordinary trade creditor in that the ordinary trade creditor cannot look to the pension for payment of the debt owing to it. She submits that in her case, the quantum of the debt is determined with reference to the pension and that the pension is an integral part of the ascertainment of net family property, of its equalization, and, in this case, of its payment.

The wife directs my attention, in particular, to section 9 of the *Family Law Act* and the powers given therein to the court to impose a charge on property for the performance of an obligation imposed by the order awarding an equalization of net family property under the Act.

Where such an order is made prior to the assignment in bankruptcy, I have no doubt that the property affected then passes to the trustee in bankruptcy subject to the charge, and the rights of the claiming spouse are protected. That is not our case. Generally speaking, an issue does not arise with respect to the charging of property after an assignment in bankruptcy because, generally speaking, there is no longer any property in the hands of the husband upon which such a charge might operate. This is an exception to that general rule. In this case we have an item of property which survives the bankruptcy. The wife submits that the interest of the trustee in bankruptcy is unaffected by these proceedings because the trustee had no claim on the pension, it being exempt in any event.

Dealing first of all with the procedural matter. With some trepidation, I accept that the case of *DiMichele v. DiMichele* (1981), 14 A.C.W.S. (2d) 411 [reported at 37 O.R. (2d) 314], a decision of the Ontario High Court under the former *Family Law Reform Act, 1978* still applies. In that case the court held that the leave of the court in bankruptcy to proceed with respect to *Family Law Reform Act, 1978* matters which had been initiated prior to the husband's bankruptcy was unnecessary but that the trustee should be served.

I am prepared to accept, for our purposes today, that it was unnecessary for the wife to obtain leave of the bankruptcy court to continue these proceedings. This, then, brings us to the substantive issue.

The wife also refers me to the case of *Boe v. Boe*, a decision of the Saskatchewan Queen's Bench (1987), 6 R.F.L. (3d) 383. In that case, proceedings under the Saskatchewan *Matrimonial Property Act* had been commenced and had come to judgment, and an award of $100,000 payable in instalments had been made to the wife. The judgment had been directed to be registered against the lands registered in the husband's name to secure payment. Subsequently, before paying the judgment, the husband made an assignment in bankruptcy. In that case it was held that the wife had a proprietary interest in the realty, and to this extent she was cured and the trustee took subject to her security.

I begin with the proposition that the family property regime which has been in effect in Ontario since the implementation of the *Family Law Act* in 1986 is one which is somewhat unique in Canada. Most, if not all, of the other common law provinces of Canada enacted family property legislation which implemented a family assets regime. Ontario led the way with the *Family Law Reform Act* in 1978. Those Acts, generally speaking, provided a class of property said in the case of the Ontario statute to constitute "family assets." Now, as Madam Justice Boland pointed out in *Stoimenov v. Stoimenov* (1982), 40 O.R. (2d) 69 (H.C.), those Acts did not confer upon a non-titled spouse an interest in the asset. What most of these statutes do is confer upon a claimant a right to claim an interest in the asset. What most of these statutes do is confer upon the claimant a right to claim an interest in the asset. Upon adjudication, the court defines the interest of the spouse. In *Re Collins* (1981), 12 A.C.W.S. (2d) 215 [[1982] W.D.F.L. 152], Mr. Justice Steele, in the context of a bankruptcy, pointed out that under a family assets regime, and, in particular, the *Family Law Reform Act* of Ontario, section 4 of that Act gave a right to both spouses in the family assets regardless of whose name the property was registered in. He pointed out that these rights had to be determined before the rights of the trustee in bankruptcy could be determined in the bankruptcy court. He pointed out that the *Family Law Reform Act* provided not only for an equal division of the assets but also provided that the court could make a division in shares that were not equal. Accordingly, it was his opinion that, at the time of the bankruptcy, there was no firm debt owing or any firm determination as to which spouse owned which particular assets. In his opinion, these issues were to be determined by the regular courts before proceedings continued in the bankruptcy court.

Generally speaking, under the family assets regimes in the provinces other than Ontario, the parties remain separate as to property. However, upon the occurrence of certain specified events, one of which invariably is the separation of the parties, certain rights arise. In the case of Saskatchewan, the right was to have either the property divided in specie between the parties or its value divided between the parties. In *Boe*, that in fact had been done, and the value had been divided and the wife's interest secured. It accordingly survived any assignment made by the husband. In *Re Roussel* (1981), 37 C.B.R. (N.S.) 262 (Ont. S.C.), Mr. Justice Hollingworth was faced with a case involving parties who had separated in 1977 and who had been divorced in December of 1978. The matrimonial home, the title to which was in the name of the husband alone, had been sold by the husband's trustee in bankruptcy in February of 1981. The trustee then applied to the court for advice as to the disposition of the proceeds. The court held that the prerequisites of the then section 4(1) of the *Family Law Reform Act, 1978* had been met, that the wife's interests had crystallized prior to the bankruptcy, and that the wife was entitled to 50 per cent of the funds realized upon the sale of that matrimonial home. In

Phillips v. Phillips (1982), 30 R.F.L. (2d) 353 (Ont. Co. Ct.), and, in particular, at page 358, 359, His Honour Judge Mossop, as he then was, distinguished the case of *Re Collins*, to which I have already referred, on the ground that in that in the *Collins's* case, the spouses had separated six months before the assignment in bankruptcy so that there had been, as he called it [at p. 358], a "triggering effect' under section 4, which was lacking in the case before him. My recollection is that in *Phillips* the separation, or the crystallizing event, had occurred subsequent to the assignment in bankruptcy. Another case on point is *Re Radovini* (1981), 22 R.F.L. (2d) 275 (Ont. S.C.), also reported in 37 C.B.R. (N.S.0 264. In that case the matrimonial home was registered in the name of the husband. It was sold and the proceeds were held by the husband's trustee in bankruptcy. The wife argued that the purpose of the *Family Law Reform Act, 1978* was to protect her and that she should be entitled to one half of the proceeds. Now, in that case, the court held that before the wife could take any interest in the matrimonial asset, one of the prerequisites in section 4(1) of the then *Family Law Reform Act, 1978* must exist. In *Radovini*, the parties in fact had not separated. The wife was held to have no inchoate right, pursuant to the *Family Law Reform Act, 1978*, to an interest in the matrimonial home.

The regime implemented by the *Family Law Act* of 1986 was dramatically different from the regime in place under the *Family Law Reform Act, 1978* and continues to be dramatically different to most, if not all, of the family property regimes in the other common law provinces of Canada. The legislature, in its wisdom, chose to abandon a family assets regime and to substitute in its place a regime which made the claimant spouse a simple creditor of the other party. The regime as implemented by the *Family Law Act* simply provides that the net family property of each party is to be determined in accordance with the provisions of that Act, and that subject to specified considerations, the value of the net family property of each party is to be equalized by an award of money from one party to the other. I an mot overlooking the provision already referred to contained in section 9 of the Act, which provides for payment by means of security against assets, and, indeed, for the transfer of assets in specie in realization of the judgment. The fact, however, remains that under the present regime or the existing regime in Ontario, the claiming spouse is simply an unsecured creditor. She or he has, in my opinion, a claim provable under the provisions of the federal *Bankruptcy Act*. While this may seem to be harsh in cases such as this, I cannot torture the law to fit the hard case. It would be a simple matter for the legislature to revert to a family assets regime and it would be an equally simple matter for the federal government to provide an exception for family asset disputes in the *Bankruptcy Act*. Neither has been done. I must apply the law as I perceive it to be.

The arguments by the wife that the pension constitutes a special type of property fails. Notwithstanding that the value of the pension is a factor to be considered in determining the husband's net family property, the pension itself is not exigible, nor is the court in a position to make any meaningful charging order against it. Under the circumstances, I must hold that the wife, while she is a creditor in the amount of $4,150, is left to her remedies in the bankruptcy court to collect that sum. It may be that she may be able to oppose an application for discharge on terms, and she may have other remedies under the *Bankruptcy Act*, but these are not of concern today...

For reasons delivered, judgment against the husband for equalization in the amount of $4,150, declaration that this constitutes a "claim provable in bankruptcy". Husband to pay costs as on a uncontested divorce, being $400, plus those disbursements. Access as agreed.

James G. McLeod and Alfred A. Mamo commented on recent court cases involving bankruptcy and family law in *2000 Annual Review of Family Law*:

A spouse's bankruptcy causes a number of problems in the context of equalization proceedings. Bankruptcy should not be used for the primary purpose of evading a debt owing to a spouse: *Re Richardson* (1998), 41 R.F.L. (4th) 141, 5 C.B.R. (4th) 280 (Ont. Bktcy.) (spousal debt not akin to commercial debt); *Coathup v. Coathup* 2000 CarswellOnt. 247 (bankruptcy not a vehicle to wipe out equalization rights); *Re Kostiuk* 2000 BCSC 400 (B.C.S.C.) (nature of matrimonial property regime relevant). A court may annul a bankruptcy as an abuse of process where a spouse has made himself insolvent by transferring away property in violation of court orders: *Stasiuk v. Stasiuk* (1999), 46 R.F.L. (4th) 382, 9 C.B.R. (4th) 182 (B.S. S.C.) [In Chambers]).

Even if a spouse is discharged from bankruptcy, he or she may retain exempt property against which the other spouse may choose to assert property rights: see *Re Gruending* (1999), 47 R.F.L. (4th) 414, 170 D.L.R. (4th) 541, 6 C.C.L.I. (3d) 1, 8 C.B.R.(4th) 246, 61 C.R.R. (2d) 338, [1999] I.L.R. I-3703, 239 A.R. 201 (Q.B.) with respect to scope of property exemption.

As well, a spouse may try to access property that is not exempt under the *Bankruptcy and Insolvency Act*, R.S.C. 1985, c. B-3, by asserting that the debtor holds the property in whole or in part on trust for her: *Cowger v. Cowger*, [1998] W.D.F.L. 1053 (N.W.T. S.C.).

Whether a person can enforce an equalization entitlement against his or her bankrupt spouse depends on the timing and nature of the property order and whether the bankrupt received an absolute discharge from bankruptcy: *Re Richardson*,[1998] W.D.F.L. 842 (Ont. Gen. Div.). A monetary judgment or entitlement will be discharged by the debtor's bankruptcy, but a property order or transfer prior to the bankruptcy should prevent the property passing to the bankrupt's trustee in bankruptcy: *Godfrey v. Godfrey* (1996), 19 R.F.L. (4th) 58 (Ont. Gen. Div.).

In *Hildebrand v. Hildebrand* (1999), 13 C.B.R. (4th) 226, 140 Man. R. (2d) 316 (Master). Master Harrison reviewed the effect of bankruptcy on a spouse's matrimonial property application and when a spouse should be allowed to continue the application with the Trustee in Bankruptcy as a party.

See also *Bankruptcy and Family Law*, Anne-France Goldwater, January 1998 *Family Law Quarterly*. Also refer to reported court cases.

- *Gough v. Gough* (1996) 92 O.A.C. 384 (Ontario Ct. of Appeal)
- *Blowes v. Blowes* (1993) 49 R.F.L. (3d) 27, 16 O.R. (3d) 318 (Ont. Ct. of Appeal)
- *Re Wale* (1996) File No. 35-063684 (Ont. Ct. Gen. Div.)
- *Re Richardson* (1998) 41 R.F.L. (4th) 141 [Ont. Ct. of Justice, Gen. Div. (In Bankruptcy)]
- *Stiles v. Stiles* (1999) 11 C.B.R. (4th) 315 (Ont. Ct. of Justice, Gen. Div.)

Notes

1   *Balyk v. Balyk* (1994) 3 R.F.L. (4th) 282, 113 D.L.R. (4th) 719.

Chapter 25

Income Tax Considerations

INTRODUCTION

Any income tax allowance deducted in valuing the pension or other assets must be reasonable. You must be able to justify the allowance with tax calculations. Some valuators arbitrarily deduct a tax allowance of 25 percent. In my experience, the rate can vary from 0 percent to 45 percent. The allowance for income tax can substantially affect the values of the assets and the equalization amount. Income tax is also important when you transfer pre-tax assets in an equalization payment.

INCOME TAX ALLOWANCE IN VALUATIONS

Pensions accumulate in the pension fund tax-free until the individual receives payments from the fund. Whether the pension is a defined contribution plan or a defined benefit plan, the income tax allowance must be calculated carefully. First, project the amount of annual pension benefit the individual will receive after he retires. Add his expected Canada Pension Plan and Old Age Security payments. Add income the individual can expect to receive from RRSPs and other income earning assets he has on the date of separation. Include the normal income tax that will be paid, but also any repayment of seniors' benefits.

A fair tax rate can reduce the value of the pension and other assets, such as RRSPs. In one case, a pension had been valued with a 25 percent reduction for income tax; the RRSPs had not been considered or reduced by an income tax allowance. There were $150,000 of RRSPs at the date of separation. I claimed an income tax allowance of 35 percent, thereby reducing the value of the pension by $10,000 and reducing the value of the RRSPs by $52,500.

If you retire before you separate and have started receiving pension payments, include the actual tax you are paying on the pension.

To calculate the income tax allowance to deduct from the survivor benefit, use the expected tax rate of the survivor, not the tax rate of the member.

INCOME TAX CONSIDERATIONS IN THE EQUALIZATION PROCESS

When you have agreed on the value of every asset and the amount of all liabilities, deductions, and exemptions, you can deduce the amount owing from one spouse to the other (the "equalization amount"). Then you must decide how this equalization amount will be paid. If you decide on a transfer of assets, remember they are subject to income tax.

Assets such as a pensions, RRSPs, real estate, or businesses have been valued in the Net Family Property statement after deducting an allowance for income tax. The person who receives an asset in the equalization settlement takes over the asset and the income tax consequences. With careful planning, these taxes can be deferred, reduced, or possibly avoided.

If a pension is being split at source under the Pension Benefits Division Act or the Pension Benefits Standards Act, consider that the after-tax value, used in determining the equalization amount, is arrived at by applying the estimated future tax rate of the payer. However, the tax rate of the recipient may be quite different. Which tax rate should be used in determining the gross amount to transfer?

If the equalization settlement is being achieved by transferring all or part of an RRSP, there should be no problem calculating the gross amount to transfer .The Income Tax Act allows for inter-spousal transfers tax free. The main consideration is any difference in future tax rates of the two parties.

If a business is one of the assets owned by one or both of the separating spouses, there may be special tax considerations and opportunities. Here is an example:

Mr. and Mrs. Jones decided to separate. Their only asset was a business that had an agreed value of $1,000,000 before income tax allowance. Mr. Jones would own and carry on the business, and Mrs. Jones would receive $500,000 less income taxes. There was cash available in the business, so Mr. Jones offered to have the company pay him a $500,000 bonus, from which he would deduct and remit $250,000 income tax. He would pay the $250,000 left to Mrs. Jones.

The tax consultant for Mrs. Jones suggested that Mrs. Jones incorporate her own company. The existing company could transfer $500,000 to Mrs. Jones's new company. Mr. Jones was left owning the old company minus $500,000 (as it would have been if his suggestion had been followed). Mrs. Jones was left with a companythat had $500,000 to invest, rather than $250,000. (This worked only because Mr. and Mrs. Jones were not divorced.)

Thre was not a tax *saving* of $250,000, but a tax deferral. Mrs. Jones could invest and earn income on an additional $250,000 until the deferred tax had to be paid.

If a portion of a pension is used to settle an equalization amount using an "If and When" agreement or court order, make sure each party pays the tax on the amount he receives. The pension administrator should issue a separate cheque and T-5 tax slip to each party.

Section 5 (1) of the Ontario Family Law Act says,

> When a divorce is granted or a marriage is declared
> a nullity, or when the spouses are separated and

> there is no reasonable prospect that they will resume cohabitation, the spouse whose net family property is the lesser of the two net family properties is entitled to one-half the difference between them.

The courts have established that the value of assets in the Net Family Property statement (NFP) is the value after income taxes. After the equalization amount has been paid, both parties should end up with the same NFP after taxes.

If the equalization amount is being satisfied with pre-tax assets, should the net amount be grossed up based on the tax rate of the person making the transfer? Or should you consider the tax rate of the person receiving the asset? The tax rate of both parties must be considered.

Assume Mr. A has net assets with a pre-tax value of $100,000 and qualifies for a tax rate of 50 percent. His NFP is $50,000. Assume Mrs. A has no NFP but qualifies for a tax rate of 25 percent. The equalization amount becomes $50,000. If the equalization is being settled by after-tax assets, you would transfer $25,000 in assets from Mr. A to Mrs. A. They both end up with NFP of $25,000 (see Exhibit 1).

Exhibit 1
Calculation and Settlement of Equalization Amount with After-Tax Assets

	Mr. A	Mrs. A
Pre-tax Value	$100, 000	0
Tax rate	50%	25%
Tax	$50, 000	0
NFP	$50, 000	0
Transfer	($25, 000)	$25, 000
NFP after transfer	$25, 000	$25, 000

If the equalization amount of $50,000 is being satisfied by a transfer of before-tax assets, should Mr. A transfer half his $100,000 of pre-tax value to Mrs. A, as shown in Exhibit 2? Since Mr. A is in a 50 percent tax bracket, this would leave him with $25,000 of NFP after the transfer. Mrs. A is in a 25 percent tax bracket; she has NFP after the transfer of $37,500. Obviously, this does not satisfy the requirements of the Ontario Family Law Act. They should both end up with the same after-tax NFP.

EXHIBIT 2
Calculation and Settlement of
Equalization Amount with Before-Tax Assets

	Mr. A	Mrs. A
Pre-tax Value	$100, 000	0
Tax rate	50%	25%
Tax	$50, 000	0
NFP	$50, 000	0
Transfer	($50, 000)	$50, 000
Pre-tax value after transfer	$50, 000	$50, 000
Tax	$25, 000	$12, 500
NFP after transfer	$25, 000	$37, 500

Exhibit 3 shows the proper amount to transfer—$40,000 of pre-tax assets—so both parties end up with $30,000 of NFP.

EXHIBIT 3
Proper Calculation and Settlement of
Equalization Amount with Before-Tax Assets

	Mr. A	Mrs. A
Pre-tax Value	$100, 000	0
Tax rate	50%	25%
Tax	$50, 000	0
NFP	$50, 000	0
Transfer	($40, 000)	$40, 000
Pre-tax value after transfer	$60, 000	$40, 000
Tax	$30, 000	$10, 000
NFP after transfer	$30, 000	$30, 000

If the two parties are in different tax brackets, consider taxes when you establish the amount of pre-tax assets to be transferred to satisfy the equalization payment. Don't gross up the equalization amount based on the tax rate of one of the parties only.

The formula to determine the amount to transfer is:

$$\frac{1 - A}{2 - A - B} \ X \ C = \text{pre-tax amount to transfer}$$

Where

A = the tax rate of the person paying the equalization payment.

B = the tax rate of the person receiving the equalization payment.

C = the difference in NFP of the two parties[1]

COMMON MISTAKES

If income taxes are to be kept to a minimum, care must be taken to adhere strictly to the provisions of the Income Tax Act. The following are mistakes that often are made:

1. Assuming that capital gains on transferred property will automatically be attributed to the new owner.

    This does not happen automatically, and may not always happen. For the gain to be attributed, the parties must:

    (a) be living separate and apart by reason of marriage breakdown,

    (b) have not resumed cohabitation within the same year,

    (c) sign and file an election form

2. Assuming that child support payments are always taxable to the recipient and deductible for the payor.

    Child support paid pursuant to an agreement after May 1, 1997, is not taxable/deductible.

    Child support paid pursuant to an agreement entered into before May 1, 1997, will not be taxable/deductible if the amount varied after May 1, 1997.

3. Assuming that all payments to third parties will be taxable/deductible.

    Third-party payments for a child are deductible only if they are pursuant to an agreement made before May 1, 1997.

    Third-party payments for a child are only deductible if the agreement or order clearly identifies the payment as being for the sole benefit of the spouse, and not for the child or children).

4. Assuming that any gain on the sale of a principal residence will not be taxable.

This is generally true when the family owns only one dwelling. If you have a cottage or other second dwelling, make sure you and your spouse agree which dwelling you will designate as your principal residence during the time you lived together.

5. Assuming that prepaid of spousal support is taxable/deductible.

To be taxable/deductible, support must be periodic. Prepaid support may be construed to be lump sum support and will not get the same treatment for tax purposes.

6. Assuming an RRSP can be pledged as security for support payments.

An RRSP cannot be pledged as security for anything.

7. Assuming that spousal support paid by an estate get the same tax treatment as spousal support paid personally.

Support payments paid by an estate do not meet the definition of "support amount" under the Income Tax Act. Such payments are not taxable to the recipient and are not deductible by the estate.

8. Assuming that the application of the income tax rules can be modified if specified in a court order or written agreement.

Income tax rules cannot be altered by an order or agreement.

SUMMARY

It may be worthwhile to retain an income tax consultant to maximize the tax allowance or to ensure all possible tax savings or tax deferrals are achieved in connection with the equalization settlement, especially if large amounts are involved. The costs of obtaining the advice may be saved many times over.

Notes

1   Developed by Kim Maika, Pension Valuator.

Chapter 26

Common Law and Same Sex Couples

One of the most interesting and oft quoted cases dealing with the sharing of assets on the breakdown of a common law relationship is the case of *Becker v. Pettkus.*[1]

The breakdown happened in 1974, after a relationship of almost twenty years. The final decision by the Supreme Court of Canada was rendered in 1980. Mr. Pettkus and Miss Becker came to Canada from central Europe separately as immigrants in 1954. He had $17 upon arrival. They met in Montreal in 1955. Shortly thereafter, Mr. Pettkus moved in with Miss Becker, on her invitation. She was thirty years old; he was twenty-five. He was earning $75 per week; she was earning between $25 and $28 per week, which later increased to $67 per week.

A short time after they began living together, Miss Becker expressed the desire that they be married. Mr. Pettkus replied that he might consider marriage after they knew each other better. Thereafter, the question of marriage was not raised, though within a few years Mr. Pettkus began to introduce Miss Becker as his wife and to claim her as such for income tax purposes.

From 1955 to 1960 both parties worked for others. Mr. Pettkus supplemented his income by repairing and restoring motor vehicles. Ms. Becker paid the rent. She bought the food and clothing and looked after other living expenses. Mr. Pettkus saved his entire income, which he regularly deposited in a bank account in his name. There was no agreement at any time to share either moneys or property placed in his name. The parties lived frugally. Due to their husbandry and parsimonious life-style, by 1960 $12,000 had been saved and deposited in Mr. Pettkus's bank account.

The two travelled to western Canada in June 1960. Expenses were shared. One reason for the trip was to locate a suitable farm on which to start a beekeeping business. They spent some time working at a beekeeper's farm.

They returned to Montreal in the early autumn of 1960. Miss Becker continued to pay the rent until October 1960. From then until May 1961, Mr. Pettkus paid rent and household expenses, as Miss Becker was jobless. In April 1961 she fell sick and required hospitalization.

In April 1961 they decided to buy a farm at Franklin Centre, Quebec, for $5,000. The purchase money came out of the bank account of Mr. Pettkus. Title was taken in his name. The floor and roof of the farmhouse were in need of repair. Miss Becker used her money to purchase flooring materials, and she assisted in laying the floor and installing a bathroom.

For about six months during 1961, Miss Becker received unemployment insurance cheques; the proceeds were used to defray household expenses. Through two successive winters, she lived in Montreal and earned approximately $100 per month as a baby-sitter. These earnings also went toward household expenses.

After purchasing the farm at Franklin Centre the parties established a beekeeping business. Both worked in the business, making frames for the hives, moving the bees to the orchards of neighbouring farmers in the spring, checking the hives during the summer, bringing in the frames for honey extraction during July and August and the bees for winter storage in autumn. Mr. Pettkus handled receipts from sales of honey; payments for purchases of beehives and equipment were made from his bank account.

The physical participation by Miss Becker in the bee operation continued over a period of about fourteen years. She ran the extracting process. For a time, she also raised a few chickens, pheasants, and geese. In 1968 and later years, they hired others to assist in moving the bees and bringing in the honey. Most of the honey was sold to wholesalers, though Miss Becker sold some door to door.

In August 1971, with a view to expanding the business, a vacant property was purchased in East Hawkesbury, Ontario, at a price of $1,300. The purchase moneys were derived from the Franklin Centre honey operation. Funds to complete the purchase were withdrawn from the bank account of Mr. Pettkus. Title to the newly acquired property was taken in his name.

In 1973 a third property was purchased, in West Hawkesbury, Ontario, in the name of Mr. Pettkus. The price was $5,500. The purchase moneys came from the Franklin Centre operation, together with $1,900 contributed by Miss Becker. The year 1973 was a prosperous one, yielding some 65,000 pounds of honey, producing net revenues in excess of $30,000.

In the early 1970s the relationship began to deteriorate. In 1972 Miss Becker left Mr. Pettkus, allegedly because of mistreatment. She was away for three months. Before she left, Mr. Pettkus threw $3,000 on the floor; he told her to take the money, a 1966 Volkswagen, and forty beehives containing bees, and "get lost." The beehives represented less than 10 percent of the total number of hives in the business.

Soon thereafter Mr. Pettkus asked Miss Becker to return. In January 1973 she agreed, on condition he see a marriage counsellor, make a will in her favour, and provide her with $500 per year so long as she stayed with him. It was also agreed that Mr. Pettkus would establish a joint bank account for household expenses, in which receipts from retail sales of honey would be deposited. Miss Becker returned; she brought back the car and $1,900 remaining out of the $3,000 she had received. The $1,900 was deposited in Mr. Pettkus's account. She also brought the forty beehives, but the bees had died.

In February 1974 they moved into a house on the West Hawkesbury property, built in part by them and in part by contractors. The money needed for construction came from the honey business, with minimal purchases of materials by Miss Becker.

The relationship continued to deteriorate. On October 4, 1974, Miss Becker again left, this time permanently, after an incident in which she alleged she had been beaten and otherwise abused. She took the car and approximately $2,600 in cash from honey sales.

At trial Miss Becker was awarded forty beehives, without bees, together with $1,500, representing earnings from those hives for 1973 and 1974.

The Ontario Court of Appeal varied the judgement at trial by awarding Miss Becker a half interest in the lands owned by Mr. Pettkus and in the beekeeping business. The Supreme Court of Canada upheld the appeal court decision.

Having won the judgement, worth about $150,000, Miss Becker spent several years trying to collect, without much success. After years of delays and costs, Miss Becker gave up. On November 5, 1987, she put a rifle to her head and killed herself.

In making their decision in *Becker v. Pettkus* the Supreme Court of Canada solidified the theory of constructive trust. They determined that the contribution of money and labour by Ms. Becker to the beehive business allowed Mr. Pettkus to acquire the property he held in his name. The question will always be whether the contribution of one party was significant enough that it allowed the other party to acquire property. This is sometimes referred to as the principle of "unjust enrichment." Justice McLachlin explained the principle in *Peter v. Beblow*[2] when he said,

> I share the view of Cory J., that the three elements
> necessary to establish a claim for unjust enrichment
> – an enrichment, a corresponding deprivation, and
> the absence of any juristic reason for the enrichment
> – are made out in this case. The appellant's house-

keeping and child-care services constituted a benefit to the respondent (1st element), in that he received household services without compensation, which in turn enhanced his ability to pay off his mortgage and other assets. These services also constituted a corresponding detriment to the appellant (2nd element), in that she provided services without compensation. Finally, since there was no obligation existing between the parties which would justify the unjust enrichment and no other arguments under this broad heading were met, there is no juristic reason for the enrichment (3rd element). Having met the three criteria, the plaintiff has established an unjust enrichment giving rise to restitution.

Establishing a constructive trust in the assets means that one party is holding assets in trust for the two of them. The second party still has the problem of trying to realize his share of the assets. The principles of unjust enrichment and constructive trust also apply to a same sex couple.

There are, of course, many cases where two people live together in a common law relationship, get married, and then their marriage breaks down. The principles of unjust enrichment and constructive trust could apply. Unjust enrichment is not easy to prove. Some people have argued that the pre-marriage period should be added to the marriage period to determine the value of the assets subject to equalization. Case law seems to be inconsistent; some lawyers resort to the unjust enrichment and constructive trust argument in an attempt to include the pre-marriage period.

In the case of *Debora v. Debora*,[3] the parties were married in a religious ceremony that did not comply with the formal requirements of the marriage act. They lived together from April 3, 1987, to July 20, 1994, when they were legally married. The Ontario

Court of Appeal decided that, based on the facts of the case, the pre-marriage period should not be included.

In the case of *MacNeill v. Pope*,[4] the parties lived together for sixteen years but were legally married for less than five of those years. The Ontario Court of Appeal decided that, on the facts of the case, the pre-marriage period should be included. The only way to be certain assets acquired during a common law relationship will be shared on the breakdown of that relationship is to have a legal written agreement, entered into before the relationship starts. However, this may change because of the decision in *Walsh v. Bona*.[5] Susan Walsh and Wayne Bona cohabited in a common law relationship for approximately ten years. Upon separation Ms. Walsh applied for a division of the assets acquired during the relationship. The definition of spouse in the Nova Scotia Matrimonial Property Act did not include common law spouses, and Ms. Walsh argued that this constituted discrimination in violation of section 15(1) of the Charter of Rights. It was determined that Ms. Walsh was right, and it was ordered that the Matrimonial Property Act be amended.

In another case, after dating for a couple of years, a woman and her boyfriend moved in together. They were both attending university and soon realized their tuition fees and living expenses were more than they could handle. They decided the woman would cut back on her course load, work more hours, and support them both while the man focused on his studies. When he completed university, he would get a full time job and the woman would quit her job and get a master's degree while the man supported them both. It didn't work out that way, of course. By the time the man graduated, the woman had been supporting them for nearly two years. It was time to start planning her return to university. That was when the man told her he could not afford to return the favour. He was working full time, but he was not going to pay for her living expenses while she got another degree.

In his book *Surviving Your Divorce*, Michael Cochrane describes a case:

Yolanda Ballard was another case involving common law spouses. She and Harold Ballard, the owner of the Toronto Maple Leafs and Maple Leaf Gardens, began living together in about 1984. They never married but she spent most of her time with him and eventually changed her last name to Ballard.

In April, 1990 Ballard died, leaving Yolanda $50,000 a year for the rest of her life. This she considered inadequate given the fact that she was his common-law spouse and had become accustomed to a higher standard of living than could be attained on $50,000 a year. She applied to the court for an interim support order of $16,050 per month. Her projected expenses included such things as $75,000 a year for clothes, $15,000 for pet care and $60,000 for vacations. Two questions arose: Was she a common-law spouse? And what did that entitle her to?

On October 2, 1990, the court awarded Yolanda Ballard interim support of $7,000 per month retroactive to April 11, 1990 to run for 6 months. She received, therefore, approximately $91,000 in support pending the final outcome of her case. She sought, incidentally, a final order of support in the amount of $381,000 per year – 7 times what Harold Ballard had in mind.[6]

SUPPORT

Seven Canadian jurisdictions have defined "spouse" in such a way as to extend an entitlement to or pay support at the end of a common-law union. Alberta, Quebec, P.E.I. and the Northwest Territories do not extend support rights and obligations to common-law spouses.

All other Canadian jurisdictions do in one form or another. Briefly, the variations are as follows:

Jurisdiction	Criteria for Common-Law Spouse
AB, QC	no common-law spouse entitlement to support
PE, NT, BC	2 years of cohabitation
MB	5 years of cohabitation and substantial dependence or 1 year of cohabitation and a child
NB	3 years of cohabitation and substantial dependence
NF	1 year of cohabitation and a child
NS	1 year of cohabitation
ON	3 years of cohabitation, or child and a relationship of some permanence
SK	3 years of cohabitation, or child and a relationship of some permanence
YK	a relationship of some permanence

When examining a common-law relationship the court asks these questions:

- Did the partners share accommodations?
- Did one render domestic services to the other?
- Was there any sharing of household expenses?
- Was there sexual intimacy between them?
- Are they of the opposite sex?
- What was the nature of their relationship?
- Were they husband and wife for all intents and purposes?

The courts have found that where there has been a relationship of such significance that it has led to the dependency of one party on another or the expectation that one will support the other in the event of financial crisis, an entitlement to support arises where there is a case of need.

The amount of the support and its duration is calculated in the same way that it is calculated for legally married spouses who separate. Aspects that can make these cases different include the length of the relationship and the court's willingness to put time limits on support orders.

In many jurisdictions the obligation to support a common law spouse might also apply with respect to an estate. If a person dies leaving a common law spouse as his survivor, the spouse may be able to obtain an order of support from the estate. This was the case with Yolanda Ballard who wanted to be considered a spouse within the meaning of Ontario's *Succession Law Reform Act*.

CHILD SUPPORT

Common law couples are subject to the child support guidelines when they separate.

PROPERTY

In Nova Scotia in 2000, a woman who was entitled to nothing after years of cohabitation challenged the court decision. She argued that denying common law partners the property rights available to married spouses was unconstitutional. The court agreed. In Nova Scotia, common law spouses have the same property rights as legally married spouses. This is the only province where that is true.

In all other provinces and territories, the matrimonial property laws deal only with married couples. Common law spouses have no statutory property rights. It doesn't matter how long they have lived together; if they do not marry, the only property to which they are entitled when they leave is their own property. This, of course, raises a problem. The courts have developed some general guidelines over the years to help couples sort out property division matters.

- In the absence of an intention to the contrary, each person may leave the relationship with any assets he brought in and any acquired in his name alone during the relationship.
- The court will not allow one person to be "unjustly enriched" at the other person's expense.
- Where one of the persons confers a benefit on the other person and suffers a corresponding deprivation as a result, and where there is no other legal reason or justification for the enrichment, the court will correct the situation by using a device called a "constructive trust." A constructive trust is simply a fancy legal way of saying to the spouse who has the property in his name—the spouse who has title—"You are holding that property or part of its value in trust for your partner." The court orders the part held in trust to be paid over to the other person. In the Rosa Becker case,. Mr. Pettkus was found to be holding part of his beekeeping operation's value in trust for Rosa. The value of the part held was the amount of the judgement.
- Each case is different. The size of an interest in a piece of property will depend on the facts of the particular case.
- A contribution does not automatically entitle a person to a half interest. The court will determine what is a fair return on the contribution.
- The court prefers a direct connection between the contribution and the property in question. It does not necessarily

have to be a contribution directly to the acquisition of the property. It could be some act that preserved the property, maintained it, or improved it.

- Being a supportive good partner or paying some household expenses will not necessarily entitle you to a share of a property. Remember, one partner must be unjustly enriched at the other's expense. The case law is evolving on this point.

- In some cases, home, child-care, and housekeeping services were considered "contributions," since the spouse who cared for the child or did the house duties freed the other spouse to earn and acquire property.

- The court will consider the intention of each person but does not insist that both have an intention. It will consider what each person reasonably expected to happen and what interest in the property they reasonably expected.

- If the property in one spouse's name was a gift from the other spouse, the court will not correct the situation. One cannot be unjustly enriched by a gift.

PENSIONS

All pension plans provide a death benefit payable if a the member dies before he retires. Many also provide a continuing lifetime pension to a non-member spouse who survives the retired member. Does a common law spouse qualify? See Chapter Twenty-Six.

You are entitled to survivor's benefits from Old Age Security and Canada Pension Plan if your common law spouse dies, just as you are if your husband or wife dies, and you may have to split your CPP pension credits if you end a common law relationship, just as you would if you divorced. Author Michael Cochrane explains:

Everyone acquires Canada Pension plan benefits over their working life. The Canada Pension Act provides that persons of the opposite sex who had been living together for at least one year and who have been separated for more than a year may apply to the Minister for a division of pension credits. So where a working spouse acquires credits, the other spouse may apply to share them. An application must be accompanied by the "necessary papers" of course! Birth certificate, Social Insurance Number, addresses (current and at cohabitation), relevant dates of cohabitation and separation and, for some reason, the reason for the separation.[7]

SUMMARY

The rights of common law and same sex couples are not the same as married couples when the relationship breaks down.

Notes

1   (1978) 5 R.F.L. (ed) 344, 20 O.R. (2d) 105, 87 (3d) 101 and (1980) 19 R.F.L. (2d) 165, 2 S.C.R. 834, 117 D.L.R. (3d) 257.
2   (1993) 44 R.F.L. (3d) 329 (S.C.C.).
3   (1999) CarswellOnt 5, 167 D.L.R. (4th) 759, 116 O.A.C. 196, 43 R.F.L. (4th) 179.
4   (1999) CarswellOnt 253, 43 R.F.L. (4th) 209, (sub nom. Pope v. Pope) 170 D.L.R. (4th) 89, (sub nom. Pope v. Pope) 117, O.A.C. 275, (sub nom Pope v. Pope) 42 O.R. (3d) 514.

5 (2000) CarswellNS 112, 2000NSCA 53, 5 R.F.L. (5th) 188, 186 D.L.R. (4TH) 50, 183 N.S.R. (2d) 74, 568 A.P.R. 74.

6 *Surviving Your Divorce*, by Michael Cochrane, page 138.

7 *Surviving Your Divorce*, by Michael Cochrane, page 145.

Chapter 27

Pre-Judgement Interest on Equalization Payments of Pension Plan Entitlements

When the major asset is a pension entitlement, the awarding of pre-judgement interest by the courts has been somewhat irregular. A pattern can be gleaned from the cases. This chapter includes comments from knowledgeable people and conclusions that may help you assess your chances of an award.

In the 1992 *Annual Review of Family Law*,[1] James G. McLeod and Alfred A. Mamo wrote:

> As a general rule, the courts have awarded pre-judgment interest on the equalization entitlement where the recipient has been deprived of the use of her money, and the payer has received some benefit or retained some benefit by not paying over the funds: see *Keelan v. Keelan* (March 22, 1991), Doc. No. London 35/38/06620/89 (Ont. Gen. Div.). Where, however, the payer has received no benefit from the funds and has not unreasonably withheld payment, pre-judgment interest may be denied. As well, in cases where had the property award been received, no support would have been payable, pre-judgment interest may be denied if support was in fact paid voluntarily or pursuant to court order during the interim between the time the cause of action arose and the time the property order was made: see *Black v.*

Black (1988), 66 O.R. (2d) 643, 31 E.T.R. 188, 18 R.F.L. (3d) 303 (H.C.).

In *Christian v. Christian*, [(1991), 37 R.F.L. (3d) 26 (Ont. Gen. Div.)] *(Citation added)*, Sutherland J. held that a spouse should be entitled to pre-judgment interest on the equalization entitlement from the date the cause of action arose. If the parties separated before the Family Law Act came into force, the interest should only run from the date of the Act. Prior to that date there was no right to the equalization entitlement and therefore, no cause of action. It seems following *Starkman v. Starkman* (1990), 75 O.R. (2d) 19, 28 R.F.L. (3d) 208, 73 D.L.R. (4th) 746, 43 O.A.C. 85, and the later cases, that pre-judgment interest will be awarded as a matter of course. The onus seems to be on the spouse opposing it to show why it should not be granted. The thrust of the recent cases seems to be reimbursing the claimant for the loss of the money, not forcing the payer to disgorge the benefit retained by non-payment. On this basis it is likely that the only way to avoid the payment is to show that the money was offered and refused or that other payments were made, as by support or payment on debts, that would not have been required if the money had been paid promptly.

In *Pelman v. Pelman* (July 25, 1991) Doc. No. ND 17117/90 (Ont. Gen. Div.), additional reasons at (September 18, 1991), doc. No. ND 17117/90 (Ont. Gen. Div.), Hamilton J. followed the normal rule and awarded pre-judgment interest at the appropriate rate on the equalization payment. On the other hand, in *Balloch v. Balloch*, supra, Greer declined to order pre-judgment interest. It is clear that Greer J. viewed pre-judgment interest as a penalty and the husband had not acted spitefully in delaying payment, and should not be penalized. If pre-judgment interest is treated as a penalty for failure to act reasonably, it will not be awarded if the payer had reasonable ground to dispute the obligation. Even on this basis it will be rare that a payer can deny all liability. Usually, what is in dispute is the quantum. The payer would be wise to pay what he or she feels is owed and dispute the rest in order to avoid pre-judgment interest: see the court's willingness to apportion pre-judgment interest in *Reeson v. Kowalik* (November 27, 1991), Doc. Nos. 42801/89, F.L. 1165/89 (Ont. Gen. Div.). Of course, in doing so, much of the bargaining leverage is lost. Is this perhaps exactly what Greer J. was trying to avoid? In the end, however, it seems that the cases do not grant or withhold pre-judgment interest as a penalty. Most cases concentrate on loss of investment funds by the payee or benefit by overholding by the payer. On balance, the former seems preferable. It encourages the payer to pay regardless of whether there is gain. In Starkman, the Court of Appeal did not indicate a penalty or an improper gain as the rationale. It seemed that the interest was awarded to compensate the payee for the loss of funds and the accompanying investment income or use, but contrast *Da Costa v. Da Costa* (1992) 7 O.R. (3d) 321, 89, D.L.R. (4ᵀᴴ) 268 (C.A.) amended (June 11, 1992), doc. No. CA 776/90 (C.A.) re supplying support and advance payments.

Although the point is not altogether free from doubt, it is suggested that the better view is that pre-judgment interest should be awarded in the ordinary course to compensate the payee for the use of his or her money. If he or she had had the money, it could have been invested at an appropriate interest rate or used for a specified end. The non-payment has deprived the payee of the use of his or her money. In many cases, the payer will have had the use of the money past the due date and may have acquired some benefit from the use of the money. If the payee has acted unreasonably in delaying proceeding it may be appropriate to deny pre-judgment interest in whole or in part on the basis that he or she is the cause of his or her own misfortune. Where the amount was reasonably in dispute and the payer did not earn interest on the money, a court may to tempted to deny interest. However, even then, the payee is out the use of the money and the payer has not had to borrow money to make the payment. While pre-judgment interest is discretionary, the discretion should be exercised on consistent principles; *Christian v. Christian*, supra; *De Mornay v. De Mornay*, supra; *Finlayson v. Finlayson* (November 12, 1991), Doc. No. Guelph 7379/88 (Ont. Gen. Div.); *Reynolds v. Reynolds*, [(Oct. 28, 1991). Doc. No. Kitchener 792/85 (Ont. Gen. Div.). Additional reasons at (Dec. 23, 1991). Doc. No. Kitchener 792/85 (Ont. Gen. Div.)](*Citation added*).

However, in *McQuay v. McQuay* (1992), 80 O.R. (3d) 111, 89 D.L.R. (4th) 40 (Div. Ct.), the Ontario Divisional Court apparently held that pre-judgment interest should not be awarded if the payer has acted reasonably and has not gained income from retention of funds. The thrust of the reasons seems to be disgorgement of benefit and not compensation for lost opportunity. See also *Lefevre v. Lefevre* (May 6,

1992), Doc. No. ND 162487/89 (Ont. Gen. Div.), to
the same effect.

In *Randolph v. Randolph* (1991), 34 R.F.L. (3D)
444 (Ont. Gen. Div.), Byers J. ordered that the equalization payment of $40,000 should be made in ten
equal annual instalments of $4,000 with no interest
unless payments were not made on the annual date.
With respect, it is difficult to see why the recipient
should not have been entitled to post-judgment interest even if no pre-judgment interest were awarded.
While inability to pay is an appropriate consideration
on support applications, it should not be an appropriate consideration on property applications.

While the inability to pay or difficulty in payment
may justify a court in extending payment through
instalments, it should not change the general
debtor/creditor rules whereby a creditor is entitled at
least to post-judgment interest. It is pointed out in
Fogel v. Fogel (1979), 24 O.R. (2d) 158 9, F.F.L. (2d) 55
(C.A.), that support is support and property is property. The considerations from one should not necessarily affect the determination in the other.

In *Berdette v. Berdette* (1991) 3, O.R. (3d) 513,
41 E.T.R. 126, 33 R.F.L. (3d) 113, 81 D.L.R. (4th)
194, 47 O.A.C. 345 (C.A.), leave to appeal to S.C.C.
refused (1991), 85 D.L.R. (4th) viii (note) (S.C.C.),
the Ontario Court of Appeal confirmed that equalization proceedings involved debtor and creditor
rights. The court applied strict property law and did
not view the legislation as allowing a court to dis-
pense palm tree justice. In awarding costs against
the wife, the court confirmed that they would not
simply do what seemed fair. The court should apply

the strict rules of law and let the chips fall where they may, but, see the special case of bankruptcy where a person should not recover more than his or her claim proved in bankruptcy in any event; *Royal Bank v. King*, [(1991) 35 R.F.L. (3d) 325, 82 D.L.R. (4th) 225 (Ont. Gen. Div.)] *(Citation added)*. On this basis, the creditor should be entitled to post-judgment interest. Just because it does not seem fair should not be sufficient to deny interest.

The income tax treatment of a pre-judgment interest award as part of an equalization judgment has as yet not been adjudicated on. It is suggested that there is no provision in law which would allow such interest to be "deductible", but that the award constitutes income in the hands of the payee and the funds would therefore attract tax at the recipient's marginal rate.

The difference in the cost to the payer and the net benefit to the payee can therefore be very significant depending on the respective tax brackets of the parties, the amount of the payment and the interest rates involved. In most cases the only real "winner" will be Revenue Canada, since the payer pays income tax on the funds when she first earns the money and then the same funds are taxed again once received by the payee.

In 1993, McLeod and Mamo wrote:

Interest on Award
Where the payment of the equalization entitlement is deferred under s. 9 of the Family Law Act, the payee is entitled to post-judgment interest unless the court orders otherwise. Since property awards are not

derived by the ability to pay, there seems no reason to deny post-judgment interest. A debt is a debt. In fact, the debtor receives a benefit not available to most debtors through the courts ability to minimize the hardship under s. 9 of the Family Law Act.

Pre-judgment interest may also be awarded on the equalization payment. The current position seems to be that pre-judgment interest will not be awarded to compensate for loss of investment capital but to disgorge benefits received on the money by the payer to discourage unreasonable delay by the payer: *Delean v. Delean*, (1992) W.D.F.L. 1405 (Ont. Gen. Div.).

In 1994 they wrote:

A court may award pre-judgment interest pursuant to the Courts of Justice Act on the equalization entitlement: s. 128, 130. Generally, the interest is awarded to deal with delay by the debtor or profit earned by the debtor on the entitlement: *McDonald v. McDonald*, (1994) W.D.F.L. 1345 (Ont. Gen. Div.) (no pre-judgment interest on portion of equalization entitlement representing home and cottage which was not available to pay entitlement and did not earn income).

In *Taylor v. Taylor*, (1994) W.D.F.L. 1234 (Ont. Gen. Div.), Kerr J. held that there was no valid reason for refusing to award pre-judgment interest on the equalization payment due to the wife because the matrimonial assets produced income which was not used for her support; see also *Khoury v. Khoury*, [(1994) CarswellNB 224, 149 N.B.R. (2d) 1, 381 A.P.R. 1] (*Citation added*) (pre-judgment interest ordered where husband had use of income earning assets); *Rostek v. Rostek*, supra (wife entitled to pre-judgment interest on equalization payment where husband paid nothing to wife since separation but disposed of $233,000 of assets after separation); *Zander v. Zander*, [(1996) 8 R.F.L. (4th) 35 (Ont. Gen. Div.)] (*Citation added*) (wife awarded pre-judgment interest where husband had assets available with which he could have paid equalization entitlement).

The Court confirmed that different principles apply in family law cases than in commercial cases: *McQuay v. McQuay* (1992) 34 R.F.L. (3d) 184 (Ont. Div. Ct.). In particular, a court may decline to award pre-judgment interest if the payor could not realize on the asset giving rise to the equalization payment and the payor had not delayed the case being brought to trial. Such would usually be the case if the main asset was the family home or a pension. In *Burgess v. Burgess* (1995) 24, O.R. (3d) 547 (Ont. C.A.), the Ontario Court of Appeal reviewed the law on awarding pre-judgment interest on an equalization entitlement and held that as a general rule, a payor spouse is required to pay pre-judgment interest on an equalization payment owing to a payee spouse in order to encourage timely settlement. In *Burgess* the Court confirmed its earlier comments in *Mollicone v. Mollicone* (1994), 9 R.F.L. (4th) 155 (Ont. C.A.) that it should deny pre-judgment interest where the major asset was a pension which, while increasing in value, did not generate funds available to pay the equalization entitlement.

A judge may depart from the pre-judgment interest percentage fixed under the Courts of Justice Act in an appropriate case: *Van Bork v. Van Bork* (1994), 3

R.F.L. (4th) 59 (Ont. C.A.), additional reasons at (1994), 5 R.F.L. (4th) 174 (Ont. C.A.); Courts of Justice Act, s. 130

In the March, 1994, issue of *Money and Family Law*,[2] Stephen Grant wrote:

> Pre-judgment interest: A PostScript
>
> Introduction
>
> A few years ago I explored the use of pre-judgment interest ("PJI") in the family law context.[3] I was particularly interested in, if you will pardon the pun, to see if our General Division judges had applied PJI with any consistency from the time of introduction of the *Family Law Act* ("the Act") in 1986 to the time of my writing. From my review of the jurisprudence I could discern a number of principles as to when PJI would not be awarded but in reality could not predict with any degree of certainty when it would. As the issues requiring judicial determination under the Act have become narrower, I thought I would take a fresh look at the situation as it exists at the beginning of 1994.
>
> Appellate Jurisprudence
>
> The appellate jurisprudence on the PJI issue is rather sparse. The Court of Appeal has addressed the point on a couple of occasions but has not seen fit to render any significant judicial pronouncement. However, two cases are modestly noteworthy.
>
> In *Milinkovic v. Milinkovic*[4] the husband owed the wife an equalization payment ("EP") and had paid nothing towards it. Moreover, he continued to live in the matrimonial home. The Court of Appeal

refused to interfere with the trial judge's discretion
to award PJI to the wife even though the assets cre-
ating the EP were not revenue producing.

Secondly, in *DaCosta v. DaCosta*[5] the court
upheld the trial judge's discretion in refusing the wife
PJI on the basis that the husband had not only made
a significant advance payment on the wife's ultimate
EP entitlement but had also paid interim support
pending trial.

The Divisional Court, too, has considered PJI
and offered some comment in *McQuay v. McQuay*[6].
The court held "that the proper test to be applied
in determining pre-judgment interest on equalization payments is not the identical test used in commercial cases" [7] but rather suggested that PJI would
be awarded:

   (a) if the assets upon which the EP was based
       were relatively liquid, were income produc-
       ing or could have been realized in some
       manner by the payer, or

   (b) if the payee could have said to have "won"
       the proceeding.[8]

McQuay was followed by White J. in *Kozuch v.
Kozuch*[9] who declined to award PJI on the basis that
the complexity of the issues really necessitated a trial
and the payee could not be said to have "won" given
the modest EP to which she was found entitled. His
Honour commented that "[t] here is all the difference
in the world between an equalization payment based
on readily ascertainable values such as cash, stocks,
bonds and marketable real estate and such recondite
values as that of tobacco in a barn, farm equipment,
band equipment and the like."[10]

Use of Funds

The most consistent application of PJI arises in cases where the payer has or has not the use of funds from which the EP is to be made. Yet, as the ineffable Professor McLeod points out in his Annotation of the *DaCosta*[11] case:

> The decisions in recent cases have been inconsistent about whether prejudgment interest should be awarded to compensate the payee for the loss of use of the equalization funds and whether the court should force the payer to disgorge the benefit received from overholding. On the former analysis, prejudgment interest will be awarded as a matter of course unless the delay is attributable to the payee or unless the payer has provided funds [as in the form of support] during the separation to make up for the loss of the equalization payment: see *Black v. Black* (1988), 18 R.F.L. (3d) 303, 31 E.T.R. 188, 66 O.R. (2d) 643 (H.C.). On the latter analysis, alternatively, prejudgment interest will be awarded only if the payer has earned income through the overholding[12].

Regrettably, while the cases seem to follow this general theme, there is no consistent application or, for that matter, identification of which alternative, if either, the courts have determined to be prevalent in the awarding of PJI.

Cases in which PJI has not been awarded include *Lefevre,*[13] *Livermore*[14] and *Bigelow.*[15]

In *Lefevre*, the matrimonial home was the parties' only asset, it had not increased in value since Valuation Day ("V-Day") and the payer husband had not delayed the proceedings.[16] While the husband in *Livermore* owned certain shares, he had no liquidity on V-Day and had derived no financial benefit from his assets since then. He had also honoured his support obligations.[17] And in *Bigelow*, the payer husband had no use of the funds from which the EP was to be made.[18]

A number of these points can also be found in Mr. Justice McCart's refusal to award PJI in *Godinek v. Godinek*.[19] His Honour declined to award PJI on the following basis:

Mrs. Godinek has had possession of the matrimonial home since separation without paying any rent. She has been receiving moneys with which she has been supporting herself far in excess of what she would have received under a court order. There was no attempt on the part of the husband to unreasonably delay payment in order to deprive Mrs. Godinek of her rightful entitlement; nor has Mr. Godinek earned income from this sum.[20]

These cases may be usefully contrasted with a number of others in which PJI was awarded to the payee spouse. First, relying on *Starkman v. Starkman*[21] and the PJI provisions of the *Courts of Justice Act*, Madam Justice Feldman awarded the wife PJI in *Reeson v. Kowalik*[22] on the basis that the husband "actually had funds available on which to earn interest"[23] and although the husband had inherited a significant sum prior to trial, he made no advance payment to the wife. However, Her Honour did not award full PJI to the wife because:

No interest was earned on the [matrimonial home owned and still occupied by the husband] nor did it appreciate in value from V-Day to trial. In those circumstances it would not be consistent with even-handedness to attribute notional interest even though technically Mr. Reeson could have sold [the home] or borrowed money against it in order to make the equalization payment.[24]

Mr. Justice Webber also awarded the wife PJI on her EP entitlement in *Docherty v. Docherty*[25] on the basis that:

> The husband has had the use of the various properties since separation. This use includes not only the income derived there-from, but also a possible capital gain. He has also extracted from the properties approximately $247,000…. In the future he will recover the capital appreciation if the properties are not sold. It is not reasonable or fair that he should not pay pre-judgment interest.[26]

In *Delean v. Delean*[27] the wife was awarded PJI of an agreed-upon sum (although her entitlement was clearly higher) on the basis that the husband had sufficient liquidity to make an advance payment but did not do so, and the wife was thus deprived of her use of the EP funds. And in *Farquharson v. Farquharson*[28] despite the fact that the husband's major assets consisted of real estate which had declined in value from V-Day to the time of trial, he was ordered to pay PJI to the wife. Regional Senior Judge MacFarland stated:

> However, the assets remain in Mr. Farquharson's name, and he is in the real estate business. [The husband's argument that PJI should be lower than the prescribed rate of 13 per cent] is predicated on the view that the value of these assets will remain lower than the V-day valuation and will be sold at a loss to

Mr. Farquharson and that view is premature at this stage. It is just as likely that if he continues to hold the assets, they may soon again attain a V-day valuation or exceed it.[29]

The trial judge did, however, approximately credit the husband for an advance payment he had made to the wife.

Finally, in *Fawcett v. Fawcett*[30] Mr. Justice Hockin held that the onus was on the payer to persuade the court to decline to award PJI. His Honour refused to accede to this request because the husband continued to reside in the matrimonial home until it was sold, failed to pay any child support until seven months after separation and then made payments that, in the trial judge's view, were wholly inadequate.

Time

It is now relatively settled that PJI will not be awarded for any period of time before the proclamation of the FLA even if V-Day precedes March 1, 1986: see *Christian v. Christian*.[31] In *Lev v. Lev*,[32] however, the Manitoba Court of Appeal awarded PJI from the date of separation rather than the date the court ordered the accounting of the parties' assets, where the husband had impeded the process.

Webber J. in *Docherty*[33] awarded the wife PJI from the date of filing her Statement of Claim (April 1989) in which the claim for PJI was made rather than from the date of issuance of her Notice of Application (August 1987) which contained no claim for PJI. And in *McCuaig v. McCuaig*[34] Kozak J. accepted the submission of the plaintiff's counsel that the case took longer than it ought to have done to reach trial and halved the PJI award from six years to three.

Recent Cases

One of the last cases issued in 1993 that dealt with PJI was *Van Bork v. Van Bork*.[35] Following Granger J. in *Heon*,[36] Madam Justice Ellen Macdonald awarded the wife PJI from the date of the Act at 11 per cent. She said:

> Most compellingly, in exercising my discretion to award pre-judgment interest in this case is that much of Mr. Van Bork's behaviour was designed to deprive Mrs. Van Bork of her entitlement.[37]

Despite the husband's conduct, however, Her Honour refused to award compound, as opposed to simple, interest although she acknowledged she had the discretion to do so, saying it should only be done where ordinary PJI will not adequately compensate the payee.

Around the same time, Mr. Justice Ferrier issued his reasons for judgment in *Bobyk v. Bobyk*[38] in which His Honour saw "no reason to deny the wife pre-judgment interest, especially in view of the fact that the husband acknowledged that his wife was entitled to one-half of the [money] held by him on deposit as of the date of separation.[39] Although the wife sought interest at 13 per cent, His Honour found 8 per cent to be the appropriate rate to be applied.[40]

Conclusion

From these cases we can safely ascertain that these principles do apply:

1. Unless there is a compelling reason to do otherwise, PJI will be awarded   on an equalization payment.

2. PJI will be awarded from the date it is claimed but, in any event, not earlier than March 1, 1986 although this aspect of the issue is now almost moot.

3. The PJI rate appears to be the rate the trial judge thinks is fair in the circumstances although some of the cases do refer to the relevant provisions of the *Courts of Justice Act* as the basis for the award.

4. Dilatory or unreasonable conduct may be a factor not only in refusing PJI but in awarding it as well.

5. Some compelling reasons to refrain from awarding PJI include:

    (a) the payer's lack of access to one or more of the assets comprising the EP entitlement, as, for example, an interest in a pension;

    (b) the payer's lack of liquid or revenue-producing assets, as, for example, a matrimonial home;

    (c) the payer's scrupulous adherence to an interim support order;

    (d) a payer's advance payment, although this may simply reduce the amount of the PJI ultimately awarded;

    (e) some blameworthy conduct on the payee's part;

(f) a persuasive argument that the determination of the EP was particularly complex and the payee did not really "win" the litigation (although why this should matter on the PJI, as opposed to the costs, part of the judgment is rather inexplicable); and

(g) all or some of these factors.

While not as consistent or predictable as family law practitioners might wish, there is now ample judicial authority outlining the circumstances (as well as time and rate) in which PJI will be awarded under the Act. In short, creative counsel will be able to fit his or her client's particular facts into this expanded jurisprudential framework to invoke the court's discretion to award or refrain from awarding PJI in the appropriate situation.

The *Annual Review of Family Law*[41] updated these comments in 2000:

A court may award pre-judgment interest pursuant to the *Courts of Justice Act*, R.S.O. 1990, c. C-43, on an equalization entitlement: *Burnett v. Burnett* (1999), 50 R.F.L. (4th) 223 (Ont. S.C.J.) (pre-judgment interest from commencement of proceedings); *Singh v. Singh* (1999), 1 R.F.L. (5th) 136 (Ont. S.C.J.) (pre-judgment interest from date of separation where husband could have paid but delayed); *Szuflita v. Szuflita Estate* 2000 CarswellOnt 1792 (Ont. S.C.J.) (scope of P.J.I.); *Jones v. Jones* (2000), 8 R.F.L. (5th) 107 (Ont. S.C.J.), additional reasons at 2000 CarswellOnt 2685 (Ont. S.C.J.), additional reasons at 2000 CarswellOnt 2684 (Ont. S.C.J.) (PJI in property proceedings). Generally, pre-judgment interest is awarded to deal with the delay by the debtor or profit earned by the debtor on the entitlement: *Burgess v. Burgess* (1995), 16 R.F.L. (4th) 388 at 395, 24 O.R. (3d) 547, 82 O.A.C. 380 (C.A.); *Kuryliak v. Kuryliak*, [1999] W.D.F.L. 148 (Ont. Gen. Div.) (delay in payment by husband causing wife to pay interest on debts incurred); *Airst v. Airst*, [1999] W.D.F.L. 218 (Ont. Gen. Div.) (pre-judgment interest awarded).

A judge may depart from the pre-judgment interest percentage fixed under the *Courts of Justice Act* in an appropriate case: *Bascello v. Bascello* (1995), 26 O.R. (3d) 342 (Gen. Div.), additional reasons at (1995), 18 R.F.L. (4th) 362 (Ont. Gen. Div.), further additional reasons at (1996), 9 O.T.C. 384 (Gen. Div.)(court restricting interest where unreasonable for either to bear full costs).

In *Nahatchewitz v. Nahatchewitz* (1999), 1 R.F.L. (5th) 395, 123 O.A.C. 319, 178 D.L.R. (4th) 496 (Ont. C.A.), additional reasons at 1999 CarswellOnt 3076 (Ont. C.A.), the Court of Appeal confirmed that a judge may deny pre-judgment interest where a spouse had the use of the main property asset through continued residence of the home during proceedings.

A judge may deny pre-judgment interest where the asset that gave rise to the equalization payment was a future entitlement to a pension or another asset that could not be enjoyed by the payor spouse prior to trial, could not be transferred to the other spouse, sold to third party, or used to generate income with which to pay the amount owing: *Attfield v. Attfield* 1998 CarswellOnt 2982 (Ont. Gen. Div.) (pre-judgment interest limited to money withheld by defendant). But see also *Bourdeau v. Bourdeau* (1996), 26 R.F.L. (4th) 117 (Ont. C.A.), where the Ontario Court of Appeal upheld an award of pre-judgment interest in respect of the portion of the wife's equalization attributable to the home notwithstanding the wife occupied the home after separation.

A court may order pre-judgment interest notwithstanding a spouse's main asset is a pension if the spouse unreasonably interfered with the prompt resolution of the dispute: *Shafer v. Shafer* (1996), 25 R.F.L. (4th) 410, 12 O.T.C. 140 (Gen. Div.), additional reasons at (1996), 25 R.F.L. (4th) 410n, 16 O.T.C. 207 (Gen. Div.), affirmed (1998), 37 R.F.L. (4th) 104 (Ont. C.A.)(delay), or if the pension can be shared in specie under pension division legislation and this was a reasonable way to deal with the pension: *Deave v. Deave* (1995), 17 R.F.L. (4th) 305 (Ont. Gen. Div.).

A court will award post-judgment interest on an equalization payment as a matter of course from the date of the order to the date of payment under the *Courts of Justice Act*: *Koiter v. Koiter* (1996), 21 O.T.C. 3 (Gen. Div.) (interest on deferred equalization payment); *Gray v. Gray* (1998), 35 R.F.L. (4th) 456 (Alta C.A.) (statutory right to post-judgment interest).

CONCLUSION

There have been at least three other reported cases of interest.

In *Sengmueller v. Sengmueller*,[42] the Ontario Court of Appeal upheld the decision of the trial judge to allow pre-judgement interest at a reduced rate because support payments had been made.

In *Price v. Price*,[43] the Ontario Court of Justice allowed pre-judgement interest at 10 percent because the husband had the use of the funds and had earned a considerable return on them.

In the case of *Schaeffer v. Schaeffer*[44] Justice Metivier said:

> Given the very long periods since separation this issue becomes of critical importance. The largest portion of this equalization payment relates to the pension and the court of appeal has clearly directed in Burgess v. Burgess and Mollocom v. Mollocom that pre-judgment interest is not to be awarded where a pension, while increasing in value, was not available for realization or was not generating income. However, the court of appeal has also provided that these factors present here, to a significant degree, are not sufficient where there is inordinate delay and/or the non-payment of support.

Justice Metivier found that Mr. Schaeffer had caused the delay in settlement and had refused to pay support. The judge awarded pre-judgement interest, including interest on the half value of Mr. Schaeffer's pension.

The arguments seem to break down like this:

For Pre-Judgement Interest

1. Normally awarded unless there is good reason against doing so. Spouse opposing must show good reason it should not be granted.
2. Recipient has been deprived of the use of the money and the payer has received some benefit by not paying the funds. Sometimes, however, for some reason, it is thought the

payor did not receive a benefit when the payment represents equalization of the value of an accrued pension benefit.

3. Payor acted spitefully in withholding payment.
4. Inability or difficulty in paying is not a good defence.

Against Pre-Judgement Interest

1. Payor has received no benefit from withholding the funds and has not withheld payment unreasonably.
2. If the award had been received, no support would have been payable.
3. Payments of amount owing offered and deferred.
4. Other payments, that were made as by support or payment on debts, would not have been required if the money had been paid promptly.
5. Payor has acted reasonably.
6. Not applicable to period prior to claim, and, in any event, not earlier than March 1, 1986.
7. The payor lacked liquid or revenue producing assets, for example where the only asset is the matrimonial home.
8. The payor has paid an advance payment that is close to the equalization amount.
9. Something blameworthy on the payee's part.

Notes

1. McLeod, James G., and Mamo, Alfred A. *Annual Review of Family Law.* 1992. Scarborough: Carswell, Thomson Professional Publishing, 1992: 200-202.

2   Grant, Stephen "Pre-judgment Interest: A Postscript." *Money and Family Law* 9.3 (1994): 21-22.

3   "Prejudgment Interest: To Award or Not to Award" (1991), *Money & Family Law* 41.

4   (1991), 37 R.F.L. (3d) 97 (Ont. C.A.).

5   (1992), 40 R.F.L. (3d) 216 (Ont. C.A.).

6   (1992), 39 R.F.L. (3d) 184 (Ont. Div. Ct.).

7   *Ibid.* at 186.

8   *Ibid.* For these principles the court cited the trial judgement of Walsh J. in *Rawluk v. Rawluk* (1986), 3 R.F.L. (3d) 113 (Ont. H.C.), *Harry v. Harry* (1987), 9 R.F.L. (3d) 121 (Ont. Dist. Ct.), *Leslie v. Leslie* (1987), 9 R.F.L. (3d) 82 (Ont. H.C.), *Humphreys v. Humphreys* (1987), 7 R.F.L. (3d) 113 (Ont. H.C.) and *Gregoric v. Gregoric* (1991), 4 O.R. (3d) 604 (Gen. Div.).

9   [1992] O.J. No. 1893.

10 *Ibid.* at 94.

11 *Supra*, note 3 at 217.

12 *Ibid.* at 220.

13 (1992), 40 R.F.L. (3d) 372 (Ont. Gen. Div.).

14 (1992), 43 R.F.L. (3d) 163 (Ont. Gen. Div.).

15 (1993), 48 R.F.L. (3d) 424 (Ont. Gen. Div.), citing B*utt v. Butt* (1989), 22 R.F.L. (3d) 415 (Ont. H.C.) as authority.

16 *Supra*, note 11 at 376-378.

17 *Supra*, note 12 at 177.

18 *Supra*, note 13 at 431.

19 (1992), 40 R.F.L. (3d) 78 (Ont. Gen. Div.).

20 *Ibid*

21 (1990), 75 O.R. (2d) 19 (C.A.).

22 (1991), 36 R.F.L. (3d) 396 (Ont. Gen. Div.) unreported supplementary reasons for judgment concerning prejudgment interest and costs, (Ont. Gen. Div.), Doc. 42801/89, F.L. 1165/89, November 27, 1991, Feldman J.

23 *Ibid.* supplementary reasons at 3.

24 *Ibid.*

25 (1992), 42 R.F.L. (3d) 87 (Ont. Gen. Div.).

26 *Ibid.* at 111.

27 [1992] O.J. No. 2949 at 6 (Gen. Div.).

28 [1992] O.J. No. 2635 (Gen. Div.).

29 *Ibid.* at 13.

30 [1993] O.J. No. 908 at 8.

31 (1991), 37 R.F.L. (3d) 26 (Ont. Gen. Div.).

32 (1992), 40 R.F.L. (3d) 404 (Man. C.A.).

33 *Supra*, note 23 at 111.

34 [1992] O.J. No. 2324 at 11 (Ont. Gen. Div.).

35 As yet unreported (Ont. Gen. Div.), Doc. D120320/84, November 10, 1993, MacDonald J.

36 (1989), 22 R.F.L. (3d) 273 (Ont. H.C.).

37 *Supra*, note 33 at 52.

38 As yet unreported, (Ont. Gen. Div.), Doc. 38867/89, November 17, 1993, Ferrier J.

39 *Ibid.* at 14-15.

40 *Ibid,* AT 15.

41 McLeod, James G., and Mamo, Alfred A. *Annual Review of Family Law.* 2000. Scarborough: Carswell, Thomson Professional Publishing, 2000: 383-384.

42 (1994) 2 R.F.L. (4th) 232, 111 D.L.R. (4th) 19 (Morden A.C.J.O. McKinlay and Carthy J.J.A.).

43 (1994) 3 R.F.L. 1 (Ont. Ct. of Justice – Gen. Div.) Walsh J. (Gen. Div.).

44 (1996) Court File No. 47942/94, Metivier J. O.F.L.R. Volume 10, Issue 6, 25 R.F.L. (4th) 410 (Ont. Gen. Div.).

Chapter 28

Is it the Law?

In any legal matter, it is important to know exactly which law applies. It is not enough to know what the law is generally. To be sure you get your fair share of the assets, you need to know which act applies, which reported cases apply, and what the applicable acts and cases say about the situation you are considering.

Divorce and support are generally federal matters and are governed by the Divorce Act, R.S.C. 1970.

The sharing of property on marriage breakdown is a provincial matter, and each province has its own matrimonial property act. Under all provincial laws, there tend to be three classes of property:

1. property that is definitely shared;
2. property that is specifically exempt from the equalization process;
3. property that may or may not be shareable based on the facts of the case and what is considered equitable.

The acts for each province and territory in Canada:

- Alberta Matrimonial Property Act
- British Columbia Family Relations Act
- Manitoba Marital Property Act, The
- New Brunswick Marital Property Act
- Newfoundland Family Law Act
- Northwest Territiories Matrimonial Property Ordinance

- Nova Scotia Matrimonial Property Act
- Nunavut Family Law Act
- Ontario Family Law Act
- Prince Edward Island Family Law Act
- Quebec Civil Code
- Saskatchewan Matrimonial Property Act
- Yukon Family Property and Support Act

Some pensions are governed by federal acts:

- Pension Benefits Standards Act
- Pension Benefits Division Act
- Public Service Superannuation Act
- Canada Pension Plan
- Canadian Forces Superannuation Act
- Royal Canadian Mounted Police Superannuation Act

These Acts override the provisions of any provincial pension legislation.

Each province has an act that sets out the minimum requirements to which most pensions registered in their province must adhere:

- Alberta Employment Pension Plans Act
- British Columbia Pension Benefits Standards Act
- Manitoba Pension Benefits Act
- New Brunswick Pension Benefits Act
- Newfoundland Pension Benefits Act
- Nova Scotia Pension Benefits Act
- Nunavut Pension Benefits Act
- Ontario Pension Benefits Act
- Prince Edward Island Pension Benefits Act
- Quebec Pension Benefits Act
- Saskatchewan Pension Benefits Act

Each pension plan is governed by a pension plan document that must meet the requirements of the particular provincial or federal pension act and be registered federally or provincially. Each pension plan must meet the requirements of the Income Tax Act.

THE COURTS

In 1998 the federal government announced a new program intended to speed up the process of settling family law cases in the courts:

> Federal Government Partners With Provinces In Unifying Family Court Services
>
> OTTAWA, March 19, 1998—Fulfilling the federal government's 1997 Budget promise to support the creation and expansion of unified family courts across Canada, Anne McLellan, Minister of Justice and Attorney General of Canada, today introduced amendments to the *Judges Act* in the House of Commons that, subject to Parliament's approval, will pave the way for 27 new federally-appointed judges for unified family courts in four provinces.
>
> The legislation follows an invitation to all provinces to express interest in the new judicial resources and several months of work with Nova Scotia, Saskatchewan, Ontario and Newfoundland to develop court models that will provide extensive community and other services to families, and make the best use of judicial resources. Women's groups and other parties have also been consulted.
>
> As a result of these discussions, Newfoundland and Saskatchewan will each receive one new UFC judge, Nova Scotia will receive eight new judges and

Ontario will receive seventeen. This brings UFCs to half the residents of Newfoundland and Ontario, most of the residents of Saskatchewan, and marks a strong beginning in Nova Scotia.

"Having a single place, a unified family court, where family members can find judicial and other services to help them resolve all legal issues is an excellent way of helping families, and especially their children. It's a single-window concept for legal and other services with simplified procedures, in a user-friendly environment," said Minister McLellan.

Savings to the provinces resulting from the new appointments will allow participating provinces to spend more on family service programs that support the work of unified courts. Easier access to services from the supporting professions, either within the courts themselves or within the community, will help families resolve their problems in a timely, more amicable and less stressful way, and reduce the potential for further conflict.

"Unified family courts are an innovative way of structuring judicial and related services for families that allows the federal government to partner with provinces and put federal monies to excellent use on behalf of families and for the long term benefit of taxpayers in general," said Minister McLellan.

Partnering with provinces and territories to support unified family courts is an element of a broad federal strategy to help children and families in need. Other complementary initiatives designed to support families and protect children include: child support guidelines that help determine appropriate amounts of financial assistance for child support on marriage breakdown; the National Child Benefit; the National Crime Prevention Council's strategy for an integrated, community-based approach to crime prevention; and tax relief for low-and middle-income Canadians announced in the recent Budget.

These amendments to the *Judges Act* are accessible on the Department of Justice's Internet homepage, under the heading "Government Bills".

Several provinces have taken steps to implement this process. For example, in Ontario:

OVERVIEW OF THE
FAMILY COURT BRANCH OF THE
SUPERIOR COURT IN ONTARIO[1]

In those areas in Ontario where the Family Court branch of the Superior Court of Justice does not exist, the jurisdiction over family law disputes is divided between the Superior Court of Justice and the Ontario Court of Justice. Cases which have divorce or property claims are brought exclusively in the Superior Court, and child protection and adoption cases must be commenced solely in the Ontario Court of Justice. Each of these two courts has jurisdiction over child and spousal support, as well as custody and access claims.

In those places where the Family Court branch of the Superior Court of Justice has been established, there is no divided jurisdiction in family law matters. It exercises a single, comprehensive jurisdiction over all legal matters and disputes related to the family. Furthermore, as a unified family court, it allows family problems to be dealt with in an integrated manner, with mediation, resource, informational and legal services attached to each court site. These services complement the judicial side of the court and mitigate the adversarial nature of court proceedings. They help in achieving non-adversarial resolutions of family disputes by narrowing down the number of contentious issues and attempting to divert as many disputes as possible from formal court hearings.

History

In July 1977, the Unified Family Court of Hamilton-Wentworth opened as a three year pilot project. It was created as a result of a federal-provincial agreement to implement law reform commission reports advocating the adoption of unified family courts. In 1982, the Unified Family Court of Hamilton-Wentworth was made a permanent entity.

The court was expanded to include four more sites in 1995 and its name was changed to the Family Court, a branch of the Ontario Court of Justice (General Division). The new courts were located in Middlesex County (London), Frontenac County (Kingston), Lennox & Addington County (Napanee) and Simcoe County (Barrie). On December 13, 1998, the court was made a branch of the Superior Court of Justice.

The Government of Ontario continued its commitment to expand the Family Court branch across the province when twelve new court sites were created, on November 15, 1999, in Ottawa, Newmarket, Oshawa, Peterborough, Lindsay, Cobourg, Bracebridge, St. Catharines, Cornwall, L'Orignal, Brockville and Perth.

Structure of the Court

The legislation setting out the structure of the Family Court branch has been amended a number of times since the original pilot project started in 1977. The current structure is set out in the *Courts of Justice Act*, R.S.O. 1990, c.43, which was most recently amended by S.O. 1998, c.20.

The Family Court is a branch of the Superior Court and is created under s.21.1 of the *Courts of Justice Act*. As part of the Superior Court, the head of the Family Court is the Chief Justice of the Superior Court. The Regional Senior Justices, who exercise the local functions of the Chief Justice in each region, are responsible for scheduling and assignment of all judicial duties in each Region of the Court. There is a Senior Judge of the Family Court branch who has enumerated duties which will be discussed below, to enhance and refine the special needs and procedures of the Family Court branch and to advise the Chief Justice on issues pertaining to the Family Court branch.

Where the Family Court branch exists, jurisdiction for all family law proceedings is consolidated into one court. The list of matters within the jurisdiction of the Family Court branch is contained in a schedule to s.21.8 of the *Courts of Justice Act*. In short, the court has jurisdiction over all claims for divorce, support, custody, access, equalization of net family property, and trust claims. Superior Court Judges also exercise the jurisdiction of an Ontario Court judge in child protection and adoption proceedings.

The Senior Judge of the Family Court branch has certain responsibilities that are defined in s.14(5) of the *Courts of Justice Act*. These include: advising the Chief Justice of the Superior Court on the education of judges sitting in Family Court branch, practice and procedure in the Family Court branch including the mediation services; the expansion of the Family Court branch; and the expenditure of funds budgeted for the Family Court branch. The *Courts of Justice Act* provides that the Senior Judge of the Family Court branch is a member of the Family Rules Committee. The senior judge is the current chair of the Rules Committee. The Senior Judge is also required to meet with the local statutory committees (described below) from time to time.

The court is made up of a core group of judges committed to family justice and who give the branch its specialized nature. Supplementing this core group are judges from the rest of the Superior Court who are rotated in on both a scheduled and as-needed basis.

Community Based Advisory Committees

Sections 21.13 and 21.14 of the *Courts of Justice Act* provide for two committees to be associated with the Family Court branch. The Community Liaison Committee is comprised of judges, lawyers, persons employed in courts administration and other residents of the community. Members of the committee are appointed by the Chief Justice of the Superior Court. The purpose of the Community Liaison Committee is to provide a forum for the regular users of the Family Court branch to discuss issues relating to its operation.

The Community Resource Committee (s.21.14) is comprised of judges, lawyers, members of social

service agencies, persons employed in courts administration and other residents of the community, as
appointed by the Chief Justice of the Superior
Court. The purpose of the Community Resource
Committee is to identify, support and promote
resources relating to family law in the community.

The Support Services ("Social Arm")
Each Family Court branch offers several support
services to litigants:

1. Family Law Information Centre;
2. Mediation services;
3. Legal Support Services;
4. Family Law Information Meetings;
5. Supervised Access and Exchange Centre.

1. Family Law Information Centre
   Every Family Court branch site has a Family
   Law Information Centre, which has resource
   material on community resources, separation
   and divorce, and information regarding legal
   services and the court system. The Information
   Centre is supported by three types of personnel:
   court staff to assist with distribution of forms and
   procedural information, social workers provided
   through the mediation service to assist in referring parties to community resources and assessing their needs and advice duty counsel who will
   provide basic legal advice within the mandate of
   Legal Aid Ontario.
2. Mediation Services
   Alternative dispute resolution is an important

aspect of the "unified family court" concept. The Ministry of the Attorney General funds mediation services operating in connection with all Family Court branch locations. The mediation services provide mediation of issues arising on family breakdown including custody, access, support and property division. At this time, the service providers do not provide mediation of child protection issues. The mediation services are offered on a fee-for-service basis, but the fee is determined on a sliding scale geared to income.

The mediation service providers' offices are located off the court site; clients can go there for mediation intake and for pre-arranged mediation sessions. In addition, an experienced mediator will be present at court on busy days (e.g., motions, first court dates). This on-site mediator will be available to do mediation intake, as well as mediate interim or discrete issues arising out of that day's court lists. The days and times that the on-site mediator will be at court will be determined locally.

3. Legal Support Services

Legal Aid Ontario provides duty counsel on motions and list days to assist litigants in court, where appropriate, and, as noted above, legal advice counsel in the Family Law Information Centre to provide short term legal assistance.

4. Family Law Information Meetings

The mediation service in each court will be responsible for providing regular information sessions on the effect of separation and divorce on children.

5. Supervised Access and Exchange Centres

Supervised access and exchange programs are in existence for all Family Court branch locations and are funded by the Ministry of the Attorney General.

The Family Law Rules

As of November 15, 1999, a new, comprehensive set of rules in family law proceedings came into effect in the Superior Court of Justice, Family Court branch and in the Ontario Court of Justice. It is no coincidence that the *Family Law Rules* came into effect at the same time as the recent Family Court expansion. Both initiatives represent major change and progress in family law. The *Family Law Rules* are the result of several years of work by the Family Rules Committee, a body created under the *Courts of Justice Act* to make rules relating to family law practice and procedure in both the Superior Court of Justice and the Ontario Court of Justice.

There are many features to the *Family Law Rules*, including its plain language approach and the comprehensive nature of the forms. Even a cursory overview of the new rules is beyond the scope of this document. However, some mention must be made of the case management approach that is integral to the rules.

Subrule 2(2) of the *Family Law Rules* states that the "primary objective" of the rules is that cases be dealt with justly. Subrule 2(5) provides that courts have a duty to promote the primary objective through active case management.

Three case management conferences are provided for in the rules (see Rule 17): a case conference, a settlement conference, and a trial management conference. In summary, the purpose of these conferences is to bring parties and their counsel to court in order to define, narrow or even settle the issues in dispute (these conferences may be consolidated where appropriate). In one of the biggest changes under the new rules, Rule 14 provides that motion materials cannot be served until a case conference is held, except in cases of urgency.

In all child protection cases, a tight time frame has been set for the completion of many of the steps in those proceedings (see Rule 33). For non-child protection cases, an outside time limit of 230 days for scheduling a hearing has been set (see Rules 39, 40). Cases involving claims for divorce or equalization of net family property are placed on a standard track (see Rule 39(7)). Cases on the standard track do not come to court until a party requests a case conference or brings an urgent motion. Once a standard case is brought to court under subrule 39(8), it will be case managed as any other case. All cases not placed on the standard track are placed on the fast track (see Rule 39(4)). These cases are assigned a first court date when the application is filed. At this first court date, a clerk will review the materials and ensure that the case is ready to proceed before a judge (see Rules 39(5), 40(4)). If the case is not ready, the parties are referred to the appropriate resources (such as the Family Law Information Centre). In both standard and fast track cases, if a case has not been scheduled for trial within 200 days from the start of the case, the court sends a notice to the parties advising them that the case will be dismissed in 30 days if no steps are taken.

Notes

1   www.ontariocourts.on.ca/family_court/overview.htm

Chapter 29

What Happens on Death

The Family Law Act of Ontario provides that when a person dies, his spouse has a choice of accepting what was left to her in the will or applying for equalization of property as set out in the Family Law Act. In effect, a spouse cannot be cut out of the will. There are extensive provisions for what happens to a person's pension when he dies, either before or after retirement.

DEATH BEFORE RETIREMENT

Generally speaking if a pension member dies before retirement, the commuted value of his pension is paid to his spouse if he has one. If not, it is paid to dependent children or to their estate. Some plans allow the member to name a beneficiary of the death benefit.

DEATH AFTER RETIREMENT

Most pensions cease on death of the member, unless the pension has been issued with a guarantee period. A guarantee period continues the payments to the named beneficiary or the estate for a specified period of time in the event the member dies before then.

In Ontario, the Pension Benefits Act requires that all pensions be issued on a Joint and Survivor basis so that when the member dies, 60 percent of his lifetime benefit must continue to the spouse for his lifetime. This benefit is generally payable to the spouse at the date of retirement. Divorce does not generally change this in Ontario private pension plans. However, divorce could extinguish the benefit for an ex-spouse if the Pension Benefits Standards Act governs the plan. The Canadian Forces Superannuation Act, for example, leaves the payment of a death benefit discretionary. The Canadian Forces Superannuation Act issues bulletins:

INFORMATION BULLETIN

Designation change of cancellation of benefit for Part II of the Canadian Forces Superannuation Act

SUPPLEMENTARY
DEATH BENEFITS PLAN

General

The Canadian Forces Superannuation Regulations now permit the designation of a beneficiary for the receipt of a Supplementary Death Benefit under Part II of the Canadian Forces Superannuation Act.

Designation of Beneficiary

The designation of a beneficiary which may be made at any time, is voluntary and remains valid until changed or cancelled by you.

PREVIOUS PROVISIONS FOR THE
PAYMENT OF BENEFITS MAY APPLY

In the case of a male pensioner who was a participant in the supplementary death benefit plan before 20 December 1975, payment of a benefit upon death will be as follows:

(a) to the widow if she was married to the participant prior to 20 December 1975 or

(b) to the estate of the participant if the widow was married to the participant after 19 December 1975 or if no widow survives the participant.

Therefore, it is not necessary to complete a designation of beneficiary form unless the benefit is to become payable to a beneficiary other than stated above.

In the case of a female pensioner who was a participant in the supplementary death benefit plan before 20 December 1975, there is no change respecting the payment of a benefit upon your death, i.e. it remains payable to your estate. Therefore, there is no necessity for you to complete a designation of beneficiary form unless you wish the benefit to become payable to a beneficiary other than your estate.

Who May Be Designated

A participant may designate one *only* of the following as beneficiary; the participant's estate, any person who is over the age of eighteen years at the date on which the form is signed and witnessed, any charitable organization, any benevolent organization or institution and any eleemosynary religious or educational organization or institution.

The full name and address of the beneficiary must be given in the space provided. If you wish to name your estate as beneficiary rather than any person, institution or organization, you insert the words "my estate" in the space provided.

Form and Manner of Designation of a Beneficiary

Should you wish to designate a beneficiary the

enclosed forms are to be completed in duplicate. A designation will not be valid until a properly completed Designation of Beneficiary form, which has been signed by you in the presence of a witness, is received by the addressee shown at the bottom of the enclosed form.

Change or Cancellation of Beneficiary
If you designate a beneficiary and subsequently wish to change or cancel the designation of beneficiary. The appropriate forms may be obtained by writing to: National Defence Headquarters, Ottawa, ON K1A 0K2: DPS-4

Designation, Change or Cancellation of Beneficiary Deemed Not to Have Taken Place

A designation, change or cancellation made by you shall be deemed to have not taken place unless the completed form is received by the addressee referred to above, prior to your death.

Payment of Benefit if Beneficiary Designated
If you designate a beneficiary, the benefit will be paid to the beneficiary; if the beneficiary designated predeceases you, the benefit will be paid to your estate and if the beneficiary dies after you, the benefit is payable to the beneficiary's estate.

The duplicate copy of the form will be returned to you as acknowledgement of its receipt.

BULLETIN
Survivors' Benefits Payable under the Canadian Forces Superannuation Act

Part I of the Canadian Forces Superannuation Act (CFSA) provides that upon the death of an annuitant, the surviving spouse is normally entitled to receive an annual allowance equal to one-half the benefit the annuitant was receiving at the time of his death, provided the marriage occurred prior to the annuitant's 60th birthday. This annual allowance is payable for life and is subject to cost-of-living adjustments.

Children of the marriage (born prior to the annuitant's 60th birthday) are normally entitled to a child's annual allowance equal to one-fifth of the surviving spouse's annual allowance per child (to a maximum of four-fifths per family). This allowance is payable until the child attains 18 years of age and may be extended to a maximum of age 25 where the child remains in uninterrupted full-time attendance in school. This benefit may be doubled where the child is orphaned (where no spouse survives the annuitant).

Where a Divorce Decree has been issued, the divorced spouse would have no entitlement to a CFSA annual allowance. In the event of a marital separation between husband and wife at the time of the annuitant's death, Treasury Board approval would be required before any benefits could be paid to the separated spouse. It would be necessary for the applying spouse to complete a Statutory Declaration confirming that the marriage had at no time been terminated by divorce.

In the event of the annuitant remarrying, the second spouse would be considered the surviving spouse for the purposes of paying the annual allowance. However, it should be noted that, regardless of whether or not it is the annuitant's first marriage, *no benefits are payable if the marriage occurred after the annuitant's 60th birthday*, unless the annuitant elected, within one year of marriage, to accept a reduction to his benefit in order to provide a survivors' benefit for his spouse.

In the case of a common-law relationship, Treasury Board would review the case and deem the person the surviving spouse if they were satisfied that they lived *as man and wife* for at least one year prior to the annuitant's death, *provided that the relationship commenced prior to the member's 60th birthday*. As Treasury Board's decision is based on the circumstances in effect at the time of the member's death, it is never possible to confirm in advance whether a common-law spouse would be entitled to CFSA survivors' benefits. It is *not* possible to "elect" a survivor's benefit after age 60 (as set out in the preceding paragraph) in a common-law situation.

Chapter 30

Financial Planning

Your divorce and equalization of assets must be considered carefully from the financial planning aspect. Which assets you keep and which assets your spouse keeps may have long-term financial results for you. Therefore, you will want to plan your finances.

THE SIX STEP PROCESS OF PERSONAL FINANCIAL PLANNING[1]

Personal financial planning focuses on the individual. In order to serve their individual client's needs best, the professional financial planning practitioner employs The Total Financial Planning Process comprising these six distinct steps:

1. The financial planner *clarifies the client's present situation* by collecting and assessing all relevant financial data such as lists of assets and liabilities, tax returns, records of securities transactions, insurance policies, wills, pension plans, etc.

2. The financial planner helps the client *identify both financial and personal goals and objectives* as well as clarify that person's financial and personal values and attitudes. These may include providing for children's education, supporting elderly parents or relieving immediate financial pressures which would help maintain the client's current lifestyle and provide for retirement. These considerations

are important in determining the client's best financial planning strategy.

3. The financial planner *identifies financial problems* that create barriers to achieving financial independence. Problem areas can include too little or too much insurance coverage, or a high tax burden. The client's cash flow may be inadequate, or the current investments may not be winning the battle with changing economic times. These possible problem areas must be identified before solutions can be found.

4. The financial planner *provides written recommendations and alternative solutions.* The length of the recommendations will vary with the complexity of the client's individual situation, but they should always be structured to meet the client's needs without undue emphasis on purchasing certain investment products.

5. A financial plan is only helpful if the recommendations are put into action. *Implementing the right strategy* will help the client reach the desired goals and objectives. The financial planner should assist the client in either actually executing the recommendations, or in coordinating their execution with other knowledgeable professionals.

6. The financial planner *provides periodic review and revision* of the client's plan to assure that the goals are achieved. A client's financial situation should be re-assessed at least once a year to account for changes in that person's life and current economic conditions.

FINANCIAL PLANNERS

You may want to retain the services of a financial planner when you begin planning for the future.

The Canadian Association of Financial Planners has a code of ethics requiring members to put a client's best interests first. The organization has more than 3,300 members. Visit their web site at www.cafp.org

---

Notes

1   www.cafp.org/six-step.html

Appendix A

Case Law by Subject

Ad-Hoc Indexing
Goulet v. Goulet
Paterson v. Paterson
Radcliff v. Radcliff
Weaver v. Weaver
Weise v. Weise

Air Travel Points
Bracewell v. Bracewell
Tibbets v. Tibbets

Bankruptcy
Canada (Attorney General) v. Gordon (Trustee of)
Balyk v. Balyk
Blowes v. Blowes
Bobyk
Gough v. Gough
Janakowski v. Janakowski
Peterson v. Peterson
Stiles v. Stiles
Wale (Re)

Canada Pension Plan
Audley v. Audley
Canada v. Blackwood
Czemeres v. Czemeres
Jones v. Asante (1995)
MacDonnell v. MacDonnell
Payne v. Payne
Snajaric v. Snajaric
Webb v. Webb

Child Support Guidelines
http://canada.justice.gc.ca/en/ps/mp/gul/intann/html - provides an extensive list of cases dealing with the Child Support Guidelines. The cases are identified with the Section they apply to. The site also provides a summary of some cases.

Common Law Relationships
Becker v. Pettkus
Bigelow v. Bigelow
Buthcher v. Hibbs
Crawford v. Rekus
Dhaliwal v. Beloud
Dorflinger v. Melanson
Farrell v. Fowler
Faufax v. Linkletter
Ford v. Werden
Forsyth v. MacDougall
Gostlin v. Kergin
Jensen v. McFadden
Keddy v. McGill
Kenny v. Martin
Madill v. Townsend
Motruck v. Thompson
Parkes v. Reidpath
Peter v. Beblow
Phillips v. Fyrie
Plattig v. Robillard
Pym v. Gieden
Ricard v. Persson
Sangster v. Sangster
Schneider v. Albrecht
Smith v. Varsanyi
Stefonavich v. Dalalla
Stewart v. Stewart
Stewart v. Whitley
Thoen v. Perrier
Tolkein v. Spurr
Toth v. Frias

Varty v. McCann
Vikander v. Parsons
Wash v. Bana
Wong v. Spencer
Woods v. Hatfield
Zegeil v. Opie

Constructive Trust
Dorflinger v. Melanson
Gregory v. Gregory
Maloney v. Maloney
Peter v. Biblow
Pettkus v. Becker
Sarochan v. Sarochan

Contingency Discounts
Ackins v. Ackins
Alger v. Alger
Bascello v. Bascello
Biblow v. Biblow
Deroo v. Deroo
Dick v. Dick
Dorriesfield v. Dorriesfield
Erion v. Erion
Ferniuk v. Ferniuk
Goulet v. Goulet
Harrop v. Harrop
Hilderley v. Hilderley
Kalytuk v. Kalytuk
Knippshild v. Knippshild
Madden v. Madden
McBurnie v. McBurnie
Richter v. Richter
Salib v. Cross
Sauder v. Sauder
Tucker v. Baudais
Weise v. Weise

Continued Employment
Bascello v. Bascello
Dick v. Dick
Kennedy v. Kennedy
Knippshild v. Knippshild
Sauder v. Sauder

Date of Valuation
Harbour v. Harbour

Death Benefits
Benson v. Los Angeles
Daker v. Daker
Dick v. Dick
Dilny v. Dilny
Gifford v. Gifford
Komori v. Malins
Lindsay v. Lindsay
Marsham v. Marsham
Miller v. Miller
Pelley v. Pelley
Phillipson v. Board of Administration
Re Bruegl
Rutherford v. Rutherford and Dennis
Thoburn v. Thoburn
Weise v. Weise
Wiebe v. Wiebe

Deferred Profit-Sharing Plan—Not Asset
Moore v. Moore

Disability Benefits
Abate v. Abate
Almeida v. Almeida
Arseneau v. Arseneau
Arvelin v. Arvelin
Artus v. Artus
Balcombe v. Balcombe
Bouey v. Bouey
Brice v. Brice
Brignolio v. Brignolio
Bullock v. Bullock
Burke v. Burke
Buske v. Buske
Canada v. Blackwood
Chafe v. Chafe
Czemeres v. Czemeres
Dixon v. Dixon
Eckert v. Eckert
Entesary v. Entesary
Fahner v. Fahner
Goldfarb v. Goldfarb
Higgins v. Higgins
Hiscock v. Hiscock
Hughes v. Hughes
Inverarity v. Inverarity
Iurincic v. Iurincic
Jarvis v. Jarvis

Jiwa v. Jiwa
Kelly v. Kelly
Le Roy v. Le Roy
Leger v. Leger
MacDonnell v. MacDonnell
McClure v. McClure
McTaggart v. McTaggart
Mead v. Mead
Meier v. Meier
Mittler v. Mittler
Murray v. Murray
Neven v. Neven
Pallister v. Pallister
Pollock v. Pollock
Rains v. Rains
Robichaud v. Robichaud
Rohl v. Rohl
Shaver v. Shaver
Smith v. Smith
Snjaric v. Snjaric
Vanderaa v. Vanderaa
Webb v. Webb
Yee v. Yee
Young v. Young

Double Dipping
Bartlett v. Bartlett
Best v. Best
Boston v. Boston
Brinkos v. Brinkos
Burtnick v. Burtnick
Butt v. Butt
Caldwell v. Caldwell
Campbell v. Campbell
Carter v. Carter
Crawford v. Crawford
Dick v. Dick
Donavan v. Donavan
Ehlers v. Ehlers
Flett v. Flett
Fogel v. Fogel
Gemmell v. Gemmell
Grainger v. Grainger
Grunwald v. Grunwald
Hutchison v. Hutchison
Inverarity v. Inverarity
LeMoine v. LeMoine
Linton v. Linton
MacLeod v. MacLeod

Mascarin v. Mascarin
McDougall v. McDougall
Moge v. Moge
Murphy v. Murphy
Nantais v. Nantais
Riegle v. Riegle
Rivers v. Rivers
Rogers v. Rogers
Schmidt v. Schmidt
Shadbolt v. Shadbolt
Strang v. Strang
Thibert v. Thibert
Vennels v. Vennels
Veres v. Veres

Economic Disadvantage—Yes
Bascello v. Bascello

Economic Disadvantage—No
Andrews v. Andrews

Equalization
Nicholas v. Nicholas

Hybrid Method
Deroo v. Deroo
Dick v. Dick
Halman v. Halman
Saunders v. Saunders
Strang v. Strang
Weaver v. Weaver
Weise v. Weise

If and When
Abate v. Abate
Andrews v. Andrews
Belyea v. Belyea
Best, T. v. Best, M.
Boudreau v. Boudreau
Bracewell v. Bracewell
Bullock v. Bullock
Carbert v. Carbert
Chaisson v. Chaisson
Daher v. Daher
Downey v. Downey
Drmanic v. Drmanic
Gardiner v. Gardiner
George v. George
Gilmour v. Gilmour

Grainger v. Grainger
Greenwood v. Greenwood
Halman v. Halman
Harrower v. Harrower
Hierlihy v. Hierlihy
Hilderley v. Hilderley
Hiscock v. Hiscock
Johnstone v. Johnstone
Jones v. Jones
Klein v. Klein
Krauss v. Krauss
Kroone v. Kroone
Lind v. Lind
Mailhot v. Mailhot
Marsham v. Marsham
McAlister v. McAlister
Monger v. Monger
Moravcik v. Moravcik
Munro v. Munro Estate
Pollock v. Pollock
Porter v. Porter
Radke v. Radke
Rauf v. Rauf
Rumpler v. Rumpler
Rushton v. Rushton
Rutherford v. Rutherford and Dennis
Scott v. Scott
Shaw v. Shaw
Simms v. Simms
Stephenson v. Stephenson
Storms v. Storms
Strahl v. Strahl
Tetz v. Tetz
Thompson v. Thompson
Touwslager v. Touwslager
Towns v. Townsend
Wettlaufer v. Wettlaufer
Woeller v. Woeller
Woodman v. Deremo

Indexing During Deferral Period
Bascello v. Bascello
Monger v. Monger

Interest on Deferred Payments
Bascello v. Bascello

Leave of Absence
Clerke v. Clerke

Lump Sum Settlement
Alger v. Alger
Arthur v. Arthur
Aylsworth v. Aylsworth
Best, T. v. Best, M.
Butt v. Butt
Cross v. Cross
Danaher v. Danaher
Davies v. Davies
Dimock-Cummings v. Cummings
Ewing v. Ewing
Fedon v. Fedon
Fitzpatrick v. Fitzpatrick
Flynn v. Flynn
Forster v. Forster
Gasparetto v. Gasparetto
Graff v. Graff
Guran v. Guran
Hodgins v. Hodgins
Hovland v. Hovland
Inverarity v. Inverarity
Kirton v. Kirton
Kopecky v. Kopecky
Leek v. Lightfoot
Lefort v. Lefort
Lovegrove v. Lovegrove
MacDougald v. MacDougald
Mamer v. Mamer
McDonald v. McDonald
Meier v. Meier
Millan v. Millan
Miller v. Miller
Morgan v. Morgan
Muir v. Muir
Nicholas v. Nicholas
Parsons v. Parsons
Purcell v. Purcell
Quintal v. Quintal
Ramsay v. Ramsay
Rednall v. Rednall
Rezler v. Rezler
Ryan v. Ryan
Salib v. Cross
Saunders v. Saunders
Stevens v. Stevens
Stokes v. Stokes and Lennox
Sykes v. Sykes
Tataryn v. Tataryn
Towns v. Townsend

Tucker v. Rudais
VanGeel v. VanGeel
Ward v. Ward
Wilson v. Wilson
Yeo v. Yeo
Yeudall v. Yeudall

Notional Costs
Cassidy v. Cassidy
Deane v. Deane
Gresham v. Gresham
Harris v. Harris
Heon v. Heon
Knippshild v. Knippshild
Lang v. Lang
Marsham v. Marsham
McClure v. McClure
McPherson v. McPherson
Melanson v. Melanson
Offset v. Offset
Sengmueller v. Sengmueller
Starkman v. Starkman
Stevenson v. Stevenson
Tanouye v. Tanouye
Tibbetts v. Tibbetts

Obligations To Produce Value
Dearing v. Dearing
Greenwood v. Greenwood

Old Age Pension
Booth v. Booth
Daly v. Daly
Goldamer v. Goldamer
Lattey v. Lattey
Podemski v. Podemski
Tumaitis v. Tumaitis

Pay Equity Award
Purcell v. Purcell

Payment over Period of Years
Bascello v. Bascello
Best, T. v. Best, M.
MacNeil v. MacNeil
McTaggart v. McTaggart
Randolph v. Randolph
Weise v. Weise

Pension Benefits Division Act
Deane v. Deane
Elgie v. Elgie
McNutt v. McNutt
Nicholas v. Nicholas
Smith v. Canada (Attorney General)
Swan v. Canada (Attorney General)
Woodley v. Woodley

Pension Benefits Standards Act
Cattran v. Cattran
Lang v. Lang
Moslinger v. Moslinger
Trew v. Canadian Pacific Ltd.

Pensions In Pay
Abate v. Abate
Bellemare v. Bellemare
Clarke v. Clarke
Datt v. Datt
Kell v. Kell
King v. King
Lapointe v. Lapointe
MacMillan v. MacMillan
McDonald v. McDonald
McNutt v. McNutt
Northorp v. Northorp
Reardigan v. Reardigan
Robichaud v. Robichaud

Pre-Judgement Interest
Best v. Best
Bigelow v. Bigelow
Black v. Black
Bolyk v. Bolyk
Bourdeau v. Bourdeau
Burgess v. Burgess
Christian v. Christian
DaCosta v. DaCosta
Deane v. Deane
Delean v. Delean
Docherty v. Docherty
Drake v. Drake
Farquharson v. Farquharson
Fawcett v. Fawcett
Finlayson v. Finlayson
Godinek v. Godinek
Ismond v. Ismond
Johnson v. Johnson

Karakatsanis v. Georgiou
Keelan v. Keelan
Kozuch v. Kozuch
Lefevre v. Lefevre
Livermore v. Livermore
McDonald v. McDonald
McQuay v. McQuay
Milinkovic v. Milinkovic
Mollicone v. Mollicone
Morettin v. Morettin
Pelman v. Pelman
Price v. Price
Purcell v. Purcell
Reeson v. Kowalik
Rostek v. Rostek
Saeglitz v. Saeglitz
Schaeffer v. Schaeffer
Sengmueller v. Sengmueller
Starkman v. Starkman
Sykes v. Sykes
Taylor v. Taylor
Van Bork v. Van Bork
Zander v. Zander
Zegil v. Opie

Property—Inclusions
Brinkos v. Brinko—right to an income stream
Corless v. Corles—right to practice law (but no value)
Duff v. Duff—agreement to Purchase and sale
Gasparetto v. Gasparetto—retirement gratuity
Hodgins v. Hodgins—accrued vacation pay
Knapp v. Knapp—life interest in a farm
Marsham v. Marsham—severance pay
Oswell v. Oswell—retirement allowance in pay
Payne v. Payne— interest in accounting practice
Poisson v. Poisson—buy-out value of a leased car.

Property—Exclusions Allowed
Balcombe v. Balcome—disability pension in pay when disability stemmed from the marriage

Caratun v. Caratun –dental licence and right to practice dentistry
De Champlain v. de Champlain—claim for damages and personal injury
Dick v. Dick –death benefit provided in pension.
Gasparetto v. Gasparetto—early retirement incentive plan
Hodgins v. Hodgins—family allowance cheques invested for children; severance pay on wrongful dismissal
Marsh v. Marsh—stock options
Marsham v. Marsham—value of spouse's survivor benefit (may be an asset of spouse)
Ormerop v. Ormerop—pre-judgement interest on motor vehicle accident settlement
Payne v. Payne –Canada Pension Plan benefits
Rickett v. Rickett—accrued sick leave gratuity
Wasylyshyn v. Wasylyshyn—wrongful dismissal payment

Property—Deductions Allowed
Heon v. Heon –notional costs of converting all assets to after-tax cash
McPherson v. McPherson—disposition costs on sale of asset required to finance equalization payment
Sengmueller v. Sengmueller—notional disposition costs based on reasonable estimate of expected date of disposition

Property—Deductions Not Allowed
Conforti v. Conforti –contingent guarantee for mortgage liability
Davies v. Davies –children's furniture
Leslie v. Leslie—contingent liability for bank loan guarantee
Nicol v. Nicol –accrued income tax liability

Pro Rata Method
Best, T. v. Best, M.
Deane v. Deane
Gilmour v. Gilmour

Goulet v. Goulet
Miller v. Miller
Porter v. Porter
Ramsay v. Ramsay
Reardigan v. Reardigan
Rutherford v. Rutherford
Sauder v. Sauder
Scott v. Scott
Tanouye v. Tanouye
Valenti v. Valenti

RRSPs
Borys v. Borys
Deane v. Deane
James v. James
Johnson v. Johnson
Saeglitz v. Saeglitz
Sengmueller v. Sengmueller
Shaw v. Shaw
Stevenson v. Stevenson

Real Interest Method
Bascello v. Bascello
Halman v. Halman

Retirement Age—Actual Retirement
Schaefer v. Schaefer

Retirement Age—Earliest Date of Unreduced Pension
Best, T. v. Best, M.
Belyea v. Belyea
Bourdeau v. Bourdeau
Buston v. Buston
Brimblecomb v. Brimblecomb
Coscarella v. Coscarella
Coathup v. Coathup
Forster v. Forster
Hilderley v. Hilderley
Huisman v. Huisman
Ledrew v. Ledrew
Leeson v. Leeson
Lock v. Lock
Marsham v. Marsham
Miller v. Miller
Monger v. Monger
Saunders v. Saunders
Stokes v. Stokes
Weaver v. Weaver

Wiebe v. Wiebe

Retirement Age—Mid Point Age
Bascello v. Bascello
Rezler v. Rezler
Reusticus v. Resticus
Schofield v. Schofield

Retirement Age—Probable Age
Alger v. Alger
Christian v. Christian
Deroo v. Deroo
Dick v. Dick
Hodgins v. Hodgins
Huisman v. Huisman
Hussein v. Hussein
Knippshild v. Knippshild
Korcek v. Korcek
Lindsay v. Lindsay
Messier v. Messier
Patrick v. Patrick
Pennock v. Pennock
Purcell v. Purcell
Quintal v. Quintal
Radcliffe v. Radcliffe
Salib v. Cross
Sanders v. Sanders
Sauder v. Sauder
Stevens v. Stevens
Weise v. Weise

Retirement Age—Normal Age
Alford v. Che-Alford
Kennedy v. Kennedy
Kirton v. Kirton
Levac-Vicev v. Vicev
Mathews v. Mathews
Skiba v. Skiba
Van Geel v. Van Geel

Retirement Method
Dick v. Dick
Knippshild v. Knippshild
Miller v. Miller
Vanderra v. Vanderra

Retiring Allowances, Bonuses and Incentives
Alger v. Alger

Blais v. Blais
Bellemare v. Bellemare
Butt v. Butt
Cameron v. Cameron
Cliché v. Cliche
Durling v. Durling
Gasparetto v. Gasparetto
Hartnett v. Hartnett
Henry v. Henry
Hilderley v. Hilderley
Hutchison v. Hutchison
Levac-Vicev v. Vicev
Leavoy v. Leavoy
Lock v. Lock
Ostapyk v. Ostapyk
Oswell v. Oswell
Pallister v. Pallister
Rickett v. Rickett
Raffey v. Raffey
Stapleton v. Stapleton
Yaschuk v. Logan

Severance Benefits and Pay
Arvelin v. Arvelin
Bellemare v. Bellemare
Berghofer v. Berghofer
Bigelow v. Bigelow
Butt v. Butt
Cameron v. Cameron
Cattran v. Cattran
Chaytor v. Chaytor
Christian v. Christian
Clerke v. Clerke
Connolly v. Connolly
Cross v. Cross
Davies v. Davies
Edminson v. Bankowski
Emond v. Emond
Hartnett v. Hartnett
Henry v. Henry
Hodgins v. Hodgins
Hutchison v. Hutchison
Jenkins v. Jenkins
Klein v. Klein
Leith v. Leith
Leavoy v. Leavoy
Lock v. Lock
M. (E.E.) v. M. (P.F.)
MacLeod v. MacLeod

Marsham v. Marsham
Melanson v. Melanson
Moslinger v. Moslinger
Offet v. Offet
Olscamp v. Olscamp
Pretty v. Pretty
Read v. Read
Sangster v. Sangster
Schaeffer v. Schaeffer
Scott v. Scott
Stapleton v. Stapleton
Stewart v. Stewart
Sykes v. Sykes
Valenti v. Valenti
Yaschuk v. Logan

Sick Leave Gratuity
Alger v. Alger
Belyea v. Belyea
Cliché v. Chiche
Deroo v. Deroo
Gasparetto v. Gasparetto
Hartnett v. Hartnett
Henry v. Henry
Hilderley v. Hilderley
Hutchison v. Hutchison
Levac-Vicev v. Vicev
McIntosh v. McIntosh
Offet v. Offet
Ostapyk v. Ostapyk
Pallister v. Pallister
Ramsay v. Ramsay
Rickett v. Rickett
Sangster v. Sangster
Sousa v. Sousa
Stapleton v. Stapleton
Tanouye v. Tanouye
Woodman v. Dememo

Stock Options
Gardiner v. Gardiner

Survivor Benefits
Belyea v. Belyea
Bracewell v. Bracewell
Brice v. Brice
Britton Estate v. Britton
Davies v. Davies
Dick v. Dick

Fiorintino v. Fiorintino
Gilman v. Gilman
Hilderley v. Hilderley
Knippshild v. Knippshild
MacMillan v. MacMillan
Marsham v. Marsham
McDougall v. McDougall
McNutt v. McNutt
Miller v. Miller
Monger v. Monger
Pevecz v. Pevecz
Shaward v. Shaward
Smiley v. Ontario Pension Board
Storms v. Storms
Weibe v. Weibe

Tax Considerations
Alford v. Che
Alger v. Alger
Armstrong v. Armstrong
Aylsworth v. Aylsworth
Bascello v. Bascello
Best, L. v. Best, M.
Borys v. Borys
Davies v. Davies
Deane v. Deane
Dick v. Dick
Drake v. Drake
Forster v. Forster
Gasparetto v. Gasparetto
Goodfield v. Goodfield
Gresham v. Gresham
Halpin v. Halpin
Harbour v. Harbour
Hilderley v. Hilderley
Hodgins v. Hodgins
Humphreys v. Humphreys
Johnson v. Johnson
Johnstone v. Johnstone
Knippshild v. Knippshild
Marsham v. Marsham
Messier v. Messier
McPherson v. McPherson
Miller v. Miller
Monger v. Monger
O'Hara v. O'Hara
Offet v. Offet
Purcell v. Purcell
Radcliff v. Radcliff

Reilly v. Reilly
Rezler v. Rezler
Richter v. Richter
Saeglitz v. Saeglitz
Salib v. Cross
Sengmueller v. Sengmueller
Starkman v. Starkman
Stevens v. Stevens
Stevenson v. Stevenson
Strahl v. Strahl
Sutherland v. Sutherland
Tanouye v. Tanouye
Van Geel v. Van Geel
Weise v. Weise
Yaschuk v. Logan

Termination Method
Alger v. Alger
Bascello v. Bascello
Belyea v. Balyea
Best, T. v. Best, M.
Deroo v. Deroo
Halman v. Halman
Hilderley v. Hilderley
Humphreys v. Humphreys
Kennedy v. Kennedy
Knippshild v. Knippshild
Marsham v. Marsham
Monger v. Monger
O'Hara v. O'Hara
Rickett v. Rickett
Salib v. Cross
Saunders v. Saunders
Schaefer v. Schaefer
Stokes v. Stokes and Lennox
Weaver v. Weaver
Weise v. Weise
Zado v. Zado

Tracing
Allgeier v. Allgeier

Unequal Division
Everson v. Rich
Ford v. Werden
Johnston v. Johnston
Merklinger v. Merklinger
Sorochan v. Sorochan
Warren v. Warren

Unjust Enrichment
Becker v. Pettkus
Ford v. Werden
Peter v. Beblow

Unvested Benefits
Askins v. Askins
Aubie v. Aubie
Austin v. Austin
Aylsworth v. Aylsworth
Bascello v. Bascello
Dimock-Cummings v. Cummings
Flynn v. Flynn
Forster v. Forster
Gardiner v. Gardiner
Gascoyne v. Gascoyne
Lauzon v. Lauzon
Lefort v. Lefort
Lock v. Lock
Lovegrove v. Lovegrove
Lowe v. Lowe
Morgan v. Morgan
Nix v. Nix
Peckford v. Peckford
Reimer v. Reimer
Ryan v. Ryan
Simms v. Simms
Stevens v. Stevens
Swallow v. Swallow
Tetz v. Tetz
Thompson v. Thompson
Ward v. Ward
Yeo v. Yeo
Yeudall v. Yeudall

Vacation Pay
Cameron v. Cameron

Hodgins v. Hodgins
Kearley v. Kearley
Lenning v. Lenning
Maloney v. Maloney
Martin v. Martin
Moge v. Moge
Offet v. Offet
Savard v. Savard
Stewart v. Stewart
Yaschuk v. Logan

Value Added Method
Best, T. v. Best, M.
Deroo v. Deroo
Huisman v. Huisman
Levac-Vicev v. Vicev
Munro v. Munro
Rusticus v. Rusticus
Shaeffer v. Shaeffer

Sykes v. Sykes

Worker's Compensation—an Asset
Almeida v. Almeida
Arvelin v. Arvelin
Clark v. Clark
Dixon v. Dixon
Girouard v. Girouard
Rohl v. Rohl
Solomon v. Solomon

Worker's Compensation—Not an Asset
Entesary v. Entesary
Buske v. Buske
Snajaric v. Snajaric

Appendix B

Child Support Guidelines

The Federal Government established the guidelines and the provinces adopted them, with slight variations. The actual guideline amounts are different for each province and are subject to change at any time. In addition to the guideline amount there may be a requirement for the parties to share special expenses.

The following table was taken from the Federal Government's web site—http://canada.justice.gc.ca

The Department of Justice Canada has a toll-free number for information on the Guidelines. On request, they will send you more detailed information as it becomes available. Call 1-888-373-2222.

Monthly Award				Monthly Award				Monthly Award			
No. of Children				No. of Children				No. of Children			
Income 1	2	3	4	Income 1	2	3	4	Income 1	2	3	4
6700	0	0	0	0	12900	104	197	227	253	19100	149	274	375	457
6800	4	4	4	4	13000	105	198	230	256	19200	151	275	376	459
6900	9	9	10	11	13100	105	200	234	260	19300	152	276	378	461
7000	14	15	16	17	13200	106	201	237	264	19400	154	278	380	463
7100	19	20	22	23	13300	107	201	240	267	19500	155	279	381	465
7200	24	25	27	29	13400	108	203	243	271	19600	157	280	383	467
7300	29	31	33	36	13500	109	205	246	275	19700	158	281	385	469
7400	34	36	39	42	13600	110	206	250	278	19800	160	283	386	472
7500	39	42	45	48	13700	111	207	253	282	19900	161	284	388	474
7600	44	47	51	54	13800	112	208	256	285	20000	163	285	390	476
7700	49	53	57	61	13900	112	210	259	289	20100	164	286	392	478
7800	54	58	62	67	14000	113	211	262	293	20200	166	287	393	480
7900	58	63	68	73	14100	114	212	266	296	20300	167	289	395	482
8000	62	67	72	78	14200	115	213	269	300	20400	169	290	397	484
8100	62	71	76	82	14300	115	215	272	304	20500	170	291	398	486
8200	63	74	80	86	14400	116	216	275	307	20600	172	292	400	488
8300	64	78	84	91	14500	117	217	278	311	20700	173	294	402	490
8400	65	81	88	95	14600	117	218	282	314	20800	175	295	403	492
8500	66	85	92	100	14700	118	219	285	318	20900	176	296	405	494
8600	67	89	96	104	14800	119	221	288	322	21000	178	297	407	496
8700	68	92	100	109	14900	119	222	291	325	21100	179	299	408	498
8800	69	96	104	113	15000	120	223	294	329	21200	181	300	410	500
8900	69	99	108	117	15100	121	224	298	333	21300	182	301	412	502
9000	70	102	112	121	15200	121	226	301	336	21400	184	302	413	504
9100	71	104	114	124	15300	122	227	304	340	21500	185	304	415	506
9200	72	106	116	126	15400	123	228	307	343	21600	187	305	417	508
9300	73	107	118	129	15500	123	229	310	347	21700	188	306	418	510
9400	74	109	120	131	15600	124	231	314	351	21800	189	307	420	512
9500	75	111	122	134	15700	125	232	317	354	21900	191	309	422	515
9600	75	112	124	136	15800	126	233	319	358	22000	192	310	424	517
9700	76	114	126	139	15900	126	234	321	361	22100	194	311	425	519
9800	77	115	128	141	16000	127	236	323	365	22200	195	312	427	521
9900	78	117	130	144	16100	128	237	324	369	22300	196	313	429	523

Monthly Award				Monthly Award				Monthly Award			
No. of Children				No. of Children				No. of Children			
Income	1	2	3	4	Income	1	2	3	4	Income	1	2	3	4

Income	1	2	3	4	Income	1	2	3	4	Income	1	2	3	4
10000	79	119	132	146	16200	128	238	326	372	22400	197	315	430	525
10100	80	121	135	149	16300	129	239	328	376	22500	198	316	432	527
10200	81	124	138	153	16400	130	241	329	380	22600	199	317	434	529
10300	81	127	142	156	16500	130	242	331	383	22700	200	318	435	531
10400	82	130	145	160	16600	131	243	333	387	22800	201	320	437	533
10500	83	133	148	164	16700	132	244	334	390	22900	202	321	439	535
10600	84	136	152	168	16800	132	245	336	394	23000	203	322	440	537
10700	85	138	155	172	16900	133	247	338	398	23100	204	323	442	539
10800	86	141	158	175	17000	134	248	339	401	23200	205	325	444	541
10900	87	144	162	179	17100	134	249	341	405	23300	206	326	445	543
11000	87	147	165	183	17200	135	250	343	409	23400	207	328	447	545
11100	88	150	168	187	17300	136	252	344	412	23500	208	330	449	547
11200	89	153	172	190	17400	136	253	346	416	23600	209	332	450	549
11300	90	156	175	194	17500	137	254	348	419	23700	210	334	452	551
11400	91	159	179	198	17600	138	255	349	423	23800	211	336	454	553
11500	92	162	182	202	17700	138	257	351	427	23900	212	338	455	556
11600	93	165	185	206	17800	139	258	353	430	24000	213	340	457	558
11700	93	168	189	209	17900	140	259	354	433	24100	213	342	459	560
11800	94	171	192	213	18000	140	260	356	435	24200	214	344	461	562
11900	95	174	195	217	18100	141	262	358	437	24300	215	346	462	564
12000	96	176	198	220	18200	142	263	360	439	24400	216	348	464	566
12100	97	179	202	224	18300	142	264	361	441	24500	217	350	466	568
12200	98	182	205	228	18400	143	265	363	443	24600	218	352	467	570
12300	99	185	208	231	18500	144	266	365	445	24700	219	354	469	572
12400	100	188	211	235	18600	144	268	366	447	24800	220	356	471	574
12500	100	190	214	238	18700	145	269	368	449	24900	221	358	472	576
12600	101	193	218	242	18800	146	270	370	451	25000	222	360	474	578
12700	102	195	221	246	18900	147	271	371	453	25100	223	362	476	580
12800	103	196	224	249	19000	148	273	373	455	25200	224	364	477	582

Monthly Award				Monthly Award				Monthly Award			
No. of Children				No. of Children				No. of Children			
Income	1	2	3	4	Income	1	2	3	4	Income	1	2	3	4

Income	1	2	3	4	Income	1	2	3	4	Income	1	2	3	4
25300	225	366	479	584	31500	277	462	600	697	37700	327	540	710	849
25400	226	368	481	586	31600	278	463	602	699	37800	328	542	712	851
25500	227	370	482	588	31700	278	465	604	702	37900	328	543	713	853
25600	228	372	484	590	31800	279	466	606	704	38000	329	544	715	855
25700	229	374	486	592	31900	280	467	608	706	38100	330	546	717	857
25800	230	375	487	594	32000	281	468	611	709	38200	331	547	718	859
25900	231	377	489	596	32100	281	469	613	711	38300	332	548	720	861
26000	232	379	491	598	32200	282	470	615	714	38400	332	549	722	862
26100	232	381	492	600	32300	283	472	617	706	38500	333	551	723	864
26200	233	383	494	602	32400	284	473	620	718	38600	334	552	725	866
26300	234	385	495	604	32500	285	474	622	721	38700	335	553	727	868
26400	235	387	497	606	32600	286	476	624	723	38800	336	554	728	870
26500	236	389	498	608	32700	286	477	627	726	38900	337	556	730	872
26600	237	390	500	610	32800	287	478	629	728	39000	337	557	732	874
26700	238	392	502	612	32900	288	479	631	731	39100	338	558	733	876
26800	239	394	503	613	33000	289	481	633	733	39200	339	559	735	878
26900	239	396	505	615	33100	290	482	635	736	39300	340	561	737	880
27000	240	398	506	617	33200	291	483	637	738	39400	341	562	738	882
27100	241	400	508	619	33300	291	484	639	741	39500	341	563	740	884
27200	242	402	509	621	33400	292	486	640	743	39600	342	564	742	886
27300	243	403	511	623	33500	293	487	642	746	39700	343	566	743	888
27400	244	405	512	625	33600	294	488	643	748	39800	344	567	745	890
27500	245	407	514	627	33700	295	489	645	751	39900	345	568	747	892
27600	246	409	516	629	33800	296	491	647	753	40000	345	570	748	894
27700	246	411	518	630	33900	296	492	648	756	40100	346	571	750	896
27800	247	413	521	632	34000	297	493	650	758	40200	347	572	752	898
27900	248	415	523	634	34100	298	494	651	761	40300	348	573	753	900
28000	249	416	525	636	34200	299	496	653	763	40400	349	575	755	902
28100	250	418	527	638	34300	300	497	655	766	40500	350	576	757	904
28200	251	420	529	640	34400	301	498	656	768	40600	350	577	759	906
28300	252	422	532	642	34500	301	499	658	771	40700	351	579	760	908
28400	253	424	534	644	34600	302	501	659	773	40800	352	580	762	910
28500	254	426	536	646	34700	303	502	661	776	40900	353	581	764	912

Monthly Award				Monthly Award				Monthly Award			
No. of Children				No. of Children				No. of Children			
Income 1	2	3	4	Income 1	2	3	4	Income 1	2	3	4
28600 254	428	538	647	34800 304	503	663	778	41000 354	583	765	914
28700 255	429	540	649	34900 304	504	664	781	41100 355	584	767	916
28800 256	430	543	651	35000 305	506	666	783	41200 356	585	769	918
28900 257	432	545	653	35100 306	507	667	786	41300 356	587	771	920
29000 258	433	547	655	35200 307	508	669	788	41400 357	588	772	922
29100 259	434	549	657	35300 308	509	671	791	41500 358	589	774	924
29200 260	436	551	659	35400 308	511	672	793	41600 359	590	776	926
29300 261	437	554	661	35500 309	512	674	796	41800 361	593	779	930
29400 261	439	556	662	35600 310	513	675	798	41900 361	594	781	932
29500 262	440	558	664	35700 311	514	677	801	42000 362	596	782	934
29600 263	441	560	666	35800 311	516	679	803	42100 363	597	784	936
29700 264	442	562	668	35900 312	517	680	806	42200 364	598	786	938
29800 265	443	564	669	36000 313	518	682	809	42300 365	600	787	940
29900 265	444	566	670	36100 314	520	683	811	42400 366	601	789	942
30000 266	446	568	672	36200 315	521	685	814	42500 366	602	791	944
30100 267	447	570	673	36300 315	522	687	816	42600 367	604	792	946
30200 267	448	572	674	36400 316	523	688	819	42700 368	605	794	948
30300 268	449	575	675	36500 317	525	690	821	42800 369	606	796	950
30400 269	450	577	677	36600 318	526	692	824	42900 370	607	798	952
30500 269	451	579	678	36700 319	527	693	827	43000 371	609	799	954
30600 270	452	581	679	36800 319	529	695	829	43100 371	610	801	956
30700 271	453	583	681	36900 320	530	697	832	43200 372	611	803	958
30800 272	454	585	682	37000 321	531	698	834	43300 373	613	804	960
30900 272	455	587	684	37100 322	533	700	837	43400 374	614	806	962
31000 273	456	589	685	37200 323	534	702	839	43500 375	615	808	964
31100 274	458	591	688	37300 324	535	703	841	43600 376	617	809	966
31200 275	459	594	690	37400 324	537	705	843	43700 377	618	811	969
31300 275	460	596	692	37500 325	538	707	845	43800 377	619	813	971
31400 276	461	598	695	37600 326	539	708	847	43900 378	621	814	973

Monthly Award				Monthly Award				Monthly Award			
No. of Children				No. of Children				No. of Children			
Income 1	2	3	4	Income 1	2	3	4	Income 1	2	3	4
44000 379	622	816	975	50300 432	704	922	1100	56500 479	780	1021	1217
44100 380	623	818	977	50400 433	705	924	1102	56600 480	781	1022	1219
44200 381	624	819	979	50500 434	707	925	1104	56700 481	783	1024	1221
44300 382	626	821	981	50600 434	708	927	1106	56800 482	784	1025	1223
44400 382	627	823	983	50700 435	709	929	1108	56900 483	785	1027	1225
44500 383	628	824	985	50800 436	711	930	1110	57000 483	786	1029	1227
44600 384	630	826	987	50900 437	712	932	1112	57100 484	788	1030	1229
44700 385	631	828	989	51000 438	713	934	1114	57200 485	789	1032	1231
44800 386	632	829	991	51100 439	715	935	1116	57300 486	790	1033	1233
44900 387	634	831	993	51200 440	716	937	1118	57400 487	791	1035	1234
45000 387	635	833	995	51300 440	717	939	1120	57500 488	793	1037	1236
45100 388	636	834	997	51400 441	719	940	1122	57600 488	794	1038	1238
45200 389	637	836	999	51500 442	720	942	1124	57700 489	795	1040	1240
45300 390	639	838	1001	51600 443	721	944	1126	57800 490	796	1042	1242
45400 391	640	840	1003	51700 444	722	945	1128	57900 491	798	1043	1244
45500 392	641	841	1005	51800 445	724	947	1130	58000 492	799	1045	1246
45600 392	643	843	1007	51900 445	725	949	1132	58100 492	800	1046	1248
45700 393	644	845	1009	52000 446	726	950	1134	58200 493	801	1048	1250
45800 394	645	846	1011	52100 447	728	952	1136	58300 494	803	1050	1252
45900 395	647	848	1013	52200 448	729	954	1138	58400 495	804	1051	1253
46000 396	648	850	1015	52300 449	730	955	1140	58500 496	805	1053	1255
46100 397	649	851	1017	52400 450	731	957	1142	58600 496	806	1054	1257
46200 398	651	853	1019	52500 450	733	959	1143	58700 497	808	1056	1259
46300 398	652	855	1021	52600 451	734	960	1145	58800 498	809	1058	1261
46400 399	653	856	1023	52700 452	735	962	1147	58900 499	810	1059	1263
46500 400	654	858	1025	52800 452	736	963	1149	59000 500	811	1061	1265
46600 401	656	860	1027	52900 453	737	965	1151	59100 500	813	1062	1267
46800 403	658	863	1031	53000 454	739	966	1153	59200 501	814	1064	1269
46900 403	660	865	1032	53100 455	740	968	1154	59300 502	815	1065	1270
47000 404	661	866	1034	53200 455	741	969	1156	59400 503	816	1067	1272
47100 405	662	868	1036	53300 456	742	971	1158	59500 503	817	1068	1274
47200 406	664	870	1038	53400 457	743	972	1160	59600 504	818	1070	1276
47300 407	665	871	1040	53500 457	744	974	1162	59700 505	820	1071	1277

Monthly Award				Monthly Award				Monthly Award			
No. of Children				No. of Children				No. of Children			
Income 1	2	3	4	Income 1	2	3	4	Income 1	2	3	4
47400 408	666	873	1042	53600 458	746	976	1164	59800 506	821	1073	1279
47500 408	668	875	1044	53700 459	747	977	1165	59900 506	822	1074	1281
47600 409	669	876	1046	53800 460	748	979	1167	60000 507	823	1076	1283
47700 410	670	878	1048	53900 460	749	980	1169	60100 508	824	1077	1284
47800 411	671	880	1050	54000 461	750	982	1171	60200 509	825	1079	1286
47900 412	673	882	1052	54100 462	751	983	1173	60300 509	826	1080	1288
48000 413	674	883	1054	54200 462	753	985	1175	60400 510	828	1082	1290
48100 413	675	885	1056	54300 463	754	986	1177	60500 511	829	1083	1291
48200 414	677	887	1058	54400 464	755	988	1178	60600 511	830	1085	1293
48300 415	678	888	1060	54500 465	756	989	1180	60700 512	831	1086	1295
48400 416	679	890	1062	54600 465	757	991	1182	60800 513	832	1088	1297
48500 417	681	892	1064	54700 466	758	992	1184	60900 514	833	1089	1298
48600 418	682	893	1066	54800 467	760	994	1186	61000 514	834	1091	1300
48700 419	683	895	1068	54900 467	761	996	1188	61100 515	836	1092	1302
48800 419	685	897	1070	55000 468	762	997	1189	61200 516	837	1093	1303
48900 420	686	898	1072	55100 469	763	999	1191	61300 517	838	1095	1305
49000 421	687	900	1074	55200 470	764	1000	1193	61400 517	839	1096	1307
49100 422	688	902	1076	55300 470	766	1002	1195	61500 518	840	1098	1309
49200 423	690	903	1078	55400 471	767	1003	1197	61600 519	841	1099	1310
49300 424	691	905	1080	55500 472	768	1005	1199	61700 520	843	1101	1312
49400 424	692	907	1082	55600 472	769	1006	1200	61800 520	844	1102	1314
49500 425	694	908	1084	55700 473	770	1008	1202	61900 521	845	1104	1316
49600 426	695	910	1086	55800 474	771	1009	1204	62000 522	846	1105	1317
49700 427	696	912	1088	55900 475	773	1011	1206	62100 523	847	1107	1319
49800 428	698	913	1090	56000 475	774	1013	1208	62200 523	848	1108	1321
49900 429	699	915	1092	56100 476	775	1014	1210	62300 524	849	1110	1323
50000 429	700	917	1094	56200 477	776	1016	1212	62400 525	851	1111	1324
50100 430	702	918	1096	56300 478	778	1017	1214	62500 525	852	1113	1326
50200 431	703	920	1098	56400 479	779	1019	1215	62600 526	853	1114	1328

Monthly Award				Monthly Award				Monthly Award			
No. of Children				No. of Children				No. of Children			
Income 1	**2**	**3**	**4**	**Income 1**	**2**	**3**	**4**	**Income 1**	**2**	**3**	**4**
62700 527	854	1116	1330	69100 566	918	1200	1430	75500 609	985	1285	1531
62800 528	855	1117	1331	69200 566	919	1201	1432	75600 609	986	1287	1533
62900 528	856	1119	1333	69300 567	920	1202	1433	75700 610	987	1288	1535
63000 529	857	1120	1335	69400 568	921	1204	1435	75800 611	988	1289	1536
63100 530	859	1121	1337	69500 568	922	1205	1436	75900 611	989	1291	1538
63200 531	860	1123	1338	69600 569	923	1206	1438	76000 612	990	1292	1539
63300 531	861	1124	1340	69700 570	924	1208	1440	76100 613	991	1293	1541
63400 532	862	1126	1342	69800 570	925	1209	1441	76200 613	992	1295	1542
63500 533	863	1127	1344	69900 571	926	1210	1443	76300 614	993	1296	1544
63600 533	864	1129	1345	70000 572	927	1212	1444	76400 615	994	1297	1546
63700 534	865	1130	1347	70100 572	928	1213	1446	76500 615	995	1299	1547
63800 535	866	1132	1348	70200 573	929	1214	1447	76600 616	996	1300	1549
63900 535	867	1133	1350	70300 574	930	1216	1449	76700 617	997	1301	1550
64000 536	868	1134	1352	70400 574	931	1217	1451	76800 617	998	1303	1552
64100 537	870	1136	1353	70500 575	932	1218	1452	76900 618	999	1304	1554
64200 537	871	1137	1355	70600 576	934	1220	1454	77000 619	1000	1305	1555
64300 538	872	1138	1357	70700 576	935	1221	1455	77100 619	1001	1307	1557
64400 539	873	1140	1358	70800 577	936	1222	1457	77200 620	1002	1308	1558
64500 539	874	1141	1360	70900 578	937	1224	1459	77300 621	1003	1309	1560
64600 540	875	1143	1362	71000 578	938	1225	1460	77400 621	1004	1311	1561
64700 541	876	1144	1363	71100 579	939	1226	1462	77500 622	1005	1312	1563
64800 541	877	1145	1365	71200 580	940	1228	1463	77600 623	1006	1313	1565
64900 542	878	1147	1367	71300 581	941	1229	1465	77700 623	1007	1315	1566
65000 543	879	1148	1368	71400 581	942	1230	1466	77800 624	1009	1316	1568
65100 543	880	1150	1370	71500 582	943	1232	1468	77900 625	1010	1317	1569
65200 544	881	1151	1371	71600 583	944	1233	1470	78000 625	1011	1319	1571
65300 544	882	1152	1373	71700 583	945	1234	1471	78100 626	1012	1320	1573
65400 545	883	1153	1374	71800 584	946	1236	1473	78200 627	1013	1321	1574
65500 545	884	1154	1376	71900 585	947	1237	1474	78300 627	1014	1323	1576
65600 546	885	1156	1377	72000 585	948	1238	1476	78400 628	1015	1324	1577
65700 546	886	1157	1379	72100 586	949	1240	1478	78500 629	1016	1325	1579
65800 547	886	1158	1380	72200 587	950	1241	1479	78600 629	1017	1327	1580
65900 547	887	1159	1382	72300 587	951	1242	1481	78700 630	1018	1328	1582

Monthly Award				Monthly Award				Monthly Award			
No. of Children				No. of Children				No. of Children			
Income 1	**2**	**3**	**4**	**Income 1**	**2**	**3**	**4**	**Income 1**	**2**	**3**	**4**
66000 548	888	1160	1383	72400 588	952	1244	1482	78800 631	1019	1330	1584
66100 548	889	1162	1385	72500 589	953	1245	1484	78900 631	1020	1331	1585
66200 549	890	1163	1386	72600 589	954	1246	1485	79000 632	1021	1332	1587
66300 549	891	1164	1388	72700 590	955	1248	1487	79100 633	1022	1334	1588
66400 550	892	1165	1389	72800 591	956	1249	1489	79200 633	1023	1335	1590
66500 550	893	1166	1390	72900 591	957	1250	1490	79300 634	1024	1336	1592
66600 551	894	1168	1392	73000 592	959	1252	1492	79400 635	1025	1338	1593
66700 552	895	1169	1393	73100 593	960	1253	1493	79500 635	1026	1339	1595
66800 552	895	1170	1395	73200 593	961	1255	1495	79600 636	1027	1340	1596
66900 553	896	1171	1396	73300 594	962	1256	1497	79700 637	1028	1342	1598
67000 553	897	1173	1398	73400 595	963	1257	1498	79800 637	1029	1343	1599
67100 554	898	1174	1399	73500 595	964	1259	1500	79900 638	1030	1344	1601
67200 554	899	1175	1401	73600 596	965	1260	1501	80000 639	1031	1346	1603
67300 555	900	1176	1402	73700 597	966	1261	1503	80100 639	1032	1347	1604
67400 555	901	1178	1404	73800 597	967	1263	1504	80200 640	1034	1348	1606
67500 556	902	1179	1405	73900 598	968	1264	1506	80300 641	1035	1350	1607
67600 556	903	1180	1407	74000 599	969	1265	1508	80400 641	1036	1351	1609
67700 557	904	1181	1408	74100 599	970	1267	1509	80500 642	1037	1352	1611
67800 558	905	1183	1410	74200 600	971	1268	1511	80600 643	1038	1354	1612
67900 558	906	1184	1411	74300 601	972	1269	1512	80700 643	1039	1355	1614
68000 559	907	1185	1413	74400 601	973	1271	1514	80800 644	1040	1356	1615
68100 559	908	1186	1414	74500 602	974	1272	1516	80900 645	1041	1358	1617
68200 560	909	1188	1416	74600 603	975	1273	1517	81000 645	1042	1359	1618
68300 560	910	1189	1417	74700 603	976	1275	1519	81100 646	1043	1360	1620
68400 561	911	1190	1419	74800 604	977	1276	1520	81200 647	1044	1362	1622
68500 562	912	1192	1421	74900 605	978	1277	1522	81300 647	1045	1363	1623
68600 562	913	1193	1422	75000 605	979	1279	1523	81400 648	1046	1364	1625
68700 563	914	1194	1424	75100 606	980	1280	1525	81500 649	1047	1366	1626
68800 564	915	1196	1425	75200 607	981	1281	1527	81600 649	1048	1367	1628
68900 564	916	1197	1427	75300 607	982	1283	1528	81700 650	1049	1368	1630
69000 565	917	1198	1428	75400 608	984	1284	1530	81800 651	1050	1370	1631

Monthly Award				Monthly Award				Monthly Award			
No. of Children				No. of Children				No. of Children			
Income 1	2	3	4	Income 1	2	3	4	Income 1	2	3	4
81900 651	1051	1371	1633	88300 694	1118	1457	1734	94700 737	1185	1542	1835
82000 652	1052	1372	1634	88400 695	1119	1458	1736	94800 738	1186	1544	1837
82100 653	1053	1374	1636	88500 696	1120	1459	1737	94900 739	1187	1545	1838
82200 654	1054	1375	1637	88600 696	1121	1461	1739	95000 739	1188	1546	1840
82300 654	1055	1376	1639	88700 697	1122	1462	1740	95100 740	1189	1548	1842
82400 655	1056	1378	1641	88800 698	1123	1463	1742	95200 741	1190	1549	1843
82500 656	1057	1379	1642	88900 698	1124	1465	1743	95300 741	1191	1551	1845
82600 656	1059	1380	1644	89000 699	1125	1466	1745	95400 742	1192	1552	1846
82700 657	1060	1382	1645	89100 700	1126	1467	1747	95500 743	1193	1553	1848
82800 658	1061	1383	1647	89200 700	1127	1469	1748	95600 743	1194	1555	1850
82900 658	1062	1384	1649	89300 701	1128	1470	1750	95700 744	1195	1556	1851
83000 659	1063	1386	1650	89400 702	1129	1471	1751	95800 745	1196	1557	1853
83100 660	1064	1387	1652	89500 702	1130	1473	1753	95900 745	1197	1559	1854
83200 660	1065	1388	1653	89600 703	1131	1474	1755	96000 746	1198	1560	1856
83300 661	1066	1390	1655	89700 704	1132	1456	1756	96100 747	1199	1561	1857
83400 662	1067	1391	1656	89800 704	1134	1477	1758	96200 747	1200	1563	1859
83500 662	1068	1392	1658	89900 705	1135	1478	1759	96300 748	1201	1564	1861
83600 663	1069	1394	1660	90000 706	1136	1480	1761	96400 749	1202	1565	1862
83700 664	1070	1395	1661	90100 706	1137	1481	1762	96500 749	1203	1567	1864
83800 664	1071	1396	1663	90200 707	1138	1482	1764	96600 750	1204	1568	1865
83900 665	1072	1398	1664	90300 708	1139	1484	1766	96700 751	1205	1569	1867
84000 666	1073	1399	1666	90400 708	1140	1485	1767	96800 751	1206	1571	1869
84100 666	1074	1400	1668	90500 709	1141	1486	1769	96900 752	1207	1572	1870
84200 667	1075	1402	1669	90600 710	1142	1488	1770	97000 753	1209	1573	1872
84300 668	1076	1403	1671	90700 710	1143	1489	1772	97100 753	1210	1575	1873
84400 668	1077	1405	1672	90800 711	1144	1490	1774	97200 754	1211	1576	1875
84500 669	1078	1406	1674	90900 712	1145	1492	1775	97300 755	1212	1577	1876
84600 670	1079	1407	1675	91000 712	1146	1493	1777	97400 755	1213	1579	1878
84700 670	1080	1409	1677	91100 713	1147	1494	1778	97500 756	1214	1580	1880
84800 671	1081	1410	1679	91200 714	1148	1496	1780	97600 757	1215	1581	1881
84900 672	1082	1411	1680	91300 714	1149	1497	1781	97700 757	1216	1583	1883
85000 672	1084	1413	1682	91400 715	1150	1498	1783	97800 758	1217	1584	1884
85100 673	1085	1414	1683	91500 716	1151	1500	1785	97900 759	1218	1585	1886

Child Support Guidelines

Monthly Award					Monthly Award					Monthly Award			
No. of Children					No. of Children					No. of Children			
Income	1	2	3	4	Income	1	2	3	4	Income	1	2	3	4

Income	1	2	3	4
85200	674	1086	1415	1685
85300	674	1087	1417	1687
85400	675	1088	1418	1688
85500	676	1089	1419	1690
85600	676	1090	1421	1691
85700	677	1091	1422	1693
85800	678	1092	1423	1694
85900	678	1093	1425	1696
86000	679	1094	1426	1698
86100	680	1095	1427	1699
86200	680	1096	1429	1701
86300	681	1097	1430	1702
86400	682	1098	1431	1704
86500	682	1099	1433	1705
86600	683	1110	1434	1707
86700	684	1111	1435	1709
86800	684	1102	1437	1710
86900	685	1103	1438	1712
87000	686	1104	1439	1713
87100	686	1105	1441	1715
87200	687	1106	1442	1717
87300	688	1107	1443	1718
93800	731	1175	1530	1821
87600	690	1111	1447	1723
94100	733	1178	1534	1826
87900	692	1114	1451	1728
94400	735	1181	1538	1831
88200	694	1117	1455	1732

Income	1	2	3	4
91600	716	1152	1501	1786
91700	717	1153	1502	1788
91800	718	1154	1504	1789
91900	718	1155	1505	1791
92000	719	1156	1506	1793
92100	720	1157	1508	1794
92200	720	1159	1509	1796
92300	721	1160	1510	1797
92400	722	1161	1512	1799
92500	722	1162	1513	1800
92600	723	1163	1514	1802
92700	724	1164	1516	1804
92800	724	1165	1517	1805
92900	725	1166	1518	1807
93000	726	1167	1520	1808
93100	726	1168	1521	1810
93200	727	1169	1522	1812
93300	728	1170	1524	1813
93400	729	1171	1525	1815
93500	729	1172	1526	1816
93600	730	1173	1528	1818
93700	731	1174	1529	1819
87500	689	1110	1446	1721
94000	733	1177	1533	1824
87800	691	1113	1450	1726
94300	735	1180	1537	1829
88100	693	1116	1454	1731
94600	737	1184	1541	1834

Income	1	2	3	4
98000	759	1219	1587	1888
98100	760	1220	1588	1889
98200	761	1221	1589	1891
98300	761	1222	1591	1892
98400	762	1223	1592	1894
98500	763	1224	1593	1895
98600	763	1225	1595	1897
98700	764	1226	1596	1899
98800	765	1227	1597	1900
98900	765	1228	1599	1902
99000	766	1229	1600	1903
99100	767	1230	1601	1905
99200	767	1231	1603	1907
99300	768	1233	1604	1908
99400	769	1234	1605	1910
99500	769	1235	1607	1911
99600	770	1236	1608	1913
99700	771	1237	1609	1914
99800	771	1238	1611	1916
99900	772	1239	1612	1918
100000	773	1240	1613	1919
87400	688	1109	1445	1720
93900	732	1176	1532	1823
87700	690	1112	1449	1724
94200	734	1179	1536	1827
88000	692	1115	1453	1729
94500	736	1182	1540	1832

Appendix C

Financial Statements

The financial statement form and Net Family Property statement will be required by your lawyer. Complete them to the best of your ability. Consider retaining an accountant or a financial advisor to assist you, as these forms can affect your financial settlement substantially.

Court File Number

(Name of Court)

At _____

Applicant(s).

Full legal name & address for service—street & number, municipality, postal code, telephone & fax and e-mail address (if any)	Lawyer's name & address—street & number, municipality, postal code, telephone & fax numbers and e-mail address (if any).

Respondent(s)

Full legal name & address for service—street & number, municipality, postal code, telephone & fax and e-mail address (if any)	Lawyer's name & address—street & number, municipality, postal code, telephone & fax numbers and e-mail address (if any).

My name is *(full legal name)*

    I live in *(municipality & province)*

    And I swear/affirm that the following is true:

1.   My financial statement set out on the following pages is accurate to the best of my knowledge and belief and sets out the financial situation as of *(give date for which information is accurate)* for

Check one or **more boxes** *as circumstances require.*

    ◻ me

    ◻ the children listed in Part 1 of this statement

◻ the following person(s): *[Give name(s) and relationship to you.]*

2.   I attach to this statement:

See the instructions in the note on the next page

        ◻ Parts 1 to 6 of this Form and the documents mentioned in Part 2 (items 9 to 12).

        ◻ Part 7 of this Form.

        ◻ Parts ◻ 8 to 10 of this Form.

        ◻ 11 to 16 of this Form.

Sworn/Affirmed before me at
 	
                             municipality
In
          province, state or country
on
    date	

Commissioner for taking affidavits *(Type or print name below if signature is illegible.)*	**Signature** **(This form is to be signed in front of a lawyer, justice of the peace, notary public or commissioner for taking affidavits.)** ***Continued on next sheet***

HOW TO FILL OUT THIS FORM

You must fill out and attach Parts 1 to 6 of this Form if this case includes:

- ☐ a claim for support;
- ☐ a claim for a change in support;
- ☐ an enforcement of a support order or of the support provisions of a domestic contract or paternity agreement;
- ☐ a claim for custody or access where the court has ordered the filing of a financial statement.
- ☐ a claim for exclusive possession of a matrimonial home and its contents; or
- ☐ a property dispute that does not involve equalization of net family property under Part 1 of the *Family Law Act.* .

You must also fill out and attach Part 7, **BUT ONLY IF THIS CASE INCLUDES A CLAIM FOR CHILD SUPPORT THAT IS DIFFERENT FROM THE TABLE AMOUNT IN THE CHILD SUPPORT GUIDE-LINES** (a claim for add-ons for special or extraordinary expenses for the child(ren); a child 18 years of age or more; a claim for undue hardship; a support claim in a case of split or shared custody; or a case where a party's annual income is over $150, 000).

Finally, you must also give information about your property and your debts. **YOU MUST FILL OUT AND ATTACH:**

(a) **PARTS 8 TO 10** if this case includes one or more of the matters mentioned above, BUT NOT a claim for equalization net family property under Part 1 of the *Family Law Act;*
   OR

(b) **PARTS 11 TO 16** if this case includes a claim for equalization of net family property under Part 1 of the *Family Law Act*, even if it also includes one or more of the matters mentioned above.

For example, if this case is only about the equalization of family property under Part 1 of the *Family Law Act*, you would skip Parts 1 to 7 and only fill out and attach Parts 11 to 16.

FURTHER IMPORTANT NOTE

As soon as you find out that:

(a) the information in this financial statement is incorrect or incomplete; or

(b) there is a material change in your circumstances that affects or will affect the information in this financial statement, you MUST serve on every other party to this case and file with the court,

(c) the correct or complete information; or

(d) a new financial statement with updated information together with any documents that back up that information.

DECLARATION

This declaration is to be filled out only if your income is tax exempt because of your Indian status.

My name is *(full legal name)*

I live in *(municipality & province)*

And I declare that the following is true:

1. I am an Indian within the meaning of the Indian Act of Canada

2. Because of my status, my income tax is exempt and I am not required to file an income tax return.

3. I have therefore not filed an income tax return for the past three years.

Declared before me at *municipality* In *province, state or country* on *date*	 **Signature** (This form is to be signed in front of a lawyer, justice of the peace, notary public or commissioner for taking affidavits.)
Commissioner for taking affidavits *(Type or print name below if signature is illegible.)*	 ***Continued on next sheet***

Form 13: Financial Statement (page 3)   Court File Number

PARTS 1 TO 6 MUST BE FILLED OUT AND ATTACHED TO THIS
FINANCIAL STATEMENT if this case includes:

◻   a claim for support;

◻   a claim for a change in support;

◻   an enforcement of a support order or of the support provisions of a
    domestic contract or paternity agreement;

◻   a claim for custody or access where the court has ordered the filing of a
    financial statement;

◻   a claim for exclusive possession of the matrimonial home and its contents;
    or

◻   a property dispute that does not involve equalization of net family prop-
    erty under Part 1 of the *Family Law Act.*

You would skip this part if this case deals only with equalization of net family property.

PART 1: NAMES AND BIRTHDATES OF CHILD(REN)

Part 1 must be filled out if this case involves a claim by you or another party;

(a)   For child support;

(b)   For the enforcement of child support; or

*(c)   For custody of or access to a child, but only where a court has ordered each party
       to serve and file a financial statement;*

(d)   For any combination of the above.

You still have to fill out this Part, even if you have decided not to oppose another
party's claim for custody or child support. Part 1 does not apply if this case contains
no claim regarding children.

CHILD'S FULL LEGAL NAME	BIRTHDATE (d, m, y)	SEX
1.		
2.		
3.		
4.		
5.		

PART 2: INCOME

For the 12 months from   to

    Include all income and other money that you get from all sources, whether taxable or not. Show the gross amount here and show your deductions in Part 5. Give the current actual amount if you know it or can find out. If you can't find out, give your best estimate. To get a monthly figure for items 13 to 28, you must multiply any weekly income by 4.33 or divide any yearly sum be 12.

---

9. I am ▢   employed by *(name and address of employer)*

           ▢   self-employed, carrying on business under the name of
                (name and address of business)

           ▢   unemployed since (date when last employed)

10. I attach to this form:

        ▢ a copy of my income tax returns that were filed with the Department of National Revenue for the past 3 taxation years, together with a copy of all material filed with the returns and a copy of any notices of assessment or re-assessment that I have received from the Department for those years.

        ▢ a statement from the Department of National Revenue that I have not filed any income tax returns for the past 3 years.

        ▢ a declaration that I am not required to file an income tax return because of the *Indian Act* (Canada) [*Use the declaration at the bottom of page 2.*]

        ▢ a direction in Form 13A signed by me to the Taxation Branch of the Department of National Revenue for the disclosure of my tax returns and assessments for the past 3 years.

IMPORTANT! *If your case requires you to fill out and attach Parts 1 to 6, the clerk of the court will NOT allow you to file this financial statement unless you have checked one of the boxes in paragraph 10 above and have attached the required document(s).*

Continued on next sheet

Form 13: Financial Statement (page 4)   Court File Number

11. _____ I attach to this statement proof of my current income, including my most recent

     ◻ pay cheque stub.   ◻ employment insurance stub.

     ◻ worker's compensation stub.   ◻ pension stub.   ◻ (*Other, specify*)

12. My total income earned so far this year is   and is detailed in items 13 to 28 below. I attach the following document(s) as proof of this year's earnings: (*Identify the document(s) being attached.*)

CATEGORY		Monthly	CATEGORY		Monthly
13.	Pay, wages, salary, including overtime (*before deductions*)		22.	Child tax benefit	
14.	Bonuses, fees, commissions		23.	Support payments actually received	
15.	Social assistance (*employment assistance, basic financial assistance*)		24.	Income received by children	
			25.	G.S.T. refund	
16.	Employment insurance		26.	Income tax refund	
17.	Workers' compensation		27.	Gifts and loans received	
18.	Pensions		28.	Other (*income from business, tips, etc. Attach statements or details.*)	
19.	Dividends				
20.	Interest		29.	INCOME FROM ALL SOURCES	
21.	Rent, board received				

PART 3: OTHER BENEFITS

Show your non-cash benefits—such as the use of a company car, a club membership or room and board that your employer or someone else provides for you or benefits that are charged through or written off by your business. If you cannot find out the actual value of these benefits, give your best estimate.

ITEM	DETAILS	Monthly Market Value
30. TOTAL		

31. GROSS MONTHLY INCOME AND BENEFITS (Add: [29] plus [30]) $

PART 4: OTHER INCOME EARNERS IN THE HOME

Fill in this part only if you are living with another person. It does not matter whether you are married to this person.

I am living with (full legal name of person)

This person has (give number)   child(ren) living in the home.

This person   ¤ works at (place of work or business)

ㅤㅤㅤㅤ¤ does not work outside the home.

35. This person   ¤ earns (give amount) $ per

ㅤㅤㅤㅤ¤ does not earn anything.

36. This person   ¤ pays for about   % of the household expenses.

ㅤㅤㅤㅤ¤ contributes no money to the household expenses.

Continued on next sheet

Form 13: Financial Statement (page 5)   Court File Number

_____

PART 5: AUTOMATIC DEDUCTIONS FROM INCOME

For the 12 months from   to

Give the current actual amount if you know it or can find out. If you can't find out, give your best estimate. To get a monthly figure, you must multiply any weekly amount by 4.33 or divide any yearly sum by 12.

TYPE OF EXPENSE	Monthly	TYPE OF EXPENSE	Monthly
37. Income tax deducted from pay		42. Group insurance	
38. Canada Pension Plan		43. Other (*Specify. If necessary attach an extra sheet.*)	
39. Other pension plans			
40. Employment insurance		44. **TOTAL AUTOMATIC DEDUCTIONS**	
41. Union or association dues			

45. NET MONTHLY INCOME (Do the subtraction: [31] minus [44]): $

PART 6: TOTAL EXPENSES

For the 12 months from   to

NOTE: This part must be completed in all cases. You must set out your TOTAL living expenses, including those expenses involving any children now living in your home. If you cannot find out the actual amount, give your best estimate. As with Part 1, convert weekly figures to monthly ones by multiplying by 4.33 or dividing yearly ones by 12.

TYPE OF EXPENSE	Monthly
Housing	
46. Rent/ Mortgage	
47. Property taxes & municipal levies	
48. Condominium fees & common expenses	
49. Water	
50. Electricity	
51. Heating fuel (natural gas, fuel oil)	
52. Telephone	
Housing	
53. Cable television & pay television	
54. Home insurance	
55. Home repairs, maintenance, gardening, snow removal, etc.	
56. Other household expenses (*Specify. If necessary, attach an extra sheet.*)	
Food, Toiletries & Sundries.	
57. Groceries	
58. Meals outside home	

TYPE OF EXPENSE		Monthly
59.	General household supplies	
60.	Hairdresser, barber, toiletries & sundries	
61.	Laundry & dry cleaning	
62.	Other (*Specify. If necessary attach an extra sheet.*)	
	Clothing	
63.	Clothing for me	
64.	Clothing for children	
65.	Other. (*Specify. If necessary, attach an extra sheet.*)	
	Transportation	
66.	Public transit	
67.	Taxis	
68.	Car insurance	
69.	Licence	
70.	Car loan payments	
71.	Car maintenance and repairs	
72.	Gasoline & oil	
73.	Parking	
74.	Other (*Specify. If necessary, attach an extra sheet.*)	

TYPE OF EXPENSE	Monthly
Health & Medical	
75. Regular dental care	
76. Orthodontal or special dental care	
77. Medicine & drugs	
78. Eye glasses or contact lenses	
79. Other (Specify. If necessary, attach an extra sheet.)	
Miscellaneous	
80. Life or term insurance premiums	
81. School fees, books, tuition, etc.	
82. School activities (Special projects, field trips, etc.)	
83. School lunches	
84. Religious School	
85. Entertainment & recreation	
86. Vacation	
87. Children's summer camp	
88. Children's activities (music lesions, clubs, sports, bicycles.)	
89. Children's allowances	

TYPE OF EXPENSE		Monthly
90.	Baby sitting	
91.	Day care	
92.	Books for home use, newspapers, magazines, audio/video tapes & discs	
93.	Gifts	
94.	Charities	
95.	Alcohol & tabocco	
96.	Pet expenses	
97.	Support actually being paid in this case	
98.	Support actually being paid in any other case	
99.	Income tax (not deducted from pay)	
100.	Other (Specify. If necessary, attach an extra sheet.)	
Debt payment (excluding mortgages)		
101	Credit cards (but not for expenses mentioned elsewhere in this statement.)	
102	Other *(Specify. If necessary, attach an extra sheet.)*	
Savings		
103.	RRSP	
104.	Other. (Specify. If necessary, attach an extra sheet.)	
105.	**Total of items [46] to [104]**	

SUMMARY OF INCOME AND EXPENSES

Net monthly income (item[45] above) =$

Subtract actual monthly expenses (item [105] above = $

ACTUAL MONTHLY SURPLUS/DEFICIT = $Form 13: Financial

IMPORTANT NOTE ABOUT THE NEXT PART

If this case deals with child support **different** from the table amount in the child support guidelines (a claim for add-ons for special or extraordinary expenses for child(ren); a child is 18 years of age or more; a claim for undue hardship; a support claim in a case of split or shared custody; or a case where the payor's annual income is over $150, 000), **THEN YOU MUST NEXT FILL OUT AND ATTACH PART 7.**

If, however, the claim for child support if this case is for the table amount in the child support guidelines or if this case does not deal with child support at all, omit Part 7 completely and instead go on to fill out and attach;

- ◻ Parts 8 to 10; **OR**
- ◻ Parts 11 to 16,

but not both. See the instruction at the top of Part 8 or Part 11 about the choice that you must make.

PART 7: EXPENSES OF THE CHILD(REN)

NOTE: DO NOT FILL OUT PART 7 UNLESS THIS CASE INCLUDES A CLAIM FOR CHILD SUPPORT THAT IS DIFFERENT FROM THE TABLE AMOUNT IN THE CHILD SUPPORT GUIDELINES (a claim for add-ons) for special or extraordinary expenses for the child(ren): a child is 18 years of age or more; a claim for undue hardship; a support claim in a case of split or shared custody; or a case where the party's annual income is $150, 000 or more).

If Part 7 applies to this case, set out the percentage of your actual total monthly living expenses in Part 6 that relates to any child(ren) now living in the household. If you cannot figure out the actual amount of each child's share of a particular expense item, give your best approximation. If there are more than three children, attach extra sheets

TYPE OF EXPENSE	% of expense attributed to child			Monthly Total
	Name: Age:	Name: Age:	Name: Age:	
Housing				
106. Rent/Mortgage				
107. Property taxes & municipal levies				
108. Condominium fees & common expenses				
109. Water				
110. Electricity				
111. Heating fuel (natural gas, fuel oil)				
112. Telephone				
113. Cable television & pay television				
114. Home insurance				
115. Home repairs, maintenance, gardening, snow removal, etc.				
Food, Toiletries & Sundries				
116. Groceries				
117. Meals outside home				
118. General household supplies				
119. Hairdresser, barber, toiletries & sundries				
129. Laundry & dry cleaning				
121. Other (*Specify. If necessary attach an extra sheet.*)				

| TYPE OF EXPENSE | % of expense attributed to child | | | Monthly Total |
	Name: Age:	Name: Age:	Name: Age:	
Clothing				
122. Clothing for children				
123. Other (*Specify. If necessary attach an extra sheet.*)				
Transportation				
124. Public transit				
125. Taxis				
126. Car insurance				
127. Licence				
128. Car loan payments				
129. Car maintenance & repairs				
130. Gasoline & oil				
131. Parking				
132. Other (*Specify. If necessary, attach an extra sheet.*)				
Health & Medical				
133. Regular dental care				
134. Orthodontal or special dental care				
135. Medicine & drugs				
136. Eye glasses or contact lenses				
137. Other (*Specify. If necessary, attach an extra sheet.*)				
Miscellaneous				
138. Life or term insurance premiums				
139. School fees, books, tuition, etc.				

TYPE OF EXPENSE	% of expense attributed to child			Monthly Total
	Name: Age:	Name: Age:	Name: Age:	
140. School residence				
141. School activities (special projects, field trips, etc.)				
142. School lunches				
143. Entertainment & recreation				
144. Vacation				
145. Children's summer camp				
146. Children's activities (music lessons, clubs, sports, bicycles)				
147. Children's allowances				
148. Baby sitting				
149. Day care				
150. Books for home use, newspapers, magazines, audio/video tapes and discs				
151. Gifts to child(ren)				
152. Gifts from child(ren) to others				
153. Charities				
154. Pet expenses				
155. Other (*Specify. If necessary, attach an extra sheet*)				
			Continued on next sheet	

TYPE OF EXPENSE	% of expense attributed to child			Monthly
	Name: Age:	Name: Age:	Name: Age:	Total
Debt Payments (excluding mortgage)				
156. Credit cards (but not for expenses mentioned elsewhere in this statement.)				
157. Other. (Specify. If necessary, attach an extra sheet.)				
Savings				
158. Other (Specify. If necessary, attach an extra sheet.)				
159. CHILD(REN)'S MONTHLY EXPENSES - TOTAL OF ITEMS [106] TO [159]				

IMPORTANT NOTE ABOUT THE NEXT PART

YOU MUST NEXT FILL OUT AND ATTACH:

- Parts 8 to 10; *OR*
- Parts 11 to 16,

But not both. See the instructions at the top of Part 8 or part 11 about the choice that you must now take.

Continued on next sheet

Form 13: Financial Statement (page)   Court File Number

IMPORTANT NOTE ABOUT PARTS 8-10

If this case includes a claim for equalization of net family property under Part 1 of the Family Law Act, skip parts 8 to 10 and go directly to Parts 11 to 16. Fill out Parts 8 to 10 ONLY IF this case involves anything else, such as:

- A claim for support;
- A change in support;
- An enforcement of a support order or of the support provisions of a domestic
- contract or paternity agreement;
- A claim for custody or access where the court has ordered the filing of a financial statement; or
- Exclusive possession of the matrimonial home or any other property dispute (except equalization of net family property).

PART 8: ASSETS IN AND OUT OF ONTARIO

PART 8(a): LAND

Include any interest in land **owned** as of the date of this statement, including leasehold interests and mortgages. Show estimated market value of your interest, but do not deduct encumbrances or costs of disposition; these encumbrances and costs should be shown under Part 9, "Debts and Liabilities". DO NOT INCLUDE LAND THAT YOU DO NOT OWN, even though you are claiming an interest in it.

For example, if you were including the matrimonial home, you might insert "Joint tenancy" in the first column on the left; and in the next column, you might write "Matrimonial home, 123 Main Street, est. value $400, 000 today".

Nature & Type of Ownership	Nature, address and estimated TOTAL value today [This total value may be different from the value of your share (set out in the last column) if the property has two or more owners.]	Estimated Market
	161. TOTAL VALUE OF LAND	

PART 8 (b): GENERAL HOUSEHOLD ITEMS AND VEHICLES

Show estimated market value, not the cost of replacement for these items owned as of the date of this statement. Do not deduct encumbrances or costs of disposition; these encumbrances and costs should be shown under Part 9, "Debts and Liabilities."

ITEM	DESCRIPTION	Tick off√ If NOT in your possession	Estimated Market Value of YOUR interest
Household goods & furniture			
Cars, boats, vehicles			
Jewellery, art, electronics, tools, sports & hobby equipment			
Other special items			
162. TOTAL VALUE OF GENERAL HOUSEHOLD ITEMS AND VEHICLES			

PART 8(c): BANK ACCOUNTS AND SAVINGS

Show the items owned by category. Include cash, accounts in financial institutions, registered retirement or other savings plan, deposit receipts, pension and any other savings.

Category	INSTITUTION	Account Number	Amount
163. TOTAL VALUE OF ACCOUNTS AND SAVINGS			

PART 8 (d): SECURITIES

Show the items owned by category. Include bonds, warrants, options, notes and other securities. Give your best estimate of their market value if the items were to be sold on the open market.

Category	Number	Description	Estimated Market Value
164. TOTAL VALUE OF SECURITIES			

PART 8(e): LIFE & DISABILITY INSURANCE

List all policies now in existence.

Company & Policy No.	Kind of Policy	Owner	Beneficiary	Face Amount	Today's Cash Surrender Value
165. TOTAL CASH SURRENDER VALUE OF INSURANCE POLICIES					

Continued on next sheet

Form 13: Financial Statement (page   )   Court File Number

_____

PART 8(f): BUSINESS INTERESTS

Show any interest in an unincorporated business owned today. A controlling interest in an incorporated business may be shown here or under "SECURITIES" in Part 8(d). Give your best estimate of market value if the business were to be sold on an open market.

Name of Firm or Company	Interest	Estimated Market value of YOUR interest
166. TOTAL VALUE OF BUSINESS INTERESTS		

PART 8(g): MONEY OWED TO YOU

Give details of all money that other persons owe to you today, whether because of business or from personal dealings. Include any court judgments in your favour and any estate money owed to you.

DETAILS	Amount Owed to You
167. TOTAL OF MONEY OWED TO YOU	

Continued on next sheet

PART 8(h): OTHER PROPERTY

Show other property or assets owned by categories. Include property of any kind not listed above. Give your best estimate of market value.

CATEGORY	DETAILS	Estimated Market Value
168. TOTAL VALUE OF OTHER PROPERTY		
169. VALUE OF ALL PROPERTY *Add items* **[161]** *to* **[168]**		

PART 9: DEBTS AND OTHER LIABILITIES

CATEGORY	DETAILS	Amount owing
170. TOTAL OF DEBTS AND OTHER LIABILITIES		

PART 10: SUMMARY OF ASSETS AND LIABILITIES

	Amounts
TOTAL ASSETS *(from item* **[169]** *above)*	
Subtract TOTAL DEBTS *(from item* **[170]** *above)*	
71. NET WORTH	

NOTE: If you have filled out Parts 8-10, then aside from any other documents that you must attach (such as income tax returns) this is the last page of this Form. Do not fill out or attach Parts 11 –16.

IMPORTANT NOTE ABOUT PARTS 11-16

Fill out Parts 11 to 16 ONLY IF this case includes a claim for equalization of net family property under Part 1 of the Family Law Act. If, however, this case deals with: A claim for support; A change in support;

An enforcement of a support order or of the support provisions of a domestic contract or paternity agreement;

A claim for custody or access where the court has ordered the filing of a financial statement; or

A claim for exclusive possession of the matrimonial home or any other property dispute (aside from equalization of net family property),

Skip parts 11 to 16 and fill out Parts 8 to 10 instead.

PART 11: ASSETS IN AND OUT OF ONTARIO

PART 11(a): LAND

Include any interest in land owned on the valuation date or as of the date of this statement, including leasehold interests and mortgages. Show estimated market value of your interest, but do not deduct encumbrances or costs of disposition; these encumbrances and costs should be shown in Part 12, "Debts and Liabilities". DO NOT INCLUDE LAND THAT YOU DO NOT OWN, even though you are claiming an interest in it.

For example, if you were including the matrimonial home, you might insert "Joint tenancy" in the first column on the left; and in the next column, you might write "Matrimonial home, 123 Main Street, est. value $400, 000 today".

The valuation date is:

Nature & Type of Ownership (Give your percentage interest where relevant)	Nature, address and estimated TOTAL value today	Estimated Market value of YOUR interest		
		On date of marriage	On valuation date	today
172. TOTAL VALUE OF LAND				

PART 11 (b): GENERAL HOUSEHOLD ITEMS AND VEHICLES					
Show estimated market value, not the cost of replacement for these items owned on valuation date or as of the date of this statement. Do not deduct encumbrances or costs of disposition; these encumbrances and costs should be shown under Part 12, "Debts and Liabilities".					
ITEM	DESCRIPTION	Tick off If NOT in your possession	Estimated Market value of YOUR interest		
			On date of marriage	On valuation date	today
Household goods & furniture					
Cars, boats, vehicles					
Jewllery, art, electronics, tools, sports & hobby equipment					
Other special items					
173. TOTAL VALUE OF GENERAL HOUSEHOLD ITEMS AND VEHICLES					

PART 11 (c): BANK ACCOUNTS AND SAVINGS					
Show the items owned on the valuation date by category. Include cash, accounts in financial institutions, registered retirement or other savings plans, deposit receipts, pension and any other savings.					
Category	INSTITUTION	Account number	Amount		
			on date of marriage	on valuation date	today
174. TOTAL VALUE OF ACCOUNTS AND SAVINGS					

PART 11(d): SECURITIES

Show the items owned on the valuation date by category. Include bonds, warrants, options, notes and other securities. Give your best estimate of their market value if the items were to be sold on the open market.

Category	Number	Description	Estimated Market value		
			On date of marriage	On valuation date	today
175. TOTAL VALUE OF SECURITIES					

PART 11(e): LIFE & DISABILITY INSURANCE

List of all policies in existence on the valuations date.

Company & Policy No.	Kind of policy	Owner	Beneficiary	Face Amount	Cash Surrender Value		
					Date of Marriage	Valuation Date	Today
176. TOTAL CASH SURRENDER VALUE OF INSURANCE POLICIES							

PART 11(f): BUSINESS INTERESTS

Show any interest in an unincorporated business owned on the valuation date. A controlling interest in an incorporated business may be shown here or under "SECURITIES" in part 11(d). Give your best estimate of market value if the business were to be sold on an open market.

Name of firm or company	Interest	Estimated Market value of YOUR interest		
		On date of marriage	On valuation date	Today
177. TOTAL VALUE OF BUSINESS INTERESTS				

PART 11(g): MONEY OWED TO YOU

Give details of all money that other persons owe to you on the valuation date, whether because of business or from personal dealings. Include any court judgments in your favour and any estate money owed to you.

DETAILS	Amount owed to you		
	On date of marriage	**On valuation date**	**Today**
178. TOTAL OF MONEY OWED TO YOU			

PART 11(h): OTHER PROPERTY

Show other property or assets owned on the valuation date. Include property of any kind not listed above. Give your best estimate of market value.

CATEGORY	DETAILS	Estimated Market value of YOUR interest		
		on date of marriage	on valuation date	today
179. TOTAL VALUE OF OTHER PROPERTY				
180. VALUE OF ALL PROPERTY OWNED ON THE VALUATION DATE Add items [172] to [179]				

PART 12: DEBTS AND OTHER LIABILITIES

Show your debts and other liabilities on the valuation date *from personal and business dealings.* List them by category such as mortgages, charges, liens, notes, credit cards, and accounts payable. Don't forget to include:

- any money owed to Revenue Canada;
- contingent liabilities such as guarantees or warranties given by you (but indicate that they are contingent); and
- any unpaid legal or professional bills as a result of this case.

CATEGORY	DETAILS	Amount owing		
		On date of marriage	On valuation date	today
	181. TOTAL OF DEBTS AND OTHER LIABILITIES			

PART 13: PROPERTY, DEBTS AND OTHER LIABILITIES ON DATE OF MARRIAGE		
Show by category the value of your property and your debts and other liabilities *as of the date of your marriage.* DO NOT INCLUDE THE VALUE OF A MATRIMONIAL HOME THAT YOU OWNED ON THE DATE OF MARRIAGE		
CATEGORY AND DETAILS	**Value on date of marriage**	
	Assets	**Liabilities**
Land (*exclude matrimonial home owned on date of marriage, unless sold before date of separation.*)		
General household items & vehicles		
Bank accounts and savings		
Securities		
Life & disability insurance		
Business interests		
Money owed to you		
Other property (*Specify.*)		
Debts and other liabilities (*Specify.*)		
TOTALS		
182. NET VALUE OF PROPERTY OWNED ON DATE OF MARRIAGE (*From the total of the "Assets" column, subtract the total of the "Liabilities" column.*)		
183. VALUE OF ALL DEDUCTIONS (*Add items* [181] *and* [182].)		

PART 14: EXCLUDED PROPERTY		
Show by category the value of property owed on the valuation date that is excluded from the definition of "net family property" (such as gifts or inheritances after marriage).		
CATEGORY	DETAILS	Value on valuation date
184. TOTAL VALUE OF EXCLUDED PROPERTY		

PART 15: DISPOSED PROPERTY		
Show by category the value of property that you disposed of during the two years immediately before the separation.		
CATEGORY	DETAILS	VALUE
185. TOTAL VALUE OF DISPOSED PROPERTY		

PART 16: CALCULATION OF NET FAMILY PROPERTY		
	Deductions	BALANCE
Value of all property owned on valuation date (from item [180]above)		
Subtract value of all deductions (from item [183] above)		
Subtract value of all excluded property (from item[184] above)		
186. NET FAMILY PROPERTY		

Appendix D

Web Resources

On the Internet there is a lot of information that could be useful to you if you are going through a divorce. Here are some sites to visit.

1. DIVORCE
Bill Ferguson's How To Divorce As Friends
www.divorceasfriends.com
This site is provided by former divorce attorney Bill Ferguson. It is promotional in that it links to his books and workshops, but it provides useful articles free. Includes links to other divorce and mediation sites.

CLFAQs: National—Divorce Act
www.law~faqs.org/nat/div-act.htm
Divorce Act FAQs

Divorce Act
www.laws.justice.gc.ca/en/D-3.4/
Consolidated Statutes and Regulations Divorce Act

Divorce Act
www.travel-net.com/~billr/divorce/divorce.html

Divorce As Friends
www.divorceasfriends.com
This site offers help with letting go, healing, resolving issues, and ending the conflict.

Divorce: Facts, Figures and Consequences
www.vifamily.ca/cft/divorce/divorce.htm
Contemporary Family Trends

DivorceSource
www.divorcesource.com

This site provides free articles and information on the financial, legal, psychological, and other aspects of divorce. It includes a directory of professionals. This comprehensive site includes a wide variety of related links.

Divorce Online

www.divorce-online.com

Divorce Online provides articles and information on the financial, legal, psychological, real estate, and other aspects of divorce. It also has a professional referral section.

Marriage, separation et divorce

www.barreau.qc.ca/feuillets/divorce.html

Smart Divorce

www.smartdivorce.com

This site is a divorce learning center providing practical solutions to divorce challenges.

2. MEDIATION

Academy of Family Mediators

www.mediate/afm

This site includes links to directory of mediation organizations, mediation training sites, conference information, bookstores, educational materials, and more.

Arbitration and Mediation Institute of Canada

www.amic.com

Association of Family and Conciliatory Courts

www.afcnet.org

Canadian Centre for Mediation

www.ccmediation.com

Canadian Department of Justice—Dispute Resolution Services

www.canada2.justice.gc.ca

Family Mediation Canada

www.fmc.ca

This site provides information on a National Conference, newsletter, as well as training for mediators in Canada. Various resources are available for purchase.

Mediation Information Resource Centre
www.mediate.com
This U.S. site provides substantial information in regards to mediation and conflict resolution. A great source for articles on-line that discuss issues of mediation, divorce, and conflict resolution. Links to forums, events, training, articles, news briefs, ethics standards, legislation, organizations, and resources for purchase.

Mediation Training Institute Canada
www.mediationworks.com

Ontario Association for Family Mediation
www.OASM.ON.CA

Ontario Mandatory Mediation Programme
www.attorneygeneral.jus.gov.on.ca

The Network
www.nicu.ca
Interaction for conflict resolution

3. COLLABORATION

Collaborative Family Law
www.theinvolvedfather.com/arts/arts
International clearing house for collaborative law groups and articles published in *The Collaborative Review*. There are forty-five family lawyers who practice what has been dubbed collaborative family law, and some of them have given up practicing adversarial law altogether.

Collaborative Family Law Group of Tampa Bay
http://collaborativedivorce.homestead.com/FAQs.html

Family Law Annual Review
www.cle.bc.ca/CLE/Analysis/Collection/01-30870-family3

The Rise of Collaborative Family Law
www.cba.org/EPIIgram/June2001/national.asp

4. SUPPORT

ACJNet: Canadian Law and Justice
http://129,128.19.162/sub/spousup/htm

Child Support
http://canada:justice.gc.ca

Spousal Support
How to avoid, reduce or terminate spousal support
www.fbfamilylaw.mb.ca/spousal.htm

Spousal Support Database
Provides a summary of reported court cases dealing with support.
http://spousalsupport.com

The Economics of Spousal Support
http://ideas.uqam.ca/ideas/data/Papers/wpawuwple9505001.html

5. PENSIONS

Acadia University Pension Plan
Admin.acadiau.ca/human/benefits/pension.html

Alberta Public Service Pension plan
www.pspp.apaco.ab.ca/

British Columbia Teachers' Pension Plan
www.bctf.ca/pensions/Pensions.html

Education Pension Plan Members
www.benefitscanada.com/planmembers.html

Financial Services Commission of Ontario
www.fsco.gov.on.ca/

Hospitals of Ontario Pension Plan (HOOPP)
www.hoopp.com

Manitoba Pension Commission
www.gov.mb.ca/labour/pen/

Newfoundland Teachers' Pension Plan
www.nlta.nf.ca/HTML_Files/html_pages/publications/pensionplan/pension.html

Old Age Security and Canada Pension Plan
www.hrdc-duhc.gc.ca/isp

OMERS Pension Plan
www.omers.com/

Ontario Law Reform Commission Report on Pensions
www.beli.org/pages/projects/pension2/menu.html

Ontario Teachers' Pension Plan
www.otpp.com/website/teachers/website.nst/Public/HomePage

OPSEU Pension Trust
www.optrust.com/

Pension Valuators of Canada
www.pension.ca
www.pension.ca/lawyer

Pension Standards Act of British Columbia
www.labour.gov.bc.ca/pbsb/

Quebec Pension Plan
www.rrq.gouv.qc.ca/an/rente/rente.htm

Quebec Private Pension Plans
www.rrq.gouv.qc.ca/an/prive/defin.htm

Saskatchewan Municipal Employees' Pension Plan
www.gov.sk.ca/deptsorgs/overviews/?8

Saskatchewan Pension Plan
www.spp.gov.sk.ca/

Superintendant of Financial Institutions
Regulates the Pension Benefits Standards Act
http://laws.justice.gc.ca/en/P-7.01/index.html

Understanding Your Pension Plan
www.fsco.gov.on.ca/Pensions/UNDRSTND.NSF?openDatabase

6. CHILDREN

Canadian Society for the Investigation of Child Abuse
www.csica.zener.com
The CSICA is a non-profit society whose activities include training child sexual abuse investigators and responding to the needs of abused children, particularly in the area of child witness court preparation.

Child Abuse Prevention Network
http://child.cornell.edu/
An online information network for professionals working with abused and neglected children. A good site for information and resources.

Child Sexual Abuse
www.commnet.edu/QVCTC/student/LindaCain/sexabuse.html
Includes legal information, statistics, journals, newsletters, and publications, books and reviews, services directories, and other resources related to child sexual abuse.

Child Visitation Interference in Divorce by Ira Daniel Turkat
www.fact.on.ca/Info/pas/turkat94.htm

Children's Institute International
http://childrensinstitute.org/index.html
A Los Angeles non-profit organization offering programs, services, and training related to domestic violence and child abuse. The related links section is an excellent resource.

Children's Pathfinder
www.childsec.gov.on.com
Offers valuable information about early childhood development, special needs, health care, education, child protection, and safety.

Divorce and Children
www.childcareinfoline.com/divorce.htm

National Clearinghouse on Child Abuse and Neglect Information
www.calib.com/nccanch
Provides access to the National Clearinghouse Documents Database, a database of more than 27,000 records. This site also provides access to NCCANH on-line publications and a catalogue that highlights publications produced by the Deptartment of Health and Human Services. Links to related child abuse sites are included.

National Data Archive on Child Abuse and Neglect
www.ndacan.cornell.edu
The NDACAN strives to facilitate the secondary analysis of research data relevant to the study of child abuse and neglect. The archive seeks to provide a relatively inexpensive and scientifically productive means for researchers to explore important issues in the child maltreatment field.

Preventing Parentectomy Following Divorce, by Frank S. Williams
www.fact.on.ca/Info/pas/willia90.htm
National Council for Children's Rights

Special Joint Committee on Child Custody and Access
www.parl.gc.ca
From the federal government Web site click on "Individual Committee Sites." Custody and Access site is found under Standing and Special committees.

Step Fathers
www.stepdads.com
A place to help stepdads develop great relationships with their stepchildren, their wives and other stepdads.

When Parents Separate or Divorce Helping Your Child Cope
www.cfc-efc.ca/docs/00000315.htm

7. OTHER

Access to Justice Network
www.acjnet.org

Accountants

www.icao.on.ca

This is the site of the National Organization of Chartered Accountants.

Canadian Bar Association (CBA)

www.cba.org

Credit Counselling Service

www.creditcanada.com

This site provides information about financial counselling, seminars, and workshops.

D.A.D.S Canada

www.dadscanada.com

Non-profit paralegal service using lawyers, accountants, doctors, and social workers to help non-custodial parents receive fair treatment in court.

Divorce Magazine

www.DivorceMagazine.com

This ultimate on-line divorce resource offers daily news, bulletin boards, more than two hundred divorce-related links and articles, and weekly columns by celebrities such as Ivana Trump and Dr. John Gray. Visit the Statistics area to view Canadian, U.S., and world stats about separation and divorce.

Family Court Review

www.hofstra.edu/Academies/Law/law_fccr_contents.cfm

Provides tables of contents for issues from 1998 to the present.

Family Violence Awareness Page

www.famvi.com

A comprehensive site with facts and statistics, hot-line and contact information, essays and other writings, as well as images and information on currently missing children.

Family Therapy Networker

www.familytherapynetwork.com

Includes the table of contents and some full text articles from the current issue of the magazine.

Financial Planners

www.cfp.ca

Kayama
www.kayama.org
A non-profit organization that provides information and assistance for obtaining a Jewish divorce (called a "get").

Mars & Venus
www.marsvenus.com
Based on the bestselling *Mars & Venus* series by Dr. John Gray. The Community section offers a chat room and an area where you can post questions for Dr. Gray; the Romance Shop features Mars & Venus materials to help you improve your relationships with the opposite sex.

National Father's Resource Center
www.fathers4kids.org
Provides fathers, children, and grandparents with information on father-related issues.

Nunavut Court of Justice
www.nunavutcourtofjustice.ca/unifiedcourt.htm

Ontario Family Law Act
www.travel-net.com/~billr/fla/fla.html

Ontario Lawyers' Links
www.lsuc.on.ca/cgi-data/legal_members_en.html

Provincial Court of Newfoundland and Labrador
www.gov.nf.ca/just/LAWCOURT/prov.htm

Single Mothers
www.singlemomz.com
Connect with other single moms facing divorce, child support, custody battles, money problems, and job-related issues.

Supreme Court of Canada
www.scc-csg.qc.ca/home/index_e.html

Supreme Court of Prince Edward Island
www.gov.pe.ca/courts/supreme

Third Age
www.thirdage.com

An on-line society of older men and women. Great information, articles, and advice on family, health, money, romance, and work.

Unified Family Court Task Force—Appendix B
www.gov.ab.ca/just/pub/Family_Court/appendixb.htm

7. WIFE
www.thirdage.com
Designed for women, this site deals mainly with financial independence, providing education, and tips for money management.

Women and Divorce...Strategies to Help You Survive and Thrive
www.womansdivorce.com/

Appendix E

Pension Plans Subject to the Pension Benefits Standards Act

The following is a partial list of the more than two thousand pension plans subject to the Pension Benefits Standards Act (PBSA). For a full list see the web site of the Office of the Superintendent of Financial Institutions at www.osfi-bsif.gc.ca

Pension Plan	Number
Canadian Fraternal Benefit Societies	13
Canadian Life Insurance Companies	52
Canadian Property and Casualty Insurance Companies	93
Co-Operative Credit Unions	7
Domestic Banks	13
Foreign Bank Representative Offices	27
Foreign Banks	44
Foreign Fraternal Benefit Societies	13
Foreign Life Insurance Companies	67
Foreign Property and Casualty Insurance Companies	110
Loan Companies	27
Trust Companies	38

Private Pension Plans (1650)

- Air Lines
- Airport Authorities
- Algoma Central
- Bus Lines
- Business Development Bank of Canada
- Cable Television Companies
- Canada Mortgage and Housing Corporation
- Canada Post
- Canadian Armed Forces
- Canadian Bankers' Association

Pension Plans Subject to the Pension Benefits Standards Act

- Courier Services
- Farm Credit Corporation
- Federal Express
- Freight Systems
- Indian Bands
- Port Authorities
- Radio Stations
- Rail Lines
- Shipping Companies
- Telephone Companies
- Television Stations
- Transport Companies
- United Steelworkers
- Van Lines
- Via Rail
- Wheat Pools

Appendix F

Canadian Divorce Statistics

(1998 except where noted)	
Marriage & Divorce	
Total divorces granted:	69,088
Rate per 1,000 population:	2.3
Province with lowest divorce rate:	
Northwest Territories. Rate per 1,000 population:	1.4
Province with the highest divorce rate:	
Yukon. Rate per 1,000 population:	3.7
Current number of divorced adults (1999):	1,417,136
Average age at divorce:	Males: 42
	Females: 39.4
Average age at marriage for divorced people:	Males: 28.3
	Females: 25.7
Average duration of marriage:	13.7
Percentage of marriages expected to end in divorce within 30 years in 1998:	36%
Year of marriage with highest divorce rate:	Fifth
Total number of single people in 1999:	Males: 6,969,698 (46% of men)
	Female: 6,063,348 (39% of women)
Total number of married people in 1999:	Males: 7,254,051 (48% of men)
	Females: 7,281,830

	(47% of women)
Total number of divorced people in 1999:	Males: 609,509
	(4% of men)
	Females: 807,627
	(5% of women)
Total number of widowed people in 1999:	Males: 271,153
	(2% of men)
	Females: 1,235,078
	(8% of women)
Province where married couples are least likely to divorce: Newfoundland. Percentage expected to divorce within 30 years:	23%
Province where married couples are most likely to divorce: Yukon. Percentage expected to divorce within 30 years:	55%
Children:	
Estimated number of dependent children involved in divorce:	36,252
Total divorce cases involving custody order for dependent children:	21,448 (31% of divorces granted)
Number of dependent children involved in custody orders in divorce cases:	37,851
Percentage of custody orders in divorce cases in which the wife received custody:	60%
Percentage of custody orders in divorce cases in which joint custody was awarded:	30%
Total single-parent families in 1996:	1,137,510 (10% of families)
Percentage of children under 12 living in a two-parent family in 1995:	84.2%

Percentage of children under 12 living in a single-parent family in 1995:	15.7%
Percentage of children under 12 living with someone other than a parent in 1995:	0.1%
Percentage of children under 12 living in a step-family in 1995:	8.6%
Percentage of children under 12 living in a blended family in which at least one child different parents as the others in 1995:	6.1%
Percentage of children in single-parent families with one or more behaviour problems in 1995:	32%
Percentage of children in two-parent families with one or more behaviour problems in 1995:	19%
Single-parent families who have children living in poverty	46%
Source: Statistics Canada	

Appendix G

Other Reading Material

There are hundreds of books, pamphlets, and articles about divorce. Some have helpful information about the financial aspects. Many books will be in your local library. The federal and provincial governments have booklets that may be helpful, as well.

Books

Annual Review of Family Law by James G. McLeod and Alfred A. Mamo

Bankruptcy and Family Law

Beat Him At His Own Divorce Mass Market Paperback

Breaking Apart: A Memoir of Divorce by Wendy Swallow

British Columbia Joint Divorce Forms: Joint Petitioners by Wayne Powell

Canadian Divorce Decisions by Julien Payne

Canadian Divorce Law and Practice by James C. MacDonald and Lee K. Ferrier, (2nd Edition)

Canadian Divorce Law and Practice by Canada, et al (Hardcover—March 2000)

Canadian Family Law and Practice: Consolidated Statues, Regulations and Forms

Cohabitation: The Law in Canada by Winifred H Holland and Barbro E. Stalbecker-Pountney

Contemporary Trends in Family Law: A National Perspective by Katherine Connell-Thouez and Barbara M. Knoppers

Creative Divorce by Mel Krantzler

Credit Splitting Upon Divorce or Separation — Canada Pension Plan

Cutting Loose: Why Women Who End Their Marriage Do So Well by Ashton Applewhite

Dealing with Divorce by Julien D. Payne and Marilyn A. Payne

Dealing with Family Law by Julien D. Payne and Marilyn A. Payne

Division of Pensions by Diane E. Pask and Cheryl A. Hass

Divorce and Beyond Participants by James Greteman

Divorce Common Sense Handbook: 180+ Things To Do and 8+ Things Not To Do Before Your Divorce by Judy Colbert

Divorce and Money: How to Make the Best Financial Decision During Divorce by Violet Woodhouse

Divorce for Dummies by John Ventura

Divorce Guide for Ontario by Sandra J. Meynick, LL.B.

Divorce Mediation by Jay Folberg and Ann Milne

Divorce Source Book by Dawn Brad Berry

Divorce: A Canadian Woman's Guide by Gail Vaz-Oxlade

Divorce: A Woman's Guide to Getting a Fair Share, by Patricia Philips

Divorcing by Melvin Belli, Mel Krantzler and Christopher S. Taylor

Family Law and Social Welfare Legislation in Canada by Ivan, Bernier and Andree Lajoie

Family Law Consolidated Statutes for Ontario.

Family Law In Canada by Christine Davies

Family Law: Dimensions of Justice by Rosalie S. Abella and Claire L'Heureux-Dube

Family Mediation: Theory and Practice of Dispute Resolution by Howard H. Irving and M. Benjamin.

Family mediation in Canada: implications for women's equality: a review of the literature and analysis of data from four publicly funded Canadian mediation programs, by Sandra A. Goundry

Good Divorce by Constance Ahrons

Growing Through Divorce by Jim Smoke

GT Divorce Mediation by Gary J. Friedman

Healing the Wounds of Divorce: A Spiritual Guide to Recovery by Barbara L. Shlemon

Help!: A Girl's Absolutely Indispensable Guide to Divorce and Stepfamilies by Nancy Holyoke

How to Survive Your Boyfriend's Divorce: Loving Your Separated Man Without Losing Your Mind by Lesley Dormen, Robyn Todd

Irreconcilable Differences by Lia Matera

It's Not the End of the World by Judy Blume

Late Divorce by A.B. Yehoshua

Law and Practice Under the Family Law Act of Ontario by James C. MacDonald and Ann Wilton, Revised Edition

Le Divorce by Diane Johnson

Let's Talk about It: Divorce by Fred Rogers

Marriage Contracts by Evita M. Roche and David C. Simmonds

Marriage in a Culture of Divorce by Karla B. Hackstaff

Marriage, Separation and Divorce in Ontario by David J. Botnick, LL.B.

Matrimonial Property Law In Canada by James G. McLeod and Alfred A. Mamo

Mediation by Jay Folberg and Allison Taylor

Men on Divorce by Penny Kaganoff

My Guy by Sarah Weeks

National Themes in Family Law by Margaret E. Hughes and Diane E. Pake

Nullity of Marriage in Canada by H.R. Hahlo

Ontario Family Law Procedures Handbook by Daniel Haden

Payne's Digest on Divorce in Canada, 1968-1980 by Julien D. Payne and Freda M. Steel and Marilyn A. Begin

Payne's Divorce and Family Law Digest by Julien D. Payne and Marilyn A. Payne

Payne on Divorce, 3rd edition by Julien D. Payne

Pension Division and Valuation - Family Lawyers' Guide by Jack Patterson, F.S.A., F.C.I.A.

Property Valuation and Income Tax Implications of Marital Dissolution by Stephen R. Cole and Andrew J. Freedman

Resolving Divorce Issues by Barbara J. MacRae, Holmes Crouch, Irma J. Crouch

Separation and Divorce a Canadian Woman's Survival Guide, by N. Gibson

Spousal Property Rights Under the Ontario Family Law Act by Julien D. Payne

Straight Talk About Divorce by Kay Porterfield

Surviving Divorce by John Bradshaw

Surviving Your Divorce: A Guide to Canadian Family Law, 2nd Edition, by Michael G. Cochrane

Tax Aspects of Divorce and Separation; America Has Become a Multiple Manage Society by Robea J. Tangi

The Complete Idiot's Guide to Handling a Breakup, by Rosanne Rosen

The Complete Idiot's Guide to Surviving Divorce, Second Edition by Pamela Weintraub

The Great Divorce, by C.S. Lewis

The Law of Family Property by Berend Hovius and Timothy G. Yudan

The Mediation Process: Practical Strategies for Resolving Conflict by Christopher Moore

The New Divorce Law by Alastair Bissett-Johnson and David Day

The Process of Divorce: How Professionals Couples Negotiate Settlements by Kenneth Kressell

The Seven Steps To A Successful Separation, by Norma Walton

The Summer of Riley by Eve Bunting

The Ties that Bind by Carol Smart

The Unexpected Legacy of Divorce: A 25 Year Landmark Study by Judith S. Wallerstein, et al

The Unofficial Guide to Divorce by Sharon Naylor

Unmarried Couple's: Legal Aspects of Cohabitation by Winifred H. Holland

When Divorce Hits Home by Beth Joselow

Winning Your Divorce by Timothy Horgan

Women on Divorce by Penny Kaganoff

World Changes in Divorce Patterns by William J. Goode

Your Divorce Advisor: A Lawyer and a Psychologist Guide You Through the Legal and Emotional Landscape of Divorce by Diana Mercer, Marsha Kline Pruett

Newsletters

Money & Family Law by Lorne H. Wolfson, Bary S. Corbin and Daniel S. Melamed
Weekly Digest of Family Law

Reports

A Conceptual Analysis of Unified Family Courts by Julien D. Payne (Law Reform Commission of Canada)

A Report on Spousal and Child Support in Canada by Danreb Inc. (Canada, Department of Justice)

An Economic Model to Assist In the Determination of Spousal Support by Richard Kerr (Canada, Department of Justice and Status of Women Canada)

Court-Based Divorce Mediation in Four Cities by C. James Richardson (Canada, Department of Justice)

Evaluation of the Divorce Act, Phase II: Monitoring and Evaluation (Canada, Department of Justice)

Family Law In Canada: New Directions by Elizabeth Sloss (Canadian Advisory Council on the Status of Women

Law and the Family in Canada (Ministry of Supply and Services, Statistics Canada)

Love, Marriage and Money by Louise Delude (Canadian Advisory Council on the Status of Women)

Report of the Attorney General's Advisory Committee on Mediation in Family Law (Ontario)

Report on Family Law (Law Reform Commission of Canada)

Report on Family Law Act (Ontario Law Reform Commission)

Report on the Rights & Responsibilities of Cohabitants under The Family Law Act (Ontario Law Reform Commission)

Studies on Divorce (Law Reform Commission of Canada)

Studies on Family Property Law (Law Reform Commission of Canada)

The Family Court (Law Reform Commission of Canada)

The War Against Women, First Report of the Sub-Committee on the Status of Women, (Canada, Department of Health and Welfare, Standing Committee on Health and Welfare, Social Affairs, Seniors and the Status of Women.

Towards Reform of the Law Relating to Cohabitation Outside Marriage Issues Paper No. 2. (Alberta Law Reform Institute)

Towards Reform of the Law Relating to Cohabitation Outside Marriage, Report No. 53 (Alberta Law Reform Institute

Women and Poverty Revisited (National Council of Welfare)

Other Reading Material

Pamphlets

An Inventory of Divorce Mediation and Reconciliation Services in Canada (Canada, Department of Justice)

Another Way: Mediation in Divorce and Separation (Canada, Department of Justice)

Divorce Law for Counselors (Canada, Department of Justice)

Divorce Law in Canada: Proposals for Change Canada, Department of Justice

Divorce Law: Questions and Answers (Canada, Department of Justice)

Family Law In Manitoba (Manitoba, Department of the Attorney General)

Introduction to Family Law (Ontario, Ministry of the Attorney General)

Marriage As An Equal Partnership A Guide to the Family Law Act (Ontario, Ministry of the Attorney General)

Your Canada Pension Plan: Disability Benefits; The Simple Facts (Canada, Department of Health and Welfare)

Your Canada Pension Plan: Retirement Pension: The Simple Facts (Canada, Department of Health and Welfare)

Your Canada Pension Plan: Survivor Benefits: The Simple Facts (Canada, Department of Health and Welfare)

Miscellaneous

Splitting Up: The Yukon Law on Separation by Lynn Gaudet (Yukon Public Legal Education Assoc.

Family Law in Ontario: A Practical Guide for Lawyers and Law Clerks by Michael G. Cochrane (Canada Law Book)

Appendix H

Glossary of Terms for Pensions, Divorce, and Support

Don't let someone embarrass you by using terminology that you don't understand. Some terms are being used by different people to mean different things. There is a lot of confusion about the meaning of certain terminology, even among professionals.

The following definitions and explanations may help you in understanding terminology that is used frequently.

Accrual of Benefits: the specific dollar amount credited, as allocated to an individual plan participant at a given point in time.

Accumulated Contributions: sum of employee contributions with interest as of a particular date.

Accrued Pension: for service up to any date, such as valuation date, is the amount of pension payable in the form of a monthly annuity commencing at retirement—in other words, it is the amount of the first monthly pension payment upon retirement excluding indexing and taxes.

Active Members: employees currently working and who are members of a pension plan.

Actuary: a person whose work is to calculate statistically risks, premiums, and life expectancies for insurance and pension plans.

Additional Voluntary Contributions: contributions to a pension plan made voluntarily by an employee in addition to those required for specific plan benefits. Extra benefits are purchased by the additional contributions, but no additional cost is borne by the employer.

Ad Hoc Adjustment: amount added to a pension after retirement or termination to compensate for increases in the cost of living on an irregular basis and not as a result of a prior commitment or contract.

Administrator: the person who administers the pension plan—arranges for pension payments, funding of the plan, and so on.

Adversarial System: Canada's court system is designed to resolve disputes between two opposing parties. The parties present their respective sides of an issue through evidence. The judge acts as an impartial arbiter, weighing the evidence and deciding how the law applies in each specific case.

Affidavit: a form of declaration made voluntarily, sworn before a lawyer or notary public, and thus admissible in court as a statement of fact.

Ancillary Benefits: benefits in addition to regular pension benefits and survivor benefits, such as bridging benefits and enriched early retirement benefits.

Annuity: in pension terminology, periodic payments (usually monthly) provided by the terms of a contract for the lifetime of an individual (the annuitant) or the individual and his or her designated beneficiary; may be a fixed or varying amount, and may continue for a period after the annuitant's death.

Appeal: when a person affected by a judge's decision believes the judge has made a mistake, he can ask a higher level of court to review the decision. The court reviewing the decision can uphold it, change it, or send the matter back to the original court for reconsideration. There are strict time limits on this type of review.

Application: a court proceeding starts with the filing of certain documents with court officers and the serving of copies of these documents on persons affected. Details of the material to be included in the application, the document format, and the filing fees are determined by provincial and territorial rules of court procedure.

Asset Mix: the proportion of various types of investments held by a pension fund, usually expressed as a percentage of total investments held in bonds, equities, and real estate.

Assign: to transfer property to another.

Attach: to take property into custody of a court by writ.

Beneficiary: in a pension plan, a person who, on the death of a plan member or pensioner, may become entitled to a benefit under the plan.

Benefit: generally, any form of payment to which a person may become entitled under the terms of a plan; often refers specifically to the normal pension provided by the plan formula.

Benefit Formula: provision in a pension plan for calculating a member's defined benefit according to years of service and earnings (career or final average), a fixed dollar amount, or flat benefit rate.

Best Five-Year Average: a defined benefit plan that applies the member's average earnings during the five years when earnings were highest.

Bridging Benefits: a temporary benefit provided to employees who retire before the age when government benefits (OAS and CPP) are available (sixty-five) in order to supplement their pension income until CPP and OAS benefits apply.

Career Average Plan: a defined benefit plan that applies the unit of benefit to earnings of the member in each year of service, and not to the final or final average earnings.

Certificate of Divorce: order that terminates the marriage and is irrevocable. It is granted after a waiting period 31 days from the date of the divorce judgement.

Chambers: the private office of a judge where the only evidence allowed is affidavit evidence. There are no witnesses or juries, simply a judge who listens to applications, peruses the affidavit evidence, and grants or refuses orders based on this evidence. It is less formal than open court and because of this can be used only to obtain certain orders.

Charge: to put a liability on; to ask as a price or fee.

Cohabitation Agreement: a domestic contract signed by a man and a woman who are living together or intend to live together but not marry. In it, they may provide for ownership and division of property, support, and any other matter affecting their relationship except custody of and access to children.

Collusion: an agreement between husband and wife that one of them shall commit, or have committed, acts constituent for divorce for the purpose of the other to obtain a divorce.

Commuted Value: amount of immediate lump sum estimated to be equal in value to a series of future payments.

Same as transfer value—the actuarial present value of the benefit to which an employee or spouse is or will be entitled. This is rarely the right value for equalization on marriage breakdown.

Common-Law Spouse: almost all the provinces recognize that some men and women live together without getting married. While the precise definition varies from province to province, it means achieving the status of a spouse for some legal purposes, such as support.

Confidentiality: people in certain relationships are protected by law from having to give any evidence in court regarding communications between them. Communications between lawyer and a client have this special protection. A court-appointed reconciliator also has this protection with regard to communications made in the course of attempting to reconcile spouses.

Most professional associations have ethical guidelines regarding the confidentiality of communications between members and their clients. These guidelines form a very important part of the professional relationship. However, they do not necessarily provide protection from disclosure in court.

The laws regarding the relationship between other professionals and their clients—clergy and their parishioners, doctors and their patients—

vary across the country. These professionals may be called upon to testify in court.

Consummation of a Marriage: the completion of a marriage by an act of sexual intercourse by a husband and wife after the marriage ceremony.

Contempt of Court: a method the court uses to control its own process. It is a willful disobedience of a court order punishable by fine or imprisonment or both.

Contested Divorce: if either the husband or wife disputes the ground for divorce, or if the spouses are unable to agree on child care or support arrangements, a court will have to resolve these matters. A hearing will be held and both sides of the dispute will be entitled to present evidence supporting their view. The judge will consider the evidence presented and impose a solution.

Contingent Vesting: upon termination of employment, the employee must leave his contributions in the pension fund and take a deferred annuity as a condition for vesting of employer's contributions.

Contingent: something that may or may not happen, a possible happening by chance, accidental, unpredictable due to dependence on chance.

Continuous Service: period during which an employee is continuously employed by the same employer; may be defined in the pension plan or by law to include certain periods of absence or service with an associated or predecessor employer. To be distinguished from credited service.

Contributory Plan: a pension plan that requires the employees to make contributions by payroll deduction to qualify for benefits under the plan.

Costs: sums payable for legal services. When matters are contested in court, a judge has the discretion to order that the losing party pay a portion of the successful party's legal costs.

Court Registry: place where all legal actions are processed. It is part of the machinery of the legal process. The employees are civil servants and not lawyers, but they are very knowledgeable in all phases of court proceedings and will help anyone who politely requests such help.

Credited Service: length of service used in the plan formula to calculate a defined benefit.

Death Benefit: A lump sum (usually), or a life annuity payable from a pension plan to the beneficiary or estate of a member who dies before retirement. May refer to a payment on death after retirement.

Decree Absolute: under the Divorce Act of 1968, a divorce only became final when a court granted a decree absolute. A decree absolute could be granted by the court three months after the day on which the court had allowed the divorce action. If the parties agreed not to appeal the divorce decision, and if special circumstances existed, the court could shorten the three-month period.

Deferred Pension: a pension benefit, payment of which is deferred until the person entitled to the pension benefit reaches the normal retirement date under the pension plan;

Defined Benefit Plan: a distinct benefit the participating member will receive upon retirement, the value of which is at least equal to the member's accumulated contributions with interest.

Defined Contribution Plan: plan sponsor contributions are defined, usually as a percentage of earnings, and usually include specific contributions to be made by the plan member. (1) At retirement, these contributions plus interest are used to purchase an annuity for former members. (2) The size of member's pension depends on the amount of contributions made by and on behalf of that member and will also vary due to interest earned on contributions and annuity rate at retirement time, exact amount of pension unknown until member reaches retirement age. There is no guarantee of specific benefit at retirement. Value is the sum of accumulated contributions with interest.

Dependant: a person who relies on someone else for financial support. In the context of divorce law, it may include a spouse or child.

Desertion: the failure of a husband or wife to live with his or her spouse. It must be a unilateral act carried out against the wishes of the other spouse. Desertion was a ground for divorce under the old divorce legislation. Under the new divorce law, it would be evidence of the separation period.

Designated Province: a province or territory of Canada that is prescribed by the regulations as a province or territory in which there is in force legislation.

Disbursements: out-of-pocket expenses incurred in a family law matter, such as the cost of paying for the petition to be issued at the court office or the cost of paying someone to deliver it to your spouse. It could also be the cost of a family law assessment.

Discoveries: a step in legal proceedings where lawyers get to ask the opposing client, under oath, questions about things said in the legal proceedings, especially in affidavits and pleadings. It is done in the presence of a court reporter, and a transcript of all questions and answers can be prepared.

Division of Pension Credits: also known as credit splitting. A provision in pension plans or pension legislation whereby one spouse, on dissolution of marriage, may obtain a share of pension credits earned by the other partner during the period of marriage or thereafter.

Divorce: the termination of the legal relationship of marriage between a husband and wife.

Eligibility Requirements: a condition such as age or length of service that must be met before an employee is permitted or required to join a pension plan. Term may refer to eligibility for certain benefits.

Employment Pension Plan: a pension plan offered by an employer or supported by a group of employers for the benefit of employees. Includes plans covering employees of governments and the private sector, but does not include the Canada Pension Plan or other public programs.

Escalated Adjustment: an adjustment made to a pension or deferred pension after the termination of a member of a pension plan where the adjustment is not capable of being determined with certainty at the time the plan or an amendment thereto is submitted for registration because the adjustment is related to the investment earnings of the pension fund or to future changes in a general wage or price index.

Execution: a writ or order, issued by a court, giving authority to put a judgement into effect.

Fifty Percent Rule: (a) OPBA, s 51 (2)—spouse never receives an amount greater than 50 percent of value of pension accrued to the member during the period when the party and the member were spouses. (Relates only to pension value.)

(b) OPBA, s 39 (3)—as of January, 1987, legislation in Ontario dictates that the sum of the contributions and interest accumulated under a pension plan made by a plan member shall not be used to provide more than 50 percent of the post-1987 commuted value on the date of termination. If the plan member is entitled to a contributory benefit, any amount above that is deemed surplus value and can be given to the member in a lump sum or returned to the value of pension (relates only to pension contributions) referred to in pension reports as Special Adjustment.

Final Order: an order that is not interim. Interim orders are effective until the end of the trial. The final order is intended to last indefinitely or until changed by the court.

Final Pay Plan: a term commonly used for a pension plan in which benefits are based on earnings in a member's last year of service.

Flat Benefit Plan: A defined benefit plan that specifies a dollar amount of pension to be credited for each year of service.

Former Member: a person who has terminated employment or membership in a pension plan and

(a) is entitled to a deferred pension payable from the pension fund,

(b) is in receipt of a pension payable from the pension fund,

(c) is entitled to commence receiving payment of pension benefits from the pension fund within one year after termination of employment or membership, or

(d)   is entitled to receive any other payment from the pension fund.

Fully Funded: a term describing a plan that at a given time has sufficient assets to provide for all pensions and other benefits in respect of service up to that date.

Funding: systematic monthly payments into a fund which, with investment earnings on these funds, are intended to provide for pensions and other benefits as they become payable.

Garnishee: a legal procedure that allows for the seizure of money owing to a person who has not paid a court-ordered debt. A court may order the debtor's bank, employer, or anyone else who may owe money to the debtor, to pay the money into court to help pay the debt.

Guaranteed Annuity: an annuity that will be paid for the lifetime of a person or for a certain period, whichever is longer, but in any event for a minimum period. For example, if an annuitant with a five-year guarantee dies after three years, payment will be continued to a beneficiary or the estate for two years.

If and When Approach: requires that once the plan member reaches retirement or leaves active service for any other reason, the spouse is entitled to a part of the pension benefits payable to the plan member. Pension is shared once it comes into pay. Share is expressed as a percentage. Upon retirement, the member pays to the non-member spouse a portion of each annuity payment according to the allocation formula agreed upon at time of divorce.

Indexing: 1. to adjust (wages, interest rates) automatically to changes in the cost of living (inflation).

2. a number used to measure change in prices, rates, or employment, showing percentage variation from an arbitrary standard (usually 100) representing the status at some earlier time.

Investment Managers: plan sponsors are frequently assisted by investment managers who help them decide how the pension funds should be invested. These managers are supervised by the plan sponsor.

Investment Return (Yield): earnings of a pension fund including interest on fixed income securities (bonds, mortgages, dividends, capital gains).

Joint and Survivor Pension Option: a mandatory reduced pension that will continue after the member's death for the lifetime of the spouse. In most cases if, at the date of commencement of pension the member has a spouse, the pension must be in the form of a joint and survivor pension paying at least 60 percent of the pension to the survivor. The benefits are not assignable. The rights to the pension benefits may be waived, but the spouse cannot be compelled to do so.

Judgement: the final decision by the court on any issues put to it during the trial. The formal piece of paper that describes who has been successful or not, and on which issues.

Life Income Fund (LIF): a prescribed retirement savings arrangement that can be purchased with funds locked in by pension legislation. Plan members, former members, and their spouses or former spouses can purchase a LIF and begin receiving an income as early as age fifty-five.

Limitation: time limits imposed by the laws and rules of court. If certain things are not done (claim support, division of property) then the right to claim is lost, unless the court grants special permission.

Locking In: the employee must leave his vested rights, including contributions made in the plan, and may receive them only in the form of a pension upon retirement.

Marriage: the voluntary union for life of one man and one woman to the exclusion of all others. In Canada, marriage involves a religious or civil ceremony that complies with the procedural requirements of the provincial or territorial laws where the marriage takes place.

Marriage creates the legal status of husband and wife and the legal obligations arising from that status.

Marriage Breakdown: the sole ground for legally ending a marriage under the terms of the Divorce Act. Marriage breakdown can be established in three ways: through evidence that one spouse committed adultery; through evidence of physical or mental cruelty; or if the spouses intentionally lived separate and apart for at least one year.

Marriage Contract: an agreement between a husband and wife outlining the spouses' respective responsibilities and obligations. Some contracts also include agreements as to how property and ongoing obligations will be shared if the marriage breaks down.

Matrimonial Home: where the family or legally married couple have resided. Common law spouses never have them (as recognized in law) because they have no statutory property rights. It is possible to have more than one matrimonial home at a time.

Mediation: a process by which people in situations of potential conflict attempt to resolve their differences and reach a mutually acceptable agreement. Neutral third parties—mediators—can often help the parties retain a focus on the problems to be solved and possible solutions, rather than on areas of personal disagreement.

Minutes of Settlement: a method of settling a case by writing out and having the parties sign an acknowledgment of how they want their problem resolved.

Motion: a request to the court for a particular order pending trial, such as interim custody or support. Filed with an affidavit.

Mortality Tables: measure the probability of a person at each age living exactly one year—a pension pays a benefit from retirement to the death of the plan member and a mortality table is required to calculate its value. The two types of tables are: 1. Life tables for Canada. developed by Statistics Canada from census data. They show mortality rates for the general population of Canada; and 2. group annuity mortality tables, developed by life insurance companies. They show mortality rates.

Motion For Judgement: a procedure by which you apply to a judge of the Ontario Court, general division, for a divorce judgement. The motion is made if the respondent is in default and has not filed an answer within the prescribed time and requires a requisition to the registrar and a notice of motion for judgement. The notice of motion sets out the documentary evidence to be relied upon, and states whether you intend to present oral evidence at the hearing; otherwise the matter will proceed by way of affidavit evidence.

Multi-Employer Pension Plan: covers employees of more than one employer, usually by agreement with a union or group of unions.

Non-Contributory Plan: a plan in which all required funding is provided by the employer.

Normal Retirement Date: the date or age specified in the pension plan as the normal retirement date of members.

Notary Public: public officer whose function is to attest and certify certain documents and to perform other official acts. (All lawyers are notaries public; not all notaries public are lawyers.)

Notice of Motion: notice in writing to the other side stating that on a certain designated day at a specific place a motion will be made to the court for the purpose or relief stated in the notice. A motion is different from a trial in that the procedure is more summary.

Ontario Court (Provincial Division): enforces applications made under the Children's Law Reform Act. Located in various districts throughout the province.

Order: the court's decision on a matter that it was asked to resolve. See Motion and Affidavit.

Partial Wind-Up: the termination of part of a pension plan and the distribution of the assets of the pension fund related to that part of the pension plan.

Participating Employer: in relation to a multi-employer pension plan, means an employer required to make contributions to the multi-employer pension plan.

Parties: the husband and wife, or anybody else who is named in the case before the court and asking for an order of any kind.

Past Service: the period of service accrued by an employee before becoming a member of a pension plan. May be used to define certain benefits that differ from those of current service or future service.

Pension: a fixed sum paid regularly to a person or surviving dependant following retirement. There are both public (Canada Pension Plan) and private (from one's employer) pensions. Some provinces consider a pension that is not yet being paid at the time of marriage breakdown to be property that must be divided.

Pension Benefit: implies periodic payments provided under the pension plan for the lifetime of the member.

Pension Benefits Act: Ontario legislation regulating employment pension plans. It specifies minimum benefit provisions, funding and solvency requirements, and investment guidelines.

Pension Benefit Credit: the value of a pension benefit at a particular time. Used in some pension distributions to share the value of the member's interest at the effective date of the assignment or order as applicable under legislation.

Pension Fund: the fund maintained to provide benefits under or related to the pension plan.

Pension Plan: a plan organized and administered to provide a regular income for the lifetime of retired members; other benefits that may be provided include payments on permanent disability or death.

Petition: written document containing an application by a person or persons and addressed to another person requesting the court to exercise its authority to redress some wrong or grant some privilege, for example, divorce.

Petitioner: person who presents the petition to the court.

Plan Sponsor: the employer sponsoring the pension plan for employees.

Pleadings: formal allegations by the parties of their respective claims and defenses submitted to the court for arbitration.

Portability: options available to an individual on termination of employment. Relates to transferring the value of accumulated pension credits to an RRSP account or to the plan of a employer to facilitate retirement planning. Under the Pension Benefits Act, an employee has these options in addition to the option of a deferred pension from the original plan at normal retirement age. See also Vesting.

Procedure: the technical rules lawyers must follow to get a case through the civil justice system. They are contained in the province's Rules of Court.

Private Pension Plan: an employment pension plan offered by an employer or by employers and unions in the private sector.

Pro Rata: according to the calculation in proportion; proportionately. For example, one tenth of total pension value is earned before marriage. Calculate the Net Present Value of whole pension and allocate nine tenths of value to marriage portion. Method assumes the value of the pension accrues equally each year.

Qualification Date: in respect Ontario, the first day of January, 1965, and, in respect of a designated province, the date on which under the law of the designated province a pension plan must be registered by the proper authority in the designated province.

Reciprocal Transfer Agreement: an agreement related to two or more pension plans that provides for the transfer of money or credits for employment in respect of individual members.

Registered Retirement Savings Plan (RRSP): a personal retirement savings plan, defined in the Income Tax Act, allows contributions to be deducted from income (which is subject to taxation), and tax is deferred on contributions and investment income until income is received as annuity payments. (locked in RRSPs may not be converted to a Registered Retirement Income Fund).

Retirement: withdrawal from the active work force because of age; may also be used in the sense of permanent withdrawal from the labour force for any reason, including disability.

Retainer: the contract by which you hire a lawyer to take your case. It can also mean the sum of money you give the lawyer to be applied to fees and disbursement.

Retirement Income: income from pension and other sources to which a retired person is entitled. May include both private and public pension payments, income from personal savings, government income supplements, and certain other sources of income, for example, free health insurance premiums.

Retirement Method: a projected accrued benefit valuation method, with salary projection where appropriate.

Requisition: instructions to the registrar to take a certain step. In the usual case, to note the respondent in default. Such a step can be taken only when the Petition for divorce has been filed with proof of service.

Respondent and Co-Respondent: person to whom the petition is addressed and usually defined as the opposing party. The co-respondent usually means the person charged with adultery with the respondent in a suit for divorce for that cause and joined as a defendant with such party if and only if some form of relief is claimed against the person. If no form of relief is claimed, the person may be named in the petition but is not a party to the action.

Rules of Court: See Procedure.

Separate: to cease living together as man and wife, possibly under the same roof but usually not. Done with the intention not to live together again.

Separation Agreement: a contract signed by the parties to settle their differences. It can deal with property, custody, access, support, and any other matter. A form of domestic contract.

Solicitor-Client Privilege: the lawyer's obligation to keep secret everything you tell him.

Spouse: a man or a woman who:

    a)   is married to the other; or,

    b)   is not married to the other and is living in a conjugal relationship;

        i)   continuously for a period of not less than three years; or,

        ii)   in a relationship of some permanence, if they are natural or adoptive parents of a child, both as defined in the Family law Act.

Spousal Support: an order that one spouse pay the other a sum of money either in a lump sum or periodically for a set period of time or indefinitely.

Statute: a law passed by the legislature of a province or the federal Parliament, for example., the Divorce Act.

Substituted Service: service upon a person in a manner other than by personal service. The method of serving substitutionally is authorized by statute, the most common being the publishing of notices in local newspapers in areas where they are most likely to be seen by the parties to whom the notices are addressed.

Surplus: OPBA, s 39 (4)—the excess of the value of the assets (member's contributions and interest made on or after January 1, 1987) of a pension fund related to a pension plan, over the value of the liabilities under the pension plan, both calculated in the prescribed manner. If a pension plan's assets exceed the plan's total liabilities, the difference is called a surplus. See Fifty Percent Rule.

Survivor Pension or Survivor Pension Benefit: a monthly benefit payable under a pension plan to the surviving spouse of a deceased employee or pensioner; usually refers to a benefit other than payments under the guaranteed annuity or joint survivor annuity provision.

Termination of Employment: severance of the employment relationship for any reason other than death and retirement.

Termination Method: an unprojected accrued benefit valuation method. No increase in accrued benefits shall be reflected, except to the extent such increases are provided to deferred vested pension plan members.

Title of Proceedings: title of the action including (in the case of divorce petitions) the court and registry numbers and the full names of the petitioner and the respondent.

Trial Cohabitation: period of separation not to be interrupted by resuming cohabitation for reconciliation during periods not totalling ninety days.

Uncontested Divorce: if neither husband nor wife disputes the ground for divorce, and if they are able to reach an agreement regarding child care and financial arrangements, it may be possible to ask a judge to grant a divorce without a lengthy court hearing. In some provinces and territories it may be possible to get a divorce without having to actually appear in court.

Unfunded Liability: generally, any amount by which the assets of a pension plan are less than its liabilities.

Updating (Benefits): applied to the occasional review and increase of accrued benefits to reflect rising wage levels where the plan does not provide for automatic improvement as in final (earnings) formula.

Valuation Date: The earliest of:
1) date spouses separate with no reasonable prospect of reconciliation,
2) date divorce is granted,
3) date marriage is declared nullity,

as outlined by the Family Law Act. In Ontario courts of law, the valuation date usually is considered to be the date of separation.

Value of Pension: always based on Net Present Value of pension at a certain date.

Value Added: this method of valuation recognizes the fact that the value of a pension increases with years of service (as salary levels increase) and usually results in a higher pension value. Two valuations are completed, (a) at date of marriage (using the purchasing value of the dollar in the year of marriage); (b) at date of separation—subtract value of (a) from value of (b).

Vested: not contingent upon anything.

Vested Benefits (Vesting): benefits to which an employee is entitled under the plan as a result of satisfying age or service requirements; usually requires locking in of contributions as a result of membership in the plan for a specified period of time (two years under the Ontario Pension Benefits Act).

Vested Interest: an established right that can't be eliminated, as to some future benefit.

Vesting: the right of an employee to a benefit from the employer's contributions whether or not he terminates employment. The benefit is usually a deferred annuity. It is taken for granted that the employee has a right to his contributions. See also Contingent Vesting and Locking In).

Winding Up, Wind Up: occurs when a pension plan ceases to operate. All members are automatically vested and entitled to receive a pension from the pension plan.

Year's Maximum Pensionable Earnings (YMPE): refers to earnings from employment on which CPP contributions and benefits are calculated. Changes each year according to a formula based on average wage levels.

Appendix I

Glossary of Terms for Business Valuation

Adjusted Cost Base: Amount (cost) of capital property from which capital gains or capital losses are measured.

Adjusted Shareholders' Equity: The shareholders' equity of a business resulting from the restatement of assets and liabilities to their fair market value.

Amortization: The annual write-off of the cost of capital or intangible assets in the determination of net earnings.

Appraised Value: The value determined by a real estate or equipment appraiser.

Arm's Length: Persons dealing on a normal commercial basis. A question of fact.

Assets Approach: Valuation procedure where assets and liabilities are restated to fair market value in valuing a business. Fair market value determination can be on either a liquidation or going-concern basis.

Blockage Discount: Discount applied to stock market price when notionally valuing a significant minority shareholding in a public corporation.

Book Value: The capitalized cost of an asset or liability less accumulated depreciation or amortization as shown on the financial statements of a business.

Business Day: A day that is not a Saturday, Sunday, or statutory holiday in the province of Ontario.

Business Valuation: The process of arriving at a determination of value for the assets or shares of a business or an interest therein.

Canadian GAAP: Generally accepted accounting principles as applied in Canada.

Capital Cost Allowance: The amount of depreciation or amortization deducted for income tax purposes on a specific class of assets based upon rates and methods set out in the Income Tax Act Regulations.

Capital Gain: Capital appreciation of an asset measured by net proceeds of disposition less adjusted cost base.

Capitalization of Maintainable Cash Flow: Valuation method where maintainable cash flow is converted into a capital sum at a valuation date.

Capitalization of Maintainable Earnings: Valuation method where maintainable earnings are converted into a capital sum at a valuation date.

Capitalization Rate: The rate of return applied to the maintainable earnings or cash flow of a business to arrive at going-concern value on an earnings based valuation. The inverse of the price/earnings multiple or price/cash flow multiple. To illustrate these relationships, we use a simple example, assuming a capitalization rate of 20 percent and maintainable earnings of $50.

$$\textit{Earnings Multiple} = \frac{100}{20\%} = 5$$

$$\textit{Capitalized Earnings} = \$50 \times 5 \text{ or } \frac{\$50}{20\%} = \$250$$

Cash Flow: Net earnings plus depreciation, amortization, or depletion and other non-cash charges.

Chartered Business Valuator (CBV): Professional designation given to individuals who successfully complete the entrance examinations and other criteria of the Canadian Institute of Chartered Business Valuators and are admitted to membership.

Closely Held Corporation: Used to describe a corporation whose shares are not listed for trading on a recognized stock exchange or traded over the counter. Also used to describe a corporation with fifty shareholders or fewer.

Control Premium: The price paid over stock market price to acquire control in a public corporation. This premium is paid for control and/or for the anticipated synergies from a combination of businesses.

De Facto Control: Where one or more persons own 50 percent or less of the outstanding share votes of a corporation but nevertheless controls the corporation. More common in public corporations.

De Jure Control: When one or more persons own in excess of 50% of the outstanding share votes of a corporation.

Deferred Income Taxes: Amounts arising from the differences in the computation of income taxes for financial statement presentation and income tax purposes.

Depreciation: The annual write-off of tangible assets in the determination of net earnings for accounting purposes. (The Canadian Institute of Chartered Accountants now uses the term "amortization.")

Depreciated Replacement Value: Used by real estate and equipment appraisers to describe the replacement cost (new) of buildings and equipment less a deduction for depreciation and obsolescence.

Discounted Cash Flow: Valuation method where a finite stream of cash flow and the residual value of a business are converted into a capital sum at a valuation date.

Discount Rate: Rate of return used to convert a stream of cash flow under the discounted cash flow method into a capital sum at a valuation date.

Discretionary Cash Flow: Operating cash flow adjusted for changes in long-term debt and fixed assets before the payment of dividends.

Earning Power: Used when referring to the economic earnings or cash flow generated by a business, as opposed to the reported earnings or cash flow.

En Bloc Value: The value of 100 percent of a business without regard to the specific shareholders therein. For example, if five individuals each owned 20 percent of the outstanding shares of a closely held corporation, en bloc value would be the value of all the outstanding shares taken together, rather than as the aggregate value of the given separate 20 percent interests.

Fair Cash Value: See Fair Market Value.

Fair Market Value: The highest price, expressed in terms of money or money's worth, obtainable in an open and unrestricted market, between informed and prudent parties acting at arm's length, neither party being under any compulsion to transact. Usually synonymous with intrinsic value, fair cash value, and real value.

Fair Value: The fair market value of a shareholding in a business determined without the application of a minority discount. Usually used in appraisal remedy or oppression remedy situations. Could include a premium for forcible taking.

Financial Leverage: Ability to borrow funds based upon the financial strength of a business when it earns more on the assets purchased with the funds than the fixed cost of financing. In the context of a merger or acquisition, the ability to finance most of the purchase price by debt instruments collateralized by the assets acquired.

Forced Liquidation Value: Price that can be obtained for an asset or a business by exposing it in the marketplace for a short period of time under restricted conditions. Not inherent in the definition of fair market value. Liquidation value is used in valuing a business that cannot be valued under the going-concern method.

Going-Concern Value: Value of a business as a going concern as opposed to the net proceeds from liquidation.

Goodwill: The difference between going-concern value and tangible assets backing. It includes those intangibles such as reputation, customer relations, location, quality of products, and similar factors that cannot be valued or identified separately but that generate economic benefits or earnings in excess of the norm. Goodwill is generally classified into the following categories: product, location, business, and personal. Personal goodwill does not have commercial value.

Group Control (Private Corporation): Control of a corporation by minority shareholders when more than 50 percent of the share votes are banded together.

Hindsight: Prospective evidence used to substantiate assumptions made at a valuation date. Usually not admissible.

Identifiable Intangible Assets: Intangible assets other than goodwill. Examples are patents, licenses, copyrights, trademarks, and franchise agreements.

Intrinsic Value: A notional value, based upon rates of return required by investors given economic and business conditions existing at the valuation date, without consideration of possible synergistic (economies of scale) benefits that might accrue in differing degrees to arm's length corporate purchasers. See also Fair Market Value.

Invested Capital: The sum of the long-term debt and shareholders' equity of a business.

Investment Approach: Valuation of a business on a going-concern basis; more common methods include capitalization of maintainable earnings, capitalization of cash flow, or discounted cash flow.

Liquidation Value: The net amount of money, if any, available to equity owners following a voluntary, orderly liquidation or a forced sale. Under this scenario a going concern is not assumed.

Maintainable Earnings: The level of earnings from operations a company can reasonably be expected to generate in the future based upon an analysis of projected earnings as well as the trend of past earnings.

Maintainable Cash Flow: Economic (adjusted) cash flow likely to be sustained by a business in the future.

Majority Interest: A shareholding of more than 50 percent of the share votes of a corporation.

Market Value: Value in exchange between a purchaser and a seller under prevailing conditions; not necessarily fair market value. Synonymous with market price or stock market price of public corporations.

Minority Discount: Adjustment made to the en bloc pro rata value of a minority interest to reflect the lack of control and liquidity (marketability) of that interest.

Minority Interest: A shareholding of 50 percent or less of the share votes of a corporation.

Multiple: Inverse of capitalization rate. See capitalization rate.

OBCA: The Business Corporations Act, 1990 (Ontario) R.S.O. 1990, C-B16.

Operating Cash Flow: Cash flow adjusted for the annual changes in working capital.

Orderly Liquidation Value: Price that can be obtained for assets or a business in the marketplace given a reasonable period of time to expose the assets or business to obtain the highest price available. Inherent in the definition of fair market value. Liquidation value is used in valuing a business that cannot be valued under the going-concern method.

Person: Includes an individual, sole proprietorship, partnership, unincorporated association, unincorporated syndicate, unincorporated organization, trust, body corporate, trustee, executor, administrator, or other legal representative of the Crown or any agency or instrumentality thereof.

Present Value of Tax Shield: Present value of tax savings that can be realized by claiming capital cost allowance on the undepreciated capital cost of depreciable assets of a business.

Public Corporation: Term used to describe a corporation whose shares are listed for trading on a recognized stock exchange or over-the-counter market.

Rateable Value: The pro rata portion of the en bloc value for a specific shareholding in a business.

Real Value: Usually synonymous with fair market value and intrinsic value.

Recapture: Taxable amount resulting from the excess of proceeds of disposition (up to capital cost) of the remaining asset over the undepreciated capital cost of that class.

Redundant Assets: Assets not employed in the day-to-day operations of a business that can be withdrawn without impairing the entity's ability to operate as a going concern. Examples include excess cash, a portfolio of marketable securities, and excess land and building.

Redundant Liabilities (Negative Redundancy): Liabilities that can be associated with redundant assets. An example would be a mortgage on excess land or building. Negative redundancy refers to a situation where a business entity is excessively leveraged and thus requires a notional capital injection.

Related Party: For securities purposes, defined extensively in Ontario Securities Commission Policy 9.1 at Part 2, paragraph 14. For income tax purposes, defined in the Income Tax Act. S. 251. The definitions are quite different.

Replacement Cost (New): The current cost of a similar new item having the nearest equivalent utility.

Reproduction Cost (New): The cost to produce an identical item at current cost.

Residual Value: The present value at a valuation date of the net assets or cash flow of a business at the end of the cash flow period when using the discounted cash flow approach.

Retention Value: Value of property in the hope that forgoing immediate returns will be rewarded with some degree of certainty in the future. A derivative of fair market value in that an open and unrestricted market for buyers and sellers is assumed.

Rules of Thumb: Methods used to estimate values of businesses in specific industries. Usually expressed as a percentage of sales volume of a business or as a combination of sales volume and assets vale. Should be corroborated with a going-concern method of valuation.

Special Interest Purchasers: Purchasers who for one or more reasons are willing to pay a higher price for an asset than are other purchasers. Generally these reasons relate to the ability of the special interest purchaser to generate higher earnings as a result of economies available to him, or to a reduced risk experienced by such a purchaser following acquisition though elimination of competition, acquisition of an assured source of supply, or retention of a viable market or key personnel. Special interest purchasers are strategic or synergistic in nature.

Stock Market Price: Price obtainable on a stock exchange or over-the-counter market. Usually represents a minority interest position.

Sustaining Capital Reinvestment: Amount of recurring annual capital investment in fixed assets required to sustain operations and provide for the ongoing replacement of existing assets of a business. Used in the capitalization of cash flow and discounted cash flow approaches.

Synergies: The benefits or economies of scale resulting from the achievement of increased earnings or cash flow as a result of the combination of two or more entities over and above the sum of earnings or cash flow of the two entities viewed separately. Could also include reduced risk thorough diversification and elimination of a competitor or ensured source of supply.

Tangible Asset Backing: Amount arrived at by restating the assets and liabilities of a business to their fair market values or realizable values. Tangible asset backing usually plays an important role in the assessment of risk of a business as a going concern.

Tax Shield: The sum of the anticipated tax savings that will accrue as a result of the claiming of capital cost allowances by the owner of the particular capital assets expressed in today's dollars.

Undepreciated Capital Cost: The capital cost for tax purposes of a class of assets on which capital cost allowance can be claimed. The sum of all properties at their original cost less proceeds of all dispositions and less all amounts claimed to date with certain other adjustments.

Valuation Date: Specific date at which assets or shares of a business are valued.

Value: The Ontario Securities Commission defines value as "fair market value, unless the context otherwise requires."

Value in Exchange: Synonymous with Market Value.

Value to the Owner: The price a person would pay for assets or shares rather than being deprived of same. Often used in expropriation matters.

Working Capital: Current assets less current liabilities.

Appendix J

Ordering a Proper Pension Valuation

Enclosed is a completed "Information Sheet" and an "Authorization Letter" signed by the pension member. Also enclosed is the information that I have about the pension and a deposit of $500.00 on account. Please send the valuation report to:

Name:_____

Address:_____

_____

Postal Code: _____

Phone Number: _____

Mail to:
Pension Valuators of Canada
785 The Kingsway
Peterborough, Ontario
K9J 6W7

LETTER OF AUTHORIZATION

DATE: _____

ATTENTION:

     NAME OF EMPLOYER _____

     NAME OF PENSION PLAN _____

NAME OF PLAN MEMBER: _____

PLAN MEMBER'S SIN: _____

PLAN MEMBER'S
EMPLOYEE NUMBER: _____

VALUATION DATE: _____

     I hereby authorize you to provide **PENSION VALUATORS OF CANADA** with any and all information requested by them regarding my income, employment, and pension plan particulars. This authorization shall remain in force until cancelled in writing by me.

_____   _____
MEMBER'S SIGNATURE   WITNESS

Appendix K

Information Sheet

INFORMATION SHEET

NAME OF PENSION PLAN MEMBER: _____

PHONE NUMBER: HOME: _____

WORK: _____

NAME OF PENSION PLAN: _____

DATE OF BIRTH:	DD/	MM/	YY/
DATE OF PLAN MEMBERSHIP:	DD/	MM/	YY/
DATE OF MARRIAGE:	DD/	MM/	YY/
DATE OF VALUATION/SEPARATION:	DD/	MM/	YY/

S.I.N.: _____

EMPLOYMENT STATUS: Salaried   ☐   Unionized   ☐
Terminated   ☐   Retired   ☐

IF RETIRED or TERMINATED PROVIDE

DATE OF RETIREMENT OR TERMINATION: _____

VALUE OF OTHER EXPECTED RETIREMENT INCOME
(i.e. RRSPs) AT DATE OF SEPARATION: _____

NAME OF EMPLOYER: _____

ADDRESS OF EMPLOYER:_____

EMPLOYER/PLAN ADMINISTRATOR _____

Phone:

_____

Fax:

EMPLOYEE NUMBER:_____

NAME OF SPOUSE:_____

Appendix L

Family Law Lawyers

A list of lawyers interested in, qualified for, and experienced in dealing with marriage breakdown.

NOVA SCOTIA
BEDFORD
Deborah E. Gillis, B.B.A., LL.B., Gillis & Walden, Barrister, Solicitors, Notaries, 1550 Bedford Highway, Suite 310, B4A 1E6, Telephone: (902) 835-6174, (902) 832-1693, Fax: (902) 835-1486, Email: dgillis@gilliswalden.ns.ca

HALIFAX
Marguerite J. MacNeil, Coady Filliter, Barristers & Solicitors, 5880 Spring Garden Road, Suite 208, B3H 1Y1, Telephone: (902) 429-6264, Fax: (902) 423-3044.

NEW WATERFORD
Charles Broderick, Barrister & Solicitor, 3316 Plummer Avenue, B1H 4K4, Telephone: (902) 862- 6471, Fax: (902) 862-9513, Email: cblaw@istar.ca

UPPER TANTALLON
Jacqueline R. Farrow, Farrow & Covan, Barristers & Solicitors, 4 Westwood Blvd, B3Z 1H3, Telephone: (902) 826-9140, Fax: (902) 826-1074, Email: jfarrow@sprint.ca

ONTARIO
AJAX
Darryl T.G. Glover, Barrister & Solicitor, 2200 Brock Road North, Units C10 & 11, L1X 2R2, Telephone: (905) 427-0646.
Michael P. Reilly, LL.B., Reilly D'Heureux Lanzi LLP, Barristers & Solicitors, 555 Kingston Road West, L1S 6M1, Telephone: (905)

427-4077, Fax: (905) 427-4042, Email: mpreilly@oak.net Web site: www.reillylegal.com

AURORA

Gordon F. Allan, B.A., LL.B., Barrister, Solicitor, Notary Public, 12 St. John's Sideroad East, Aurora, ON L4G 3G8, Telephone: (905) 895-3425, Fax: (905) 726-3098.

BARRIE

Douglas J. Manning, Burgar, Rowe LLP, Barristers, Solicitors & Trade Mark Agents, 90 Mulcaster Street, L4M 4Y5, Telephone: (705) 721-3377, Fax: (705) 721-4025, Email: dmanning@burgarrowe.com Web site: www.burgarrowe.com

John C. Rogers, Barrister, Solicitor & Notary Public, 25 Poyntz Street, L4M 3N8, Telephone: (705) 734-0057, Fax: (705) 734-0306.

Judith Turner-Macbeth, Barrister & Solicitor, P.O. Box 295, 86 Worsley Street, Barrie, ON L4M 4T2, Telephone: (705) 721-5907, Fax: (705) 728-7642.

BOLTON

Marilyn Conway Jones, Barrister & Solicitor, 284 Queen Street South, Bolton, ON L7E 4Z5, Telephone: (905) 951-0504, Fax: (905) 951-0074.

Patrick G. Muise, B.A., LL.B., Palmateer & Muise, Barristers & Solicitors, 58 King Street West, L7E 5T5, Telephone: (905) 857-0847, Fax: (905) 857-4410, Email: pmuise@caledonlaw.com, Web site: www.caledonlaw.com

BRACEBRIDGE

Michael Anne MacDonald, Barrister and Solicitor, Notary Public, 25 Ontario Street, Box 509, P1L 1T8, Telephone: (705) 645-7858, Fax: (705) 645-4746.

Daniel J. Wyjad, M. Sc., LL.B., Pinckard Wyjad Associates, Barristers, Solicitors, Notaries, 39 Dominion Street, P1L 1T6, Telephone: (705) 645-8787, Fax: (705) 645-3390, Email: dwyjad@on.aibn.com

BRAMPTON

Barbara J. Byers, Barrister & Solicitor, 167 Queen Street West, L6Y 1M5, Telephone: (905) 453-0078, Fax: (905) 453-0095.

BRANTFORD

Lawrence J. Brock, B.A., LL.B., Barrister, Solicitor & Notary Public, 36 King Street, N3T 3C5, Telephone: (519) 751-3325, Fax: (519) 758-8857.

BURLINGTON

Henri J. Charlebois, B.A., LL.B., Hastings, Charlebois, Barristers & Solicitors, 3513 Mainway, L7M 1A9, Telephone: (905) 332-1888, Fax: (905) 332-0021, Residence: (905) 689-8058, Email: hjcharlebois@hclawyers.ca Web site: www.hclawyers.ca

June P. McAskie, Barrister & Solicitor, 1414 Ontario Street, L7S 1G4, Telephone: (905) 639-9407, Fax: (905) 639-6166.

CAYUGA

Shawn Richarz, B.A. (Hons.) LL.B., Barrister, Solicitor & Notary Public, 1 Cayuga Street, N0A 1E0, Telephone: (905) 772-3513, Fax: (905) 772-5918, Email: sricharz@yahoo.com, Web site: www.richarzlaw.ca

COBOURG

Rodger F. Cooper, Lawyer, Mediator, 253 Division Street, K9A 3P9, Telephone: (888) 251- 1945, (905) 372-8727, Fax: (905) 372-0720.

COCHRANE

Dominique Boucher, B.A., LL.B., Boivin Beaudoin Boucher, Barristers & Solicitors, P.O. Box 1898, 174-4th Avenue, P0L 1C0, Telephone: (705) 272-4346, Fax: (705) 272-2991.

CORNWALL

Thomas M. Byrne, B.A., LL.B., Wilson Poirier Byrne, Barristers & Solicitors, 132 Second Street West, K6J 1G5, Telephone: (613) 938-2224, Fax: (613) 938-8005.

FORT FRANCES

Barbara J. Morgan, R.N., B.Sc.N., LL.B., Morgan Associates, Barristers & Solicitors, 436 Scott Street, P9A 1H2, Telephone: (807) 274-5361, Fax: (807) 274-0414, Email: morgan@jam21.net, Web site: www.morgan.on.ca

GUELPH

Randy S. Brant, SmithValeriote, Barristers & Solicitors, 285 Woolwich Street, N1H 6N1, Telephone: (519) 821-0010, Fax: (519) 821-6821.

M. Wesley Philp, Barrister & Solicitor, 176 Woolwich Street, N1H 3V5, Telephone: (519) 826-6952, Fax: (519) 829-2971.

HAMILTON

John Alexander Bland, B.Mus., M.Ed., LL.B., Barrister & Solicitor, The Union Gas building, 801—20 Hughson Street South, L8N 2A1,

Telephone: (905) 524-3533, Fax: (905) 524-5142.

Caroline E. Brown, Barrister & Solicitor, 117 Hunter Street East, L8N 1M5, Telephone: (905) 540-8999, Fax: (905) 540-9250.

Michael P. Clarke, Barrister & Solicitor, 25 Main Street West, Suite 700, L8P 1H1, Telephone: (905) 527-4399, Fax: (905) 577-7775.

Earl R. Cranfield, Q.C., Barrister & Solicitor, 20 Hughson Street South, Suite 901, L8N 2A1, Telephone: (905) 528-0089, Fax: (905) 528-7692.

Richard F. Gaasenbeek, B.A., Barrister, Solicitor, Notary Public, 131 John Street South, Suite 203, L8N 2C3, Telephone: (905) 528-8369, Fax: (905) 528-8066.

Gordon T. Gardner, B.A., LL.B., Cain, Gzik & Gardner, Barristers & Solicitors, 340 Main Street East, L8N 1J1, Telephone: (905) 528-7933, Fax: (905) 528-1326.

Mary Elizabeth Kneeland, Barrister & Solicitor, 131 John Street South, L8N 2C3, Telephone: (905) 572-7737.

Tamra A. Mann, Barrister & Solicitor, 105 Main Street East, Suite 501, L8N 1G6, Telephone: (905) 308-8308, Fax: (905) 308-9984.

David J. Sherman, B.A., LL.B., Thoman, Soule, Gage LLP, Barristers & Solicitors, 46 Jackson Street East, LCD 1, Box 187, L8N 3C5, Telephone: (905) 529-8195, Fax: (905) 529-7906, Email: shermada@tsg-legal.com Web site: www.tsg-legal.com

Gary L. Waxman, Barrister, Solicitor, Notary Public, 1367 Upper James Street, L9B 1K2, Telephone: (905) 388-0585, Fax: (905) 574-1991

HANOVER

Kevin W. McMeeken, LL.B., Halpin & McMeeken, Barristers & Solicitors, 478 Tenth Street, N4N 1R1, Telephone: (519) 364-5505, Fax: (519) 364-0165, Email: halpinandmcmeeken@on.aibn.com

HILLSBURGH

Robert P. Harper, 115 Main Street, P.O. Box 10, N0B 1Z0, Telephone: (519) 855-4961, Fax: (519) 855-4029.

KINCARDINE

William S. Mathers, B.A., LL.B., Barrister & Solicitor, 6-777 Queen Street, N2Z 2Y2, Telephone: (519) 396-4147, Fax: (519) 396-1872.

KINGSTON

John F. Black, B.A.(Hons.), LL.B., Racioppo, Zuber, Coetzee, Dionne LLP, Law Firm, 574 Princess Street, Suite 201, K7L 1C9, Telephone: (613) 544-1482, Fax: (613) 546-3633.

Douglas Slack, Barrister & Solicitor, 817 Blackburn Mews, K7P 2N6, Telephone: (613) 384-7260, Fax: (613) 384-7262, Email: dmslack@utoronto.ca

KITCHENER

C. Richard Buck B.A., LL.B and Roger M. Hunt LLB, Smith Hunt Buck, Barristers & Solicitors, 53 Roy Street, Maplecroft House, N2H 6L1, Telephone: (519) 579-3400, Fax: (519) 741-9041.

William C. Cline, LL.B., Shuh Cline & Grossman, Barristers and Solicitors, 17 Weber Street West, N2H 3Y9, Telephone: (519) 578-9010, ext. 228, Fax: (519) 578-1590.

Richard Herold, B.A., M.B.A., LL.B., Barrister & Solicitor, Notary Public, 53 Roy Street, N2H 4B4, Telephone: (877) 369-5353(toll free), (519) 749-0555 (Kitchener), Fax: (519) 741-9041, Email: herold-lawyers@on.aibn.com

Michael David Lannan, B.A., L.B., Barrister & Solicitor, 15 Charles Street East, N2G 2P3, Telephone: (519) 579-8558, Fax: (519) 579-8856, Email: mdl@golden.net

Tracy Miller, Lawyer, 7 Duke Street West, Suite 203, N2H 6N7, Telephone: (519) 745-1912.

Sandra M. Spiegelberg, B.A., LL.B., Protopapas & Spiegelberg, Barristers, Solicitors, Notaries, 22 Frederick Street, Suite 1016, N2H 6M6, Telephone: (519) 772-1047, Fax: (519) 772-1051, Email: Sandra@pslaw.ca

LASALLE

Ute Wigley-Mueller, LL.B., DR. jur., Barrister, Solicitor, Notary Public, 1620 Front Road, N9J 2B6, Telephone: (519) 734-1303, Fax: (519) 978-3845, Email: legal2@wincom.net, Web site: germancanadian-lawfirm.com

LINDSAY

A. Ronald Cork, B.A., LL.B., Warner & Cork, Barrister & Solicitor, 82 Kent Street West, P.O. Box 333, K9V 4S3, Telephone: (800) 461- 0373 (toll free), (705) 324-6196, Fax: (705) 324-7440.

R. Dan Cornell, LL.B., Cornell, Mortlock & Sillberg, Barrister, Solicitor, Notary Public, 272 Kent Street West, K9V 4S5, Telephone: (705) 324-4312, (705) 324-8511, Fax: (705) 324-7525.

Drew S. Gunsolus, Hons. B.A., LL.B., Staples, Swain & Gunsolus, Barristers, Solicitors, Notaries, 10 William Street South, K9V 3A4, Telephone: (705) 324-6222, Fax: (705) 324-4168.

Helen McMorrow, Barrister, Solicitor, Notary Public, Suite 207, Kent

Place Mall, 189 Kent Street West, K9V 5G6, Telephone: (705) 878-1234, Fax: (705) 878-1042, Email: hmcmorrow@on.aibn.com
Philip Watson, Barrister & Solicitor, 26 Peel Street, Telephone: (705) 878-9494, Fax: (705) 878-9959.

LONDON

E.P. Mandy Heyninck, Kelly, Barnes, Chapman, Hayes & Heyninck, Associates at Law, 305 Oxford Street East, N6A 1V3, Telephone: (519) 672-1075, Fax: (519) 672-1292.
R. Jonathan McKinnon, B.A., LL.B., Barrister & Solicitor, 64 Fullarton Street, N6A 1K1, Telephone: (519) 672-2227, (519) 473-0675, Fax: (519) 679-6576.
Maria G. Mendes, B.A.(Hons.), LL.B., 123 King Street, N6A 1C3, Telephone: (519) 438-0808, Fax: (519) 432-5455, Email: mmendes@ mendeslawfirm.ca Web site: www.mendeslawfirm.ca
M. Anne Robinson, Robinson Blokker, Barristers & Solicitors, 735 Wonderland Road North, Suite 202, N6H 4L1, Telephone: (519) 657-8985, Fax: (519) 657-7286, Email: anne@robinsonblokker.com

MANOTICK

Jacqueline F. Dunbar, B.A. (Psych.) LL.B., Barrister & Solicitor, 5548 Main Street, K4M 1A3, Telephone: (613) 692-0130, Fax: (613) 692-1747.

MARKHAM

E. Bruce Solomon, B.C.L., LL.B., Barrister & Solicitor, 7507 Kennedy Road, L3R 0L8, Telephone: (905) 479-1900, Fax: (905) 479-9793, Email: solo@total.net

MILTON

Dale F. Fitzpatrick, Furlong Collins, Barristers & Solicitors, 64 Ontario Street North, L9T 2T1, Telephone: (905) 878-8123, Fax: (905) 878-2555, Email: dale@furlongcollins.ca
Ronald Flannagan, Q.C., Barrister & Solicitor, 13 Charles Street, Suite 105, L9T 2G5, Telephone: (877) 443- 4409, (905) 878-2804, Fax: (905) 878-5610, Email: rflannagan@stn.net
Nigel A. Gunding, B.A. (HONS.) LL.B., Barrister, Solicitor, Notary Public, 350 Main Street East, Suite B, L9T 1P6

MISSISSAUGA

Gordon Zlatko Bobesich, Barrister-at-Law, 20 Hurontario Street, L5G 3G7, Telephone: (905) 891-1533, (905) 849-1741, Fax: (905) 891-0169.

Michael F. O'Connor, Barrister & Solicitor, 4275 Village Centre Court, L4Z 1V3, Telephone: (905) 896-4370, Fax: (905) 896-4926.

Michael Woods, Barrister & Solicitor, 203—120 Traders Blvd. East, L4Z 2H7, Telephone: (905) 568-3810, Fax: (905) 568-1206.

Janice E. Younker, Barrister & Solicitor, 20 Hurontario Street, Suite 100, L4Z 1V3, Telephone: (905) 271-2784, Fax: (905) 271-5960, Email: younker@the-wire.com

NAPANEE

Steven M. P. Starbuck, B.A., LL.B., Madden, Sirman & Cowle, Barristers & Solicitors, 3 Bridge Street East, P.O. Box 37, K7R 3L8, Telephone: (877) 969-9959 (toll free), (613) 354-2161, Fax: (613) 354-5027, Email: msclaw@ihorizons.net

NEWMARKET

Debra L. McNairn, LL.B., Kinahan, McNairn, Barristers & Solicitors, 465 Davis Drive, Suite 222, L3Y 2P1, Telephone: (905) 836-1371, Fax: (905) 898-2050.

Peter S. Oliver, B.A., LL.B., Barrister & Solicitor, 178 Victoria Street, L3Y 4E1, Telephone: (905) 836-4946, Fax: (905) 836-0364.

NIAGARA FALLS

David A. Crowe, Barrister & Solicitor, 6617 Drummond Road, L2G 4N4, Telephone: (905) 356-7755, Fax: (905) 356-7772.

NORTH BAY

Nathalie Gregson, B.A., LL.B., Lawyer, 461 McIntyre Street West, P1B 2Z3, Telephone: (705) 476-1110, Fax: (705) 472-1485.

NORTH YORK

Garfin, Zeidenberg, Michael E. Garfin, B.BA., LLB ,Peter A. Grunwald, B.A., LL.B, Alan Chun, B.A., M.L.S., LL.B., Asha Gafar, LL.B.,., Lawyers, 6400 Yonge Street, Centerpoint Mall, M2M 3X4, Telephone: (416) 512-8000, Fax: (416) 512-9992, Email: pag@garfinzeidenberg.com akmc@garfinzeidenberg.com ag@garfinzeidenberg.com meg@garfinzeidenberg.com

Peter J. Lewarne, Steinberg Morton Frymer, Barristers & Solicitors, 5255 Yonge Street, Suite 810, M2N 6P4, Telephone: (416) 225-2777 ext. 214 or 219, Fax: (416) 225-7112, Email: peter@smflaw.com

Kenneth C. Vaughan, Barrister, 50 Gervais Drive, Suite 505, M3C 1Z3, Telephone: (416) 441-6313, Fax: (416) 441-2999.

OAKVILLE

Diane F. Daly, B.A., LL.B., Barrister & Solicitor, 251 North Service Road West, L6M 3E7, Telephone: (905) 844-5883, Fax: (905) 844-9765.
Mary-Anne Kril, O'Connor MacLeod Hanna LLP, Barristers & Solicitors, 700 Kerr Street, L6K 3W5, Telephone: (905) 842-8030, Fax: (905) 842-2460, Email: kril@omh.ca
Barbara J. McLeod, Barrister & Solicitor, 233 Robinson Street, P.O. Box 100, L6J 4Z5, Telephone: (905) 842-8600, Fax: (905) 842-4774.
Lydia Moritz, B.A., M.Ed., LL.B., Barrister & Solicitor, 251 North Service Road West, Suite 100, L6M 3E7, Telephone: (905) 337-1535, Fax: (905) 844-9765.
Karen A. Thompson, B.A., LL.B., Barrister & Solicitor, 251 North Service Road, Suite 100, L6M 3E7, Telephone: (905) 338-7941, Fax: (905) 844-9765, Email: katlaw@cgocable.net

OSHAWA

Kelly A. Aitchison, Aitchison Law Office, Oshawa Centre Office Galleria, 419 King Street West, Suite 185, L1J 8L8, Telephone: (905) 433-1174, Fax: (905) 433-1645.
Jeffrey G. Brown, Brown & Bell LLP, Barristers & Solicitors, 200 Bond Street West, Suite 202, L1J 2L7, Telephone: (905) 571-1301, Fax: (905) 576-5022, Email: bblaw@brownandbell.ca
Barry L. Evans, B.A., LL.B., Barrister & Solicitor, 419 King Street West, Suite 208, L1J 2K5, Telephone: (905) 433-1200, Fax: (905) 433-2555.
Brian J. R. Hall, B.A., (Bil.), LL.B., Creighton, Victor, Alexander, Hayward & Morison, Barristers and Solicitors, 235 King Street East, Box 26010, L1H 8R4, Telephone: (905) 723-3446, Fax: (905) 432-2323
Jayne E. Hughes, B.A., LL.B., Elliott & Hughes, Barristers, Solicitors, Notaries, 106 Stevenson Road South, L1J 5M1, Telephone: (877) 272-5220, (905) 571-1774, Fax: (905) 571-7706, Email: jayne@jaynehughes.com Web site: www.jaynehughes.com
Brian S. Korb, Kelly Greenway Bruce Korb, Barristers and Solicitors, 114 King Street East, L1H 7N1, Telephone: (905) 723-2278, (905) 686-5156 (Toronto), Fax: (905) 432-2663, Email: bkorb@oshawalawyers.com
Josef Neubauer, Barrister & Solicitor, 106 Stevenson Road South, L1J 5M1, Telephone: (905) 433-1991, Fax: (905) 433-7038.
Margot Poepjes, B.A., (Hons.), LL.B., Barrister, Solicitor & Mediator, 231 King Street East, 2nd Floor, L1H 1C5, Telephone: (905) 433-4020, Fax: (905) 433-7028.

OTTAWA

Philip W. Augustine, LL.B., LL.M (CANTAB), Augustine, Bater, Polowin LLP, 141 Laurier Avenue West, Suite 1100, K1P 5J3, Telephone: (613) 569-9500, Fax: (613) 569-9522, Email: pwa@abplaw.com

Kevin J. Cantor, Merovitz Potechin, Barristers & Solicitors, 301—200 Catherine Street, K2P 2K9, Telephone: (613) 563-7544, Fax: (613) 563-4577, Email: cantor@merovitzpotechin.com Web site: merovitzpotechin.com

Darrin L. Clayton, Clayton Law Offices, Barrister & Solicitor, 2571 Carling Avenue, Suite 207, K2B 7H7, Telephone: (613) 596-1350, Fax: (613) 596-2664, Web site: www.ottawafamilylaw.com Branch Office: 30 Emily Street, Carleton Place, ON K7C 1S2.

Susan E. Galarneau, B. Soc. Sc., LL.B., Galarneau & Associates, Barristers & Solicitors, 2831 St. Joseph Blvd., K1C 1G6, Telephone: (613) 830-7111, Fax: (613) 830-7108, Email: susan-galarneau@galarneau-law-offices.on.ca

Anne B. Gregory, Barrister & Solicitor, 200 Elgin Street, Suite 203, Ottawa, ON K2P 1L5, Telephone: (613) 236-7575, Fax: (613) 236-2208

Marc-Nicholas Quinn, B.A., LL.B., Plant, Quinn, Thiele LLP, Barristers & Solicitors, 200 Elgin Street, Suite 1107, K2P 1L5, Telephone: (613) 563-1131, Fax: (613) 230-8297, Email: mquinn@PQTlaw.com Web site: www.PQTlaw.com

Ernest G. Tannis, B.A., LL.B., C. Med., The ADR Centre, Solicitor & Mediator, 251 Bank Street, Suite 500, K2P 1X3, Telephone: (613) 567-9715, Fax: (613) 567-9722, Email: ernestgtannis@adrcentre.org

OWEN SOUND

Herbert E. Boyce, LL.B., Barrister, Solicitor, Notary Public, 887 Third Avenue East, Dominion Place, Suite 103, N4K 6H6, Telephone: (519) 371-4160, Fax: (519) 371-1604.

PEMBROKE

Adrian R. Cleaver, LL.B., Barrister & Solicitor, 156 MacKay Street, K8A 6Y6, Telephone: (613) 732-1377, Fax: (613) 732-3899.

PETERBOROUGH

Paula Armstrong, Howell Fleming LLP, Barristers & Solicitors, 415 Water Street, K9J 6Y5.

W.F. (Bill) Hampton, B.A., LL.B., Barrister, Solicitor, Notary Public & Mediator, 184 Charlotte Street, K9J 2T8, Telephone: (705) 876-6900, Fax: (705) 876-6922, Web site: www.ontariobusiness.net

Terence Gain, Barrister and Solicitor, 469 Water Street, K9H 3M2,

Telephone: (705) 749-6633, Fax: (705) 749-9765.

Robert McGillen, B.A., LL.B., McGillen, Ayotte, Barristers, Solicitors, Notaries Public, 244 Aylmer Street North, P.O. Box 1718, K9J 7X6, Telephone: (705) 748-2241, Fax: (705) 748-9125, Residence: (705) 292-5424, Email: bmcgillen@thelawoffices.net

Jane Rutherford, Howell Fleming LLP, Barristers & Solicitors, 415 Water Street, K9J 6Y5.

PICKERING

Darryl T.G. Glover, Barrister & Solicitor, 2200 Brock Road North, Units C10 & 11, L1X 2R2, Telephone: (905) 427-0646.

Allan R. Rowsell, Walker Head, Barristers & Solicitors, 200-1305 Pickering Parkway, L1V 3P2, Telephone: (905) 839-4484, (905) 683-3444 (Whitby), Fax: (905) 420-1073, Email: rowsell@walkerhead.com www.walkerhead.com

PORT DOVER

A.M. Lee Gaunt, B.A., LL.B., 110 St. Andrew Street, N0A 1N0, Telephone: (519) 583-1411, (519) 443-8676, Fax: (519) 583-1110, Second practice: Birnie & Gaunt, 70 Alice Street, Waterford, ON N0E 1Y0, Telephone: (519) 443-8676, Fax: (519) 443-5596.

PORT HOPE

J. Douglas Mann, B.A., LL.B., Brooks, Harrison, Mann & McCracken, Barristers & Solicitors, 114 Walton Street, L1A 1N5, Telephone: (905) 885-2451, if busy call, (905) 885-7291, Fax: (905) 885-7474, Email: dmann@porthopelaw.com

Allan T. McCracken, B.A., LL.B., Brooks, Harrison, Mann & McCracken, Barristers & Solicitors, 114 Walton Street, L1A 1N5, Telephone: (905) 885-2451, Fax: (905) 885-7474, Email: amccracken@porthopelaw.com

RICHMOND HILL

Nancy E. Macivor, B.A., R.N., LL.B., Barrister & Solicitor, 109 Highland Lane, L4C 3S1, Telephone: (905) 883-1829, Fax: (905) 883-0293, Email: nancy@nancymacivor.com

Norman Ronski, MacDonald, Ronski, Lawyers, 15 Wertheim Court, Suite 702, L4B 3H7, Telephone: (905) 731-9251, Fax: (905) 731-7989, Email: nronski@macronlaw.com

Paul H. Veugelers, M.A., LL.B., Stong, Blackburn, Machon, Bohm, Barristers & Solicitors, 10350 Yonge Street, 4th Floor, L4C 5K9, Telephone: (905) 884-9242, Fax: (905) 884-5445, Email: pveugelers@SBMBLAW.COM

SARNIA

Paul R. Beaudet, Barrister & Solicitor, 251 Exmouth Street, P.O. Box 2162, Sarnia, ON N7T 7L7, Telephone: (519) 337-1529, Fax: (519) 336-2569, Email: beaudet@ebtech.net Web site: www.sarnia.com/beaudet

SAULT STE. MARIE

Bonnie L. Ostroski, B.A., LL.B., Sarlo O'Neill, Barristers & Solicitors, 116 Spring Street, P6A 3A1, Telephone: (705) 949-6901, Fax: (705) 949-0618, Email: bostroski@sarlo-oneill.com Web site: www.sarlo-oneill.com

SIMCOE

Cobb & Jones, Barristers & Solicitors, Two Talbot Street North, P.O. Box 548, N3Y 4N5, Telephone: (519) 428-0170, Fax: (519) 428-3105, Email: cobblaw@cobbjones.ca

Anthony G. Lados, Barrister & Solicitor, 58 Peel Street, P.O. Box 677, Simcoe, ON N3Y 1S2.

Robert F. MacLeod, Cline Backus Nightingale McArthur, Barrister & Solicitor, 39 Colborne Street North, N3Y 4N5, Telephone: (519) 426-6763, Fax: (519) 426-2055, Email: Macleod@clinebackus.com

ST. CATHARINES

Frederick Cameron, Barrister & Solicitor, 6 Clark Street, L2R 5G2, Telephone: (905) 688-8002, Fax: (905) 688-8026.

Margaret Ramanauskas, Martens Lingard Maddalena Robinson & Koke, Barrister & Solicitor, 195 King Street, L2R 3J6, Telephone: (905) 687-6551, Fax: (905) 687-6553.

Kevin H. Robins, B.A., LL.B., Reid McNaughton, Barrister—Solicitor, 63 Ontario Street, L2R 6T8, Telephone: (905) 685-5435, Fax: (905) 685-3143, Email: lawyers@reidlaw.com

ST. THOMAS

Robert J. Upsdell, B.A., LL.B., Barrister & Solicitor, 59 Metcalfe Street, N5R 3K4, Telephone: (519) 633-7100, Fax: (5190 633-8984

SUDBURY

Guy A. Hurtubise, B.A., LL.B., Conroy Trebb Scott Hurtubise LLP, Barristers, Solicitors, 164 Elm Street, P3C 1T7, Telephone: (800) 627-1825, (705) 674- 6441, Fax: (705) 673-9567, Email: gahurtubise@sudburylegal.com Web site: www.sudburylegal.com

R.B. Michael Keenan, Q.C., Desmarais, Keenan, LLP, Lawyers, 30 Durham Street, Suite 100, P3C 5E5, Telephone: (800) 290-5465, (705)

675-7521, Fax: (705) 675-7390, Email: keenan@desmaraiskeenan.com
Web site: www.desmaraiskeenan.com
Christopher D. McInnis, Weaver, Simmons, Barristers, Solicitors &
Notaries, 233 Brady Street, P3B 4H5, Telephone: (705) 674-6421, Fax:
(705) 674-9948, Email: cdmcinnis@weaversimmons.com
Nicola S. Munro, B.A., LL.B., Conroy Trebb Scott Hurtubise LLP,
Barristers, Solicitors, 164 Elm Street, P3C 1T7, Telephone: (800) 627-1825,
(705) 674- 6441, Fax: (705) 673-9567, Web site: www.sudburylegal.com
R.A. Sullivan, Weaver, Simmons, Barristers, Solicitors & Notaries, 233
Brady Street, Sudbury, ON, P3B 4H5, Telephone: (705) 674-6421, Fax:
(705) 674-9948, Email: rasullivan@weaversimmons.com

THORNHILL
D. Todd Morganstein, B.A., LL.B., Barrister & Solicitor, Notary
Public, Gazebo of Thornhill, 8111 Yonge Street, Suite 110, L3T 4V9,
Telephone: (905) 881-8289, Fax: (905) 881-2696.

THUNDER BAY
Michael B. Carter, Barrister, Solicitor, Notary Public, Suite 702, 34
N. Cumberland Street, P7A 4L3, Telephone: (807) 343-0313, Fax:
(807) 343-9022.

TILBURY
Robert M. Jutras, LL.B., Jutras Law Office, 50 Queen Street South,
N0P 2L0, Telephone: (519) 682-3100, Fax: (519) 682-3622.

TILLSONBURG
Olie Mandryk, Q.C., Barrister & Solicitor, 65 Bidwell Street, N4G 3T8,
Telephone: (519) 842-4228, Fax: (519) 842-7659, Email: mhlaw@oxford.net
Robert B. Stewart, B.A., M.A., LL.B., Barrister & Solicitor, 65 Bidwell
Street, N4G 3T8, Telephone: (519) 842-4228, Fax: (519) 842-7659,
Email: mhlaw@oxford.net

TIMMINS
Kim E. Cogar, B.A., (Hons.), LL.B., Ellery, Ellery & Cogar, Barristers
& Solicitors, 135 Algonquin Blvd. East, P4N 1A6, Telephone: (705) 360-
5879, Fax: (705) 264-3297, Email: ellery-j@ntl.sympatico.ca
Luc E. Maisonneuve, LL.B., Racicot, Maisonneuve, Labelle, Gosselin,
Barristers and Solicitors, 15 Balsam Street South, P4N 2C7, Telephone:
(705) 264-2385, Fax: (705) 268-3949.

TORONTO

Denise M.F. Badley, Barrister, Solicitor, Notary, 2069 Danforth Avenue, 2nd Floor, M4C 1J8, Telephone: (416) 690-9195, Fax: (416) 690-6271, Email: dbadley@connection.com

Rochelle F. Cantor, Barrister and Solicitor, 204—100 Lombard Street, M5C 1M3, Telephone: (416) 861-1625.

G. Bruce Clark, B.Math., LL.B., Clark, Farb, Fiksel, Barristers & Solicitors, 144 Front Street West, Suite 400, M5J 2L7, Telephone: (416) 599-7761, Fax: (416) 977-8587, Email: bclark@cfflaw.com

Gene C. Colman, B.A., LL.B., Author of "Fuss About Pensions— Practical Suggestions", *Money & Family Law*, Vol. XI, No.8, 25 Bowring Walk, Toronto, ON M3H 5Z8, Telephone: (416) 635-9264, Fax: (416) 635-5468, Email: gcolman@4famlaw.com   Web site: www.4famlaw.com

Vanessa A. D'Souza, Barrister, Solicitor & Notary Public, 2680 Lawrence Avenue East, Suite 204, M1P 4Y4, Telephone: (416) 615-1087, Fax: (416) 615-2981, Email: dsouzafamlaw@hotmail.com

Grant W. Gold, Goodman and Carr LLP, Barristers and Solicitors, Suite 2300, 200 King Street West, M5H 3W5, Telephone: (416) 595-2300, Fax: (416) 595-0567, Web site: www.goodmancarr.com

Kenneth D. Goldstein, B.A., Hons., LL.B., Goldstein & Grubner, Barristers and Solicitors, 3459 Sheppard Avenue East, Suite 212, M1T 3K5, Telephone: (416) 292-0414, Fax: (416) 292-4508, Email: k.goldstein@rogers.com

Eric B. Gossin, B.Sc.,B.Ed., LL.B., Stancer Gossin Rose LLP, Barristers and Solicitors, 230 Sheppard Avenue West, Suite 300, M2N 1N1, Telephone: (416) 224-1996, Fax: (416) 224-1997, Email: egossin@sgrllp.com

Stephen M. Grant, McCarthy Tétrault, Barristers & Solicitors, 4700 TD Bank Tower, PO Box 48, Stn. Toronto Dom., M5K 1E6, Telephone: (416) 362-1812, Fax: (416) 868-0673, Email: toronto@mccarthy.ca Web site: www.mccarthy.ca

A. John Hodgins, Barrister & Solicitor, 677 Brown's Line, M8W 3V7, Telephone: (416) 251-9390, Fax: (416) 251-0449.

Paul Jacobs, Q.C., Elkind, Lipton & Jacobs LLP, Barrister & Solicitor, Mediator, Arbitrator, One Queen Street East, Suite 1900, M5C 2W6, Telephone: (416) 367-0871, Fax: (416) 367-9388, Email: pjacobs@eljlaw.com   Web site: www.eljlaw.com

Cori Kalinowski, Barrister & Solicitor, 69 Elm Street, M5G 1H2, Telephone: (416) 598-9495, Fax: (416) 971-9092, Email: kalinowski@sympatico.ca

Pirkko Kuronen, Barrister and Solicitor, 35 Old Orchard Grove, M5M 2C8, Telephone: (416) 544-8889, Fax: (416) 544-8890.

Shirley E. Levitan, B.Sc., LL.B., Barrister & Solicitor, 69 Elm Street, M5G 1H2, Telephone: (416) 585-2626, Fax: (416) 971-9092, Email: shilev@idirect.com

Henry N. Lowi, (of the Ontario and the Israel Bars), Advocate, Barrister & Solicitor, 120 Eglinton Avenue East, Suite 1100, M4P 1E2, Telephone: (877) 980-0901 (toll free), (416) 480-0901, Fax: (416) 480-0902, Email: lowi@attcanada.net

Linda J. Meldrum, Barrister, 3 Rowanwood Avenue, M4W 1Y5, Telephone: (416) 925-4385, Fax: (416) 867-1873, Email: lmeldrum@ rfeasible.com

Sandra J. Meyrick, B.A., M.Sc., LL.B., Barrister & Solicitor, 920 Yonge Street, Suite 900, M4W 3C7, Telephone: (416) 975-8255, Fax: (416) 969-9173, Email: meyrick@idirect.com

Mary Lou Parker, Barrister & Solicitor, 2 St. Clair Avenue East, Suite 800, M4T 2T5, Telephone: (416) 920-4708, Fax: (416) 920-3819, Email: mlparker@tor.axxent.ca

Laurie H. Pawlitza, Goodman and Carr LLP, Barristers and Solicitors, Suite 2300, 200 King Street West, M5H 3W5, Telephone: (416) 595-2300, Fax: (416) 595-0567, Web site: www.goodmancarr.com

Evelyn Kohn Rayson, Rayson Wallach, Barristers & Solicitors, 3845 Bathurst Street, Suite 302, M3H 3N2, Telephone: (416) 630-5600, Fax: (416) 630-5906.

Gary R. Reid, Mills & Mills LLP, Barristers & Solicitors, 2 St. Clair Avenue West, M4V 1L5, Telephone: (416) 682-7113 (Direct Line), (416) 863-0125, Fax: (416) 863-3997, Email: garyr@millslawyer.com

Ricketts, Harris Family Law Practice Group, Anne McLaughlin, Family Law Clerk, 181 University Avenue, Suite 816, M5H 2X7, Telephone: (416) 364-6211, Fax: (416) 364-1697, Email: jgm@rickettsharris.com Web site: www.familylawcentre.com

Hugh R. Scher, Scher & De Angelis LLP, Barristers & Solicitors, 69 Bloor Street East, Suite 210, M4W 1A9, Telephone: (416) 515-9686, Direct Line: (416) 969-1812, Fax: (416) 969-1815, Email: hscher@interlog.com

Louise A. Scrivener, Barrister & Solicitor, 8 King Street East, Suite 100, M5C 1B5, Telephone: (416) 869-0950.

Joseph J. Sheridan, Sheridan, Ippolito, Barristers & Solicitors, 2 Jane Street, Suite 506, M6S 4W3, Telephone: (416) 763-3399, Fax: (416) 763-3443.

Gary E. Shortliffe, barrister / avocat, Family law in English and French, 84 McGill Street, M5B 1H2, Telephone: (416) 596-0202, Fax: (416) 348-

8879, Email: shortliffe@canada.com

Anne M. Silverman, B.A., LL.B., Barrister and Solicitor, 5075 Yonge Street, Suite 301, M2N 6C6, Telephone: (416) 250-0045, Fax: (416) 250-1984, Email: asil23@sprint.ca

Alvin G. Starkman, M.A., LL.B., Banks & Starkman, Lawyers, 200 Ronson Drive, Suite 310, M9W 5Z9, Telephone: (416) 243-3394, Fax: (416) 243-9692, Email: astarkman@banksandstarkman.com, Website: www.banksandstarkman.com

Gordon E. Wood, EnfieldAdair LLP, Partner, One Queen Street East, Suite 810, M5C 2W5, Telephone: (416) 941-5865, Fax: (416) 863-1241, Email: gwood@enfieldadair.com

UNIONVILLE

McGee & Fryer, Barristers & Solicitors, Notaries Public, 4961 Hwy. #7, Suite 201, L3R 1N1, Telephone: (905) 940-1598, Fax: (905) 940-1730, Email: heather@mcgeefryer.net

WATERLOO

Peter J. Brennan, Amy, Appleby & Brennan, Barristers & Solicitors, 372 Erb Street West, N2L 1W6, Telephone: (519) 884-7330, Fax: (519) 884-7390, Email: aab-lawoffffice@rogers.com

W. Marlene Fitzpatrick, Barrister, Solicitor, Notary, 421 King Street North, N2J 4E4, Telephone: (519) 725-9500, Fax: (519) 725-2379.

WHITBY

Helen E. Brooks, LL.B., Brooks, Whittington, Barristers, Solicitors & Notaries Public, 326 Dundas Street East, L1N 2J1, Telephone: (905) 430-1755, Toronto Line: (905) 686-5246.

Debra J. Sweetman, Barrister, Solicitor, Notary, 340 Byron Street South, L1N 4P8, Telephone: (905) 666-8166, Fax: (905) 666-8163

WINDSOR

Larry M. Belowus, Barrister & Solicitor, 100 Ouellette Avenue, Seventh Floor, N9A 6T2, Telephone: (519) 973-1900, Fax: (519) 973-0225.

Cheryl A. Hodgkin, Corrent & Macri, Barrister and Solicitor, 110 Tecumseh Road East, N8X 2P8, Telephone: (519) 255-1390, Ext. 249, Fax: (519) 255-9123.

Lou Ann M. Pope, B.A., LL.B., Pope Law Office, Barrister, Solicitor & Notary Public, 880 Ouellette Avenue, Suite 200, Windsor, ON N9A 1C7, Telephone: (519) 977-1177, Fax: (519) 977-1199, Email: lawyerpope@aol.com

Derek R. Revait, B.A., LL.B., Barrister, Solicitor & Notary Public, Royal Windsor Terrace, 380 Pelissier Street, Suite 209, N9A 6W8, Telephone: (519) 258-7030, Fax: (519) 258-2629.

William A. Salem, B.A., LL.B., Salem & McCullough, Barristers & Solicitors, 2828 Howard Avenue, N8X 3Y3, Telephone: (519) 966-3633, Fax: (519) 972-7788, Email: salmcc@on.aibn.com

Tamara Stomp, Barrister & Solicitor, 4510 Rhodes Drive, Suite 205, N8W 5K5, Telephone: (519) 948-9778, Fax: (519) 948-4033, Email: stomp@mnsi.net

WOODBRIDGE

Lorraine A. Bortolussi, B.A., LL.B., Bortolussi & Associates, Barristers and Solicitors, 7050 Weston Road, Suite 302, L4L 8G7, Telephone: (905) 856-1816, Fax: (905) 856-6682.

John Lo Faso, LL.B., Barrister & Solicitor, 3800 Steeles Avenue West, Suite 300, West Building, L4L 4G9, Telephone: Toronto Line: (416) 746-7420, (905) 850-8550, Fax: (905) 850-9969.

Appendix M

Family Law Mediators

A list of mediators who have indicated they are interested, qualified, and experienced in dealing with marriage breakdown.

ONTARIO

BRAMPTON

Colm Brannigan, M.A., LL.B., Mediator, 4 Burwash Court, L6Z 4M3, Telephone: (905) 840-9882, Fax: (905) 840-4809, Email: colm@mediate.ca
Victoria L. Smith, LL.B., C.Med, Cert.CFM (FMC) Collaborative Family Lawyer, Mediator, Simmons Da Silva & Sinton L.L.P., 201 County Court Blvd., Suite 200, Brampton, ON L6W 4L2, and 2454 Bloor St. W. (At Jane St.), Toronto, M6S 1R2, Telephone: (905) 457-1660, Fax: (905) 457-5641, Email: vsmith@lawcan.com Web site: www.lawcan.com

GODERICH

Norman B. Pickell, LL.B., Lawyer, Mediator & Arbitrator, 58 South Street, N7A 4C7, Telephone: (519) 524-8335, (519) 524-1530, Email: pickell@normanpickell.com Web site: www.normanpickell.com

GUELPH

Susan Garrod-Schuster, Cert. CFM (FMC), Acc.FM (OAFM), Resolve Mediation Services, 221 Woolwich Street, Guelph, ON N1H 3V4, Telephone: (519) 836-0281, Fax: (519) 836-0455, Email: susan@resolve-mediation.on.ca

HAGERSVILLE

James R. Baxter, Barrister-at-Law, 19 King Street West, N0A 1H0, Telephone: (905) 768-3363, Fax: (905) 768-1550, Residence: (905) 768-5771.

HAMILTON

Angelo Procopio, Mediator, Ontario Association for Family Mediation, 247 Kenilworth Avenue South, L8K 2T6, Telephone: (905) 548-9544, Fax: (905) 548-6375, Email: angelo@workaid.net Web site: www.workaid.net

KITCHENER

David Ryan, B.A., M.A., Animated Resolutions, Mediation—Facilitation—Arbitration—Training, 34 Simeon Street, N2H 1S1, Telephone: (519) 496-5756, Fax: (519) 576-0055, Email: animated.resolutions@sympatico.ca Web site: www3.simpatico.ca/animated.resolutions/

NEWMARKET

Christopher M. Murphy, Murphy & Lewis, Barristers, Solicitors, Family Mediation, 30 Prospect Street, Suite 301, L3Y 3S9, (800) 262-2659, (905) 836-4750, Fax: (905) 836-6691

OSHAWA

Bea Hancock, MSW, RSW, Family Services of Durham, 850 King Street West, L1J 8N5, Telephone: (905) 721-6100, Fax: (905) 579-8455, Email: hancock@speedline.ca

OTTAWA

Heidi N. Ruppert, B.A. (Hon), LL.B., Lawyer and Accredited Family Mediator (OAFM), 136 Lewis Street, K2P 0S7, Telephone: (613) 567-5065, Fax: (613) 567-7164, Email: heidir@cyberus.ca

POINT EDWARD

Peter Westfall, Barrister & Solicitor, Mediation Services, 805 N. Christian Street, Suite 104, N7V 1X6, Telephone: (519) 344-1155, Fax: (519) 344-1842, Email: peter@westfall.net

SCARBOROUGH

Rev. Dr. J. Kent Clayton, Clayton & Associates Inc., Family Counselor & Mediator, 27 Silver Spruce Drive, M1W 1V6, Telephone: (416) 490-8801, Fax: (416) 490-8831, Email: revkclayton@sympatico.ca Web site: www.myfamilymediator.com

THORNHILL

Rita Czarny, B.A.(Hons.) C.Med, Accredited Family Mediator (OAFM), Roster Mediator, OMMP (Ontario Mandatory Mediation Program),

Ottawa/Toronto, Telephone: (905) 771-1100, Fax: (905) 889-8472, Email: peacefully_yours@hotmail.com

Mervyn N. Rosenstein, B.A., B.C.L., The Resolution Alternative, Mediation & Arbitration Services, 182 Bayview Fairways Drive, L3T 2Y8, Telephone: (905) 889-2069, Fax: (905) 889-2486, Email: mrosenstein@idirect.com

WINDSOR

David Osmun, MSW, Counselling Mediation, Therapy, 95 Giles Blvd. East, N9A 4B8, Telephone: (519) 258-8255, Fax: (519) 969-0595.

SASKATCHEWAN
SASKATOON

Robert Gillies, M.S.W., R.S.W., Vickers, Ish, Gryba & Gillies, Professional Counselling and Mediation, #4—505 23rd Street East, S7K 4K7, Telephone: (306) 934-5898, Fax: (306) 934-5812.

VIBANK

Linda Haroldson, Mediator, Rainbow Mediation Services, Box 262, S0G 4Y0, Telephone: (306) 762-4509, Cell: (306) 596-1098.

Appendix N

Accountants

A list of accountants interested in assisting you preparate your Net Family Property statement.

BRITISH COLUMBIA
VANCOUVER

Scott Bannatyne, CA, CBV, Partner, SmytheRatcliffe, Chartered Accountants, 7th Floor, Marine Building, 355 Burrard Street, V6C 2G8, Telephone: (604) 688-4675, Fax: (604) 687-1231, Email: bannatyne@smytheratcliffe.com

ONTARIO
SAULT STE. MARIE

Thomas C. Ambeault, B. Comm., C.A., CBV, BDO Dunwoody LLP, Chartered Accountants and Consultants, 747 Queen Street East, P6A 5N7, Telephone: (800) 520-3005, (705) 945-0990, Ext. 206, Residence: (705) 759-3415, Fax: (705) 942-7979, Email: tambeault@bdo.ca

THUNDER BAY

Brian Randle, CA, CBV, ASA, Partner (Valuations and Financial Advisory Services), BDO Dunwoody LLP, 1095 Barton Street, P7B 5N3, Telephone: (800) 465-6868, (807) 625-4444, Fax: (807) 623-8460, Residence: (807) 683-8240, Email: brandle@bdo.ca Web site: www.thunderbay.bdo.ca

Appendix O

Business Valuators

A list of chartered business valuators.

BRITISH COLUMBIA
ABBOTSFORD
Joe S. Bring, CA, CBV, West-Can Consulting Corp., Business Valuations, Mergers & Acquisitions, Corporate Finance, P.O. Box 316 Main, V2S 4N9, Telephone: (604) 864-9464, Cell: (604) 855-5562, Fax: (604) 864-9438, Email: jbring@direct.ca

ONTARIO
BRANTFORD
Ron Sciannella, B.B.A, C.A., C.M.A., C.B.V., Millard, Rouse & Rosebrugh LLP, Chartered Accountants, 96 Nelson Street, N3T 5N3, Telephone: (519) 759-3511, Fax: (519) 759-7961, Voice Mail:(519) 759-3708, ext.228, Mobile: (519) 770-8505, Email: rsciannella@millards.com Web site: millards.com

BRAMPTON
Mario Re, President, Blue Water Financial Services, 350 Rutherford Road South, Plaza 1, Unit 7, L6W 3P6, Telephone: (877) 877-8575 (toll free), (905) 457-1044, ext. 226, Fax: (905) 457-6845, Email: mario.re@bluewaterfinancial

HAMILTON
Michael R. Carnegie, Bcomm, CA, CBV, President, Talyor Leibow Valuations Inc., Effort Square, 7th Floor, 105 Main Street East, Hamilton, ON, L8N 1G6, Telephone: (905) 523-0000, Ext.250, Fax:(905) 523-4681, Email: mcarnegie@tlval.com Web site: www.tlval.com

HUNTSVILLE
Peter J. Schwarzl, C.B.V., C.A., BDO Dunwoody LLP, Chartered

Accountants and Consultants, 2 Elm Street, P1H 2K8, Telephone: (705) 789-4469, Fax: (705) 789-1079, Residence: (705) 385-0650, Email: pjschwarzl@bdo.ca

NORTH YORK

Tom Strezos, CA, CBV, CFE, ASA, Partner, Mintz & Partners Financial Services, 100—1446 Don Mills Road, M3B 3N6, Telephone: (416) 644-4377, Fax: (416) 644-4378, Email: tom_strezos@mintzca.com Web site: www.mintzca.com

OWEN SOUND

L. Clarke McLeod, C.A., CBV, Business Valuations, Insurance Claims and Litigation Services, BDO Dunwoody LLP, 1717 2nd Avenue East, N4K 5P7, Telephone: (519) 376-6110, Fax: (519) 376-4741, Email: cmcleod@bdo.ca

PETERBOROUGH

Brad J. Huggins, CA, CBV, Partner, Morrison & Hollingsworth, Chartered Accountants, 425 Water Street North, K9H 3L9, Telephone: (705) 745-4657, Fax: (705) 745-6246, Email: bhuggins@morrisonca.com

PORT PERRY

William A.D. Selby, CA, CBV, CFP, Caledonia Consultants Inc., P.O. Box 899, Port Perry, ON L9L 1A7, Telephone: (905) 982-0197, Fax: (905) 982-0198.

SCARBOROUGH

Thomas A. Koger, B.Comm, CA, CBV, Koger Valuations Inc., Business Valuation and Litigation Support, 45 Coalport Drive, M1N 4B5, Telephone/Fax: (416) 690-7717, Residence: (416) 694-4633.

THUNDER BAY

Brian W. Randle, CA, CBV, BDO Dunwoody LLP, Financial Advisory Services, 1095 Barton Street, P7B 5N3, Telephone: (807) 625-4444, Fax: (807) 623-8460, Web site: www. bdothunderbay.com
Donna Bain Smith, CA, IFA, CBV, BDO Dunwoody LLP, Financial Advisory Services, 1095 Barton Street, P7B 5N3, Telephone: (807) 625-4444, Fax: (807) 623-8460, Email: dbsmith@bdo.ca Web site: www.bdothunderbay.com

TORONTO

Farley J. Cohen, MBA, CA, IFA, CIRP, CBV, ASA, Kroll Lindquist Avey, The Risk Consulting Company, One Financial Place, One Adelaide Street East, 30ᵗʰ Floor, Toronto, ON, M5C 2V9, Telephone: (416) 777-2440, Direct: (416) 777-2477, Fax: (416) 777-2441, Email: fcohen@kroll-worldwide.com   Web site: www.krollworldwide.com

Krofchick Valuation Partners, Gordon Krofchick, B.Comm, C.A., C.B.V., Investigative Accountants and Business Valuators, The Annex Centre, 344 Dupont Street, Suite 202, M5R 1V9, Telephone: (416) 922-9889, Fax: (416) 922-3056.

Scott Schellenberg, CA, CBV, CFA, BDO Dunwoody LLP, 2005 Sheppard Avenue East, Suite 302, M2J 5B4, Telephone: (416) 498-6010, Fax: (416) 498-6786, Email: sschellenberg@bdo.ca

QUEBEC

MONTREAL

Richard M. Wise, FCA, CA, IFA, FCBV, ASA, MCBA, CFE, Wise, Blackman, CA, Business Valuation, Forensic Accounting, The Royal Bank of Canada Building, Suite 3430, 1 Place Ville Marie, H3B 3N6, Telephone: (514) 875-8100, (514) 875-9109, Email: rmwise@wbbusval.com

Appendix P

Financial Planners

A list of financial planners.

ALBERTA

CALGARY

James Buchan, CFP, BEd, Investors Group Financial Services, Senior Financial Consultant, 1816 Crowchild Trail NW, T2M 3Y7, Telephone: (800) 347-0296, (403) 284-0494, Fax: (403) 289-9674, Email: james.buchan@investorsgroup.com

Rose Raimondo, B.B.A., R.F.P. CFP, Raimondo & Associates, Financial and Employee Benefit Consulting, 305—4625 Varsity Drive NW, Suite 329, T3A 0Z9, Telephone: (403) 288-8561, Fax: (403) 288-8705, Email: rose@raimondo-associates.com

Russell Todd, RFP, CFP, Todd & Associates, Registered Financial Planner, Certified Financial Planner, 305, 4625 Varsity Drive NW, Suite 364, T3A 0Z9, Telephone: (403) 547-0328, Fax: (403) 547-7828.

Robert S. White, PriceWaterhouseCoopers, Financial Advisory Services, 639 5th Avenue SW, Suite 2100, T2P 0M9, Telephone: (403) 509-7345, Fax: (403) 781-1825, Email: robert.s.white@ca.pwcglobal.com

BRITISH COLUMBIA

CAMPBELL RIVER

Cecil Baldry-White, CFP, RFP, Cartier Partners Securities Inc., Certified Financial Planner, 101—909 Island Highway, V9W 2C2, Telephone: (800) 667-2554, (250) 287-4933, Email: baldrywhitec@cartierpartners.ca

KAMLOOPS

David W. Page, CFP, Investors Group Financial Services, Senior Consultant, Executive & Corporate Division, 1735 Bearcroft Court, V2B 8M2, Telephone: (250) 554-2468, Fax: (250) 376-3025, Email: david@dwpage.com Web site: dwpage.com

Financial Planners

VANCOUVER
Fran Goldberg, MA, CFP, RFP, , Registered Financial Planner, President, Sage Planning Ltd., 333—1275 West 6th Avenue, V6H 1A6, Telephone: (604) 738-0036, Fax: (604) 738-0046, Email: fgoldberg@sageplanners.com

NEWFOUNDLAND
ST. JOHN'S
Donald Cuff, B. Comm, CFP, RFP, DWC Financial Planning, Certified Financial Planner, 70 Portugal Cove Road, Suite 101, A1B 2M3, Telephone: (800) 900-2833, (709) 753-8100, Email: don@dwcfinancial.com Web site: www.dwcfinancial.com

ONTARIO
ANCASTER
George Van Arragon, CFP, Bick Financial, 241 Wilson Street East, L9G 2B8, Telephone: (905) 648-9559.

BRAMPTON
Blue Water Financial Services, 350 Rutherford Road South, Plaza 1, Unit 7, L6W 3P6, Telephone: (877) 877-8575 (toll free), (905) 457-1044, ext. 226, Fax: (905) 457-6845, Email: mario.re@bluewaterfinancial.ca ATTN: Mario Re

Steve Robinson, B.Sc., F.C.S.I., RBC Dominion Securities, Vice President, Investment Advisor, 50 Queen Street West, Suite 300, L6X 4H3, Telephone: (800) 844-7906, (905) 450-5946, Fax: (905) 451-3414, Email: steve-robinson@RBCDS.com

BURLINGTON
Timea Sarkozi, Hons. B.A., CFP, CDP, Sarkozi & Associates, Certified Financial Planner, Certified Divorce Planner, 185 Plains Road East, Suite 9, L7T 2C4, Telephone: (905) 632-4999, Fax: (905) 632-5632, Email: timea@sympatico.ca

DRYDEN
Fred R. Van Vogt, CFP, RFP, Investors Group Financial Services Inc., Senior Financial Consultant, 31 Whyte Avenue, P8N 1Z2, Telephone: (807) 223-5440, Cell: (807) 221-8126, Fax: (807) 223-7771, Email: vanvvf1@investorsgroup.com

OAKVILLE

Frank Lipka, eplanning solutions, 2829 Sherwood Heights Drive, Suite 102, L6J 7R7, Telephone: (905) 829-5277, Fax: (905) 829-5205

RJ McBain, Strategic Tax Planners, 2829 Sherwood Heights Drive, Suite 102, L6J 7R7, Telephone: (877) 366-9787 (toll free), (905) 829-5277, Fax: (905) 829-5205, Email: rmcbain@strategictaxplanners.com

Lisa Warll, Financial Strategies, Miles Santo and Associates, 356 Trafalgar Road, Oakville, ON L6J 3H4, Telephone: (905) 338-8286, Fax: (905) 338-7174, Email: lisa.warll@sympatico.ca

ORLEANS

Bill Goodwin, M.Ed, CFP, Armstrong & Quaile Associates Inc., Certified Financial Planner, #204—2451 St. Joseph Blvd., K1C 1E9, Telephone: (866) 837-7117, (613) 837-7177, Ext.225, Fax: (613) 837-4224, Email: billgaq@magma.ca Web site: comsearch-can.com/A-Q1.htm

OTTAWA

Ronald P. Harvey, B. Comm., CGA, CFP, Money Concepts, Vice President, Ottawa Central, 275 Bank Street, Suite 304, K2P 2L6, Telephone: (613) 238-7818, Fax: (613) 238-8035, Email: ron@money-conceptsoc.on.ca

John H. Murray, CFP, R.F.P., Senior Investment Advisor, TD Evergreen, Constitution Square, 360 Albert Street, Suite 100, K1R 7X7, Telephone: (613) 783-6623, Fax: (613) 783-4075, Email: murraj5@tdbank.ca

Anne Rounding, CFP, CIM, FMA, FCSI, Investment Advisor, Dundee Securities Corporation, 210- 1770 Woodward Drive, K2C 0P8, Telephone: (613) 523-4156, Fax: (613) 523-3222, Email: rounding@sympatico.ca Web site: www.dundeewealth.com

PETERBOROUGH

Jolley Financial Services, David Jolley, Accountant/Financial Advisor, 785 The Kingsway, K9J 6W7, Telephone: (705) 748-6481, Fax: (705) 748-5018.

SUDBURY

Sandra L. Mews, CFP, Cartier Partners Financial Group, 176 Larch Street, Suit 102, P3E 1C5, Telephone: (800) 720-9829, (705) 525-5811, Email: regal@vianet.on.ca

TORONTO

Allan Kalin, CFP, SB & C, Financial Growth Associates, 272 Lawrence

Financial Planners

Avenue West, Suit 203, M5M 4M1, Telephone: (800) 787-3983, (416) 787-4517, Fax: (416) 787-5763, Email: akalin@fingrowth.com Web site: www.fingrowth.com

WINDSOR

Jason Campbell, B.Comm, CFP, Sterling Mutuals Inc., Vice President, Insurance, Certified Financial Planner, 880 Ouellette Avenue, Suite 704, N9A 1C7, Telephone: (800) 354-4956, (519) 256-1002, Fax: (519) 256-2682, Email: jc@sterlingmutuals.com

SASKATCHEWAN
PRINCE ALBERT

Patricia Weir, B. Comm, CFP, Cartier Partners Financial Services, 460 South Industrial Drive, S6V 7L8, Telephone: (306) 922-2020, Fax: (306) 922-0535, Email: patweir@sk.sympatico.ca

Index